TŪ RANGA RANGA

TŪ RANGA RANGA

Rights, responsibilities and global citizenship in Aotearoa New Zealand

Edited by Sharon McLennan, Margaret Forster, Rand Hazou, David Littlewood and Carol Neill

MASSEY UNIVERSITY PRESS

Contents

Kupu Māori / Glossary
page 8

PART ONE:
TE TAKE, THE BASE

01. Tuia te here tangata: The threads that connect us
Margaret Forster
& Sharon McLennan
page 14

02. Global encounters
David Littlewood & Carol Neill
page 26

03. Globalisation
Sharon McLennan
page 44

04. Encountering global citizenship
Sharon McLennan, Margaret Forster & Rand Hazou
page 63

05. Rights
Shine Choi, Margaret Forster
& Beth Greener
page 81

06. Responsibilities
Tracey Hepi, Krushil Watene
& Carol Neill
page 96

PART TWO:
TE RITO, THE CENTRAL SHOOTS

07. Encountering climate change
Sharon McLennan & Axel Malecki
page 116

08. Climate change, tourism and the Pacific
Apisalome Movono &
Sharon McLennan
page 127

09. Tangata whenua responses to climate change
Lucy Kaiser & Christine Kenney
page 141

10. Writing the climate crisis
Ingrid Horrocks & Tom Doig
page 161

11. Encountering conflict
David Littlewood
page 180

12. Responsibility to Protect: Using armed force to counter atrocity crimes
Damien Rogers
page 190

13. Conflict commodities, rights and responsibilities
Vanessa Bramwell, Glenn Banks, Nicholas Holm & Sy Taffel
page 206

14. Arts and conflict: Banksy, art and Palestinian solidarity
Rand Hazou
page 223

15. Encountering inequality and poverty
Carol Neill & Samantha Gardyne
page 237

16. Poverty, inequality and the SDGs: Transforming our world for whom?
Samantha Gardyne & Axel Malecki
page 248

17. Covid-19 and inequality in Aotearoa
Margaret Forster, Sharon McLennan & Catherine Rivera
page 264

18. Shifting the poverty lens for sustainable livelihoods: Pasifika perspectives on better quality of life
Siautu Alefaio-Tugia, Malcolm Andrews, Emeline Afeaki-Mafile'o, Petra Satele, Stuart Carr, Jarrod Haar, Darrin Hodgetts, Jane Parker, James Arrowsmith, Amanda Young-Hauser & Harvey Jones
page 282

PART THREE:
TE PUĀWAI, THE FLOWERS

19. Agency and action
Margaret Forster &
David Belgrave
page 298

20. Reflections on global citizenship
Sharon McLennan
page 311

About the contributors
page 319

Index
page 327

Kupu Māori / Glossary

Word or phrase	Description
ahikā	keeping the home fires burning
aho	threads that act as a cross-stitch
Aotearoa	generic Māori name for New Zealand
aroha	love
atua	deities
awa	river
hapori	community
hapū	subtribes
harakeke	flax bush
harirū	handshakes
hongi	a greeting involving the pressing together of noses
iho atua	an origin narrative derived from a Māori world view
iwi	tribes
kaimahi	social service workers
kaimoana	seafood
kāinga	settlements
kaitiaki	to care and look after the environment and natural resources
kaitiakitanga	stewardship over the environment
kaupapa Māori services	services designed by Māori for Māori
Kāwanatanga Karauna	state governance
kihi	kiss
mahinga kai	food gathering sites
mana	authority
mana tangata	elevate the human condition
mana whenua	exercise of tribal authority over a specific domain
manaaki	caring for one another
manaaki manuhiri	care of visitors
Māori	the first peoples of Aotearoa
mātauranga/ mātauranga Māori	Māori knowledge
mauri	life essence
mihimihi	greeting

moana	sea
Ngā ipukarea	ancestral homelands
Ngāi Tahu whānui	the broader Ngāi Tahu tribe
Pākehā	non-Māori
papakāinga	housing developments on Māori land and marae
pā wars	tribal sporting event
poutiriao	to place in the world, guardians
pouwhenua	marking of the land
rāhui	temporary restriction of access to protect the health and wellbeing of people and the environment
rangatahi	youth
rangatira	chiefs
rangatiratanga	Māori authority
raranga	the customary practice of weaving using the harakeke or flax plant
Rātana	a prophetic movement
Ringatū	a prophetic movement
rohe	region
rūnanga	tribal council
Tairāwhiti	Gisborne, East Coast of Aotearoa
takiwā	area
tangata	people
tangata tiriti	non-Māori with rights to citizenship established through te Tiriti o Waitangi
tangata whenua	Māori, Indigenous people of Aotearoa
taonga/taonga tuku iho	treasures handed down
taunahanaha	naming of the land
te ao Māori	the Māori world, Māori world views
te pō	the darkness
te puawai	the flowers of the flax bush
te reo	the Māori language
te rito	the central shoot of the flax bush
te take	the base of the flax bush
te Tiriti o Waitangi	the Treaty of Waitangi
tikanga	customs

tino rangatiratanga	absolute tribal authority
tupuna/tūpuna	ancestor/ancestors
tūrangawaewae	an affiliation and authority associated with tribal territory, tribal base
uha	earthly female element
urupā	burial grounds
wāhi tapu	sacred places
waiora	health and wellbeing
waka hourua	double-hulled sailing vessels
Whai Rawa	a Ngāi Tahi savings and investment scheme
whakapapa	genealogical sequences
whakataukī	proverb
whānau	family
whānau ora	state policy
Whanganui iwi	Whanganui tribe/people
whenua	land

PART ONE:
TE TAKE, THE BASE

01.

Tuia te here tangata
The threads that connect us

Margaret Forster & Sharon McLennan

E koekoe te tūī, Ketekete te kākā, Kūkū te kererū.
Iere mai nei ngā manu, he reo karanga ki ngā iwi o te ao.

The tūī chatters, the parrot gabbles, the wood pigeon coos.
The birds sing a welcoming call to all peoples.

This is a book about global encounters as told from the context of Aotearoa. We open with a mihimihi or greeting composed by our colleague Hone Morris (Ngāti Kahungunu, Rangitāne) that uses the metaphor of birds and birdsong to introduce key themes explored in this book. The forest represents the interconnected world where various birds live and interact — the tūī, the kākā and the kererū. Our collective wealth is linked to recognising and celebrating the distinctiveness of each bird. Myriad encounters are possible in this world, and this is revealed by birdsongs that range from harmonious compositions to a cacophony of sound. These metaphors illustrate encounters that make visible both our obligations to each other and the dynamic, evolving and interconnected nature of global issues. This intent is reflected by the book's title, *Tū Rangaranga*, literally meaning 'to weave together' or establish connections.

Connections are also visualised through the metaphor associated with raranga or the customary practice of weaving using the harakeke or flax plant. Raranga is synonymous with unity, togetherness and strength, as reflected by the following whakataukī or proverb:

E kore e taea e te whenu kotahi ki te raranga i te whāriki, kia mohio tātau kia tātou, mā te mahi o ngā whenu, mā te mahi o ngā kairaranga, ka oti tēnei whāriki i te otinga, me titiro ki ngā mea pai ka puta mai ā tana wā, me titiro hoki ki ngā raranga i makere, mā te mea, he kōrero kei reira.

A strand of flax is nothing in itself but woven together it is strong and enduring. Let us look at the good that comes from it and, in time, we should also look at those stitches that have been dropped, because they also have a message.

This whakataukī is a reminder that collective efforts often result in more meaningful and enduring outcomes. How can multiple strands be brought together to create enduring connections that shape our rights and responsibilities as global citizens? And what about those stitches that have been dropped? Not all encounters are positive or enduring — many are violent and disruptive.

Implicit in this challenge is the importance of manaaki, a Māori concept that encapsulates the notion of caring for one another. This intent is also reflected in the raranga metaphor, as the harakeke plant represents the family unit and the key roles and functions of family. For example, the leaves of this plant are organised in a fan structure. In the middle is the newest growth or youngest members of the family, the children. The children are surrounded by the adult leaves, and on the outer edges of the fan are the grandparent leaves. This visual imagery emphasises the importance of protecting and looking after members of the family. The various parts of the harakeke provide the structure of this book.

In this chapter we provide the context and foundations of the book and explain the harakeke and weaving structure and metaphors. The first section explains the foundations of this book and its roots in Aotearoa, the way in which different knowledges are woven into the book, and the use of Māori perspectives through iho atua (origin narratives). The chapter then introduces the key themes of global citizenship, rights and responsibilities, before giving an overview of the organisation of the book.

The foundations

In this section we set out the foundational basis of the book, the underlying priorities that guide its design, and the narrative threads that run through it. This includes acknowledging our tūrangawaewae, the place from where we stand and start this journey, in Aotearoa, and the presence of Māori as tangata whenua, and explains why we have chosen the various voices represented in the book.

Situating the encounter in Aotearoa

In Aotearoa, the presence of Māori as first peoples of this land and our collective colonial history shape any local framing of the concept of citizenship and our responses to the wider world. Situating this book on global citizenship in Aotearoa means we need to acknowledge and make visible the contemporary relevance of Indigenous ways of knowing that have been subjugated through colonial hierarchies of power.

To ensure this book is rooted in the place it is taught, and to centre Māori perspectives on global encounters and citizenship, we began this introduction with a mihimihi and whakataukī, and foregrounded the notion of manaaki as a platform for ethical behaviour. This centring continues throughout the book, with each chapter beginning with an iho atua, an origin narrative derived from a Māori world view that provides a Māori knowledge-based or disciplinary reflection on the various issues addressed. These commentaries are derived from customary narratives that encapsulate core cultural values and practices as set by the ancestors. Iho atua, therefore, provide a guide to contemporary responsibilities and actions that are grounded in Māori culture, and are a way to localise the global and globalise the local. The iho atua are a deliberate strategy to ensure a plurality of voices is present in this book.

We also signal the centrality of Indigenous peoples and the importance of the history of Aotearoa at the beginning of Chapter 2, through a focus on Indigenous voyaging in the Pacific. Some tribal histories trace their presence in Aotearoa to migration from the Pacific beginning in 1200 CE (Anderson et al., 2014), while other histories show tribes originating in this land. Consequently, there are still strong connections between Māori and Pacific Island communities, alongside many similarities in world views, social organisation and language. By exploring these connections, Indigenous globalisation is rendered visible and becomes the first strand in the book, as indicated in the opening whakataukī. Māori perspectives are highlighted throughout the book, particularly Māori approaches to citizenship (Chapter 4), rights (Chapter 5) and responsibilities (Chapter 6), as well as responses to climate change (Chapter 9) and to the Covid-19 pandemic (Chapter 17).

Weaving Indigenous and marginalised voices and perspectives

The metaphors of weaving and braiding invoked in the whakataukī at the beginning of this chapter are often used in educational contexts where Indigenous world views and knowledges are woven into courses and curriculum (see Jimmy & Andreotti, 2019; Kimmerer, 2013; Sockbeson, 2009; Synot et al., 2020). As Snively and Williams (2018) discuss, in weaving and braiding there is reciprocity and tension among the strands in a braid, but each strand remains a separate entity, coming together to form the whole. Braiding Indigenous knowledge with Western knowledge affirms both ways of knowing as legitimate, and the metaphor reflects our approach to this book in promoting a range of voices on global encounters and citizenship.

Importantly, the content in this book was curated to highlight the voice and agency of the speakers. Much of the discourse around global challenges focus on victimhood, with Indigenous and marginalised groups spoken for, and portrayed as in need of help. As Macfarlane (2019) asks:

> is it appropriate to seek solutions to the impact of climate change, poverty, inequality, and human rights violations that threaten peace and sustainability worldwide, solely from a Western approach? Or are there lessons to be learnt from Indigenous perspectives of 'place' and 'authority'? (p. 99)

In our view as editors the answer to Macfarlane's second question is an unequivocal 'Yes'. Indeed, and to restate the centrality to this book of the metaphor of weaving, throughout the book we highlight and share the voices of those directly affected by the challenges and concerns we discuss. This not only enables us to see the problems as defined by those affected, but also to become aware of the myriad solutions and responses missed by mainstream media and scholarship, enabling much more positive, hopeful and mana-enhancing or empowering conversations about responsibility.

Encounters from a Māori perspective

The global encounters explored in this book are complex, multifaceted and represent a diverse range of perspectives. A Māori perspective of these encounters can be derived from Māori origin narratives. Encounters feature in many of these narratives as a reminder of the challenges and triumphs of the atua or deities and deeds of the ancestors as they shaped the world. Origin narratives are instructional and aspiring. They are a blueprint for understanding our world, our roles, and our rights and responsibilities. These narratives emphasise that identity, belonging and ethical behaviour are a useful foundation for global citizenship. Furthermore, a Māori perspective draws attention to the continued impacts of colonisation and, therefore, becomes a tangible expression of Māori resistance, self-determination and hope. The first iho atua is provided here.

IHO ATUA

Margaret Forster (Rongomaiwāhine, Ngāti Kahungunu)

According to a Māori perspective the first global encounter is revealed through origin narratives about the world created by the first parents — Ranginui, Skyfather, and Papatūānuku, Earth Mother.

> Te Pō
> The darkness is a womb, it has nurtured us but
> we cannot stay within its confines forever.
> (Ihimaera & Hereaka, 2019, p. 23)

Ranginui and Papaptūānuku were bound together in a loving embrace. Their children were born into the space between them, a world of darkness that protected and sheltered. Their world was confining and cramped — a necessary condition at the onset to nurture and establish life. In one origin narrative, some of the children escaped from their parents' embrace through the menstrual flow of Papatūānuku (Whatahoro, 1913). In another, the children peeked out of her armpits (Best, 1924). Both encounters exposed the children to a world beyond their own, and the unknown sparked a curiosity that inspired within our people the potential for change, transformation and expansion. These ideals are encapsulated within a well-known origin narrative about how Ranginui and Papatūānuku as sky and earth were separated so that the natural world could evolve and create the conditions for humans to flourish and prosper.

Te Pō

The darkness, O the darkness that has nurtured us,
that has oppressed us and defined us. The darkness
that is us, must inevitably arc into light.

Ki te whaiao, ki te ao mārama. (Ihimaera & Hereaka,
2019, p. 23)

Encounters, therefore, provide opportunities for growth and
expansion, and inevitably involve navigating new terrain and
dealing with uncertainty. Overcoming adversity and responding to
contests and conflicts are reoccurring themes in the pursuit of new
opportunities that sustain and strengthen the family and amplify
the interconnectedness of the world. Māori have a long legacy of
engaging with new ideas, commodities, economies and people
from around the globe (see, for example, Petrie, 2006). Some of
these global encounters have been mutually beneficial; others have
threatened Māori sovereignty or authority and Māori culture. A
contemporary challenge, therefore, is engaging in global encounters
that advance Māori priorities, that actively promote Māori interests
and political agendas, that allow Māori to realise their full potential in
the constant arc that reaches from absence, exclusion and 'darkness'
into attendance, inclusion and 'light'. This includes revisiting the
past to re-evaluate contemporary notions of citizenship, rights and
responsibilities, to better reflect present-day Māori notions of identity,
belonging and ethical behaviour.

Citizenship and global citizenship

This book explores our connections, impacts and roles in the world, and how we might respond to global issues. How should we respond to the climate crisis, conflict or inequality? What are our responsibilities to those who live beyond our national borders? And how will we connect and work with others to address issues of social justice and weave a better world? These are complicated and complex issues that are difficult to address, but at the heart of these responses is the need to develop an ethical awareness, to encourage rights and responsibilities that are globally informed, collective in orientation, and that strive for social justice.

The term 'citizenship' is commonly used in a narrow, legal sense to refer to membership of a nation-state or a particular geographical or political context, or, in a broader sense, to refer to membership of any community (Brown, 2017; Kahu, 2022). This may be a workplace, educational institution or family. Membership in a community brings a range of obligations, including fostering a sense of identity and belonging, and legitimising participation and voice. We broaden our conceptualisation of citizenship even further, taking into account the way globalisation has changed the way we live and how we connect with others (and who we can connect with). Many of us now have connections and allegiances well beyond our national borders and beyond the communities in which we live and work, and we utilise products and services that connect us daily with communities and individuals across the globe. Contemporary globalisation provides new opportunities to make societies richer and more connected, but it also links us to global concerns, from environmental degradation and climate change to conflict, inequality and injustice. These global connections complicate notions of citizenship, as explored in Chapters 3 and 4, and have significant implications for how we understand the rights and responsibilities of citizenship, and the tension between individual and collective rights and responsibilities.

Complicating rights and responsibilities

This book explores global citizenship as a means to examine how we think, act, relate and respond to global issues. The topics we introduce are examples of global issues that make claims and require a response that goes beyond narrow state and locally based conceptions of citizenship. Throughout the book, we present the rights concerns related to each topic and explore any corresponding responsibilities. You might disagree with some of these, or approach things differently. Regardless, our challenge to you is to think about the implications of the global changes and connections discussed in this book, and what this means in terms of rights and responsibilities — for Aotearoa as a nation, for our communities and for ourselves as individuals.

The concepts of rights and responsibilities are introduced in Chapters 5 and 6 and are woven throughout the book. The concept of rights is a difficult one from an Indigenous standpoint. Discourses of rights are considered to be one way in which patriarchal white sovereignty exercises its power, enabling the law and government to intervene in the lives of Indigenous people (Moreton-Robinson, 2009). The very concept of universal rights is derived from 'state-centric forums while "Indigenous nations" responsibilities to the natural world originate from their long-standing relationships with their homelands — relationships that have existed long before the development of the state system' (Corntassel, 2012, p. 92).

To acknowledge this, and to complicate and trouble the concept of rights, discussions of human rights and the Universal Declaration of Human Rights in this book occur in tandem with discussions of collective rights, which are deliberately embedded in Māori conceptions of rights as derived from their status as tangata whenua or people of the land as expressed through tūrangawaewae — an affiliation and authority associated with tribal territory. Then there is the issue of non-human rights. How do we acknowledge and respond to the rights of the environment or animals or birds? They are an important part of the global world and global encounters, as well as being affected by human activity related to climate change, conflict and inequality.

The question of responsibility is also fraught. A key critique of global citizenship is that it positions a global elite as being endowed with superior knowledge, a superior world view, and a responsibility to 'improve' the lives of others (Shultz, 2018, p. 253). As Pashby (2011), notes, transforming notions of responsibility and agency is key. Throughout the book, we aim to shift from forms of thinking that emphasise rights as individualistic, and responsibilities as something the privileged do for others within or outside our borders, to a more critical understanding of collective responsibility towards the planet and all forms of life.

The organisation of this book

Building on the notion of weaving that is inherent in the book's title, the various parts of the harakeke are used to organise the content (see Figure 1). Part One is Te Take or the base, where key concepts are introduced associated with encounters, engagements, citizenship, rights and responsibilities. Part Two is Te Rito or the central shoot of the harakeke. This section introduces key global issues with a focus on implications for rights and responsibilities. The final part of the harakeke is called Te Puāwai, the flowers, and focuses on aspects of agency and action, exploring a range of collective responses to particular global issues.

In Te Take, we introduce key concepts and explore the notion of global encounters and how the ideas, processes and events associated with colonialism and globalisation shape our understanding of citizenship, rights and responsibilities in the context of Aotearoa. In Chapter 2, 'Global encounters', David Littlewood and Carol Neill explore global encounters through a historical lens. This chapter sets the scene for understanding globalisation by examining the intersections of the global and the local in the human history of Aotearoa. It proceeds from

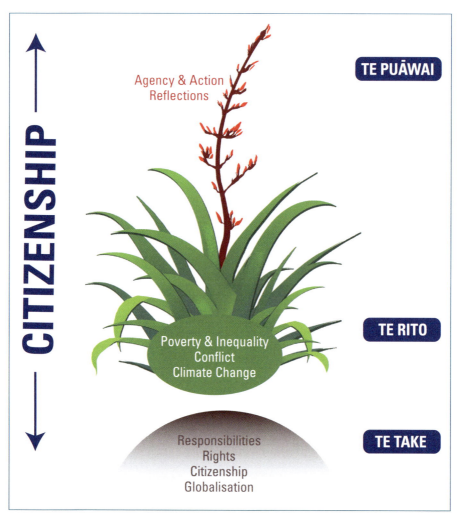

FIGURE 1: A harakeke showing te take (the base), te rito (the central shoot) and te puāwai (the flowers).
DESIGNED BY LIZA HAARHOFF

first settlement by Māori as part of a chain of Pacific migration, through waves of European exploration and engagement, to modern networks of communication, interaction and trade.

In Chapter 3, 'Encountering globalisation', Sharon McLennan explores the various ways that globalisation has been defined, and makes explicit the links between processes of globalisation, particularly neoliberalism, and the local challenges we face. Throughout the chapter, she introduces some key questions about the inequitable impacts of globalisation and the implications of these for rights and responsibilities.

In Chapter 4, 'Encountering global citizenship', Sharon McLennan, Margaret Forster and Rand Hazou introduce various understandings of global citizenship. One of the key arguments underscoring conceptions of global citizenship is that nation-state citizenship is limited and insufficient for accommodating the multiple expressions of identity and belonging that globalisation brings. They introduce the concept of global citizenship as a way of moving beyond these limitations and creating a more inclusive and socially just world.

In Chapter 5, 'Rights', Shine Choi, Margaret Forster and Beth Greener explore the notion of human rights from a politics, international relations and Māori policy disciplinary lens. This chapter explores the various ways that human rights can be conceptualised, and how power and politics interplay to determine whose rights are recognised.

The final chapter in Te Take, Chapter 6, 'Responsibilities', by Tracey Hepi, Carol Neill and Krushil Watene, asks how constructions of identity, belonging and citizenship in a global world shape the nature and extent of our relationships and, more importantly, our responsibilities to one another. Together, the chapters in Te Take provide a grounding or a base from which to encounter and explore various rights issues from around the globe. Te Take also provides a shared vocabulary of key concepts that will deepen your engagement with the various global issues that are presented in Te Rito.

In Te Rito, or the central shoots, we introduce some key challenges facing the world and explore these in relation to rights and responsibilities. The chapters in Te Rito are subdivided into three main areas covering climate change, conflict, and poverty and inequality. These are each introduced by summary chapters that highlight some of the key strands that run through the accompanying chapters. The first of these is climate change. In Chapter 7, 'Encountering climate change', Sharon McLennan and Axel Malecki provide an overview of climate change and its consequences, particularly for people in vulnerable places and for those already marginalised. The chapters in this section focus on responses to the environmental crisis, namely Pacific Island responses (Movono & McLennan, Chapter 8), Māori responses (Kaiser & Kenney, Chapter 9), and creative responses (Horrocks & Doig, Chapter 10).

The second section focuses on conflict. In Chapter 11, 'Encountering conflict', David Littlewood examines the repercussions of conflict for Aotearoa and describes the frequency of, and most persistent causes for, conflict in the early twenty-first century. Chapters in this section explore the multifaceted links between conflict and human rights violations and responses to these, including the Responsibility to Protect concept (Rogers, Chapter 12), conflict commodities (Bramwell et al., Chapter 13), and finally artistic and creative responses (Hazou, Chapter 14).

The final section of Te Rito explores poverty and inequality. Chapter 15, 'Encountering inequality and poverty', by Carol Neill and Samantha Gardyne, examines how socio-economic or material inequality can be problematised through understandings of, and responses to, poverty. The chapters in this section explore global and local responses to inequality. Chapter 16 (Gardyne & Malecki) explores the Sustainable Development Goals as a global response, while Chapters 17 and 18 examine responses here in Aotearoa. Chapter 17, by Margaret Forster, Sharon McLennan and Catherine Rivera, examines Māori responses to Covid-19 and inequality, while Chapter 18, by Siautu Alefaio-Tugia and colleagues, explores Pasifika perspectives on income inequality and sustainable livelihoods. Each of the chapters in Te Rito deploys disciplinary perspectives from across the humanities and social sciences and offers very different considerations, but they are all structured in similar ways, introducing an issue of global relevance, highlighting the issue in relation to a consideration of rights, and then offering some thoughts or provocations on what our responsibilities might be as individuals and collectives.

Throughout all of Te Take and Te Rito chapters, we provide a series of aho or threads. Some of these aho are short, focused, stand-alone commentaries responding to or deepening the content in each chapter, while others provide links to videos and websites that provide access to other voices and perspectives on the issues presented. The aho ensure a multidisciplinary lens and remind us that there are many ways to view, understand and respond to complex global issues.

Two final chapters comprise the puāwai or flowers of the harakeke. Chapter 19 by Margaret Forster and David Belgrave focuses on agency and action and the potential for transformation that can emerge when we engage collectively with messy and complicated global issues. In the final chapter, Sharon McLennan reviews the concepts introduced in Te Take and the global challenges discussed in Te Rito in a reflection on the dropped stitches, tangled threads and unfinished edges of global citizenship as a concept and practice.

References

Anderson, A., Binney, J., & Harris, A. (2014). *Tangata Whenua: An illustrated history*. Bridget Williams Books.

Best, E. (1924). *Māori Religion and Mythology, Part 2*. Hasselberg. http://nzetc.victoria.ac.nz/tm/scholarly/tei-Bes02Reli.html

Brown, A. (2017). Introduction. The citizen: From ancient to post-modern. In A. Brown & J. Griffiths (Eds.), *The Citizen* (pp. 9–22). Massey University Press. https://doi.org/10.1093/nq/s5-VIII.193.188-d

Corntassel, J. (2012). Re-envisioning resurgence: Indigenous pathways to decolonization and sustainable self-determination. *Decolonization: Indigeneity, education and society, 1*(1), 86–101.

Ihimaera, W., & Hereaka, W. (Eds.). (2019). *Pūrākau: Māori myths retold by Māori writers*. Vintage.

Jimmy, E., & Andreotti, V. (2019). *Towards Braiding*. Musagetes. https://decolonialfutures.net/towardsbraiding

Kahu, E. (2022). Identity and citizenship in Aotearoa New Zealand. In E. Kahu, R. Shaw & H. Dollery (Eds.), *Tūrangawaewae: Identity & belonging in Aotearoa New Zealand* (2nd ed). Massey University Press.

Kimmerer, R. W. (2013). *Braiding Sweetgrass: Indigenous wisdom, scientific knowledge and the teachings of plants*. Milkweed Editions.

Macfarlane, S. (2019). He rarunga o te ao — Global citizenship: A Māori perspective. *Curriculum Matters, 15*, 99–103. https://doi.org/10.18296/cm.0039

Moreton-Robinson, A. (2009). Imagining the good indigenous citizen: Race war and the pathology of patriarchal white sovereignty. *Cultural Studies Review, 15*(2), 61–79. https://search.informit.org/doi/10.3316/informit.699352291848041

Pashby, K. (2011). Cultivating global citizens: Planting new seeds or pruning the perennials? Looking for the citizen-subject in global citizenship education theory. *Globalisation, Societies and Education, 9*(3–4), 427–442. https://doi.org/10.1080/14767724.2011.605326

Petrie, H. (2006). *Chiefs of Industry: Māori tribal enterprise in early colonial New Zealand*. Auckland University Press.

Shultz, L. (2018). Global citizenship and equity: Cracking the code and finding decolonial possibility. In I. Davies, D. Kiwan, C. Peck, A. Peterson, E. Sant, & Y. Waghid (Eds.), *Palgrave Handbook of Global Citizenship and Education* (pp. 245–255). Palgrave MacMillan.

Snively, G., & Williams, W. L. (2018). *Knowing Home: Braiding Indigenous science with Western science, book 2*. University of Victoria Libraries.

Sockbeson, R. C. (2009). Waponaki intellectual tradition of weaving educational policy. *Alberta Journal of Educational Research, 55*(3), 351–364. https://doi.org/10.11575/ajer.v55i3.55332

Synot, E., Graham, M., Graham, J., Valencia-Forrester, F., Longworth, C., & Backhaus, B. (2020). Weaving First Peoples' knowledge into a university course. *The Australian Journal of Indigenous Education*, 1–7. https://doi.org/10.1017/jie.2019.29

Whatahoro, H. T. (1913). *The Lore of the Whare-wananga: Te Kauwae-runga, or 'things celestial'; Or teachings of the Māori College on religion, cosmogony, and history*. Polynesian Society.

02.
Global encounters

David Littlewood & Carol Neill

Introduction

Movement and contact between places and peoples have been ongoing for millennia. Indeed, global connections existed between Indigenous groups long before European colonialism. But while flows of people, goods, capital and information have a long history, the roots of modern globalisation are commonly dated to the 1950s or attributed to mass air travel and advances in telecommunications technology. Such interconnections — both old and new — have had profound implications in Aotearoa. Here, political, economic, social and cultural trends have long been influenced by outside factors, while migration, trade and the dissemination of ideas in the opposite direction have also produced lasting impacts.

This chapter sets the historical scene for understanding globalisation as we encounter it today, by examining how the global has been localised and the local globalised throughout the human history of Aotearoa. It proceeds from first settlement by Māori as part of a chain of Pacific migration, through waves of European exploration and engagement, to modern networks of communication, interaction and trade. A recurring theme is that although global interconnectedness has confronted the peoples of this country with significant challenges, it has also brought them a range of opportunities.

IHO ATUA

Margaret Forster (Rongomaiwāhine, Ngāti Kahungunu)

The origin narrative about Hine-ahu-one, the woman fashioned from clay, is useful for understanding encounters within an Aotearoa context.

> I sneezed and therefore I lived . . . It was Papatūānuku, the earth mother, who kept me hidden, keeping secret the hiding place of the uha [earthly female element] . . . Then, when all was ready on earth for mortal being, she told Tāne to form woman from the clay at Kurawaka . . . Within my human shape, I, Hine-ahu-one, held first human life. (Grace, 2019, pp. 53–54)

Māori people, through genealogical connections to Hine-ahu-one, are of the land, as signified by the expression tangata whenua. Consequently, Māori culture, values and practices are grounded in whenua. This is a reminder of the immutable and intimate connection to the local that established a series of binding cultural obligations and responsibilities. Manaaki is one such obligation. The hongi or greeting act that involves the pressing of noses is a constant reminder of the shared breath of life that first awoke Hine-ahu-one. It is a physical expression of manaaki that provides a blueprint for appropriate relations and interactions. Manaaki involves elevating the mana or authority and presence of others. It is associated with acts of love and generosity, promoting relations that are welcoming, protective and purposeful; these are referred to as mana-enhancing relations and are synonymous with respect, good health and wellbeing. Māori encounters with the global are grounded in manaaki, as exemplified by Bishop Manu Bennett when he described the constitutional basis of Aotearoa as 'a promise of two peoples [Māori and Pākehā/non-Māori] to take the best possible care of each other' (Waitangi Tribunal, 1992, p. 8).

Pacific voyaging

Global encounters in an Aotearoa context were initially led by Pacific peoples, whose advances in seafaring vessels and navigation technology enabled long-distance voyaging after 1050CE. The first arrivals to Aotearoa were part of the 'burst of Polynesian exploration that, over a few hundred years, reached the Kermadec Islands, Norfolk Island and the sub-Antarctic Auckland Islands' (Davidson, 2019, p. 37). Migration to Aotearoa from Hawaiki, an island(s) located to the east or north-east, is dated around 1200CE (Anderson, 2014). The permanent habitation of Aotearoa has varying understandings in different iwi histories, but there was certainly longstanding and widespread settlement by the seventeenth century. While connections to the Pacific were essentially lost following the era of great Māori/Polynesian travel (O'Malley, 2015), there is evidence that early Polynesian settlers passed down their navigational knowledge and maintained their ties with Pacific relatives through return voyaging (Anderson, 2014). This was particularly apparent with Tupaia, who guided Cook and the HMS *Endeavour* from Tahiti to Aotearoa in 1769.

European exploration and colonialism

European nations began exploring the globe after 1400CE during a period of rapid economic development. Population growth and technological advances combined to generate significant increases in agricultural and industrial production, which in turn stimulated the beginnings of a commercial middle class with capital to invest in overseas ventures. Technological innovations also facilitated improvements in shipbuilding and navigation, while the influence wielded by the Christian churches fed a widespread missionary zeal. What better way for the rulers of European nations to demonstrate their power, gain resources and win converts to Christianity than by finding new lands (Abernathy, 2000)?

The 'Age of Discovery' quickly developed a momentum of its own. In 1492 Christopher Columbus sailed into Central America, before Vasco De Gama rounded the bottom of Africa and established a sea route to India. Ferdinand Magellan then led the first known circumnavigation of the globe between 1519 and 1522 (Thomas, 2003). Returning explorers added to knowledge about ocean currents and helped draw up more reliable maps. They also spread tales of the riches and wonders to be found. With Spain, Portugal, Britain, France and the Netherlands locked in competition for supremacy, they all poured resources into trying to locate new lands before their rivals.

The achievements of European exploration came with devastating consequences.

There were many instances of exploitation and violence, particularly because the Europeans tended to regard the peoples they encountered as racially inferior. The desire for gold and silver caused them to carve a bloody path through South America, while they also instigated the dreadful suffering of the trans-Atlantic slave trade. Less deliberate, but no less deadly, was the spread of European diseases among Indigenous populations who lacked any built-up immunity (Crosby, 1972).

The Enlightenment of the seventeenth and eighteenth centuries prompted certain changes in emphasis, but slight change in outcomes. A growing belief that all humans were endowed with natural rights led some people to criticise outrages like the slave trade, and to maintain that Europeans should engage with Indigenous peoples via negotiation, rather than by force. However, this 'humanitarianism' was still based on a particular set of beliefs. Convinced they were at the forefront of scientific and intellectual reasoning, Europeans held that the resources of the world were properly theirs and that they had a right, even a duty, to dominate racially different peoples. Whether they set out to exploit or to 'civilise', Europeans invariably proceeded from an assumption that they were superior and that other peoples should move aside or assimilate (Skinner & Lester, 2012).

Māori encounters with Europeans

Māori first encountered Europeans during the seventeenth and eighteenth centuries. The first to arrive off Aotearoa was an expedition led by Dutchman Abel Tasman in 1642, although this never made landfall after a violent incident with Ngāti Tūmatakōkiri. Contact between Māori and Europeans then lapsed until 1769, after which a series of expeditions visited on a quest for riches and scientific knowledge. The most famous were those led by British Captain James Cook, but there were others by French, Spanish, American and Russian explorers. When these expeditions returned to their homelands, they spread tales of the resources available — timber, flax, whales and seals — alongside the prospect of converting Māori to Christianity.

For the next 50 years, the European presence in Aotearoa consisted of traders and missionaries. Their numbers were small — an estimated 2000 by 1840 — and they remained confined to coastal areas. Many Māori viewed establishing social and economic relationships with the new arrivals as a means of demonstrating their capacity for generous hospitality, of acquiring goods, technologies and innovations, and as an opportunity to enhance their mana (Easton, 2020). They were likewise eager to acquire reading and writing skills that enabled them to expand their existing communication and recording strategies (Walker, 2004).

AHO 2.1 EARLY MĀORI GLOBAL ENCOUNTERS: TE PAHI AND HIS MEDAL

In 1805 Ngāpuhi chief Te Pahi left his home in the Bay of Islands bound for the Australian settlement of Port Jackson (Sydney). He took his four sons with him and for three months they were the guests of the British Governor of New South Wales, Philip King. Te Pahi was one of a growing number of Māori in the early nineteenth century who took the opportunity of boarding European vessels to explore the world beyond Aotearoa. The son of Te Pahi, Matara, had spent time in New South Wales with King previously and had brought back gifts to his father. Te Pahi wanted to establish further opportunities to cement trade and cultural relations that would benefit his tribe (Stocker, 2015).

While there, King presented him with a silver medal, inscribed on both sides and now considered to be one of the earliest examples of Australian silver smithery. Stocker (2015) suggests it was one of the first official trans-Tasman taonga (treasures) to be exchanged, boosting the mana of Te Pahi on his return home due to its metal composition.

The promising trade links established between Te Pahi and King were scuttled by the burning and murder of the crew of the ship *Boyd* in 1809 in Whangaroa Harbour. Te Pahi was unfairly blamed for the incident and his house and village destroyed in a revenge attack by British soldiers.

It is thought that in the attack a soldier took the Te Pahi medal and somehow it made its way back to Australia, where it disappeared until 1899 when it turned up in the will of Edward du Moulin. It appeared again in 2014 at Sotheby's auction house in Sydney. The medal was bought in a joint purchase by the Museum of New Zealand Te Papa Tongarewa and Auckland War Memorial Museum, a venture made at the urging of and in collaboration with Ngāti Rua, Ngāti Torehina ki Matakā and Ngāpuhi, and after 200 years it made its way back home to Aotearoa, a symbol of both the peaceful and fiery nature of global encounters.

Reference

Stocker, M. (2015). A silver slice of history: The Te Pahi medal. *Tuhinga, 26*, 31–48.

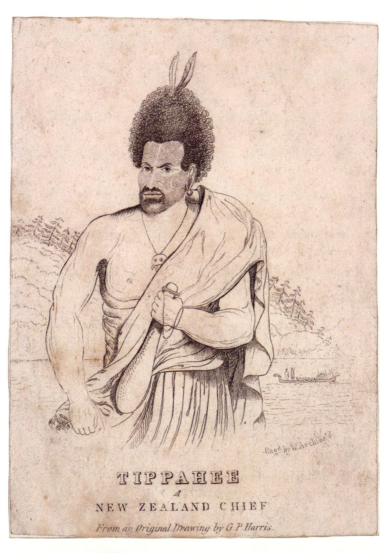

ABOVE: William Archibald, '[Te Pahi] A New Zealand Chief', 1827, after a drawing by George Prideaux Harris.
ALEXANDER TURNBULL LIBRARY, A-092-007

LEFT: Te Pahi Medal.
TĀMAKI PAENGA HIRA AUCKLAND WAR MEMORIAL MUSEUM, 2014.59.1, 56858

GLOBAL ENCOUNTERS

Yet the arrival of Europeans also caused significant disruption. Not only did they introduce a range of diseases, but the importation of muskets upset the balance of power between iwi and caused a significant increase in conflict. Iwi with access to more muskets were able to defeat those with fewer, prompting cycles of invasion and forced migration. By the time the Musket Wars of the 1820s and 1830s finally tapered off, an estimated 20,000 Māori had been killed (Ballara, 2003).

The colonisation of Aotearoa

The European presence in Aotearoa changed irrevocably with te Tiriti o Waitangi in 1840. Around 500 rangatira (Māori chiefs) signed te Tiriti o Waitangi, although many, especially in the central North Island, did not. For those who did, there were multiple motives. Some saw it as a way of implementing a governance system that would control the growing population of Pākehā (non-Māori) settlers — something a petition by Northern rangatira to the King of England had already sought to achieve (Walker, 2004). The signatories also desired to enhance their global connections and strengthen the trading networks that had already begun to develop (Henare, 2011). Māori tended to view te Tiriti o Waitangi as formalising a partnership of equals and offering new opportunities to enhance their mana — as a means of sharing power, rather than giving it away (Williams, 1989). The agreement would cement the right of Europeans as tangata tiriti (non-Māori with rights to citizenship established through te Tiriti o Waitangi) to be in the country and purchase some of its land, but the two peoples would live side by side according to their separate traditions. This would enable Māori self-determination and tino rangatiratanga (absolute tribal authority) to be preserved (Orange, 2011).

From the British perspective, te Tiriti o Waitangi arose from several imperatives. One held that if Britain did not incorporate Aotearoa into its empire, it would fall under French control. Another stemmed from the concept of humanitarianism, whose adherents were horrified by the impact of the Musket Wars and European diseases, and asserted it was Britain's responsibility to intervene before Māori were wiped out. But the greatest driver of colonisation was a sense that the European dominance of an Indigenous people was necessary and preordained. How could Britons and Māori live side by side as equals when Britons were superior? How could Māori achieve law and order without British oversight? And how could the resources of Aotearoa be properly exploited except under British direction? The answers to these questions resided in the British belief in their 'civilising mission' that also informed their writing of te Tiriti o Waitangi (Belich, 1996).

The following two decades contained several warning signs of challenges to come. Trade between Māori and Europeans continued to flourish, with certain iwi and hapū (subtribes) achieving success by building flour mills, supplying food or providing transport (Petrie, 2006). There were also some amicable land sales by Māori to Europeans for the establishment of new towns. Yet these partnerships did not mean an absence of conflict. The Northern War broke out when Hone Heke reacted to European attempts to transfer the capital from Kororāreka (Russell) in the Bay of Islands to Auckland and impose customs duties by cutting down the same flagstaff three times. Other disputes centred on whether British law or tikanga (Māori customs) should hold sway, while settlers were especially perturbed by the decision of several iwi to unite behind the pan-tribal Kingitanga movement — a step that overtly demonstrated Māori expectations of autonomy and equality (Sorrenson, 1992).

These disputes erupted into full-scale conflict in the 1860s. For Māori as tangata whenua (Indigenous people of Aotearoa), the land possessed great spiritual significance and provided a crucial connection to their ancestors. For the newly arrived Europeans, land was a commodity, the purchase of which would enable them to achieve security and independence. The frequent refusal of Māori to sell or vacate, therefore, prompted considerable resentment, with warfare over land ownership breaking out in Taranaki during 1860. Much larger battles followed in the Waikato and Bay of Plenty, as imperial forces attempted to crush the Kingitanga. Despite winning several victories, Māori were eventually overwhelmed (Belich, 1986). Europeans punished certain iwi through confiscations — particularly of their most fertile land — and subjected the whole country to the activities of the Native Land Court. That body worked to 'Europeanise' land by replacing iwi collective ownership with individual ownership over designated plots, something that made it far easier to pressure Māori into sales (King, 2003).

European dominance increased over the following decades. Māori were not passive victims of this process, frequently resisting by military means or by attempting to avoid European measures (Hill, 2004). But the pressure they came under was immense. The European population reached 100,000 in 1861, grew to 300,000 in 1874, and then exploded to half a million by 1882. At the turn of the century, it stood at over 750,000. In contrast, disease, land loss and warfare caused the Māori population to decline from around 60,000 in 1858 to 48,000 in 1874, before reaching its nadir of around 42,000 in 1896 (Pool, 1991). Through confiscation and the activities of the Native Land Court, Māori land ownership declined from 80 per cent of the North Island in 1861 to 40 per cent in 1891, then 25 per cent by 1911. Europeans also mounted efforts to assimilate Māori through schooling and the attempted eradication of the Māori language (Williams, 2001).

AHO 2.2 FROM TENANT FARMER TO LANDOWNING SETTLER

When researching his family's history, Richard Shaw was disturbed to uncover the role played by his ancestors in European colonisation and the alienation of Māori land.

'Whenever I visit my mother in New Plymouth, we drive out around the Taranaki coast to visit the old family farms, chugging along the South Road that was built to carry the Armed Constabulary (AC) forces that invaded Parihaka on November 5th, 1881. My great-grandfather worked on that road. As a member of the AC he was also at Parihaka as the sun rose on the morning of te Pāhua (the sacking). In time, he and his wife would own two farms on the coast and lease a third. All their farms were part of the 1,199,622 acres of land confiscated from Māori . . .

'My great-grandfather and his wife eventually controlled 412 acres of Taranaki land, on which a small economic and social revolution took place. For a start, the three farms allowed my great-grandparents to transform themselves from poor Irish migrants into settler landowners. The scale of the economic transformation was breathtaking. My great-grandfather was one of ten children, the son of tenant farmers who paid £26 a year to the local (English) squire for the lease on a 29-acre tenement in County Limerick. When he died, the combined property he and his wife held sway over on the Taranaki coast was 16 times the size of the farm he was born on. He was born the son of an Irish tenant farmer and died a landowning British settler. It is an extraordinary economic and social transformation in a single generation. And it is built upon land that the colonial state had taken from other people.' (Shaw, 2021)

For more on Richard Shaw's story, check out his book *The Forgotten Coast* (2021) from Massey University Press.

Reference

Shaw, R. (2021). From Parihaka to He Puapua: It's time Pākehā New Zealanders faced their personal connections to the past. *The Conversation.* https://theconversation.com/from-parihaka-to-he-puapua-its-time-pakeha-new-zealanders-faced-their-personal-connections-to-the-past-164553

Troops march along the beach, with Mount Taranaki in the background, February 1865.
E. A. WILLIAMS, A STROLL ON THE BEACH – MT EGMONT IN THE DISTANCE – 16 FEB. Y65 – DAYBREAK. AFTER MARCHING ALL NIGHT. WANGANUI CAMPAIGN, 1865, HOCKEN COLLECTIONS, UARE TAOKA O HĀKENA, UNIVERSITY OF OTAGO, 75/162 A13210

Enduring and deepening connectedness

British colonisation continues to exert a major influence over the political, economic and social structures of Aotearoa, as do the consequences of advantage and disadvantage for Pākehā and Māori. However, the flows generated by successive waves of migration and engagement were never one way; they were global encounters that produced worldwide connections and exchanges that interacted with and transformed the local. Indeed, pursuits of opportunity through the expansion of connections beyond Aotearoa have always compelled people to look for means to better their chances of survival and flourishing. In particular, the notion of Aotearoa 'trading its way' through global economic booms and busts has been ever-present (Neill, 2010).

Economic connections through trade were primary drivers of links between Aotearoa and the rest of the world, and these were highly influenced by Britain. The development of a farming economy, on the back of Māori land acquisition by conquest and statute, was based on notions of settler capitalism that exploited the land to produce goods for export back to Britain (McAloon, 2002). Māori engagement with the world became overshadowed by the activity of Pākehā settlers, whose economic connections with Britain intensified when refrigerated shipping enabled trade in perishable agricultural goods from 1882. That development provided the catalyst for farming expansion throughout both the North and South Islands, and embedded sheep and dairy farming as staples of the economy (Sinclair, 2000). The notion of Aotearoa being 'Britain's farm in the South Pacific' continued until Britain's entry into the European Economic Community (EEC — now the European Union) in the 1970s. Britain was not only the predominant source of export income but also of consumer and cultural goods and fashions.

Economic opportunity was the principal avenue through which the colonial government marketed Aotearoa to prospective British migrants. For many who made the voyage, Aotearoa offered greater possibilities for land ownership, social mobility and wealth generation. The economic and social structures that were established deliberately gave British migrants distinct advantages over Māori, and over any 'others' who arrived in pursuit of new opportunities. The disadvantages were particularly obvious for Chinese migrants, who were subjected to a 'poll tax' in the early twentieth century (Ip, 2009). That little had progressed for non-European migrants was evident in the 'Dawn Raids' on Pacific migrants in the 1970s.

The approach of Aotearoa to foreign policy further reflected its close ties to Britain. In both the South African War and the First World War, the government immediately offered Britain its full support and committed to sending soldiers overseas (Laking, 1980). Both conflicts also witnessed an outpouring of pro-British sentiment, with many New Zealanders enlisting to fight and many others taking part in patriotic activities and fund-raising. While the country's foreign policy had become slightly more independent by the outbreak of the Second World War, Prime Minister Savage still spoke for most New Zealanders when he said 'where [Britain] goes, we go; where she stands, we stand'. Most of the armed forces were again sent to Europe and the Middle East to support Britain directly (Rabel, 2009). Among them was 28 (Maori) Battalion, which won a formidable reputation as a fighting force and was seen by many Māori as paying 'the price' of full citizenship (Ngata, 1943).

Expanding connections — Pacific orientation

Aotearoa connections and allegiances started to expand after the Second World War, particularly through the adoption of the Statute of Westminster in 1949. Aotearoa engaged independently in international post-war restructuring, as states rallied to address the causes of a horrific conflict and develop systems that would ensure cooperation in the future. Its leaders were involved in the establishment of the 'Bretton Woods' system in 1944, which heralded today's major international financial and trade organisations, such as the International Monetary Fund, the World Bank and the General Agreement on Tariffs and Trade (GATT — later the World Trade Organization [WTO]) (Neill, 2010). Aotearoa also enthusiastically joined the new United Nations (UN) on its establishment in 1945. These multilateral organisations quickly became leaders in globalisation, as they developed cooperation agreements between states through many spheres of political and economic engagement. Integration of Aotearoa into such global systems effected change away from British models of economic and political management; this was at first gradual but became more pronounced from the 1980s.

The shift away from Britain was also built on a growing orientation towards the Pacific and Asia. The establishment of the ANZUS alliance with Australia and the United States in 1951, and particularly the military involvement of Aotearoa in the Vietnam War, demonstrated a shift in foreign policy priorities. As Britain commenced moves to join the EEC from the early 1960s, the close trading ties also came under threat (Easton, 2020). The growing connections and diversifying trade in Aotearoa fostered a more independent national identity, while a shift in focus to the Pacific region meant 'Britishness' increasingly took a back seat.

Changes in the economy provided the basis for social change across communities in Aotearoa. Post-Second World War industrial development led many Māori to migrate to urban centres for employment and establish new urban communities (Harris & Williams, 2014; Walker, 2004). This was accompanied in the 1950s and

AHO 2.3 CHINESE MIGRATION EXPERIENCES IN AOTEAROA

Kirsten Wong's explanation of her grandfather's experience highlights multiple dimensions of global connectedness in Chinese migration during the late nineteenth century.

'In the 1890s, when my grandfather was a young man in China, he dreamed of going to Canada. He was almost on his way when his friend, a fellow villager, said, "Don't go to Canada. Come to New Zealand with me." And he did.

'My grandfather, Chun Yee-Hop, arrived in Wellington on 5 December 1895 on board the Hauroto. He was 25 years old. Born into a poor rural family, he was in many ways a typical migrant, although hardly a pioneer. By the time he was born in 1870, a mass exodus was already in progress. Driven out by poverty, war and civil unrest, young men from all over Guangdong province were leaving their homeland in search of ways to make a living and support their families. In many villages, the export of young men was the principal source of income.

'The area in which Yee-Hop was born, Bak Shiek village in the Guangdong county of Jung Seng, was a fertile source of migrants. In fact, almost all the Chinese migrants to North America and Australasia came from three neighbouring counties: Jung Seng, Poon Yu and Seyip (comprising Toishan, Sun Wui, Hoy Ping and Yun Ping).

'Of the thousands who left, however, few set out with the intention of settling permanently in a new country. They saw themselves as sojourners, or temporary migrants. Their dream was to pay back the costs involved in migrating, find some work, support their families in China and eventually return with savings to last a lifetime. Unfortunately for many migrants, the last part of this dream went unfulfilled.

'To understand the early migrants properly, it is worth looking at turn-of-the-century New Zealand from their point of view. One of the first things they would have realised was that the world outside China was not a welcoming place — and this would surely have reinforced the migrants' sojourner identity. Yee-Hop's first experience of it would have been the £10 poll tax he had to pay when he disembarked at Wellington's Customhouse Quay. The poll tax was levied on all Chinese migrants and was specifically designed to discourage Chinese from entering the country. No other ethnic group had to pay this tax.' (Wong, 2003, pp. 114–115).

To learn more about Chinese migrants to Aotearoa, use the QR code to have a look at this report and video from Te Ao Māori News.

Chinese migrants Ah Sam and Joe Quin prepare vegetables for market in Roxburgh, Central Otago, c. 1903.
ALEXANDER TURNBULL LIBRARY, PACOLL-7581-96

Reference

Wong, K. (2003). A place to stand: The Chun family experience. In M. Ip (Ed.), *Unfolding History, Evolving Identity: The Chinese in New Zealand* (pp. 113–135). Auckland University Press.

1960s by government invitations to Pacific migrant workers to fill low-skilled jobs in factories (Mila, 2017), who in turn created Pacific neighbourhoods across the associated urban areas (Salesa, 2017; see also Chapter 18). Such processes started to build diversity into what had become a Pākehā–Māori dichotomy, although diversity would not be acknowledged as a characteristic of society in Aotearoa for some decades. As 1980s neoliberalism unlocked constraints on migration policies, the scope and breadth of immigration further contributed to a more diverse population. The new groups that have emerged, with their social, cultural, economic and political links reaching all parts of the world, have added complexity and richness to global connectedness in Aotearoa and led to it being described as 'superdiverse' (Spoonley, 2015).

Personal connections have also grown through outward migration and travel. Māori and Pākehā have long histories of moving across the world in pursuit of new opportunities, whether for short or long terms. Many pursued higher education studies overseas, especially in Britain and the United States. New Zealanders have settled and made their own lives in many countries — in 2013, for example, one in five Māori were recorded as living in Australia (Harris & Williams, 2014).

Global leadership?

While global connections have often caused local changes, Aotearoa has at times been viewed as a leader in global developments. A common narrative describes this country as punching above its weight, with its political influence outweighing its demographic and geographic smallness. Closer to home, the idea of Aotearoa being a 'first adopter' of domestic policies started in the 1890s, with social security measures and the granting of voting rights to women. In the 1980s, the Fourth Labour Government's economic reforms were seen to lead the world in taking up the neoliberal ideas practised under Margaret Thatcher in Britain, and Ronald Reagan in the United States. While the changes had substantial (and in many sectors dire) impacts on the domestic economy, they also increased the country's international leverage in GATT/WTO trade negotiations (Neill, 2010).

Claims about global leadership provided by Aotearoa have continued in recent years. The adoption of a 'living standard framework' by the Labour-led government in 2018 was viewed as continuing the tradition of Aotearoa as a 'social laboratory' (Hartcher, 2018). Similarly, the response of New Zealanders to the 2019 Christchurch Mosque attacks and the Covid-19 pandemic have cast this country's political management into the spotlight and given Prime Minister Jacinda Ardern strong global recognition.

Civil society groups have also made connections across, and even led, global action. The enduring and multifaceted work of Māori and Pacific activists and academics through the 1960s and 1970s, extending in the community support networks established across urban centres (Walker, 2004), built strong links with civil and Indigenous rights groups throughout the world. In the 1980s, activism against apartheid through the opposition to the 1981 Springbok rugby tour, the protests against nuclear testing in the Pacific, and the implementation of a national nuclear-free policy highlighted that New Zealanders were not afraid to assert their concerns against more powerful nations (McKinnon, 1993).

Individual New Zealanders have made names for themselves as global leaders in a range of fields. These include Ernest Rutherford in splitting the atom; Edmund Hillary in climbing Mount Everest; Kiri Te Kanawa in becoming a leading opera singer; Steven Adams's professional basketball career; and Lorde's many awards for songwriting and performing. Collectively, the outward migrants and representatives of Aotearoa continue in personal, professional and often public ways to maintain and build global connections.

Conclusion

Aotearoa has long been shaped by political, economic, social and cultural forces brought by migration, trade and diplomacy. After first being settled as part of a widespread Pacific exchange community, colonial Aotearoa was then built on deep ties to Britain. As those bonds gradually loosened after the Second World War, new connections were forged with the United States and other countries, especially through the development of global political and economic organisations. The intensity of those links has increased and diversified in recent decades, to a point where the peoples of Aotearoa are part of an intricate web of global connections.

The consequences of this longstanding interconnectedness have been, and remain, double-edged. It has caused Māori to undergo the trauma of European colonisation, led many New Zealanders to be killed or wounded during overseas wars, and brought the effects of global economic downturns to these shores. Yet engagement with the world has also generated opportunities for many individuals and groups to increase their wealth and influence, gain knowledge, experience new things, and enhance their mana. Every facet of life in Aotearoa is shaped in some way by centuries of localising the global and globalising the local.

References

Abernathy, D. R. (2000). *The Dynamics of Global Dominance: European overseas empires, 1415–1980*. Yale University Press.

Anderson, A. (2014). Pieces of the past: AD 1200–1800. In A. Anderson, J. Binney, & A. Harris (Eds.), *Tangata Whenua: An illustrated history* (pp. 56–87). Bridget Williams Books.

Ballara, A. (2003). *Taua: 'Musket wars', 'land wars' or tikanga? Warfare in Māori society in the early nineteenth century*. Penguin.

Belich, J. (1986). *The New Zealand Wars and the Victorian Interpretation of Racial Conflict*. Auckland University Press.

Belich, J. (1996). *Making Peoples: A history of the New Zealanders from Polynesian settlement to the end of the nineteenth century*. Allen Lane.

Crosby, A. W. (1972). *The Columbian Exchange: Biological and cultural consequences of 1492*. Greenwood.

Davidson, J. (2019). Explorers and pioneers: The first Pacific people of New Zealand. In S. Mallon, K. Mahina-Tuai, & D. Salesa (Eds.), *Tangata o le Moana: New Zealand and the people of the Pacific* (pp. 37–56). Te Papa Press.

Easton, B. (2020). *Not in Narrow Seas: The economic history of Aotearoa New Zealand*. Victoria University Press.

Grace, P. (2019) Hine-ahu-one. In W. Ihimaera & W. Hereaka (Eds.), *Pūrākau: Māori myths retold by Māori writers* (pp. 53–54). Vintage.

Harris, A., & Williams, M. M. (2014). Te ao hurihuri: The changing world. In A. Anderson, J. Binney, & A. Harris (Eds.), *Tangata Whenua: An illustrated history* (pp. 352–487). Bridget Williams Books.

Hartcher, P. (2018, March 6). Jacinda Ardern's New Zealand a social laboratory for the world. *Stuff*. www.stuff.co.nz/national/politics/102001865/jacinda-arderns-new-zealand-a-social-laboratory-for-the-world

Henare, M. (2011). Lasting peace and the good life: Economic development and the 'ato noho' principle of te Tiriti o Waitangi. In V. M. H. Tawahi & K. Gray-Sharp (Eds.), *Always Speaking: The Treaty of Waitangi and public policy* (pp. 224–235). Huia Publishers.

Hill, R. S. (2004). *State Authority, Indigenous Autonomy: Crown–Maori relations in New Zealand/Aotearoa, 1900–1950*. Victoria University Press.

Ip, M. (2009). *The Dragon and the Taniwha: Māori and Chinese in New Zealand*. Auckland University Press.

King, M. (2003). *The Penguin History of New Zealand*. Penguin.

Laking, G. (1980). The evolution of an independent foreign policy. In J. Henderson, K. Jackson, & R. Kennaway (Eds.), *Beyond New Zealand: The foreign policy of a small state* (pp. 10–15). Methuen.

McAloon, J. (2002). Gentlemanly capitalism and settler capitalists: Imperialism, dependent development and colonial wealth in the South Island of New Zealand. *Australian Economic History Review, 42*(2), 204–223.

McKinnon, M. (1993). *Independence and Foreign Policy: New Zealand in the world since 1935*. Auckland University Press.

Mila, K. (2017). Deconstructing the big brown tail/tales: Pasifika peoples in Aotearoa New Zealand. In V. Elizabeth, A. Bell, M. Wynyard, & T. McIntosh (Eds.), *Land of Milk and Honey? Making sense of Aotearoa New Zealand* (pp. 68–86). Auckland University Press.

Neill, C. (2010). Trading Our Way: Developments in New Zealand's trade policy 1930s to 1980s [unpublished doctoral thesis]. Massey University.

Ngata, A. T. (1943). *The Price of Citizenship: Ngarimu, V.C.* Author.

O'Malley, V. (2015). *Haerenga: Early Māori journeys across the globe*. Bridget Williams Books.

Orange, C. (2011). *The Treaty of Waitangi* (2nd ed.). Bridget Williams Books.

Petrie, H. (2006). *Chiefs of Industry: Māori tribal enterprise in early colonial New Zealand*. Auckland University Press.

Pool, I. (1991). *Te Iwi Maori: A New Zealand population, past, present and projected*. Auckland University Press.

Rabel, R. (2009). New Zealand's wars. In G. Byrnes (Ed.), *The New Oxford History of New Zealand* (pp. 245–262). Oxford University Press.

Salesa, D. (2017). *Island Time: New Zealand's Pacific futures*. Bridget Williams Books.

Sinclair, K. (2000). *A History of New Zealand*. Penguin.

Skinner, R., & Lester, A. (2012). Humanitarianism and empire: New research agendas. *Journal of Imperial and Commonwealth History, 40*(5), 729–747. https://doi.org/10.1080/03086534.2012.730828

Sorrenson, M. P. K. (1992). Māori and Pākehā. In G. W. Rice (Ed.), *The Oxford History of New Zealand* (2nd ed., pp. 141–166). Oxford University Press.

Spoonley, P. (2015). New diversity, old anxieties in New Zealand: The complex identity politics and engagement of a settler society. *Ethnic and Racial Studies, 38*(4), 650–661.

Thomas, H. (2003). *Rivers of Gold: The rise of the Spanish Empire, from Columbus to Magellan*. Random House.

Waitangi Tribunal. (1992). *Te Roroa Claim — Wai 38*. https://forms.justice.govt.nz/search/Documents/WT/wt_DOC_68462675/Wai38.pdf

Walker, R. (2004). *Ka Whawhai Tonu Matou — Struggle without end*. Penguin.

Williams, D. V. (1989). Te Tiriti o Waitangi: Unique relationship between Crown and tangata whenua? In I. H. Kawharu (Ed.), *Waitangi: Māori and Pākehā perspectives of the Treaty of Waitangi* (pp. 64–91). Oxford University Press.

Williams, D. V. (2001). *Crown Policy Affecting Māori Knowledge Systems and Cultural Practices*. Waitangi Tribunal.

03.
Encountering globalisation

Sharon McLennan

Introduction

Never has the interconnectedness of the world been more evident than in the Covid-19 pandemic. As we put together this book, Aotearoa was experiencing a second nationwide lockdown, with case numbers rising, and potentially tragic consequences for many. Much of the writing was completed at home, at laptops on dining tables and away from the conveniences and camaraderie of the office. Yet, despite the physical isolation that lockdown imposes, we remained connected through never-ending Zoom meetings, multiple apps and chat groups, and video calls with loved ones. The pandemic also highlighted our reliance on imported goods, both through the products we bought — such as coffee from Papua New Guinea or bananas from Ecuador — and in the inconvenience caused by shipping delays resulting in empty shelves. As such, the pandemic illuminated both the risks and opportunities of globalisation.

But what exactly is globalisation? In the previous chapter, we used a historical lens to explore how global connections and encounters have brought change to Aotearoa and helped establish our place in the wider world. These global encounters set the scene for contemporary globalisation, and the challenges and opportunities it entails, including our exposure and response to the global pandemic. In this chapter we explore the concept of globalisation further,

IHO ATUA

Margaret Forster (Rongomaiwāhine, Ngāti Kahungunu)

Potentiality is a prevalent theme in Māori narratives. It is embedded in whakapapa or genealogical sequences, such as Te Kore — Te Pō —Te Ao Mārama that refers to the transformation from the nothingness to the darkness to the world of light. And light in this context signified a shift, creating space for innovation and change. A specific reference to change is seen in another whakapapa sequence Te Ao Mārama — Te Ao Hurihuri — Te Ao Hou, which acknowledges transitions between the world of light, the ever-changing world and the new world.

Te Ao Hurihuri has specific implications for globalisation. This term is often associated with modernity and the contemporary world. It is a reminder that things are constantly changing and of the need to adapt tikanga or our ethical practices in response to change, so that culture remains central, appropriate and relevant. In the context of globalisation, Te Ao Hurihuri is reflective of the opportunities and challenges that arise from engaging with new knowlege, new technology, increased mobility and new peoples. It is also a reminder of the need to be mindful of the impact of the global on the Māori world to ensure the centrality of Māori priorities and aspirations and the retention of mana — the authority and dignity of people, communities and the environment. There is considerable potential in a globally interconnected world, if the risks can be navigated.

outlining different forms of contemporary globalisation and some of their impacts. We finish the chapter with some curly questions — is globalisation slowing? What might be the impact of the rise of nationalism and populism, and the Covid-19 pandemic? What do these changes mean for our place in the world?

Defining globalisation

Contemporary globalisation is the process by which the world is becoming increasingly interconnected through flows of ideas, commodities, finance and people, made possible through improvements in transport, technology and communications. It is a broad phenomenon that provides new opportunities to make societies richer and more connected and facilitates the global encounters that continue to shape local communities and our understanding of, and interactions with, the wider world. Globalisation has been defined by Anthony Giddens (1990) in *The Consequences of Modernity* as 'the intensification of worldwide social relations which link distant localities in such a way that local happenings are shaped by events occurring many miles away and vice versa' (p. 64). These links contribute to greater interconnectedness and interdependence among the world's places, people and institutions (Greiner, 2014).

Conceptualising globalisation as flows that connect different geographical places emphasises the increased movement of people, ideas, capital and commodities through space and time and the connections and encounters that result from that. Prior to the pandemic, unprecedented numbers of people were moving between nations. Some of this travel was for leisure and work, while others migrated temporarily or permanently, contributing to the hyper-diversity of cities like Auckland (Cain, 2017). Ideas move with people as people travel and communicate, and through the entertainment industry, media and social media. International trade and finance markets move vast amounts of goods and finances around the globe. Arguably, commodities and capital now flow further and faster than people, and those commodity chains link us all to places we will never see and know little about. With these flows comes risk. Globalisation can threaten, particularly in its neoliberal form, by exacerbating inequality and precarity, by further endangering Indigenous people, by its frightening implications for the environment, and through the emergence of global pandemics such as Covid-19. Before exploring these risks, this chapter first outlines the three main forms of globalisation — economic, political, and social and cultural.

Economic globalisation

When globalisation is mentioned in the media and popular discourse, it is often used as shorthand for economic globalisation. This use of the term refers to the integration of economies into a 'borderless' world, the internationalisation of production, and increasing migration for labour purposes. Most discussions of globalisation focus on the economic dimensions for good reason. As Rhoads & Szelényi (2011) argue, we cannot examine contemporary globalisation without looking at its economic features and the increasing role that capitalism and free-market ideology play around the world. The process of economic globalisation rapidly accelerated in the 1980s, when neoliberalism emerged as a key mechanism for facilitating economic globalisation.

Neoliberalism is an ideology and policy model that emphasises markets, minimal states and individual choice as the means for ensuring economic and social wellbeing. As noted in Chapter 2, it came to prominence as an economic model in the West during the 1980s, particularly under the governments of Ronald Reagan in the United States (US) and Margaret Thatcher in the United Kingdom (UK), before spreading throughout much of the world. Neoliberal policies were introduced in Aotearoa during the 1980s. Named after the neoliberal economic reforms introduced by Roger Douglas, a Minister of Finance in the Fourth Labour Government, 'Rogernomics' is regarded by some as moving the country from 'what had probably been the most protected, regulated and state-dominated system of any capitalist democracy to an extreme position at the open, competitive, free-market end of the spectrum' (Nagal, 1998, p. 223).

Some commentators talk about neoliberalism as a new form of colonisation, since it defines success in terms of individual rights, monetary accumulation and competition, and at a very basic level involves the 'extension of the market mechanism into areas of the community previously organised and governed in other ways' (Bargh, 2007, p. 1). Under neoliberalism, every entity is seen to have an economic value. This includes things like medical care, public hygiene, prisons, and environmental features such as oceans, lakes and land. The state is seen as an inefficient provider of basic services and infrastructure, resulting in the increasing privatisation of previously public roads, hospitals, and utilities like water and telecommunications. The role of the state is therefore minimised and limited to providing the infrastructure to support the market, such as police to protect individual property rights. Neoliberals argue the state should interfere as little as possible with markets through taxes or subsidies, as well as allowing capital to flow unhindered across borders, hence the support for 'free trade' agreements. There is a strong focus on the individual as the master of their own success, where one sells their human capital to the market in return for wages. The good citizen is, therefore, one who is 'entrepreneurial and responsible for themselves' (Hardin, 2014, p. 208). As Thorsen (2010) points out, under neoliberalism, 'the virtuous person is one who is able to access the relevant markets and function as a competent actor . . . Individuals are also seen as being solely responsible for the consequences of the choices and decisions they freely make' (p. 202).

Political globalisation

From a political viewpoint, globalisation refers to the engagement of nation-states in international political cooperation and diplomacy, the increasing trend towards multilateralism (organised relationships between groups of three or more states) and to the possibility of a cosmopolitan or transnational state apparatus. As outlined in the previous chapter, the twentieth century saw the establishment of a series of institutions designed to address the causes of conflict and to develop systems for peace and cooperation, including the United Nations (UN), the European Union (EU), the International Monetary Fund (IMF) and the General Agreement on Tariffs and Trade (GATT). All of these organisations have played a powerful role in the acceleration of globalisation.

The growth of these international and regional mechanisms of government has also had an impact on nation-states, with national decision making increasingly restricted by agreements and rules stemming from these international bodies. Some suggest the free flow of capital has also weakened the control of governments over their economies and led to a 'retreat' and/or transformation of the state (Bellone Hite et al., 2015, p. 15). However, although the nation-state may be weakening, the size and complexity of worldwide political and governance systems continue to grow. This includes not only governmental and intergovernmental organisations but also global civil society, such as international non-governmental organisations and social movement organisations.

Social and cultural globalisation

Alongside, and accelerated by, economic and political globalisation are profound social and cultural changes. Globalisation is linked to cultural shifts and changes, and with flows of human (through migration, diaspora, tourism and travel) and non-human connections (e.g. finance, commodities and information, but also flora and fauna, and micro-organisms and viruses such as Covid-19). Think, for example, of the ubiquity of stars such as Beyoncé, the global reach of social media, and how Coca-Cola can be found in every corner of the globe — even reaching places international aid struggles to find (Byfield, 2015). This can also be seen as a process of Westernisation or, as some term it, McDonaldisation (Ritzer, 2009) or Coca-Colonisation (Greiner, 2014).

However, since the early days of colonialism, cultural artefacts and social practices have also moved the other way. Today, we regularly eat food that originates far from our home communities and nation, and enjoy music, movies and art from across the globe. Celebrities such as South Korean boy band BTS gather massive international followings. The global movement that is the BTS Army (fandom) illustrates the emergence of transcultural identities and hybridisation of popular cultures — in the case of the Army, these identities are based on solidarity and shared 'experiences of hardship, mental health, and political, economic, and social uncertainty' (McLaren & Jin, 2020, p. 122). This process, whereby information, commodities, popular culture, media, and to some degree people, flow easily around the globe is, somewhat paradoxically, contributing both to a more homogenised world, and to a more diverse one.

These processes are clear in Aotearoa. The nation is increasingly being described as 'superdiverse' with complex social formations that 'produce a dynamic interplay of country of origin, ethnic identification, migration pathways, languages spoken, religious affiliation and socio-cultural practices and values' (Cain, 2017, p. 35). This has led to unique challenges, particularly the need to balance a growing multicultural society and the bicultural relationship between Māori and Pākehā (a relationship based in te Tiriti o Waitangi and officially recognised in state policy). Balancing respect for Indigenous rights with multicultural responsibilities in a culturally diverse society is an ongoing challenge (Ward & Liu, 2012).

Impacts of globalisation

As should be clear from the preceding discussion, the increased connections and flows of globalisation have many impacts. Our phones may be connected to exploitative mining practices in Africa, our food to the use of pesticides or unsustainable agricultural practices in South America, and our transport to unsafe factory working conditions in Asia. The rapid growth of transport, technology and manufacturing in recent decades has presented significant challenges to the global community, contributing to climate change, local and international conflicts, and rising poverty in many parts of the globe. These will be explored in depth in later chapters. While it would be impossible to provide a comprehensive list of impacts, in this chapter we discuss some of the more profound changes to help deepen considerations of the positive and negative impacts of globalisation.

The positives: Economic growth, opportunity and connection

Economic and political globalisation enables businesses to source raw materials where they are least expensive, and to take advantage of lower labour costs in some parts of the world, while being able to access the technical expertise and experience of more developed economies. This means different parts of a product may be made in different regions of the world. Services can also be globalised. For example, call centres or information technology services may be outsourced to places like India. This decreases business costs and enables us to have access to a wide range of products and services at cheaper prices. It can also have a positive effect on national economies and result in a higher standard of living.

Globalisation has also opened up communication and transportation networks, enabling significant, world-changing flows of ideas and inter-personal connections around the globe. The processes of globalisation and networking are closely connected, with transnational networks of advocacy groups, Indigenous movements and other organisations in geographically distant parts of the globe now able to communicate and work together in real-time. As the introduction to this chapter highlighted, online connections have been particularly important in the Covid-19 pandemic, with global networks and relationships maintained through online networking at a time when travel and face-to-face encounters are difficult or impossible.

The negatives: Neo-colonialism, inequality and instability

Globalisation and Indigenous peoples

Indigenous peoples were and are significantly impacted by encounters with colonialism and early globalisation. Furthermore, the processes of contemporary globalisation have had a profound impact on Indigenous peoples, perpetuating and exacerbating the inequities created by colonialism. The loss of land to colonial powers continues in land grabs by multinational corporations and governments. Neoliberal reforms also have profoundly negative impacts on Indigenous groups around the world. We can see this in Aotearoa, where Māori were disproportionately affected by the economic reforms of the 1980s and 1990s (Bargh, 2007).

While the appropriation and alienation of land under colonialism left many Māori impoverished and marginalised from their tūrangawaewae (tribal base), that poverty has deepened under neoliberalism — Māori and Pacific ethnic groups typically have poverty rates that are around double those of the European/Pākehā ethnic group, regardless of the measure used (Marriott & Sim, 2014). Continuing structural discrimination in public services including the health sector also means, for example, that Māori have disproportionately high mortality and morbidity and are less likely to be treated for similar health conditions than Pākehā (Rashbrooke, 2013). Under neoliberalism, a response has been to emphasise restructuring and the shifting of service delivery to the private sector (Bargh, 2007, p. 37). This has led to cuts in health, education and welfare — often framed as attacks on 'welfare dependency'. The response from Māori has been to take responsibility for their own development, and, over the past three decades, there has been a concurrent rise in the number of Māori health and social service providers. These initiatives align with Māori aspirations to self-manage and take control of their futures (key goals of rangatiratanga or Māori authority), although some commentators point out Māori are now providing services that are part of the government's social equity responsibilities and, as such, providing support for the continued roll-out of neoliberal policies (see Bargh, 2007).

In addition to the disproportionate impacts of neoliberal globalisation on Indigenous peoples, the expansion of Western ideas, values, lifestyles and technology (Smith et al., 2000) has resulted in the continuation of the loss of languages, cultural memories and artefacts that began with colonisation. And while, as discussed above, globalisation enables the sharing of ideas and culture, and two-way movement of cultural artefacts and ideas, this process also facilitates cultural appropriation, thereby threatening Indigenous intellectual property.

Inequality and the growth of the precariat

Economic and political globalisation, along with the spread of neoliberal policies, have been highly successful in creating wealth. However, rather than 'trickling down' to the poor as predicted, since the 1990s we have witnessed significantly greater disparities in wealth and income, as well as increased poverty. For example, workers in the developed world compete with those in lower-cost markets for jobs, while the working conditions of people in some parts of the world are deplorable. The garment industry in Bangladesh — which provides clothing to many retailers in Aotearoa — employs an estimated four million people, but the average worker earns less in a month than a US worker earns in a day, and human rights abuses and fatal accidents are common (HRW, 2015). This situation is worsening with the Covid-19 pandemic, with order cancellations and factory closures meaning that around 2.8 million workers, most of them women, are facing poverty and hunger (Islam, 2020).

AHO 3.1 GLOBALISATION AND FAST FASHION

One of the ways in which globalisation is present in our everyday lives is through the products that we buy. Many of these products are made overseas from components that are themselves grown or produced in a different country from where they are assembled. One of these products is clothing. Organisations such as Tearfund have critiqued the garment industry for promoting 'fast fashion': badly made clothes that last for a season and are often made by unethical means, including low-paid and dangerous labour practices, and environmental damage. Jeans, for example, can cause water pollution when blue dye is washed into waterways. Clothes are also a concern at the end-of-life, with many old clothes from the West being shipped to poorer countries where they may flood local markets and/or create a waste problem.

The non-governmental organisation (NGO) Tearfund has responded to fast fashion by producing an 'ethical fashion guide'. Scan the QR code to see the report and to read more about the impacts of climate change, Covid-19 and modern slavery on the fashion industry.

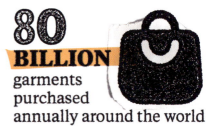

OVER **50 MILLION** people work in the global garment industry

10% of Greenhouse **GAS** emissions come from the global fashion industry

Covid-19 continues to impact – garment workers have lost more than **NZ$16 BILLION** in wages

FASHION is among the **TOP 5** industries at risk of modern slavery

WWW.TEARFUND.ORG.NZ/ETHICALFASHIONGUIDE

ENCOUNTERING GLOBALISATION 53

Economic globalisation has also prompted the rise of a group of people called the precariat, a global class in the making characterised by precarious jobs, uncertain occupational identities and career pathways, and limited rights (Horner & Hulme, 2017; Standing, 2015). 'Precariat' is a blend of the words 'precarious' and 'proletariat' — the latter a word used in Marxist ideology to describe the working class. The term was first used in the 1980s and is linked to the growing prominence of the neoliberal economic system. Guy Standing (2011) defines precarity as a condition of 'precarious existence' — one that involves a 'temporary status of some kind' (p. 11). Standing mainly applies the notion to an analysis of insecure labour conditions in the global economy, although he also links it to various groups of people who have had their civil, cultural, social or political rights restricted or limited in some way — 'those whose lives are dominated by insecurity, uncertainty, debt and humiliation. They are becoming denizens rather than citizens, losing cultural, civil, social, political and economic rights built up over generations' (Standing, 2011, p. x). This situation was exacerbated by the Covid-19 pandemic, with workers trapped in precarious employment being those most affected by increased unemployment and reduced hours, abuse, barriers to health care, and lack of access to safety and virus control measures (Matilla-Santander et al., 2021).

The rise of inequality and the precariat has been well-documented in Aotearoa (see for example, Groot et al., 2017), and evidence is emerging that the pandemic is also exposing and deepening social inequities here (Elers et al., 2021; Masselot & Hayes, 2020). Although, as discussed in this chapter, the neoliberal economic reforms were successful in strengthening the economy and were considered an international success story, as discussed in this chapter many people suffered as a result (Kelsey, 2015; Rashbrooke, 2013), and this has contributed to inequality and a growing precariat (Rua et al., 2019). This precariat is likely to be disproportionately Māori and Pasifika and will be significantly impacted by the pandemic.

Instability and the pandemic

Trade and travel have long been recognised as significant determinants of the spread of disease, as has the rise in urbanisation and the closer integration of the world economy (Shrestha et al., 2020). Covid-19 is far from the first disease to be spread via globalisation. The bubonic plague caused by *Yersinia pestis* was transmitted from China to Europe through trade routes; the influenza pandemic of 1918 that led to over 50 million deaths worldwide followed the movement of armies in the First World War; the Asian flu of 1957 (influenza A H2N2) was reported in 20 countries and primarily spread via land and sea travel; and the

Hong Kong flu pandemic (influenza A H3N2) was spread extensively through air travel (Shrestha et al., 2020).

Globalisation exacerbates this situation by influencing the dynamics of the disease as it changes patterns of human interaction, by giving rise to scenarios in which new infectious agents have more opportunities to originate and by facilitating the spread of already existing agents. As a result, the Covid-19 pandemic has been unprecedented in its capacity to take advantage of modern globalisation, allowing for massive transborder spread at a surprising speed. So, although humanity has survived previous pandemics, the changing world and massive scale of global connections unavoidably increase the probability of future pandemics, perhaps worse than Covid-19 (Mas-Coma et al., 2020).

Slowing globalisation

Globalisation has long been the focus of critique and resistance. In the 1990s and 2000s, the speed and impacts of globalisation were heavily criticised by anti-globalisation protestors and nationalist politicians — for very different but converging reasons. Over the past decade, the speed of globalisation appeared to slow and in January 2019, before the emergence of the Covid-19 pandemic, *The Economist* coined the term 'slowbalisation' for a new era of global economic sluggishness. Does this signal a slow down or potential reversal of globalisation? While there is not enough space here to explore all the factors that have had an impact on globalisation in recent years, this section outlines the impact of anti-globalisation protests, as well as the rise of far-right nationalism and the impact of the pandemic.

Indigenous resistance and anti-globalisation movements

While globalisation seems unstoppable, it has had many critics. In particular, Indigenous peoples have been resisting globalisation and globalisation-like forces for millennia (Hall & Fenelon, 2008). The forms of resistance have changed over time, but, in general, Indigenous groups are less interested in changing the system than in preserving autonomy and their own political and cultural spaces. This is the case in Aotearoa, where resistance to globalisation — including the neoliberal changes of the 1980s and 1990s and opposition to the free trade agreements of the 2000s — is rooted in tino rangatiratanga, absolute tribal authority. For Teanau Tuiono (in Bargh, 2007), tino rangatiratanga is about recognising the original resistance from the 1800s and the resistance processes that have evolved to the present day, including activism around Waitangi Day, land occupations and

AHO 3.2 THE STORY OF IOANE TEITIOTA

Migration is one of the most visible and significant flows of globalisation as people move within and between nations to find better employment and lifestyle opportunities. People also move to escape environmental and social problems including conflict and, increasingly, climate change.

Consider the case of Ioane Teitiota, a man from the Pacific Island nation of Kiribati. In 2007, Teitiota moved from Kiribati to Aotearoa to work. There is a long history of Pacific peoples migrating to Aotearoa for employment, and Teitiota was one of 186 i-Kiribati granted work permits for Aotearoa in 2007 (FigureNZ, 2021). However, his motivation for migrating was more than just economic — the family struggled living on poor-quality land, frequently inundated by high tides and flooding, which was worsening due to climate change.

Teitiota's wife became a caregiver in an Auckland nursing home, and he found work on nearby farms. In 2011, Teitiota inadvertently overstayed his visa after a miscommunication. His case was then taken on by another attorney who decided to present Teitiota as a casualty of climate change — and to set out to change international law. Mr Teitiota's attorney claimed that he was entitled to be recognised as a refugee on the basis that changes to his environment in Kiribati caused by sea-level rise associated with climate change threatened his and his family's health and safety. An asylum claim was lodged under Section 198 of the Immigration Act 2009 which would allow Teitiota the right to remain in Aotearoa as a refugee under the terms of the UN 1951 Refugee Convention to which New Zealand is a state party. However, he was declined refugee status, and this decision was upheld by the Immigration and Protection Tribunal. Appeals were declined by both the High Court and the Court of Appeal.

Mr Teitiota was subsequently arrested by police and immigration officials at his West Auckland home for overstaying his permit and was deported to Kiribati. Following deportation, Teitiota complained to the UN Human Rights Committee, arguing that by deporting him, New Zealand had violated his right to life. Although the Committee determined that New Zealand's courts did not violate his

Sea levels are rising in Kiribati.
GOVERNMENT OF KIRIBATI, WIKIMEDIA, CC-BY-3.0

right to life. Committee expert Yuval Shany noted at the time that 'this ruling sets forth new standards that could facilitate the success of future climate change-related asylum claims' (UNHCR, 2020).

To read more about Teitiota's case, scan the QR code.

References

FigureNZ. (2021). People from Kiribati granted work visas for New Zealand. https://figure.nz/chart/RKUyBz3iVVpyUEM2-SJRnkMe158XYualY

UNHCR. (2020). *Historic UN Human Rights case opens door to climate change asylum claims.* www.ohchr.org/EN/NewsEvents/Pages/DisplayNews.aspx?NewsID=25482

Further reading

Behrman, S. & Kent, A. (2020). The Teitiota Case and the limitations of the human rights framework. *Questions of International Law: Zoom In, 75,* 25–39.

te reo (Māori language) revitalisation activities. This activism has changed over the decades, with a focus on the new colonialism that is neoliberalism. As Bargh (2007) notes, this includes returning land to communal ownership, pursuing development activities that differ from mainstream ways of doing business, strengthening practices that reaffirm values and world views that differ from neoliberal norms, and reaffirming a world that neoliberal practices and agendas do not control through local community initiatives, the development of local economies, mātauranga or Māori knowledge, and Indigenous decision-making practices (Bargh, 2007).

Arguably, these practices offer deeper challenges to neoliberalism than other movements, but recent anti-globalisation activism has had a considerable impact, particularly in raising awareness around inequities. Sometimes termed the Global Justice Movement, the Movement of Movements or the alter-globalist movement, the anti-globalisation community of the 1990s and early 2000s was diverse and included activists, non-governmental organisations (NGOs) and a variety of peace, conservation, labour, fair trade, and debt-relief activities. The movement was particularly visible in the 1990s and early 2000s, inspired by the works of authors and activists such as Vandana Shiva, Arundhati Roy and Naomi Klein. The general tenets included opposition to neoliberal economic integration, with a particular emphasis on the impacts of globalisation as experienced by the Global South (Horner et al., 2018). These movements were visible in large protests, particularly at the Seattle WTO meetings in 1999 and Washington meetings of the IMF and World Bank in 2000 and 2002.

Trump, Brexit and Covid-19

In the past decade, the world has shifted again. While globalisation remains a powerful process, you may wonder about the impact of nationalism as seen in Brexit and Donald Trump's presidency, or the effect the pandemic will have on the global economy and politics. In particular, commentators have pointed to nation-states reasserting their legitimacy in global affairs, a process which has seen a reterritorialisation of national borders. This has been accompanied by protests against economic forms of globalisation that are seen to disadvantage local markets and workers.

In addition, Norris and Inglehart (2019) argue that a tipping point has been reached in Western democracies, with a backlash against the cultural change that has become increasingly prominent in recent decades, including policies such as environmental protection, same-sex marriage and gender equality. They also note that immigration flows, especially from lower-income countries, changed the ethnic makeup of advanced industrial societies, contributing to anti-immigrant sentiments and growing nationalism.

This has led to the rise of populism, a political stance that is characterised by the division of society into two groups, 'the people' and 'the elite', and increased support for populist, charismatic leaders, reflecting a deep mistrust of the 'establishment' and mainstream parties. The simplest definition of populism is 'a political approach that strives to appeal to "ordinary people" who feel that their concerns are disregarded by established "elite" groups' (Urbinati, 2018, p. 77). Politics (and politicians) are seen as the problem and a populist leader will claim to represent the will of the people by opposing an enemy, often embodied by the current system. In recent years, the two most widely cited examples of populism are the presidency of Donald Trump in the US and the pro-Brexit movement in the UK. These both assert a desire to shake up the established political order and to aid certain 'downtrodden' groups in society — particularly the white working class. In addition, both oppose aspects of globalisation.

Where the anti-globalisation movements of the 1990s and early 2000s were primarily left-wing and concerned with impacts on the Global South, much of the recent opposition to globalisation has come from the right and emerged from concerns with its impact on the Global North[1] (Horner et al., 2018). For example, Trump promoted US industries by raising tariffs on imports, and sought to restrict immigration; while pro-Brexit groups wanted to take back control from the EU, particularly over immigration and trade policy. Both movements can also be described as nationalist (in that they believe in taking care of their own citizens first) and both talk of returning their respective countries to a 'golden-age' that existed before globalisation and mass immigration, and before 'political-correctness' (e.g. 'Make America Great Again', the 'Blitz Spirit'). However, populism is not restricted to the political right, nor does it occur only in wealthier nations (for example, the election of Jair Bolsonaro in Brazil and Rodrigo Duterte in the Philippines).

Nationalism and populism have also been on the rise during the pandemic (Stavrakakis et al., 2020; Su & Shen, 2020; Vieten, 2020). As Vieten (2020) notes, 'although some aspects of public normality of our 21st century urban, cosmopolitan and consumer lifestyle have been disrupted with the pandemic

---

1 The division of the world into the Global North and South is based on the Brandt Line. This was developed in the 1980s to show the world is geographically split into relatively richer and poorer nations. According to this model, most of the world's richer countries are located in the Northern Hemisphere (the exceptions being Australia and Aotearoa), while most of the poorer countries are located in the Southern Hemisphere. While this is imperfect, we use the terms Global North / Global South in this book to differentiate between socio-economically richer and poorer nations.

curfew, the underlying gendered, racialised and classed structural inequalities and violence have been kept in place' (p. 164), and that digitalised 'pandemic populism' during lockdowns might have pushed further the mobilisation of the far right.

Conclusion

While there has been considerable backlash and challenges to globalisation in recent years, and while the movement of people has slowed dramatically, flows of information, finance, commodities and other non-human flows have continued and even expanded since the start of the pandemic. The rise of nationalism and the pandemic has not killed globalisation, with global economic and political powers continuing to push for neoliberal policy. The powerful global elites who benefit from the global flow of capital, less tax and less regulation will continue to back globalisation.

As such, the positive and negative effects of globalisation continue to be fiercely debated. This is not unlike previous debates about colonisation, and although colonialism is largely (although not entirely) consigned to history, its shadow lies under the processes of contemporary globalisation. Critical scholars argue that the processes of globalisation mimic the goals and outcomes of colonialism, ensuring that flows that benefit the rich and powerful continue to do so, while just enough attention is given to the needs of weaker nations, the poor and Indigenous groups to prevent the collapse of the system. The question is, will contemporary globalisation provide solutions to the problems facing our world, including the difficult problems of climate change, conflict and inequality, or is it exacerbating them? And what are the implications for citizenship, and our identities, rights and responsibilities?

References

Bargh, M. (2007). *Resistance: An Indigenous response to neoliberalism.* Huia Books.

Bellone Hite, A., Roberts, J. T., & Chorev, N. (2015). Globalisation and development: Recurring themes. In J. T. Roberts, A. Bellone Hite, & N. Chorev (Eds.), *The Globalisation and Development Reader: Perspectives on development and social change* (pp. 1–18). Wiley-Blackwell.

Byfield, S. (2015). Should Australia partner with Coke in the Pacific? *Devpolicy Blog.* http://devpolicy.org/should-australia-partner-with-coke-in-the-pacific-20150714

Cain, T. (2017). Demographic diversities. The changing faces of Aotearoa New Zealand. In T. Cain, E. Kahu, & R. Shaw (Eds.), *Tūrangawaewae: Identity & belonging in Aotearoa New Zealand* (pp. 33–53). Massey University Press.

The Economist. (2019, January 24). Slowbalisation: The steam has gone out of globalisation. www.economist.com/leaders/2019/01/24/the-steam-has-gone-out-of-globalisation

Elers, C., Jayan, P., Elers, P., & Dutta, M. J. (2021). Negotiating health amidst COVID-19 lockdown in low-income communities in Aotearoa New Zealand. *Health Communication, 36*(1), 109–115. https://doi.org/10.1080/10410236.20 20.1848082

Giddens, A. (1990). *The Consequences of Modernity.* Stanford University Press.

Greiner, A. (2014). *Visualizing Human Geography.* John Wiley and Sons.

Groot, S., Tassell-Matamua, N., Van Ommen, C., & Masters-Awatere, B. (Eds.). (2017). *Precarity: Uncertain, insecure and unequal lives in Aotearoa New Zealand.* Massey University Press.

Hall, T. D., & Fenelon, J. V. (2008). Indigenous movements and globalization: What is different? What is the same? *Globalizations, 5*(1), 1–11. https://doi.org/10.1080/14747730701574478

Hardin, C. (2014). Finding the 'neo' in neoliberalism. *Cultural Studies, 28*(2), 199–221. https://doi.org/10.1080/09502386.2012.748815

Horner, R., Haberly, D., Schindler, S., & Aoyama, Y. (2018). How anti-globalisation switched from a left to a right-wing issue — and where it will go next. *Global Development Institute Blog.* http://blog.gdi.manchester.ac.uk/how-anti-globalisation-switched-from-a-left-to-a-right-wing-issue

Horner, R., & Hulme, D. (2017). Converging divergence? Unpacking the new geography of 21st century global development. *Global Development Institute Working Paper Series 2017–010.* https://doi.org/10.2139/ssrn.3144281

Human Rights Watch (HRW). (2015). 'Whoever raises their head suffers the most': Workers' rights in Bangladesh's garment factories. *Human Rights Report.* www.hrw.org/report/2015/04/22/whoever-raises-their-head-suffers-most/workers-rights-bangladeshs-garment

Islam, M. A. (2020, July 1). Coronavirus measures give Bangladeshi workers for global clothing chains a stark choice: disease or starvation. *The Conversation.* https://theconversation.com/coronavirus-measures-give-bangladeshi-workers-for-global-clothing-chains-a-stark-choice-disease-or-starvation-138549

Katsampekis, G., & Stavrakakis, Y., (Eds.). (2020). Populism and the Pandemic:

A collaborative report. *POPULISMUS Interventions No. 7.* Loughborough University. https://repository.lboro.ac.uk/articles/report/Populism-and-the-pandemic-A-collaborative-report/12546284

Kelsey, J. (2015). *The New Zealand Experiment: A world model for structural adjustment?* Bridget Williams Books.

Marriott, L., & Sim, D. (2014). *Indicators of Inequality for Māori and Pacific People* (Working Papers in Public Finance 09/2014). Victoria University of Wellington.

Mas-Coma, S., Jones, M. K., & Marty, A. M. (2020). COVID-19 and globalization. *One Health, 9* (April). https://doi.org/10.1016/j.onehlt.2020.100132

Masselot, A., & Hayes, M. (2020). Exposing gender inequalities: Impacts of Covid-19 on Aotearoa New Zealand employment. *New Zealand Journal of Employment Relations, 45*(2), 57–69. http://doi.org/10.24135/nzjer.v45i2.21

Matilla-Santander, N., Ahonen, E., Albin, M., Baron, S., Bolíbar, M., Bosmans, K., Burström, B., Cuervo, I., Davis, L., Gunn, V., Håkansta, C., Hemmingsson, T., Hogstedt, C., Jonsson, J., Julià, M., Kjellberg, K., Kreshpaj, B., Lewchuk, W., Muntaner, C., ... Bodin, T. (2021). COVID-19 and precarious employment: Consequences of the evolving crisis. *International Journal of Health Services, 51*(2), 226–228. https://doi.org/10.1177/0020731420986694

McLaren, C., & Jin, D. Y. (2020). 'You can't help but love them': BTS, transcultural fandom, and affective identities. *Korea Journal, 60*(1), 100–127. https://doi.org/10.25024/KJ.2020.60.1.100

Nagal, J. (1998). Social choice in a pluralitarian democracy: The politics of market liberalization in New Zealand. *British Journal of Political Science, 28,* 223–269.

Norris, P., & Inglehart, R. (2019). *Cultural Backlash: Trump, Brexit and authoritarian populism.* Cambridge University Press.

Rashbrooke, M. (2013). *Inequality: A New Zealand crisis.* Bridget Williams Books.

Rhoads, R. A., & Szelényi, K. (2011). *Global Citizenship and the University: Advancing social life and relations in an interdependent world.* Stanford University Press.

Ritzer, G. (Ed.). (2009). *McDonaldization: The reader*. SAGE.

Rua, M., Hodgetts, D., Stolte, O., King, D., Cochrane, W., Stubbs, T., Karapu, R., Neha, E., Chamberlain, K., Te Whetu, T., Te Awekotuku, N., Harr, J., & Groot, S. (2019). Precariat Māori households today. *Te Arotahi Paper*, May, 1–16.

Shrestha, N., Shad, M. Y., Ulvi, O., Khan, M. H., Karamehic-Muratovic, A., Nguyen, U. S. D. T., Baghbanzadeh, M., Wardrup, R., Aghamohammadi, N., Cervantes, D., Nahiduzzaman, K. M., Zaki, R. A., & Haque, U. (2020). The impact of COVID-19 on globalization. *One Health, 11*, 100180. https://doi.org/10.1016/j.onehlt.2020.100180

Smith, C., Burke, H., & Ward, G. K. (2000). Indigenous peoples: Threat or empowerment? In C. Smith & G. K. Ward (Eds.), *Indigenous Cultures in an Interconnected World* (pp. 1–24). Routledge.

Standing, G. (2011). *The Precariat: The new dangerous class*. Bloomsbury Academic.

Standing, G. (2015, June 13). A new class: Canada neglects the precariat at its peril. *The Globe and Mail*. www.theglobeandmail.com/report-on-business/rob-commentary/a-new-class-canada-neglects-the-precariat-at-its-peril/article24944758/

Su, R., & Shen, W. (2020). Is nationalism rising in times of the COVID-19 pandemic? Individual-level evidence from the United States. *Journal of Chinese Political Science, 7*, 169–187. https://doi.org/10.1007/s11366-020-09696-2

Thorsen, D. E. (2010). The neoliberal challenge: What is neoliberalism? *Contemporary Readings in Law and Social Justice, 2*(2), 188–214.

Urbinati, N. (2018). Antiestablishment and the substitution of the whole with one of its parts. In C. de la Torre (Ed.), *Routledge Handbook of Global Populism* (pp. 1–28). Routledge. https://doi.org/10.4324/9781315226446

Vieten, U. M. (2020). The 'new normal' and 'pandemic populism': The COVID-19 crisis and anti-hygienic mobilisation of the far-right. *Social Sciences, 9*(9), 1–14. https://doi.org/10.3390/SOCSCI9090165

Ward, C., & Liu, J. H. (2012). Ethno-cultural conflict in Aotearoa/New Zealand: Balancing Indigenous rights and multicultural responsibilities. In D. Landis & R. A. Albert (Eds.), *Handbook of Ethnic Conflict: International perspectives* (pp. 45–70). Springer. https://doi.org/10.2307/2758075

04.
Encountering global citizenship

Sharon McLennan, Margaret Forster & Rand Hazou

From sending a text message to eating a banana or getting in a car, our daily activities connect us to people and places around the globe in ways that we are often unaware of. As highlighted in the previous chapter, globalisation means that our phones may connect us to exploitative mining practices in Africa, our food to the use of pesticides or unsustainable agricultural practices in South America, and our transport to unsafe factory working conditions in Asia. In addition, our identities and sense of belonging are becoming less tied to one place or nation. For example, you may have been born and raised in Aotearoa, but identify as Chinese, Indian or Fijian. You might identify with a nation whose borders are not internationally recognised (the Kurds, for example, or the Palestinians). Similarly, some Indigenous people might not identify with the colonial/settler state that they now find themselves inhabiting (or confined by) — for example, many Māori primarily identify themselves by whakapapa, hapū and iwi, and through connections to the land and their tūrangawaewae, rather than as New Zealanders. These identities and connections have significant implications for citizenship.

In this chapter, we explore these implications. How does globalisation affect citizenship? How do Māori and other Indigenous peoples view citizenship and global connections? And what is global citizenship and why is it a contested

IHO ATUA

Margaret Forster (Rongomaiwāhine, Ngāti Kahungunu)

The origin narrative of the first family is useful for understanding a Māori view of citizenship centred around identity, belonging and ethical behaviour.

> They're exploring, the novelty of having so much room is still new to them. They've made this place their own; each staking out their territory, busy with their interests. Rongo will be nearby in the garden, digging neat furrows into the ground. Tāne and Haumia will be in the bush — Tāne has probably climbed the tallest tree and Haumia will be hanging out in the scrub land. Tangaroa will be at the beach. Tū could be with any of them, it depends on his mood or if he's annoyed his brothers — which he often was. (Hereaka, 2019, p. 40)

Ranginui, Papatūānuku and their children are the first family. Their exploits fashioned the natural world — Earth — revealing a shared kinship between nature and humanity. Kinship connections and obligations bind the first family together, and us as their descendants. The continued presence in the world of the first family as atua provides a regulatory system to guide encounters with each other and within the various domains — the garden, the bush and the beach. Citizenship from a Māori viewpoint therefore is premised on kinship, establishing a strong sense of belonging and obligation to the community. The intent is to elevate mana tangata or the human condition and secure community advancement and prosperity. The challenge today involves traversing the often-rocky terrain of recognition and balancing of rights and responsibilities as citizens of te ao Māori, the nation-state and the world.

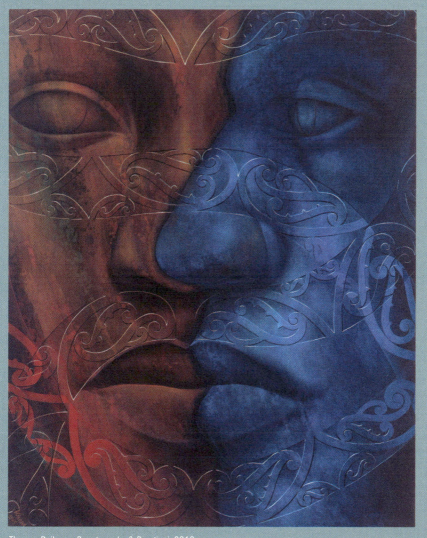

Theresa Reihana, *Papatuanuku & Ranginui*, 2018. COURTESY OF THE ARTIST

concept? To answer these questions, the chapter begins with a discussion of notions of Indigenous and Māori citizenship and an overview of Western, state-based conceptions of citizenship before examining the concept of global citizenship. In doing so, we introduce concepts that will reappear throughout this book and begin exploring global issues that require responses that go beyond narrow state-based responsibilities of citizenship.

Māori views of citizenship

Citizenship for Māori is founded on tangata whenua status and being part of a tribal community connected through Papatūānuku the Earth Mother and Ranginui the Sky Father to the world *and* through ancestors to a specific geographical area. These connections to place shape identity and belonging and construct a Māori understanding of citizenry that emphasises obligations and responsibilities to others. Therefore, the idea of citizenship — as generally premised on the responsibility to protect and care for each other — is clearly evident in Māori thought.

One way to understand these responsibilities is through the purpose and roles of poutiriao. Poutiriao literally means to place in the world. It refers to guardians (often atua) who were tasked with looking after specific domains or bounded territory by setting expectations, standards and behaviours. For example, Tāne and Hinetūparimaunga have rangatiratanga or authority over mountains and cliffs. One of their offspring Parawhenuamea (loosely translated as 'water that springs forth from the land') in partnership with Tūtoto have rangatiratanga over freshwater environments (Best, 1924).

The presence of atua is critical for understanding appropriate actions, particularly the need to maintain order through balance and harmony — their role is protective and regulatory, much like that of the modern state. Tangata whenua as tribes are also associated with a tribal territory and assert a specific form of rangatiratanga or local authority over the territory known as mana whenua. Their authority, however, is subject to the presence of poutiriao and the guidelines that have been set for appropriate behaviour.

Colonisation introduced new 'Western' forms of citizenship (discussed in the next section) and imposed a new set of rules over these territories, natural resources and peoples. These rules disregarded the presence of poutiriao and assumed that Māori notions of citizenship were incompatible and irrelevant to the new emerging and 'modern' nation-state. Māori have continuously challenged these assumptions and the often conditional nature of citizenship for Māori,[1] with contestation being an early and enduring feature of Māori nation-state relations (Walker, 1984). This can be observed through te Tiriti o Waitangi politics, the New Zealand Wars, various sovereignty movements such as the Kingitanga and Kotahitanga, prophetic movements such as Ringatū and Rātana, and more recent pan-tribal health and wellbeing initiatives such as the Māori Women's Welfare League, urban authorities and Māori health and social service providers.

A common thread running through all of these initiatives is the assertion of tino rangatiratanga — in this context Māori control and sovereignty — to resist attempts by the state to dispossess tangata whenua of their authority, tribal estate, culture and lifestyles (Harris, 2004; Taonui, 2012). Unfortunately, this approach has had little impact on disrupting colonisation and nation-state sovereignty. Despite this, Māori demands to exercise rangatiratanga remain strong and are a high priority. Shifting to a more global perspective provides a key opportunity to challenge and perhaps circumvent the power of the state. This focus does not negate local tribal responsibilities or relations with the nation-state. Rather, it builds on responsibilities associated with guardianship of Indigenous lands (as determined by tangata whenua, Indigenous or first nation status) and care for visitors (Macfarlane, 2019), which in an Aotearoa context extends to tangata tiriti — those people whose rights are derived from te Tiriti o Waitangi as manuhiri or visitors. This way of thinking extends Indigenous responsibilities to include the need to resolve pressing global interests and concerns (Tawhai, 2020), such as lobbying for the rights of Indigenous peoples, advocating for decolonisation and enacting obligations that promote the socio-political and life-sustaining capacity of the environment.

These enduring global connections and networks are dependent on mutual and beneficial engagement. From a Māori perspective, these types of relations are guided by the intersection of aroha or love and manaaki manuhiri or care of visitors. The responsibility of tangata whenua to care for and protect visitors in a manner that is empowering is inherent in this way of thinking. This commitment also extends to tangata whenua as they move beyond their own tribal territory to live or whenever travelling and working (Macfarlane, 2019). This is a Māori framework for enacting global citizenship. As Tawhai (2020) notes, these responsibilities 'extend to global issues that needed the urgent attention and collective efforts of all citizens, be that locally, regionally or globally, to resolve' (p. 293), including the protection of lands,

---

1   Māori have often identified as being treated as 'second-class citizens', as highlighted, for example, in the differential treatment of Māori returned servicemen after the Second World War (Humpage, 2008, p. 127).

waters and the environment. Tawhai cites LaDuke to emphasise the importance of relationships in this, that citizens are members of collectives with common responsibilities on local, regional and global levels. According to LaDuke:

> We are all children of Mother Earth. That is perhaps a different way of saying that we are all global citizens. We are children of Mother Earth, and we have responsibilities as humans who are here to treat all of our relatives with respect, whether they have hands or fins, or roots or paws. That is the bottom truth. (2020, p. 298)

These connections are not new. While the next section of this chapter explores the emergence of global citizenship from a Western perspective, it is important to remember that connections between Indigenous groups throughout the world existed long before colonialism, and continue today. For example, as Hau'ofa (1994) notes in his seminal essay, 'Our Sea of Islands', a widespread exchange community extended across the Pacific before colonialism, which he describes as 'a large world in which peoples and cultures moved and mingled, unhindered by boundaries of the kind erected much later by imperial powers' (p. 154). As will be discussed later in this chapter, and throughout the book, many of these networks and connections have persisted, and new connections are emerging, and these continue to be of vital importance to the health and wellbeing of the planet and all peoples.

Citizenship in the context of nation-states

Citizenship is a term used to refer to membership of a community, both in the formal, legal sense of the nation-state, and membership of communities and interest groups that operate at the sub-state level. This membership provides a sense of identity and belonging, legitimises participation and voice, and brings a range of rights and responsibilities (Brown, 2017; Kahu, 2022). However, although there are enormous tensions between different traditions and positions within 'the West', citizenship from a Western perspective is most often understood as a legal relationship between the individual and the state. As such, Andrew Brown (2017) suggests that citizenship is 'a balance between the duties owed to the state and rights expected from it; as a sense of belonging to the state, and the degree of participation within it' (p. 9). This idea of citizenship can be traced back to ancient Athens in the fifth century BCE. Athens is considered the birthplace of democracy, and citizenship was an idea linked to urban city-states in ancient Greece.[2]

Since that time, the concept of citizenship has constantly evolved in the Western tradition. Brown (2017) notes three key changes to the definition of citizenship in the Western tradition. The first is from a smaller, urban-based notion of citizenship to one focused on the larger nation-state. The idea of a citizen as the subject of a state and as a legal entity emerged within the Roman Empire; and was evident in the medieval West, but really took hold in revolutionary Europe and America in the late eighteenth century. Alongside this development, there was also a second shift from citizens taking an active role in society and governance to adopting a more passive function. This began with the shift from urban to national-level citizenship — even Aristotle recognised that active participation in political life may not be possible in a city-state that was 'excessively large' (Brown, 2017, p. 10). As such, most members of a modern nation-state cannot be full citizens in Aristotle's sense, and the democratic role of citizens is now expressed in more passive ways, with citizenship engagement being mediated through representatives, so that voting rather than direct participation is the norm. The third key change was a shift in emphasis from a focus on 'duties' to one privileging 'rights'. The strong emphasis on the obligations required of active citizens in the ancient world, and on the virtue of fulfilling them, was replaced in the modern world by an emphasis on the civil rights that citizens could demand of their nation-state.

However, in the globalised world in which we now live, where national borders are more porous than ever (or were until the shutdowns and border closures of the Covid-19 pandemic), and technological and other advances mean our lives are touched daily by global concerns, the idea of citizenship becomes more complicated, and a fourth change may be underway. This change moves citizenship beyond the confines of the nation-state and the communities in which we live to acknowledge global connections and identities. As Williams and Death (2017) note, 'questions about who is owed what, and by whom, have become increasingly complicated in nature because of the increasing interdependence of our world and the sense in which our fate is increasingly tied to the activities of people and agencies all over the world' (p. 2).

The term 'global citizen' has been used to describe this global belonging and interdependence, and the rights and responsibilities that flow from it. This expansion of citizenship to the global level is the focus of the remainder of this chapter.

---

2   An important point to note is that the term citizenship has never been particularly inclusive. The citizens in Athens were male, Greek, property owners. Women, slaves and migrants to the city (also known as 'denizens') were excluded from citizenship and therefore had no say in decision making. Arguably, citizenship continues to be used as much to exclude as to include people, particularly when narrow and legal definitions of citizenship are utilised.

Global citizenship

Before we examine the idea of global citizenship as it has come to be understood, it is important to acknowledge — as discussed above — that global identities and perspectives on rights and responsibilities are not limited to Western thought and philosophy. The identity of Indigenous peoples is rooted in a connection to the earth that transcends national borders and local places. In Western traditions, the idea of citizenship beyond geographical borders also has a long history. Like the idea of citizenship itself, contemporary global citizenship has roots in the ancient European world, and specifically in the notion of cosmopolitanism, a term which derives from ancient Greek ideas of universality, where the 'cosmos' (universe/world) is one's 'city' (living place/community) (Oxley & Morris, 2013, p. 305). Indeed, around 450 BCE Socrates insisted that he was 'not an Athenian or a Greek, but a citizen of the world' (Bowden, 2003, p. 349). One hundred years later, Diogenes the Cynic made a similar declaration as a 'citizen of the world', and in the second century CE Marcus Aurelius issued his famous declaration, 'my city and country so far as I am Antonius is Rome; but so far as I am a man, it is the world' (Bowden, 2003, p. 353).

As a political theory, cosmopolitanism gained traction during the enlightenment, when philosophers such as Kant argued that individuals have rights as citizens of the Earth rather than as citizens of particular states (Kleingeld & Brown, 2014). This interest in cosmopolitanism emerged partly in response to the development of the European nation-state system through which states exercised complete legitimate power over clearly defined territories. The nation-state system was supposed to regulate and limit wars and promote order and peace, but the continued frequency of wars prompted some to think of other ways to achieve more permanent peace, including advocating for world government, or more commitment to universal moral principles (Dower & Williams, 2016).

In the twentieth century, there was renewed interest in the notion of cosmopolitan or global citizenship, as individuals began to see themselves as capable of playing a part in world affairs. The events of the first half of the twentieth century — including the two world wars — persuaded many that radical reform of the international system was necessary (Dower & Williams, 2016). At the same time, scholars and social activists were looking for a new language of politics to challenge the belief that an individual's key obligations are to the nation-state, and to promote collective and individual responsibility at a global level (Linklater, 2002). This resulted in a new type of world citizen evoked by the Universal Declaration of Human Rights (UDHR) (1948). As Eglin (2020) notes, this citizen was still defined in relation to the nation-state; however, 'the rights-bearing individual of the Declaration is "born free and equal in dignity and rights" and is thereby nominally a member of a single, universal "human family", a noble ideal' (p. 12). Those who saw themselves as world citizens were often keen supporters of the United Nations or poured their energies into the peace movement through organisations such as the Campaign for Nuclear Disarmament (CND) (Dower & Williams, 2016).

From the 1970s, this focus on peace and the problem of war began to give way to concerns about world poverty and responses to this, including aid programmes and the reformation of international trade; and to environmental concerns such as resource depletion and pollution (Dower & Williams, 2016). Human rights violations also began to garner increased attention, as regimes such as the Khmer Rouge in Cambodia and Idi Amin in Uganda were brought to the public's attention through the rapidly growing international media. It was also from this time that the process of globalisation began to accelerate, which became not only the cause of many of the global problems we face but also 'the context in which individuals increasingly see themselves as involved in the wider world and are thus more likely to see themselves as "world citizens"' (Dower & Williams, 2016, p. 4).

Since the 1990s, with the acceleration of globalisation and what some argue is the decline of the nation-state, the idea of global citizenship has gained considerable traction. Dower and Williams (2016) give a broad definition that makes a useful starting place for a discussion of twenty-first-century global citizenship, describing a global citizen as:

> a member of the wider community of all humanity, the world or a similar whole that is wider than that of a nation-state or other political community of which we are normally thought to be citizens. This membership is important in the sense that it involves (or would involve if people accept that they are global citizens) a significant identity, loyalty or commitment beyond the nation-state. (p. 1)

Taking this a step further, Mansouri and others (2017) define global citizenship as 'one's identity as a social, cultural, and economic being, with rights and responsibilities to act locally, nationally, and globally' (p. 3). What this looks like in practice, and, indeed, whether global forms of citizenship are even possible, are disputed. But our responsibilities to act and respond to rights issues within local, national and global contexts remain important considerations in our globalised world.

AHO 4.1 EARTHRISE

In December 1968, the space shuttle *Apollo 8* arrived to orbit the moon. On Christmas Eve one of the astronauts aboard the vessel, William Anders, took a photo that would change how people viewed Earth and their place on it. This photo came to be called *Earthrise*. The blue ball that is planet Earth is seen rising over the moon's horizon, a small dot in the vast blackness of space. For the first time, humans were able to get a physical view of their home in comparison to the size of the cosmos. *Earthrise* drew attention to the fact that we are all inhabitants of a small planet, and this is the only place in the universe where we can survive. It has been suggested that the photo helped to kick-start the modern environmental movement, as it visibly demonstrated that the Earth is a holistic and interconnected entity.

Earthrise. WILLIAM ANDERS, PUBLIC DOMAIN

Critical perspectives

While the idea of global citizenship has increased in popularity and application worldwide, it remains a controversial and contested concept. As Mansouri and others (2017) note, the term 'citizenship' commonly implies membership of and belonging to a nation-state, while 'global' invokes a sense of an attachment to an imagined global community transcending the nation-state. They argue that global citizenship is 'more of an aspirational ethical framework that reflects how the traditional notion of citizenship, defined within the contours of the nation-state, is progressively being challenged and transformed within the context of globalisation and transnational mobility' (Mansouri et al., 2017, p. 3). However, some critics find it:

> overly romantic, dangerously vague, completely unfeasible, and/or ultimately undesirable . . . [a] rosy idea that connotes a set of goals inseparable from those for which a good national citizen should strive: open-mindedness, awareness of other cultures, tolerance of difference, and so on. (Levi & Durham, 2015, p. 411)

Others see global citizenship as rooted in Western, liberal traditions, and argue that global forms of citizenship could advance particular (Western) political interests and 'are generally framed, and thus limited, by a common metanarrative: the modern/colonial imaginary' (Pashby et al., 2020, p. 146) which naturalises a Western/European stand-point and a corresponding set of colonial and capitalist social relations. In this way, efforts to promote rights and duties that apply to all human beings may be seen as a form of neo-colonialism and cultural imperialism (Linklater, 2002, p. 317). As such, global citizenship can be viewed as a historical framework that masks the impacts of colonial violence and the material relationships that produce some as privileged, and hence capable of being active global citizens, and some as in need of support or aid.

This ahistorical framework underpins what Andreotti (2014) terms 'soft' global citizenship, an individualist approach that emphasises the responsibility of the privileged (usually Northern/Western, white) to help others around the world. These soft forms of global citizenship construct global inequality through a Northern lens that is ahistorical, depoliticised and ethnocentric, offering simple solutions that reflect Northern paternalism and salvationism (Andreotti 2012). Soft global citizenship is also closely aligned to the rise of popular events such as Make Poverty History and Live 8, and with what Eglin (2020) and Jefferess (2021) describe as the neoliberal global citizenship nexus — the dominant discourse of global citizenship articulated by a group of interrelated, 'ruling' institutions, including educational institutions, multinational corporations, advocacy groups, community service organisations and some national governments.

The connection of global citizenship with individualism, and with Western, liberal traditions and neoliberalism is particularly problematic for many Indigenous scholars and groups. As Tawhai (2020) explains, there are concerns that global notions of citizenship can be associated with an assimilationist agenda in which all citizens are perceived through a homogeneous lens, and that forms of global citizenship are being promoted that draw on a predetermined set of 'common' values and aspirations for society and the creation of a (pseudo) peace around these values and aspirations, thereby diminishing the distinct identities of Indigenous peoples. This can lead to the suppression of 'Indigenous worldviews, understandings, priorities and perspectives that clash with states' predetermined frameworks of common values about what global, cosmopolitan citizenship is asserted as meaning' (Tawhai, 2020, p. 287). There are also concerns that global forms of citizenship reaffirm the legitimacy of coloniser peoples' presence upon and control of Indigenous homelands, resulting in further exploitation, as global citizens may have a false sense of belonging or claim a right to belong to wherever they wish (Tawhai, 2020).

While these are important critiques, there is considerable support for the idea of global citizenship. Supporters argue that the definition of citizenship used by critics of global citizenship is too restrictive and that the concept of global citizenship is necessary to galvanise moral commitments to others, particularly those whom the nation-state has failed. Linklater (2002) argues that 'as the ties between the citizen and the state loosen, it would be foolish to assume that efforts to extend the achievement of national citizenship into the global realm are bound to be frustrated' (p. 330), while Baillie Smith (2016) notes:

> the fact that particular ideas of global citizenship have gained particular policy and strategic purchase in the global North should not obscure the breadth and diversity of expressions of global citizenship within and between the global South, nor the emergence of new global civic spaces within which new global citizenships are emerging. (p. 109)

International Indigenous rights movements are a contemporary example of these connections, representing the idea that 'indigenous identity is actually a manifestation, rather than the antithesis, of global citizenship' (Levi & Durham, 2015, p. 396). The conceptualisation of Indigenous identity as a type of global citizenship is particularly compelling when global citizenship is defined in terms of collective identity or political activity. While we must be careful not to homogenise or romanticise Indigenous cultures and groups, the global networks and connections to land and sea held by Indigenous peoples present a compelling alternative to neoliberal globalisation.

Global citizenship, rights and responsibilities

While the language of citizenship varies, ideas of community and subjectivity beyond the local is expressed in multiple ways by diverse groups globally and over time (Baillie Smith, 2016). This is particularly relevant in the context of Aotearoa, where Western notions of citizenship sit alongside Māori conceptions, and our understanding of global citizenship is influenced by Māori understandings of rights and responsibilities.

In this book, citizenship is conceptualised as an identity that results in a particular set of rights and responsibilities. In traditional notions of citizenship formed around the nation-state, citizens have certain rights (e.g. the right to vote) and duties (e.g. paying taxes and obeying the laws of the land). However, as we have attempted to show, this rather narrow and legalistic notion of citizenship is becoming increasingly complicated by globalisation and the changes in the role of the nation-state. What does citizenship mean for those whose identity and place of belonging were fractured by colonisation? Or when millions are stateless refugees? Do they have rights and responsibilities? What are our responsibilities when we enjoy food, clothing and devices produced in myriad geographical locations around the globe, especially when conditions of production might be exploitative or impinge on the health and rights of workers overseas?

These questions address issues of rights. A right is a moral or legal entitlement to have or do something. Cosmopolitans argue that all humans have rights based on personhood or common humanity that are the same for everyone equally (this is the principle of universality). This commitment to individual, universal rights is expressed in the concept of human rights, which will be explored further in Chapter 5. At this point, it is important to note that the idea of universal rights is integral to most conceptions of global citizenship and that these rights have attendant responsibilities, obligations or duties that may apply at international, national and individual levels.

While the responsibilities related to global citizenship are usually premised on the idea of common humanity, some scholars argue for a deeper sense of shared responsibility. They maintain that all who contribute by their actions to

AHO 4.2 **IHUMĀTAO**

Ihumātao is believed to be one of the first places in Tāmaki Makaurau where Māori settled and farmed. Archaeologists have estimated that Māori occupied the area from around 1450. Mana whenua continued to occupy and farm the land at Ihumātao through the early years of colonisation, until 1863. After the New Zealand Wars ended, most of the Māori land on the Ihumātao peninsula was confiscated under the New Zealand Settlements Act and sold to British immigrants. Mana whenua returned to a small reserve at Ihumātao, where their descendants continue to live today; however, most of the land remained in the hands of Pākehā settlers as a privately owned farm for 150 years.

In 2014 the land was designated as a special housing area in the city, and in 2015 Pania Newton, along with relatives and other locals, started a campaign which they called SOUL — Save Our Urban Landscape. They opposed the development because of the historical, cultural and archaeological significance of the land, and argued it should be left an open space or returned to mana whenua. Despite this, in 2016 the land was sold to Fletcher Residential, who planned to build 480 houses there. In November 2016,

about 20 members of the community started camping by the side of the road to protest against the development. Some continued to live there, sleeping in caravans, sheds and tents.

The campaign at Ihumātao also had global connections. One of these links was through formal channels when the campaigners took their fight to the United Nations in 2017, hoping to address alleged breaches under the UN Declaration on the Rights of Indigenous People (UNDRIP). The UN report recognised that consultation and consent from Māori had not been adequately sought and recommended the government evaluate the plan's compliance with the Treaty of Waitangi and UNDRIP, and in June 2019 the UN Chief Human Rights Commissioner visited Ihumātao.

SOUL's actions were also successful in drawing world attention to Ihumātao, and headlines appeared in news outlets around the globe, and gained interest from interconnected webs of Indigenous activists, especially through social media. Many saw the stand-off as part of a global movement to assert Indigenous rights that includes protests at Mauna Kea in Hawai'i, North Dakota, Uluru, West Papua, and the Amazon rainforest in Brazil. The height of

SOUL protestors outside the old Manukau City Council chambers during resource consent hearings for the special housing area at Ihumātao, 2016. STUFF LIMITED

the protests at Ihumātao coincided with the Mauna Kea protests, where Indigenous Hawaiians were demonstrating against a $1.4-billion observatory on their sacred mountain, Mauna Kea. Much support was expressed back and forth between the groups and other Indigenous activists, including visitors from around the world.

Scan the QR code to watch a waiata from Ihumātao, sung in solidarity with those protecting Mauna Kea.

ENCOUNTERING GLOBAL CITIZENSHIP   77

the structural processes that produce injustice have responsibilities to work to address the injustices (Young, 2006). This means that if you benefit from a structural injustice — for example, a company making a profit that results from a system that abuses workers, or buying goods from that company — you may be seen as sharing some responsibility for addressing those concerns. Similarly, there is a growing critical awareness of the need to confront 'white privilege' and address the benefits secured through colonialism as a means of challenging racial disparities in countries that experienced colonialism (Davids et al., 2021). There are growing concerns about the nature and limits of these responsibilities, and vast differences in how they are understood by people around the globe. However, in general, there is increasing acceptance internationally of the need for shared responsibility in addressing rights and justice issues. This will be discussed further throughout this book.

The topics we introduce in this book are examples of global issues that invoke rights and require a response that goes beyond narrow state-based conceptions of citizenship. Each section of the book engages with rights concerns and discusses the responsibilities these might entail. You might disagree with some of these, or approach things differently. Regardless, our challenge to you is to think about the implications of the global changes and connections discussed, and what this means in terms of rights and responsibilities — for Aotearoa as a nation, for our communities, and for ourselves as individuals. This means thinking about:

- what rights human beings possess by virtue of being human
- what obligations these rights impose on others
- how far these obligations extend
- what specific actions these obligations require.[3]

There are no simple or single answers to these questions. Indeed, as this chapter indicates, these are questions that philosophers and scholars have grappled with for centuries, and for which there are a wide range of responses. However, while we live on land that connects us to the past and the future of this place, we are also part of the wider world. We are affected by events and activities in far-away places, and the choices we make and decisions we take here in Aotearoa have a habit of rippling out into the world. As such, we would argue that in this increasingly connected and globalised world in which we live, it is more important than ever that we consider if and how we should respond to various

---

3 Adapted from Cameron (2014, p. 26)

rights issues around the world, not just as citizens of Aotearoa, but as members of a global community.

References

Andreotti, V. (2012). Editor's Preface: Heads up. *Critical Literacy: Theories and practices, 6*(1): 1–3.

Andreotti, V. (2014). Soft versus critical global citizenship education. In S. McCloskey (Ed.), *Development Education in Policy and Practice* (pp. 21–31). Palgrave Macmillan. https://doi.org/10.1057/9781137324665_2

Baillie Smith, M. (2016). Global citizenship and development: From benevolence to global justice? In J. Grugel & D. Hammett (Eds.), *The Palgrave Handbook of International Development* (pp. 99–117). Palgrave Macmillan. https://doi.org/10.1057/9781137352217

Best, E. (1924). *Māori Religion and Mythology, Part 2*. Hasselberg. http://nzetc.victoria.ac.nz/tm/scholarly/tei-Bes02Reli.html

Bowden, B. (2003). The perils of global citizenship. *Citizenship Studies, 7*(3), 349–362. https://doi.org/10.1080/13621020302213

Brown, A. (2017). Introduction. The citizen: From ancient to post-modern. In A. Brown & J. Griffiths (Eds.), *The Citizen* (pp. 9–22). Massey University Press. https://doi.org/10.1093/nq/s5-VIII.193.188-d

Cameron, J. (2014). Grounding experiential learning in 'thick' conceptions of global citizenship. In R. Tiessen & R. Huish (Eds.), *Globetrotting or Global Citizenship? Perils and potential of international experiential learning* (pp. 21–42). University of Toronto Press. https://doi.org/10.3138/9781442616707-003

Davids, N., Tyson, K., Driscoll, K., Della Sudda, M., Terriquez, V., & Zayas, V. (2021, September 14). White privilege: What it is, what it means and why understanding it matters. *The Conversation*. https://theconversation.com/white-privilege-what-it-is-what-it-means-and-why-understanding-it-matters-166683

Dower, N., & Williams, J. (2016). *Global Citizenship: A critical introduction*. Routledge.

Eglin, P. (2020). Introduction. In D. Chapman, T. Ruiz-Chapman, & P. Eglin (Eds). *The Global Citizenship Nexus: Critical studies* (pp. 3–21). Routledge.

Harris, A. (2004). *Hikoi: Forty years of Māori protest*. Huia.

Hau'ofa, E. (1994). Our sea of islands. *The Contemporary Pacific, 6*(1), 147–161.

Hereaka, W. (2019). Papatūānuku. In W. Ihimaera & W. Hereaka (Eds.). *Pūrākau: Māori myths retold by Māori writers* (pp. 37–45). Vintage.

Humpage, L. (2008). Talking about citizenship in New Zealand. *Kōtuitui: New Zealand Journal of Social Sciences Online, 3*(2), 121–134.

Jefferess, D. (2021). On saviours and saviourism: lessons from the #WEscandal. *Globalisation, Societies and Education, 19*(4), 420–431. https://doi.org/10.1080/14767724.2021.1892478

Kahu, E. (2022). Identity and citizenship in Aotearoa New Zealand. In E. Kahu, R. Shaw & H. Dollery (Eds.), *Tūrangawaewae: Identity & belonging in Aotearoa New Zealand* (2nd ed.). Massey University Press.

Kleingeld, P., & Brown, E. (2014). Cosmopolitanism. *The Stanford Encyclopedia of Philosophy*. https://plato.stanford.edu/archives/fall2014/entries/cosmopolitanism/

LaDuke, W. (1999). *All Our Relations: Native struggles for land and life*. South End Press.

Levi, J. M., & Durham, E. (2015). Indigeneity and global citizenship. In W. J. Jacob, S. Y. Cheng & M. K. Porter (Eds.) *Indigenous Education: Language, culture and identity* (pp. 395–428). Springer. https://doi.org/10.1007/978-94-017-9355-1_15

Linklater, A. (2002). Cosmopolitan citizenship. In E. F. Isin & B. S. Turner (Eds.), *Handbook of Citizenship Studies*. Sage. https://doi.org/https://doi.org/10.4135/9781848608276.n20

Macfarlane, S. (2019). *GCED — a Māori perspective*. New Zealand Commission for UNESCO. Retrieved from https://unesco.org.nz/1852-2/

Mansouri, F., Johns, A., & Marotta, V. (2017). Critical global citizenship: Contextualising globalisation. *Journal of Citizenship and Globalisation Studies, 1*(1), 1–9.

Oxley, L., & Morris, P. (2013). Global citizenship: A typology for distinguishing its multiple conceptions. *British Journal of Educational Studies, 61*(3), 301–325. https://doi.org/10.1080/00071005.2013.798393

Pashby, K., da Costa, M., Stein, S., & Andreotti, V. (2020). A meta-review of typologies of global citizenship education. *Comparative Education, 56*(2), 144–164. https://doi.org/10.1080/03050068.2020.1723352

Taonui, R. (2012). Māori urban protest movements. In D. Keenan (Ed.), *Huia Histories of Māori: Ngā tāhuhu kōrero* (pp. 230–259). Huia.

Tawhai, V. M. H. (2020). A red-tipped dawn: Teaching and learning about indigeneity and the implications for citizenship education [doctoral dissertation, Massey University]. http://hdl.handle.net/10179/16332

Walker, R. J. (1984). The genesis of Māori activism. *The Journal of the Polynesian Society, 93*(3), 267–281.

Williams, H. L., & Death, C. (2017). *Global Justice: The basics.* Routledge Classics.

Young, I. M. (2006). Responsibility and global justice: A social connection model. *Social Philosophy and Policy, 23*(1), 102–130.

05.
Rights

Shine Choi, Margaret Forster & Beth Greener

Introduction

Human Rights can be defined in several ways. Some suggest that human rights are universal moral natural rights endowed to us simply by virtue of being human. But even if we accept this basic premise, other questions endure. What exactly are rights, who has them, whose rights can trump other people's rights and in what situations, and how are rights to be fulfilled and by whom? And, finally, if the authority of rights regimes — the grounds for claiming and protecting human rights — does not come from shared values, political belonging and 'humanity', what could be the basis of strengthening people's claims?

This chapter begins with mainstream discussions about the nature of rights; discussions that might seem like 'common sense', and that are baked into the disciplines of politics and international relations. However, it will soon become apparent that matters are much more complex because the mainstream view is always a product of power politics. Throughout this chapter, we will note points of divergence and sites of resistance to these mainstream approaches, seeking to make visible the effects of power and spotlighting the alternative visions of rights that have always been present. Alternative visions, by their nature, often speak in ways that escape the existing legal regime. That is, alternative approaches not only seek to realise rights under existing political, legal and cultural frameworks,

IHO ATUA

Margaret Forster (Rongomaiwāhine, Ngāti Kahungunu)

There are other ways to interpret the origin narrative about the first family that helps to understand rights in contemporary settings.

> Her boys are strong willed. Tangaroa, changeable Tangaroa — calm one moment, a tantrum the next. Tāwhirimātea, strident in his beliefs, always trying to stir something up. Tū is smart, cunning even, and is always looking for a fight. Haumia is tough and wild, she's given up trying to tame him; and Rongo, the quiet one, the peace broker, steadfast, stoic and stubborn. (Hereaka, 2019, p. 37)

This narrative illustrates the various qualities of the atua as a reminder of the multiplicity of views and interests that exist within the world. Contemporary rights involve navigating this expansiveness if fairness and justice are to be realised.

Global encounters had a horrendous impact on Māori rights, as the success of colonisation was dependent on the deliberate and systematic suppression of Māori sovereignty. Māori, like other Indigenous peoples, never accepted and continuously resisted the absolute sovereignty of the coloniser. Whawhai tonu mātou is a whakatauākī or saying meaning 'our struggle continues'. It is a reminder of the need to be vigilant and engage in decoloniality, or the unravelling of the logic and matrices of power associated with colonisation that continue to challenge the legitimacy of indigeneity today. Decoloniality is one mechanism for the meaningful acknowledgement of Māori rights and the delivery of more equitable outcomes for Māori.

but also challenge the authorised discourses and understandings of what rights are, emphasising that people have sought to shift the very grounds on which the rights regime sits. In short, rights are one of the political sites where power meets resistance, dominant narratives meet subjugated histories, and those outside the system demand to be heard on their own terms. At the heart of this is the need to recognise how colonialism and imperialism have fundamentally shaped our understanding of human rights as an institution. Therefore, we illustrate the usefulness of understanding the history and politics of human rights as a multi-levelled and multi-located site, one where north and south, east and west, meet.

Rights according to human needs and nature?

The idea that there are such things as 'human' rights is often based on arguments about humankind's capacity for reason (this is particularly strong in the Western liberal tradition [Kant, [1785] 2019]), or the fact that humans are endowed with a conscience (this has been advocated from a Sinophone perspective of humanity [Sun, 2016]). That is, many suggest that humans have rights simply by virtue of being human. Note, however, that rights scholars, especially those coming from Indigenous traditions, have increasingly questioned the anthropocentric assumptions built into the human rights discourse that began to be institutionalised at the end of the Second World War.

From here, some might suggest that human rights could potentially be related to the basic needs for survival that all living entities have, such as food, shelter and the ecological conditions to thrive. Others might argue that rights also come from our moral and social nature, not just from the fact that we are a particular kind of animal species or that we have shared needs with other species. Thus, some theorists suggest that it is not acceptable for humans to be ill-treated or ill-educated, as this does not allow the possibility of living a full 'human life' — 'each human being possesses an intrinsic worth that should be respected . . . some forms of conduct are inconsistent with respect for this intrinsic worth' (McCrudden, 2008, p. 723). We can see echoes of these scholarly ideas in policy, with former Secretary General Kofi Annan's *In Larger Freedom* report calling for UN member states to ensure 'freedom from fear, freedom from want and freedom to live in dignity' (2005, p. 55).

These varying approaches to understanding what human rights might consist of, or what they might require of others, clearly have differing implications for how we conceive of a desirable political, economic and social life.

Positive and negative rights?

In seeking to further explicate what rights might be, we can suggest that rights could be understood in either 'positive' or 'negative' ways (Berlin, 1969). Negative rights are those that focus on freedom from interference, such as the right not to be tortured or the right to conscientious objection. Alternatively, we might think that this is insufficient to fulfil the needs outlined above, hence positive rights start from the premise that it is not enough to 'do no harm'. Economic and social rights, such as welfare to keep people alive and public education, are said to be examples of positive rights. Putting positive rights into practice is, however, a challenging affair. Implementation of positive rights for all may also not necessarily be enough, particularly if we come from a social justice perspective concerned with prioritising the most marginalised and creating more just and equitable structures.

Rights as capabilities?

Some scholars have, therefore, advocated for conceiving of rights as 'capabilities'. After all, if we cannot exercise a right, does it really exist? The 'capabilities approach' suggests that understanding what activities we can do and what kind of persons we are able to be are central to notions of rights (Sen, 1979). This approach also changes our focus from thinking about what 'means' (resources, etc.) people can access, to 'ends' — that is, to thinking about what different people can do and what they are able to be with those means. It also helps raise the threshold for the importance of the right to choose. For example, the right to choose one's sex and sexual orientation is reconceptualised not just as a right to be left alone, but as a social responsibility that all must be involved to ensure it is fully realised (Weinman, 2011).

Different families of rights?

The Universal Declaration of Human Rights (UDHR) is a key document in our attempts to better understand the question of what human rights might consist of. The UDHR lists 30 potential human rights. Taking these alongside the rights listed in other international treaties, such as the United Nations Declaration on the Rights of Indigenous People (UNDRIP), some scholars suggest that rights can be grouped into seven 'families'. These are: security rights that protect against phenomena such as murder and genocide; due process rights that protect against arbitrary punishments and that require fair trial; liberty rights that protect freedoms in areas such as belief, freedom of association, etc.; political rights that protect the right to participate in politics; equality rights that support equal citizenship and equality before the law; social rights that insist governments help to provide goods such as education and an adequate standard of living; and minority and group rights, which protect women, racial and ethnic minorities, Indigenous peoples, children, migrant workers and the disabled (Nickel, 2021). This final 'family' brings us to another way in which we might think about the notion of rights.

Individual or collective rights?

In the West, conceptions of human rights have centred on the idea that humans are autonomous, rational individuals. This emphasis can be traced all the way back to the Stoics, who highlighted the natural equality of all rational beings (Gosepath, 2021). The beginning of the Renaissance in the fourteenth century saw further emphasis placed on the importance of the individual, again informed by the notion that humankind had the capacity to reason, while the American and then the French Revolutions helped to cement the idea that individuals had particular rights. The liberty of individuals became central to the development of liberal democratic societies.

Although not all societies held to this individualist conception of rights, the rise of the West through colonisation, the two world wars, and then through the hegemony exercised by the United States at the end of the Cold War, helped to consolidate the notion that 'human rights' were essentially about individual rights. But we can understand rights as being collective, too.

Pushing back against a perceived emphasis on individualism and political rights, the 'Asian Values' debate of the early to mid-1990s suggested that Asian populations were more likely to: prioritise community over the individual; privilege order and harmony over personal freedom; emphasise family loyalty, a savings-based economy and a strong work ethic; emphasise respect for political leadership; and pursue a strong connection between government and business (Langlois, 2001).

This way of attributing the strength of collective over individual rights to a culture or a whole geographical location has also been critiqued. Some note that this approach can 'provide dominant elites in particular societies opportunities to oppress individuals and other religious and cultural minorities who do not fit their self-serving conceptions of traditional values' (Ishay, 2004, p. 366). Others point out how the 'Asian Values' debate was shaped by the pressures of global capitalism and the need for formerly colonised societies to 'catch up' in an

AHO 5.1 UNIVERSAL DECLARATION OF HUMAN RIGHTS

The Universal Declaration of Human Rights is a product of post-Second World War politics and is one of the key early documents of the newly emerging international system institutionalised through the United Nations. Representatives of the Republic of China, Great Britain, the Soviet Union and the United States came together in 1944 to plan for a new peace and security organisation, which became the United Nations. Its founding charter created the Human Rights Commission in 1946, which was tasked to write an international bill of rights. The Commission was headed by Eleanor Roosevelt of the United States, with Peng-Chun Chang from China as vice-president (Zhao, 2015).

Eclectic, well-seasoned minds on legal, civilisational, social justice and philosophical issues framed the international human rights language. The early framing and drafting work in the Human Rights Council and beyond produced not only the UDHR, which is a declaration (and retains the universal in its title), but also two legally binding international human rights covenants that were developed in the 1960s.

When the declaration passed in the December 1948 UN General Assembly with no dissenting vote, this was less because the universality of the ideas enshrined in the declaration existed in practice, and more because a consensus on the universality of these rights had been developed at each stage in the creation of the UDHR. Many representatives were participating in the formulation of a universalist international document for the first time, and it is not surprising that the human rights debates became closely linked to debates on ending colonial rule via independence and self-determination.

The international human rights regime that the UDHR upholds began formal institutionalisation in Aotearoa through the New Zealand Human Rights Commission, which was established in 1977. By design, international covenants must be enshrined in national legislation to gain 'legal teeth' — the Human Rights Act of 1993 provides this basis.

View the text of the UDHR by scanning the QR code.

international environment that they had little say in shaping (Han & Ling, 1998). Nonetheless, even in more historically attuned analyses, it is important to know that individualism and individual rights are viewed as foreign imports in much of the non-Western world and that their manifestations in these societies are seen as sites of cultural and political negotiation for survival in a Western-dominated international order.

Instead of an emphasis on individuals and their rationality bestowing upon them the right to political and civil rights, discussing the relative importance of dignity in our conceptions of human rights becomes important. The emphasis on humans only being 'human' within a society and community allows people to approach and make sense of human rights as centrally linked to the cultural, economic and political conditions of realising and ensuring human dignity in all. To put this another way, understanding rights as a collective issue rather than an individual one is a way for less powerful populations to push back against being deemed less important in the social and political hierarchy of international relations.

In global, regional and national arenas, then, we need to recognise that there are different conceptions of the notion of rights (Donnelly, 2003), particularly in terms of disagreements between those who emphasise individual liberty, rationality and the centrality of political and civil rights, and those who emphasise community, reciprocity, duty, the notion of conscience and the centrality of social, cultural and economic rights.

Individual and collective rights in tension

A recent case arising from the first Covid-19 lockdown in Aotearoa helps to further demonstrate how individual and collective rights — as well as rights and law — can be in tension.

On 25 March 2020, the government declared a state of national emergency in response to the coronavirus pandemic and initiated a stay-at-home order, known as a lockdown. Lawyer Dr Andrew Borrowdale spearheaded a legal campaign that challenged the legal basis of the lockdown. Borrowdale's legal team argued that the orders passed by the Director-General of Health, Dr Ashley Bloomfield, did not provide an adequate legal basis to make people stay at home. By July 2021, Borrowdale had won part of the case in the High Court, which ruled that the first nine days of the alert level 4 lockdown were 'justified but unlawful' (Cardwell, 2021, para. 2).

The case brings into focus questions about the rights of individuals to move about their daily lives, freedom to cross state-defined borders, and the need to protect more vulnerable individuals and vulnerable communities. In the case of Covid-19, the need to protect others has been paramount in decisions to limit the rights of individuals, and it has also been significant in terms of driving uptake of vaccination. This also highlights the fact that the state's protection of certain rights can sometimes be seen to impinge on other rights — the right to liberty may at times be in tension with the responsibility of the state to provide security, for example. Moreover, we also need to recognise that those in marginal political positions — for example, migrants, international students and the displaced — can often bear the brunt individually for the sharp policy detours in emergency decisions made for the public good (Fonseka, 2020, 2021).

This case further highlights that there can be a dynamic hierarchy of rights. The state exercised its sovereignty in deciding who was subject to these constraints (citizens and non-citizens within their territory) and in deciding that the right to wellbeing trumped some economic rights or individual rights to freedom of movement.

Tensions between human rights and state sovereignty

Another key site of tension is when human rights come into conflict with state sovereignty. The idea of state sovereignty is that the state exercises 'supreme legitimate authority within a given territory' (Philpott, 1995, p. 357). This is codified in international law. The UN Charter, for example, emphasises the importance of human rights in its preamble, but it also reifies the central importance of state sovereignty, particularly in Articles 2 and 51.

As noted in Rogers' chapter in this book (Chapter 12), the tension between human rights and state sovereignty came to a head throughout the 1990s, with the development of the concept of humanitarian intervention and the subsequent creation and adoption of the responsibility to protect (R2P). The emphasis here is on the notion that state sovereignty should not be available as something to hide behind when significant human rights abuses are occurring — abuses that threaten the lives and wellbeing of individual people. But this also brings us to another site of contest that is more about how state sovereignty can, at times, be in tension with the rights of groups to political self-determination.

State sovereignty and self-determination

Self-determination is the idea that political communities can decide their own destinies (Philpott, 1995). State sovereignty became the main way the right to self-determination was institutionalised and consolidated, first in Europe and then through the mid-century decolonisation of Asia, Africa and Latin America that ended the European empires. However, becoming a sovereign nation could also be a process of 'deferring' decolonisation and realising self-determination, just as the end of the British, French and Lusophone empires can be seen as a continuation of imperialism when the old extractive economic ties and paternalistic political relations remain in place. In short, it would be a historical inaccuracy to claim that the emergence of sovereign states and the formal end to empires and colonial outposts led to the full realisation of self-determination for the world's majority (Bhambra & Shilliam, 2009; Rutazibwa & Shilliam, 2018). Neo-colonial and imperial arrangements have led to the continued suppression of the substantial formation and flourishing of the 'self' in self-determination; for example, the presence of US military bases in South Korea and Japan; the occupied territories that US military/foreign policy depends on, such as Hawai'i, Guam and Puerto Rico; the occupation of Kashmir by the Indian state, and of Palestine by the Israeli state; the settler-colonial conditions in Canada, the United States, Aotearoa and Australia that makes self-determination of the Indigenous populations a constant struggle; the economic hold that white Africans have over Indigenous Black populations despite the formal national independence, and so on.

Sovereign states have also created new conditions of political suppression; for example, two-tier citizenships along gender differences; religious persecution in the name of national unity of populations exercising forms of autonomy; and anti-democratic measures that curtail not only freedom of the press, but also people's right to contest and be heard. In short, state sovereignty has created new problems for meaningful realisation of self-determination of all humans and all groups, and in all contexts, especially when the claim to self-determination challenges the existing global order and power structures. Considering this stark reality, Nelson Mandela's words about the interconnectedness of struggles for freedom are particularly relevant: 'We know too well that our freedom is incomplete without the freedom of the Palestinians' (in Davis, 2016, p. 53). Put differently, nothing happens in isolation; self-determination requires a constant struggle for freedom from all structures of oppression. So let us take a closer look at one of those sites of ongoing struggle.

Māori sovereignty and self-determination

In Aotearoa, absolute state sovereignty was built on the oppression of Māori sovereignty. Contemporary demands for Māori sovereignty, therefore, represent a site of resistance constantly challenging mainstream discourses with the intent to shift the terms on which rights regimes exist. Māori sovereignty is derived from the status of tangata whenua, expressed through rangatiratanga as tribal authority and autonomy and enacted through the practice of tūrangawaewae — rights and responsibilities associated with residency in the tribal territory and belonging as established through whakapapa. These political and group rights are clearly visible in Article Two of both the reo and English versions of te Tiriti o Waitangi (te Tiriti). Unfortunately, at least for Māori, the 'promise to respect rangatiratanga (in any of its definitions) has been violated endemically by the Crown' (Hill, 2004, p. 14), as evident in myriad reports from the Waitangi Tribunal.

Consequently, there is a long tradition in Aotearoa of contests over recognition and protection of Māori collective *and* citizenship rights. Some gains have been achieved as the state responds to Māori demands for justice and reconciliation. However, these responses are limited, as the ability of Māori to be 'free and self-determining' (Te Aho, 2017, p. 117) is constrained by the indivisible sovereignty of the state. In more recent decades, there is hope that an emphasis on universal rights and the presence of UNDRIP will provide international standards and assert political pressure on the state to honour te Tiriti promises (Human Rights Commission, 2016). Although this is dependent of course on the international declarations being enshrined in national legislation; this has not really eventuated in any substantive form. It is also important to remember that one of the reasons UNDRIP exists is because Indigenous people remain among the most marginalised people in the world, despite the presence of the UDHR. At the end of the day, if Indigenous lives remain precarious and Indigenous languages and cultures struggle to flourish, then there is a disconnect between the aspirations reflected by international rights instruments and the lived realities of Indigenous peoples.

Māori rights

Māori have a long tradition of fighting for rights. For example, survival of the hapū and whānau required securing access to territory and associated resources to harvest birds, fish, seafood, flax and other weaving material, traditional medicine, and much more. Several practices were developed to establish and maintain these customary rights. One of the most well-known practices is ahikā — keeping the home fires burning. Hapū and whānau protected their interests by naming and marking the land, mountains and rivers (known as taunahanaha and pouwhenua), residing on the land, and regularly using natural resources. The customary right to exercise sovereignty over the territory is encapsulated in the concept of mana whenua and the practice of tūrangawaewae. Violations of these rights by other hapū and whānau were met with swift retribution. Hapū furiously defended their territory, and there are numerous tribal histories that provide accounts of skirmishes over territory and mana whenua.

Encounters with the West and British colonisation transformed Māori politics, social organisations and lifestyles, directly challenged Māori sovereignty, and violated Māori customary rights. New strategies and responses emerged from Māori communities in an attempt to protect rights to tribal resources and culture (Harris, 2004; Taonui, 2012; Walker, 1984, 1989). In this context te Tiriti is an important instrument. Te Tiriti has been described as a bill of rights (Human Rights Commission, 2011) setting out the terms for peaceful and beneficial co-existence (Preamble). Rangatira granted the Crown a form of authority (Article One), the Crown recognised the continuance of rangatiratanga (i.e. tangata whenua rights) (Article Two) and granted Māori the same rights as a British subject (i.e. citizenship rights) (Article Three) (Orange, 1987). By the 1870s, these promises were quickly disregarded as an emphasis on immigrant interests emerged (see for example, Ward, 1995; Williams, 1999). Despite this, Māori consider te Tiriti to be a sacred covenant signed by our ancestors (Ngā Puhi Nui Tonu, 2012) and have continuously and actively lobbied government to honour the spirit of te Tiriti, including the right to Māori sovereignty and self-determination.

Today the status of te Tiriti is tenuous. It is widely recognised as part of the constitutional arrangements of this country (Constitutional Advisory Panel, 2013) but its spirit and promises are not legally binding unless recognised in statute. This means it is difficult 'for Māori to invoke the Treaty provisions in defence of their rights before the courts and in negotiations with the Government' (Stavenhagen, 2006, p. 5). Despite this, in recent decades te Tiriti policy has increasingly played a more significant role in government and institutional life. For example, the Ministry of Health (2020) recently released *Whakamaua: Māori Health Action Plan 2020–2025* to help achieve better health outcomes for Māori. Te Tiriti provisions and principles and Māori notions of health and wellbeing are the foundation of this plan. Through this plan, the ministry has clearly acknowledged an obligation to honour te Tiriti and recognise Māori political, collective and citizenship rights as a step towards realising healthy futures for Māori.

Te Tiriti is not the sole instrument used to promote and protect Māori rights. Investigating and settling historical injustices are key functions of the Waitangi Tribunal (a commission of inquiry) and the Office of Treaty Settlements. Aotearoa has a Bill of Rights Act, constitutional rights and conventions. This includes the statutory protection of Māori interests in the form of acknowledging te Tiriti

AHO 5.2 UNDRIP AND THE TREATY

In Aotearoa Te Tiriti o Waitangi is an important instrument in the promotion and protection of Māori rights. But how does this relate to global instruments such as UNDRIP? In 2016 the NZ Human Rights Commission published a booklet on the rights of Indigenous peoples, which included this useful comment on the relationship between UNDRIP and the Treaty of Waitangi:

'The Treaty and Declaration are strongly aligned and mutually consistent. The Declaration assists with the interpretation and application of the Treaty principles.

'Partnership: Which entails good faith cooperation and shared decision making.

'Protection: Protection of rangatiratanga (self-determination) and taonga such as reo (language), tikanga (customs), mātauranga (knowledge), land and resources.

'Participation: Participation in society on an equal basis to others, and freedom from discrimination.

'UNDRIP affirms the status of treaties between indigenous people and States. It helps explain how international rights standards apply and how treaty promises can be achieved.'

To learn more from the Human Rights Commission about Indigenous rights in Aotearoa, scan the QR code to read the full booklet.

principles, Māori groups rights and Māori citizenship rights. While this regime might appear progressive and wide-ranging, questions arise as to comprehensiveness and extent of implementation. Several Māori law scholars argue that while much has been achieved, there are significant gaps (Te Aho, 2017) and therefore much more to accomplish in this space. This is where the UNDRIP could be influential by lending international might and pressure for greater recognition of the rights of Māori (Erueti, 2017). The declaration recognises both individual and collective rights; cultural rights and identity; rights to education, health, employment, language and others. It encourages harmonious and cooperative relations between states and Indigenous peoples and declares discrimination against Indigenous peoples unlawful. It promotes full and effective participation and the freedom to remain distinct and pursue Indigenous priorities in economic, social and cultural development.

In Aotearoa, recognising Māori rights is a highly contested and fluid space made problematic by the collision of rangatiratanga and state sovereignty. Domestic right instruments accommodate some Māori interests, and it is hoped that the UNDRIP will facilitate a shift in power towards greater recognition of Māori rights. How UNDRIP can support Māori political aspirations particularly through greater recognition of te Tiriti was the focus of a report commissioned by the New Zealand Government in 2019. *He Puapua* (Charters et al., 2019) offered a roadmap for achieving UNDRIP goals and some of the recommendations for pursuing equality will be discussed in more detail later in Chapter 17.

Conclusion

This chapter has discussed a range of ideas about what human rights might be, what they might consist of and who might have them. In doing so, it has highlighted tensions between different conceptualisations of rights (e.g. negative and positive, individual and collective) as well as noting how concepts such as universalism, sovereignty and self-determination contain particular relevance for thinking about how we might realise those rights, linking us to the preceding chapter on global citizenship. The discussion about Māori rights in this chapter further shows us the interrelationship of these contested and contesting ideas in action. This case study thus helps to illuminate how certain universal ideals have not translated into lived realities, by demonstrating that the role of the state has been important but limited (and limiting), with some rights being prioritised over others and some being denied altogether. For example, the focus on human rights has rendered invisible non-human rights. From a Māori perspective, the environment, animals and birds are all part of the wider whānau. How are their rights acknowledged within existing rights regimes? What are our responsibilities towards recognising the rights of the environment? Some of these issues are picked up in the next chapter.

Moreover, although a shallower version of states, statehood and national citizenship has more recently been brought about by globalisation and hegemonic neoliberalism, the state nonetheless remains important in the protection and delivery of rights. The implementation of conventions such as the UDHR or UNDRIP, for example, remains dependent on state endorsement. This highlights the fact that the idea of 'universal rights' is a complicated one and the ability to enforce rights remains challenging. The next chapter picks up on this problem of enforcement in discussing how contemporary global systems act to both constrain and enable socio-environmental relationships.

References

Annan, K. (2005). *In Larger Freedom: Towards development, security and human rights for all* (Report of the Secretary General. A/59/2005). https://undocs.org/A/59/2005

Berlin, I. (1969). Two concepts of liberty. In I. Berlin (Ed.), *Four Essays on Liberty* (pp. 118–172). Oxford University Press.

Bhambra, G. K., & Shilliam, R. (Eds.). (2009). *Silencing Human Rights: Critical engagements with a contested project.* Palgrave Macmillan.

Cardwell, H. (2021, July 7). *Level 4 Lockdown Legality: Appeal Court reserves decision.* RadioNZ. www.rnz.co.nz/news/covid-19/446410/level-4-lockdown-legality-appeal-court-reserves-decision

Charters, C., Kingdon-Bebb, K., Olsen, T., Ormsby, W., Owen, E., Pryor, J., Ruru, J., Solomon, N., & Williams, G. (2019*). He Puapua: Report of the working group on a plan to realise the UN Declaration of the Rights of Indigenous Peoples in Aotearoa/New Zealand.* Te Puni Kōkiri. www.tpk.govt.nz/docs/undrip/tpk-undrip-he-puapua.pdf

Constitutional Advisory Panel. (2013). *A Report on a Conversation/He kōtuinga kōrero mō te kaupapa ture o Aotearoa.* Ministry of Justice. www.justice.govt.nz/assets/Documents/Publications/Constitutional-Advisory-Panel-Full-Report-2013.pdf

Davis, A. (2016). *Freedom is a Constant Struggle: Ferguson, Palestine, and the foundations of a movement.* Haymarket Books.

Donnelly, J. (2003). *Universal Human Rights in Theory and Practice* (2nd ed.). Cornell University Press.

Erueti, A. (2017). *International Indigenous Rights in Aotearoa New Zealand.* Victoria University Press.

Fonseka, D. (2020, May 21). 'Forgotten' migrants locked out. Newsroom. www.newsroom.co.nz/forgotten-migrants-locked-out

Fonseka, D. (2021, August 8). What is behind the immigration delays, and why are some proposing an amnesty to resolve the deadlock? *Stuff.* www.stuff.co.nz/business/opinion-analysis/125940580/what-is-behind-the-immigration-delays-and-why-are-some-proposing-an-amnesty-to-resolve-the-deadlock

Gosepath, S. (2021). Equality. In E. N. Zalta (Ed.), *The Stanford Encyclopedia of Philosophy.* https://plato.stanford.edu/archives/sum2021/entries/equality

Han, J., & Ling, L. H. M. (1998). Authoritarianism in hypermasculinized state: Hybridity, patriarchy, and capitalism in Korea. *International Studies Quarterly, 42*(1), 53–78. https://doi.org/10.1111/0020-8833.00069

Harris, A. (2004). *Hikoi: Forty years of Māori protest*. Huia.

Hereaka, W. (2019). Papatūānuku. In W. Ihimaera & W. Hereaka (Eds.), *Pūrākau: Māori myths retold by Māori writers* (pp. 37–45). Vintage.

Hill, R. S. (2004). *State Authority, Indigenous Autonomy: Crown–Māori relations in New Zealand/Aotearoa, 1900–1950*. Victoria University Press.

Human Rights Commission. (2011). *Te Mana i Waitangi: Human Rights and the Treaty of Waitangi*.

Human Rights Commission. (2016). *The Rights of Indigenous Peoples: What you need to know*. www.hrc.co.nz/files/5814/5618/4456/NZHR_Booklet_12_WEB.pdf

Ishay, M. (2004). What are human rights? Six historical controversies. *Journal of Human Rights, 3*(3), 359–371. https://doi.org/10.1080/1475483042000224897

Kant, I. ([1785] 2019). *Groundwork for the Metaphysics of Morals* (Ed. and Trans. by C. Bennett, J. Saunders, & R. Stern). Oxford University Press.

Langlois, A. (2001). *The Politics of Justice and Human Rights: Southeast Asia and universalist theory*. Cambridge University Press.

McCrudden, C. (2008). Human dignity and judicial interpretation of human rights. *European Journal of International Law, 19*(4), 655–724. https://doi.org/10.1093/ejil/chn043

Ministry of Health. (2020). *Whakamaua: Māori health action plan 2020–2025*. www.health.govt.nz/system/files/documents/publications/whakamaua-maori-health-action-plan-2020-2025-2.pdf

Ngā Puhi Nui Tonu. (2012). *Ngāpuhi Speaks: He wakaputanga o te rangatiratanga o nu tireni and te Tiriti o Waitangi: Independent report on Ngāpuhi Nui Tonu claim*. Network Waitangi Whangarei, Te Kawariki.

Nickel, J. (2021). Human rights. In E. N. Zalta (Ed.), *The Stanford Encyclopedia of Philosophy*. https://plato.stanford.edu/archives/fall2021/entries/rights-human

Orange, C. (1987). *The Treaty of Waitangi*. Bridget Williams Books.

Philpott, D. (1995). Sovereignty: An introduction and brief history. *Journal of International Affairs, 48*(2), 353–368.

Rutazibwa, O. U., & Shilliam, R. (Eds.). (2018). *Routledge Handbook of Postcolonial Politics*. Routledge.

Sen, A. (1979). Equality of what? In S. M. McMurrin (Ed.), *Tanner Lectures on Human Values* (pp. 197–220). Cambridge University Press.

Stavenhagen, R. (2006). *Economic and Social Council (ESC) Report of the Special Rapporteur on the Situation of Human Rights and Fundamental Freedoms of Indigenous Peoples* (E/CN.4/2006/78/Add.3). Rodolfo Stavenhagen, Addendum: Mission to New Zealand.

Sun, P. (2016). Chinese discourse on human rights in global governance. *The Chinese Journal of Global Governance, 1*(2), 192–213. https://doi.org/10.1163/23525207-12340011

Taonui, R. (2012). Māori urban protest movements. In D. Keenan (Ed.), *Huia Histories of Māori: Ngā tāhuhu kōrero* (pp. 230–259). Huia.

Te Aho, L. (2017). The 'false generosity' of Treaty settlements: Innovation and contortion. In A. Erueti (Ed.), *International Indigenous Rights in Aotearoa New Zealand* (pp. 99–117). Victoria University Press.

Walker, R. J. (1984). The genesis of Māori activism. *The Journal of the Polynesian Society, 93*(3), 267–281.

Walker, R. J. (1989). The Treaty of Waitangi as the focus of Māori protest. In I. H. Kawharu (Ed.), *Waitangi: Māori and Pākehā perspectives of the Treaty of Waitangi* (pp. 263–279). Oxford University Press.

Ward, A. (1995). *A Show of Justice: Racial 'amalgamation' in nineteenth century New Zealand*. Auckland University Press.

Weinman, M. (2011). Living well and sexual self-determination: Expanding human rights discourse about sex and sexuality. *Law, Culture and the Humanities, 7*(1), 101–120. https://doi.org/10.1177/1743872109355577

Williams, D. V. (1999). *Te Kooti Tango Whenua: The Native Land Court, 1864-1909*. Huia.

06.
Responsibilities

Tracey Hepi, Krushil Watene & Carol Neill

Introduction

Just as our notions of rights are informed by culture and context, so too are our understandings of responsibility. The construction of identity, belonging and citizenship frame assumptions about the nature and extent of our relationships in a global world. In this chapter, we first examine responsibilities as they feature within Indigenous communities. This allows us to delve into the conceptual underpinnings of Indigenous philosophies and provide a platform for thinking about how the global political system constrains and/or enables our relationships and responsibilities. In doing so, we secondly explore tensions within dominant political power structures that characterise global society. We conclude with a discussion of some of the ways that Indigenous notions of responsibility push the boundaries of thought and practice in the realms of rights and governance.

Indigenous philosophies and responsibility

Recognising the need to motivate socio-environmental responsibilities to stem patterns of consumption and biodiversity loss, global agendas and reports are looking to Indigenous philosophies and frameworks for guidance (IPBES, 2019; UN, 2015; UNDP, 2020; see also: Watene & Yap, 2015; Yap & Watene, 2019). These

IHO ATUA

Margaret Forster (Rongomaiwāhine, Ngāti Kahungunu)

Responsibilities from a Māori viewpoint are encapsulated in origin narratives that inspire and encourage exploits that serve the greater good and secure community advancement and prosperity; this is called mana tangata and involves engaging in mana-enhancing practices. The most renowned exploits are those associated with the ancestor Māui.

> One day, Hina would plait the sacred rope that Māui would use to snare the sun, pulling it like a fish from the darkness and flooding the world with light.
>
> He would charm their grandmother Mahuika so much that she would give him every single one of her magical glittery nails. Each nail would hold a flame, and he would bring fire back into the world . . .
>
> Using the jawbone of his other grandmother, Murirangawhenua, he would fish up a new, clean land, full of life, with forests and rivers and trees. That land would become their home. (Grace-Smith, 2019, p. 102)

There is an expectation that 'citizens' act in the best interests of the collective by acknowledging the importance of ancestral connections and engaging in encounters that secure sovereignty and wellbeing for all — keeping in mind that community includes atua, the environment and natural resources. At an individual level this means realising your full potential and being of service to others. Such practices strengthen identity and a sense of belonging and are a foundation for citizenship and action.

global developments meet with longstanding calls by Indigenous communities themselves to centre thriving human–nature relationships — echoed in collective Indigenous socio-environmental statements, socio-environmental movements, and tribal environmental management and planning strategies (Indigenous Environmental Network, 2012; Matike Mai Aotearoa, 2016; Ngāti Whātua Ōrākei, 2018; UNPFII, 2007; World People's Conference, 2010). These and other Indigenous statements and movements begin from the contention that we have deep attachments to people, places and the natural world more broadly. Out of this contention stems the idea that particular kinds of relationships generate responsibilities, and that these responsibilities extend to include people, more than human animals, and natural entities such as rivers, mountains, land and seascapes. The world, from this starting point, is full of relatives (Wildcat, 2013).

More specifically, Māori and other Indigenous philosophies think of all things existing within a complex system of relationships (Marsden, 2003a, 2003b; Marsden & Henare, 1992; Royal, 2001, 2009, 2014). This complex network or whakapapa animates both our connections and separations — the places where our lives meet and the spaces in between. Furthermore, whakapapa captures how our relationships connect us both to a past that we were not part of and to a future that we will not live to see ourselves — stretching backwards and forwards in time, and outwards to connect (in some form or another) all communities in the present.

By highlighting the significance of our interactions, Indigenous philosophies highlight the ways in which our practices shape our relationships. When we fail to relate well, our lives are diminished. If we fail to meet our relational responsibilities, we neglect the importance of each other and the network in which our lives are lived (Whyte & Cuomo, 2016). Indigenous philosophy, in this way, recognises the interdependence of the collective for living well. In doing so, Māori and other Indigenous relational philosophies ground value systems that mediate and prioritise both personal and collective responsibility (Kawharu, 2000; Murdock, 2018; Sioui, 2020).

Examples abound across Indigenous societies. For the Yawuru community of Broome in north-western Australia, good connections with other people and the natural environment play a vital role in mabu liyan or living a good life (Yap & Yu, 2016). In North America, relationships, as well as the need for cooperation and justice between all beings, ground the Anishinaabe good-living concept of minobimaatisiiwin (McGregor, 2013). In South America, reciprocity in human interactions with nature is fundamental to the Quechua people's good-living notion of allin kawsay (Huambachano, 2017).

Significantly, these responsibilities and the practices that enact them are grounded in a deep sense of belonging to nature (Murdock, 2018). For the Yucatec Mayan (Indigenous people of Xuilub, Yucatán, Mexico), the land provides a spiritually informed way of seeing the world that grounds 'a sense of *being part of the land, rather than a sense of having rights to or on it*' (emphasis added: Sioui, 2020, p. xv). Understanding identity as bound up with land, water and non-human entities frames the scope of these responsibilities. As such, not only are relational responsibilities significant, but they also include 'our responsibility to the world, our responsibility to the animals, our responsibilities to all of the things that surround us' (Virtual Museum of Canada, 2012, para. 1). For Indigenous peoples everywhere, navigating our complex responsibilities for people and other living things in ways that enrich our existence is fundamental.

So, too, is navigating responsibilities to both the past and future — with our relationships to ancestors and descendants as central for understanding our places in the universe (Sioui, 1999, as cited in Sioui, 2020, p. x). Present generations not only have a responsibility to honour learning from the past but also to build on this knowledge by leaving behind a world in which future generations can do the same. The complex network of relationships expands to include those in the cosmos and the natural world who no longer exist and are yet to exist. For Native Hawaiians, he aliʻi ka ʻāina; he kauwā ke kanaka — land is the chief and people are the stewards (Kawena Pukui, 1983, as cited in Sproat & Tuteur, 2019, p. 193). As with many Indigenous societies, the relationship to natural and cultural resources is familial:

> [L]and is an ancestor; fresh water is deified as a physical embodiment of one of our principal gods; and we as younger siblings have a kuleana — a unique cultural duty — to care for these resources as a public trust for present and future generations. For us, kuleana infuses responsibility that must be shouldered before any 'right' may be claimed. (Sproat & Tuteur, 2019, p. 193)

Spirituality is, thus, also an important dimension of this relational philosophy, leaving room for the centrality of spiritual connections, nourishment and responsibility. As Cajete (2000) points out, this emphasises the ontological and epistemological roots of Indigenous philosophies, but it also highlights (we should add) the significance of spirituality in our lives — both within the Pacific region and globally. Similarly, Sāmoa's former head of state, His Highness Tusi Atua Tupua Tamasese Taʻisi Efi, articulates the importance of this relationship, emphasising the place of God in this kinship web, and describing all of creation 'the environment, the animals, the plants, the trees, the water, and so on and so forth', as family and worthy of our protection (2019, p. 131).

In short, responsibilities within Indigenous philosophies are rich and complex. Stemming from a commitment to relating well to all of creation, these responsibilities are distributed across a network inclusive of local, global, multi-species, intergenerational and spiritual dimensions. Not only does this complex understanding of responsibility offer new ways of framing how we ought to live well as individuals and communities, but it also differs radically from contemporary mainstream views. We turn to examine those views next.

Responsibilities in the global context

Contemporary, 'mainstream' understandings of responsibilities have grown out of Western thinking that for a long time disregarded the Indigenous approaches we have outlined above. Resource exploitation, rather than guardianship, has driven the development of the modern global political/economic/social systems of today. Those systems were built historically through European imperialist endeavours that assumed rights to acquire and conquer new lands, natural resources and Indigenous peoples for the progress of empire. The state system developed since the seventeenth-century Treaty of Westphalia, and through the political and industrial revolutions of the eighteenth and nineteenth centuries, entrenched European anthropogenic thinking about the superiority and entitlements of humans to use the natural resources of the Earth to their own means and progress, in deep contrast to Indigenous approaches. Global power structures today remain as legacies of those historical developments.

The state system is dominant globally, with modern societies having been formed and maintained around the idea of the nation-state. Sovereignty underlies international order so that states have equal status, and each state government has ultimate responsibility over their people and territories (Hocking, 2014). Global instruments for cooperation between states seek to build a sense of community across nations and societies, especially through the 1945 formation of the United Nations (UN) and the Universal Declaration of Human Rights (UDHR) and its covenants. However, state self-interest, enabled by sovereignty, tends to create obstacles to authentic cooperation across societies (Weitz, 2019), and relationships between people across states are moderated by the entitlements and obligations attached to their respective national citizenships. Attempts by the UN and other intergovernmental organisations to pursue and realise a global community remain hampered and limit the possibilities for making the most of diverse, cross-cultural thinking (Wehi et al., 2021).

As an institution based on Western cultural understandings (Parida et al., 2021), the modern state privileges individual citizenship and determines culpability and responsibility through constitution, laws, statutes or contracts. As such, the state sits centrally in citizens' views of responsibility, accountability and political participation, but with requirements that are stripped of moral, ethical or cultural concerns for relationships between people and the environment (Herr, 2018; Watene & Yap, 2015). Responsibilities are set down as minimum requirements of citizens; for example, to register and vote, pay taxes and meet certain regulations so that wider, more in-depth political participation is up to individuals to decide. How much citizens choose to voluntarily take part differs across states, communities and groups, and is mediated by the individual's sense that they are recognised and have the right to engage and participate. A major consequence of the privileging of these liberal individualist approaches politically has been the associated benefitting and empowerment of Western peoples, and the marginalisation of Indigenous and other minority local communities (Kymlicka, 1995). Indigenous peoples and other vulnerable peoples regularly face discrimination, lack of political representation or means for participation, economic marginalisation and poverty, and barriers in access to social services (UNPFII, n.d.).

The setting down of minimal state requirements for political citizen participation sets an extremely low bar for community engagement and the enactment of voluntary civic duties. The spread of neoliberalism across Western societies since the 1970s has centralised the private, market-focused sector above the public domain in many people's lives, so that civic participation has become extraordinary rather than a norm within modern lifestyles. The centrality of the market — production, labour and consumer markets that now range to once 'public' goods such as health care and education — has promoted ideas of individual rationality and action in self-interest.

Living standards are measured by income and property acquisition calculations, further distancing Western peoples from relationships with each other and with the Earth. Furthermore, care is relegated to lower-valued and paid jobs in the labour market, or as things people do voluntarily — and with little social recognition — outside of market participation (HRC, 2012; Waring, 2018). Despite some philosophical roots in relationality and connection to nature, it is only recently that dominant Western modes have shifted to thinking about wellbeing. This has started to awaken realisation of the inadequacies of standard economic measures in either understanding 'progress', or in enabling people to take responsibility for the best interests of themselves and their communities.

Much of the contestation of political power structures and policies that does occur is through civil society, defined as 'dense networks of groups, communities,

AHO 6.1 THE GREAT CHAIN OF BEING

For centuries, the 'Great Chain of Being' was a foundational idea in Western thinking. Originating with the Greek philosophers, the idea was developed further as an understanding of social order in the Middle Ages and was still influential for eighteenth-century scientists and 'discoverers'. Anthropologist Anne Salmond (1997) points out that the first European visitors to Aotearoa came with this mindset, seeking to impose an order that would literally change the physical landscape of the country and be instrumental in the oppression of Māori. She explains:

'In the Age of Discovery, new plants, animals and people were 'discovered' simultaneously, and by 1770 the project of sorting them was well under way. The "Great Chain of Being" had long offered one device for ordering all forms of life, with God ruling over angels, humans, animals, plants and rocks, in a strict analogy with European social arrangements at the time. Entities were further sorted into "kingdoms" and "tribes", for as Linnaeus, the Swedish naturalist, commented in 1760, "we must pursue the great chain of nature till we arrive at its origin . . .". While European kingdoms were being placed under bureaucratic control, so too were the plant and animal "kingdoms". Linnaeus' own taxonomic system was used by scientists on Cook's voyages [to Aotearoa] and gave a straightforward means of sorting plant and animal life into species and genera. On the Great Chain of Being, "primitive" and "barbaric" peoples were just one step up from the "higher" animals, so it was logical to handle them in the same way. As fellow human beings, they might have their own ideas on how their lives were organised, but emergent European anthropology saw this as irrelevant.' (Salmond, 1997, pp.146–147)

Reference

Salmond, A. (1997). *Between worlds: Early exchanges between Maori and Europeans 1773–1815.* Viking.

Didacus Valades, *The Great Chain of Being*, 1579. PUBLIC DOMAIN, WIKIMEDIA COMMONS

networks and ties that stand between the individual and the modern state' (Kenny, 2016, para. 1). As an arena of pluralism and contestation (Kaldor, 2003), civil society is complex and variable in how individuals engage, whether that be in non-governmental organisations, social movements, or civic engagement, community networks that may operate locally, nationally or globally. Those civil society actors that operate at the global level tend to be organised as corporatised bodies to achieve long-lasting funding and operational models. This can challenge the heart of the 'neoliberal global citizenship "nexus"' (Jefferess, 2021, p. 421), where civic responsibility is negotiated between the powers of the market and dominant political structures.

Developing strong 'brand' recognition can build an organisation's power and competitiveness in the civil society 'marketplace', but also necessitate the organisation's strategic focus towards securing support rather than advancing founding goals. Directing energies to build alliances with state actors so the organisation is 'at the table' in global political fora can mean that limited resources are given to political manoeuvring rather than grassroots action. Decision making may become undemocratic and undermine the ability of locally based actors to have any significant positive impact on existing challenges.

Western forms of traditional community engagement have been recognised by scholars such as Robert Putnam (2000) as having declined over the past half-century, indicated by the decline in community group memberships, and shifts to 'digital' rather than physical interactions online (Millard et al., 2018). However, such activities remain important for the social fabric of societies. A core element is that community participation is voluntary, needing to be done outside of people's work and other more 'formal' commitments, which can make them difficult to prioritise. Community engagement can thus be ad hoc and short term. Such participation contrasts with Indigenous peoples, where, more often than not, individual norms and life choices are centred on lifetime commitments to family and community, as are their work and leisure choices.

Lack of recognition and trust in political processes can also be at the root of non-participation. Whereas in Aotearoa, for example, the growth of apathetic generations is pointed out through declining numbers of young voters, larger systemic causes tend to be ignored. It is important to acknowledge that generations of disconnected citizens have become resigned to the disproportionate experiences of unemployment and poverty, the negative effects of poor education, insecure and low income, and low housing affordability, in large part due to the results of an economic model they had no part in creating (Dean, 2015). Considering the resulting loneliness and sense of not belonging to many communities, it is understandable why these generations may not participate in civil society engagement. Why should they, when society has made living in Aotearoa such a struggle?

The idea of development as a means of advancing living standards for all peoples has been dominated historically by anthropogenic, 'first world' Western views of progress. Consequently, action to help disadvantaged or marginalised peoples still tends to be driven by humanitarian assumptions of what is needed, and what development should look like for those people. History is littered with stories of humanitarian action where the goals were not fit for purpose for the recipients, causing more challenges than benefits in the long term. Likewise, 'white saviourism' creates problems where humanitarian action is driven more by self-interest and the pursuit of heroism, rather than by authentically considering the long-term needs and empowerment of the recipients, and in blurry lines between not-for-profit and profit-making endeavours of some organisations (Jefferess, 2021; McLennan, 2021). Such humanitarianism essentially works to entrench — rather than disrupt — unequal global power structures.

Within modern societies, business development and economic innovation are looked to as the best hope for progress. In saying this, the profit imperative of businesses has meant that responsibility has historically been limited to meeting business and employment regulations, contractual obligations and guidelines for accountability to investors and clients. However, corporate social responsibility (CSR) has grown to influence notions of corporate 'citizenship' with 'a company's duties and obligations as a member of civil society: to obey the law, contribute to the commonwealth, participate in governance, and to demonstrate respect for other citizens' (Frederick, 2018, p. 21). Further, social enterprises — examples in Aotearoa include Will & Able, Joy of Giving NZ, and The Fearless Kitchen (Social Enterprise Auckland, 2021) — challenge conventional business approaches by centring values-driven and positive social goals. Social responsibility drives their business strategies and operations. Despite these positive developments, a criticism of such approaches is that, regardless of their positive social goals, such entities tend to only 'tinker' around the edges of dominant neoliberal, Westernised business paradigms, serving to maintain their power rather than deconstructing them (McLennan & Banks, 2019).

Much work has been done at the global level to build cooperation between states, civil society and market-based actors to address challenges wrought through historical inequalities and power imbalances. The United Nations and other intergovernmental fora have grown to engage with non-state actors, recognising the need to engage beyond levels of political leadership — the Sustainable Development Goals (SDGs) are a prominent example. However, slow, negative

AHO 6.2 WHAT ARE THE SDGS?

In 2015, the United Nations (UN) adopted 17 Sustainable Development Goals (SDGs). The goals, described as a 'shared blueprint for peace and prosperity for people and the planet, now and into the future' (UN, n.d., para. 1), were designed to not only guide government action but cross all spheres and levels of society, including civil society and the private sector. The SDGs are part of a wider UN resolution called the *2030 Agenda for Sustainable Development*, and advocate for worldwide sustainable betterment of health, food security, gender equality, environmental protections and more. (See Chapter 16 for a more in-depth discussion of SDGs, poverty and inequality.)

United Nations' 17 Sustainable Development Goals. UNITED NATIONS DEPARTMENT OF GLOBAL COMMUNICATIONS, HTTPS://SDGS.UN.ORG/GOALS

and even backwards progress in international action to truly address global challenges such as climate change, ongoing conflict, and poverty and inequality has highlighted the inadequacy of state-based power in dealing with big global challenges as they are, and it is commonly agreed that new ways of working together, incorporating wider ways of thinking, need to be found. The next section will consider examples that present the possibilities of meaningful partnerships, led by Indigenous peoples, for enabling effective positive change.

Rethinking global responsibilities

Indigenous people worldwide employ a variety of traditional governance approaches that can potentially provide viable alternatives to narrower Western economic-centred visions of progress and development (Alfred & Corntassel, 2005; Pierotti & Wildcat, 2000). Indigenous societies continue to keep their Indigenous Knowledge Systems (IKS) alive, despite being undermined by state institutional and legal configurations (Battiste, 2000; Radcliffe, 2012; Sherman, 2008; Sioui, 2020; Zimmerer, 2000). The insights from these land-related cultural knowledge systems may be used to better elaborate and implement more sustainable, and culturally respectful, development and conservation efforts, while validating the world view of Indigenous people, in an effort to renegotiate dominant ethnocentric policies.

Most recently, and beginning in Latin America, Indigenous communities have helped to inspire transformations in law, with the granting of legal personhood to natural entities in their own right. By viewing the natural world as a living and legal entity, rights of protection and guardianship may be afforded to mountains, lakes and rivers and other natural formations. In 2008, Ecuador adopted a new constitution establishing rights for nature and identifying the commensurate duties of human responsibility. This constitution is explicitly stated to be underpinned by the Indigenous concept of sumac kawsay (Constitution of Ecuador, 2008) which is simply translated as 'living in harmony with nature'. However, sumac kawsay also sees nature as 'an inherent part of the social being' (Chuji, 2017, as cited in Magallanes, 2019, p. 219) rather than merely a resource to be exploited.

In Aotearoa, the Whanganui River is seen as an ancestor for the Whanganui iwi. In March 2017, the New Zealand Parliament afforded legal personhood to the river with the name, Te Awa Tupua, endorsing the river as a legal person with the incumbent rights, powers, duties and liabilities (Te Awa Tupua [Whanganui River Claims Settlement] Act 2017, section 14). One key difference from other examples of legal personality and rights of nature is the vesting of ownership of the riverbed

AHO 6.3 LAST WARNING CAMPAIGN

If you woke up this morning, had a coffee and cut up a banana to put on your porridge, you may have already been complicit in some of the processes that are destroying the Amazon rainforest and other natural environments. The Amazon is the lungs of the Earth and key to planetary survival, but it is being cut down to supply global trade in agricultural and forestry products.

The Last Warning Campaign (LWC) was started by the Huni Kui people, an Indigenous group that lives in the Amazon. As Hunt et al. (2021) explain: 'Last Warning does not tell us how to shift away from our current paradigm and make space for a wiser one to emerge; it does not claim to have the answers. Instead, it offers a new educational compass — a way of orienting ourselves away from reproducing harm and toward fostering more generative possibilities for co-existence, without glossing over the difficult elements of this work . . .

'Responsibility here is understood as an affirmation of our interdependence, including the debts we have to specific communities and to the Earth. It also involves facing humanity in all of its complexities and paradoxes: the good, the bad, the broken and the messed up within and around us.' (Hunt et al., 2021, para. 20, 22)

Scan the QR code to learn more about the Last Warning Campaign and to hear from some of the activists.

Reference

Hunt, D., Ahenakew, C., Stein, S., Andreotti, V., & Valley, W. (2021, November 2). From the Amazon, Indigenous peoples offer a new compass to navigate climate change. *The Conversation.* https://theconversation.com/from-the-amazon-indigenous-peoples-offer-new-compass-to-navigate-climate-change-167768

Tropical rainforest is cleared for agriculture.
SHUTTERSTOCK

RESPONSIBILITIES 109

in Te Awa Tupua itself. Another is the creation of statutory guardians to uphold the interests of the river. A third is the recognition of the river's own intrinsic value. Iorns Magallanes argues it is an attempt to uphold Indigenous rights and an Indigenous concept of kinship with and responsibility for the river; yet the focus is responsibility rather than rights (2019, p. 221). Thus, such an evolving legal landscape can begin to create the kinds of partnerships that go some way to recognising the right of Indigenous peoples to relate to nature in ways grounded in their philosophies and practices.

Conclusion

Despite structures that privilege Western approaches in laws, policies and political agendas, Indigenous peoples and other local communities have found ways to enact their responsibilities to the Earth and each other consistent with their values. Humanity's actions have brought us to the tipping point of irreversible damage in ecosystems and Earth's climate system (IPCC, 2018), and with the world's population facing challenges like the climate change crisis, it has become increasingly apparent that the human–Earth relationship needs to be prioritised. Indigenous societies the world over have implemented Indigenous Knowledge Systems with the aim of producing a sustainable future based on philosophical concepts and practical observation of living reciprocally with the Earth. Together these local movements offer insights for global change. There is, therefore, much to be gained in listening to, learning from and working together with Indigenous peoples.

References

Alfred, T., & Corntassel, J. (2005). Being Indigenous: Resurgences against contemporary colonialism. *Government and Opposition: An international journal of comparative politics, 40*(4), 597–614. https://doi.org/10.1111/j.1477-7053.2005.00166.x

Battiste, M. A. (2000). *Reclaiming Indigenous Voice and Vision*. UBC Press.

Cajete, G. (2000). *Native Science: Natural laws of interdependence*. Clear Light Publishers.

Constitution of Ecuador. (2008). *Preamble*. www.constituteproject.org/constitution/Ecuador_2008.pdf

Dean, A. (2015). *Ruth, Roger and Me: Debts and legacies*. BWB Texts.

Frederick, W. C. (2018). The origins and development of Corporate Social Responsibility. In J. Weber & D. M. Wasieleski (Eds.), *Corporate Social Responsibility* (pp. 3–38). Emerald Publishing.

Grace-Smith, B. (2019). Born. Still. The birth and return of Māui-Tikitiki-a-Taranga (as observed by his sister, Hina). In W. Ihimaera & W. Hereaka (Eds.), *Pūrākau: Māori myths retold by Māori writers* (pp. 97–102). Vintage.

Herr, R. S. (2018). Indigenous peoples' collective self-determination in the age of legal globalisation. In E. Yahyaoui (Ed.), *Human Rights and Power in Times of Globalisation* (pp. 11–41). Brill.

His Highness Tusi Atua Tupua Tamasese Ta'isi Efi. (2019). An ethic of responsibility in Samoan customary law. In B. Martin, L. Te Aho, & M. Humphries-Kil (Eds.), *ResponsAbility: Law and governance for living well with the Earth* (pp. 126–134). Routledge.

Hocking, B. (2014). The state system. In B. Hocking & M. Smith (Eds.), *World Politics: An introduction to international relations* (pp. 50–73). Routledge.

Huambachano, M. (2017). Through an Indigenous Lens Food Security is Food Sovereignty: Case studies of Māori people of Aotearoa and Andean people of Peru [unpublished doctoral dissertation, University of Auckland].

Human Rights Commission (HRC). (2012). *Caring Counts: Tautiaki tika.* New Zealand Human Rights Commission.

Indigenous Environmental Network. (2012). Kari-Oca 2 Declaration: Indigenous Peoples Global Conference on Rio+20 and Mother Earth. www.ienearth.org/kari-oca-2-declaration

Intergovernmental Panel on Biodiversity and Ecosystem Services (IPBES). (2019). *Summary for Policymakers of the Global Assessment Report on Biodiversity and Ecosystem Services of the Intergovernmental Science-Policy Platform on Biodiversity and Ecosystem Services.* https://uwe-repository.worktribe.com/output/1493508

Intergovernmental Panel on Climate Change (IPCC). (2018). Global Warming of 1.5°C. www.ipcc.ch/sr15

Jefferess, D. (2021). On saviours and saviourism: Lessons from the #WEscandal. *Globalisation, Societies and Education, 19*(4), 420–431. https://doi.org/10.1080/14767724.2021.1892478

Kaldor, M. (2003). The idea of global civil society. *International Affairs, 79*(3), 583–593. https://doi.org/10.1111/1468-2346.00324

Kawharu, M. (2000). Kaitiakitanga: A Maori anthropological perspective of the Maori socioenvironmental ethic of resource management. *The Journal of the Polynesian Society, 110*(4), 349–370.

Kenny, M. (2016). Civil society, social science. *Encyclopaedia Brittanica.* www.britannica.com/topic/civil-society

Kymlicka, W. (1995). *Multicultural Citizenship.* Oxford University Press.

Magallanes, C. I. (2019). From rights to responsibilities using legal personhood and guardianship for rivers. In B. Martin, L. Te Aho, & M. Humphries-Kil (Eds.), *ResponsAbility: Law and governance for living well with the Earth* (pp. 216–239). Routledge.

Marsden, Rev. M. (2003a). The achievement of authentic being: God, man and universe, a Māori view. In C. Royal (Ed.), *The Woven Universe: Selected writings of Rev. Maori Marsden* (pp. 2–23). The Estate of Rev. Maori Marsden.

Marsden, Rev. M. (2003b). The natural world and natural resources: Māori value systems and perspectives. In C. Royal (Ed.), *The Woven Universe: Selected writings of Rev. Maori Marsden* (pp. 24–53). The Estate of Rev. Maori Marsden.

Marsden, Rev. M., & Henare, T. A. (1992). Kaitiakitanga: A definitive introduction to the holistic worldview of Māori. [Unpublished paper].

Matike Mai Aotearoa. (2016). He Whakaaro Here Whakaumu Mō Aotearoa: The Report of Matike Mai Aotearoa — The Independent Working Group on Constitutional Transformation. www.converge.org.nz/pma/MatikeMaiAotearoaReport.pdf

McGregor, D. (2013). Indigenous women, water justice and *zaagidowin* (love). *Canadian Woman Studies, 30*(2/3), 71–78.

McLennan, S. (2021). New Zealanders as international volunteers: Who, what, why . . . and should I? In D. Belgrave & G. Dodson (Eds.), *Tūtira Mai: Making change in Aotearoa New Zealand* (pp. 192–210). Massey University Press.

McLennan, S., & Banks, G. (2019). Reversing the lens: Why corporate social responsibility is not community development. *Corporate Social Responsibility and Environmental Management, 26*(1), 117–126. https://doi.org/10.1002/csr.1664

Millard, A., Baldassar, L., & Wilding, R. (2018). The significance of digital citizenship in the well-being of older migrants. *Public Health, 158,* 144–148. https://doi.org/10.1016/j.puhe.2018.03.005

Murdock, E. G. (2018). Storied with land: 'Transitional justice' on Indigenous lands. *Journal of Global Ethics, 14*(2), 232–239. https://doi.org/10.1080/17449626.2018.1516692

Ngāti Whātua Ōrākei. (2018). Te Pou o Kāhu Pōkere: Iwi Management Plan for Ngāti Whātua Ōrākei. https://ngatiwhatuaorakei.com/wpcontent/uploads/2019/08/58087_Ngati_Whatua_Orakei_Iwi_Management_Plan_FINAL.pdf

Parida, B., Dash, S. S., & Sharma, D. (2021). Role of culture-specific rights, responsibilities and duties in industry 4.0: Comparing Indic and Western perspectives. Benchmarking: An *International Journal, 28*(5), 1543–1557. https://doi.org/10.1108/BIJ-05-2020-0257

Pierotti, R., & Wildcat, D. (2000). Traditional ecological knowledge: The third alternative (commentary). *Ecological Applications, 10*(5), 1333–1340. https://doi.org/10.1890/1051-0761(2000)010[1333:TEKTTA]2.0.CO;2

Putnam, R. D. (2000). *Bowling Alone: The collapse and revival of American community*. Simon & Schuster.

Radcliffe, S. A. (2012). Development for a postneoliberal era? Sumak kawsay, living well and the limits to decolonisation in Ecuador. *Geoforum, 43*(2), 240–249. https://doi.org/10.1016/j.geoforum.2011.09.003

Royal, T. A. C. (2001). Indigenous worldviews: A comparative study. Written for Ngāti Kikopiri, Te Wānanga o Raukawa, Te Puni Kōkiri, Fullbright New Zealand, Winston Churchill Memorial Trust.

Royal, T. A. C. (2009). Mātauranga Māori: Perspectives. (Monograph five of Te Kaimānga: Towards a new vision for Mātauranga Māori). MKTA.

Royal, T. A. C. (2014). Indigenous ways of knowing. In Argos Aotearoa (Eds.), *The University Beside Itself* (pp. 27–41). Argos Aotearoa.

Sherman, P. (2008). *Dishonour of the Crown: The Ontario resource regime in the Valley of the Kiji Sibi*. Arbeiter Ring Publishing.

Sioui, M. (2020). *Indigenous Geographies in the Yucatan: Learning from the responsibility-based Maya environmental ethos*. Springer Nature.

Social Enterprise Auckland. (2021). Member spotlights. www.socialenterpriseauckland.org.nz/spotlight-stories

Sproat, K., & Tuteur, M. (2019). The power and potential of the public trust: Insight from Hawai'i's water battles and triumph. In B. Martin, L. Te Aho, & M. Humphries-Kil (Eds.), *ResponsAbility: Law and governance for living well with the Earth* (pp. 193–215). Routledge.

Te Awa Tupua (Whanganui River Claims Settlement) Act 2017, s 14. (2017). www.legislation.govt.nz/act/public/2017/0007/latest/DLM6830851.html?src=qs

United Nations (UN). (2015). Transforming our world: The 2030 Agenda for Sustainable Development. https://sdgs.un.org/2030agenda

United Nations Development Programme (UNDP). (2020). *The Next Frontier: Human development and the Anthropocene* (Human Development Report 2020). http://report.hdr.undp.org

United Nations Permanent Forum for Indigenous Issues (UNPFII). (n.d.). Factsheet: Who are Indigenous peoples? www.un.org/esa/socdev/unpfii/documents/5session_factsheet1.pdf

United Nations Permanent Forum for Indigenous Issues (UNPFII). (2007). United Nations Declaration on the Rights of Indigenous Peoples. www.un.org/esa/socdev/unpfii/en/drip.html

Virtual Museum of Canada. (2012, January 15). *Testimony of F. Henry Lickers / The story continues / The St. Lawrence Iroquoians*. www.virtualmuseum.ca/sgc-cms/expositions-exhibitions/iroquoiens-iroquoians/descendants_fh_licker-story_continues_fh_licker-eng.html

Waring, M. (2018). *Still Counting: Wellbeing, women's work and policy-making*. Bridget Williams Books.

Watene, K., & Yap, M. (2015). Culture and sustainable development: Indigenous contributions. *Journal of Global Ethics, 11*(1), 51–55. https://doi.org/10.1080/17449626.2015.1010099

Wehi, P. M., van Uitregt, V., Scott, N. J., Gillies, T., Beckwith, J., Rodgers, R. P., & Watene, K. (2021). Transforming Antarctic management and policy with an Indigenous Māori lens. *Nature*

Ecology and Evolution, 5, 1055–1059. https://doi.org/10.1038/s41559-021-01466-4

Weitz, E. D. (2019). *A World Divided: The global struggle for human rights in the age of nation-states.* Princeton University Press.

Whyte, K., & Cuomo, C. (2016). Ethics of caring in environmental ethics: Indigenous and feminist philosophies. In S. M. Gardiner & A. Thompson (Eds.), *Oxford Handbook of Environmental Ethics* (pp. 234–247). Oxford University Press.

Wildcat, D. R. (2013) Introduction: Climate change and Indigenous peoples of the USA. In J. K. Maldonado, B. Colombi, & R. Pandya (Eds.), *Climate Change and Indigenous Peoples in the United States.* Springer. https://doi.org/10.1007/978-3-319-05266-3_1

World People's Conference on Climate Change and the Rights of Mother Earth. (2010). Universal Declaration of the Rights of Mother Earth, Cochabamba, Bolivia.

Yap, M., & Yu, E. (2016). Operationalising the capability approach to develop indicators of wellbeing: An Australian example. *Oxford Development Studies, 44*(3), 315–331. https://doi.org/10.1080/13600818.2016.1178223

Yap, M. L., & Watene, K. (2019). The Sustainable Development Goals (SDGs) and Indigenous peoples: Another missed opportunity? *Journal of Human Development and Capabilities, 20*(4), 451–467. https://doi.org/10.1080/19452829.2019.1574725

Zimmerer, K. S. (2000). Rescaling irrigation in Latin America: The cultural images and political ecology of water resources. *Ecumene: A journal of cultural geography, 7*(2), 150–175. https://doi.org/10.1177/096746080000700202

PART TWO:

TE RITO, THE CENTRAL SHOOTS

07.
Encountering climate change

Sharon McLennan & Axel Malecki

Introduction

What comes to mind when you think about climate change? Melting polar ice caps? Growing deserts? Storms, fires, floods? Climate change will have (and is already having) wide-ranging environmental impacts. But it is more than an environmental crisis. The consequences for all life on Earth and for all peoples are immense and will have a significant impact on the nature and scope of global citizenship in the twenty-first century.

This summary chapter provides important context for the chapters in this section. It begins with an overview of climate change and its consequences, particularly for people in vulnerable places and for those already marginalised, including Indigenous groups. We then link this to our framework of rights and responsibilities. The chapters in this section focus on responses to the crisis, namely Pacific Island responses (Movono & McLennan, Chapter 8), Māori responses (Kaiser & Kenney, Chapter 9), and creative responses (Horrocks & Doig, Chapter 10).

Climate change: An overview

Climate change refers to change in the climate that persists for an extended period. In recent decades, it has come to mean the shift in weather phenomena

IHO ATUA

Margaret Forster (Rongomaiwāhine, Ngāti Kahungunu)

Change is inevitable. In the narrative about the separation of Ranginui and Papatūānuku, it is expressed as a transition from darkness to light, a precursor to growth and expansion leading to the evolution of the natural world. It is seen in the exploits of Māui as he bound the sun to slow time and form the seasons to bring forth the conditions for cultivation. Change is also a necessary reaction to pain and trauma as seen through the experiences of Hinetītama as she engages in a courageous act of rangatiratanga as a precursor to healing and recovery.

> Hine-tītama achieved her transcendence. She became Hinenuitepō which some have translated as 'The Goddess of Death'. I say to you, look to the literal translation of her name: just as the full name of Tāne is Tānenuiārangi, Great Father of the Overworld, let us acknowledge Hinenuitepō's nurturing role as Great Mother of the Underworld. Hers is the redemptive role and it is through her that we achieve forgiveness. (Ihimaera & Hereaka, 2019, p. 90)

Consequence is a constant companion of change. And the consequences associated with climate change are substantive. The speed and scale of change is potentially catastrophic for the environment and for people. All the superpowers and wisdom of the atua and ancestors will be needed to keep the world safe and protected and to navigate the impacts of climate change.

associated with an increase in global average temperatures. Our world is now about one degree Celsius hotter than it was between 1850 and 1900. Projections for the remainder of the twenty-first century vary, with scientists warning global temperatures are likely to reach 1.0 degree to 5.7 degrees Celsius higher than pre-industrial averages by 2100 (IPCC, 2021).

This warming results from human activity that generates an excess of long-lived greenhouse gases (GHGs). Life on Earth is dependent on a layer of gases in the lower atmosphere that traps heat from the sun. However, increasing levels of GHGs (particularly carbon dioxide) are now trapping too much heat near the Earth's surface, causing rising temperatures. Although a range of natural phenomena can affect the climate, scientists overwhelmingly agree that global warming and its resultant climatic effects are anthropogenic — that is, human made. According to the IPCC's sixth assessment report, increases in GHG concentrations since 1750 are unequivocally caused by human activities (IPCC, 2021, p. 5). This has occurred mainly through the burning of fossil fuels, while deforestation has reduced the amount of plant life available to turn carbon dioxide into oxygen.

There is now more carbon dioxide in the atmosphere than at any time in at least 800,000 years. Indeed, although the effects of Covid-19-related lockdowns, such as scaled-back manufacturing processes, helped to reduce the annual emissions of GHGs in 2020 and 2021, the actual concentration of GHGs in the Earth's atmosphere continued to increase. These emissions could double or nearly triple by 2100, greatly amplifying climate change. And because carbon dioxide lives long in the atmosphere, this will effectively lock the Earth and future generations into a range of impacts, some of which could be severe. These include:

- more intense rainfall and flooding in some regions, and more intense drought in others
- continued sea-level rise, contributing to more frequent and severe coastal flooding in low-lying areas
- changes to the ocean, including warming, more-frequent marine heatwaves, acidification, and reduced oxygen levels affecting both ocean ecosystems and the people who rely on them
- changes to the geographical distribution of plants and animals, affecting crop production, human and animal health, and contributing to species extinction. (IPBES, 2019; IPCC, 2021)

Climate inequality

Although it has become standard to refer to climate change as anthropogenic, humans do not share equal responsibility for excess GHG emissions. Climate change, industrialisation and neoliberal globalisation have progressed hand in hand. For example, a study by the Stockholm Environment Institute and Oxfam (Kartha et al., 2020) showed that the wealthiest 10 per cent of people are responsible for about half of all carbon emissions. The United States (US) military alone produces as much GHG emissions as 140 countries. Between 1854 and 2010, the 90 largest producers of coal, oil, natural gas and cement were responsible for approximately two-thirds of the total industrial emissions of carbon dioxide and methane. Moreover, there are several corporate manufacturers who not only produce fossil fuels, but also fight to ensure their activities will be unhindered by environmental or climate policies.

Meanwhile, the populations of the world's poorest nations and Indigenous peoples, who do not drive, fly or consume material goods in large quantities, contribute very little to GHGs. Indeed, the poorest 50 per cent, or about 3.5 billion people, are responsible for only 10 per cent of global carbon emissions (Kartha et al., 2020). And it is this bottom 50 per cent who bear the brunt of climate change, as their lives and livelihoods are often precarious and they are already more vulnerable to water shortages, reductions in food production, damaging weather events, sea-level rises and the spread of disease.

Climate change and rights

Climate change threatens all human rights, particularly among those whose lives are already precarious. As Atapattu (2016) notes:

> The rights affected include the right to life, right to property and the right to a livelihood, while those living on small island states are facing the risk of extinction as their island nations are threatened with submergence associated with sea-level rise. Other communities are facing the likelihood of losing their traditional way of life, their culture and their traditional lands. (p. 67)

Yet climate change was not considered a human rights issue until recently, and early action was confined to environmental bodies (Atapattu, 2016). It was not until 2009 that the Human Rights Council noted that climate change poses an immediate and far-reaching threat to people and communities and has

AHO 7.1 INDIA LOGAN-RILEY COP26 SPEECH

In October 2021, young Māori activist India Logan-Riley stood before an international audience at the UN COP26 summit in Scotland and told them that refusal to act on climate change was a 'colonial project'. Logan-Riley argued that it was Indigenous people who had been at the forefront of efforts to address climate change because they know the destruction that occurs when greed for natural resources and a 'profit at all costs' mentality overrule respect for nature. She linked the climate crisis with imperialism and colonialism, explicitly pointing out the role of the English empire, while British Prime Minister Boris Johnson sat uncomfortably by:

'Two-hundred-and-fifty-two years ago invading forces sent by the ancestors of this presidency arrived at my ancestors' territories, heralding an age of violence, murder and destruction enabled by documents, like the Document of Discovery, formulated in Europe.'

To see more of India Logan-Riley's COP26 speech, scan the QR code.

Reference

RNZ News. (2021, November 1). Māori climate activist tells COP26 challenge modern 'colonial project' or be complicit in death. www.rnz.co.nz/news/te-manu-korihi/454669/maori-climate-activist-tells-cop26-challenge-modern-colonial-project-or-be-complicit-in-death

India Logan-Riley speaks at the UN COP26 summit in Scotland, 2021. UNCLIMATECHANGE, WWW.FLICKR.COM/PHOTOS/UNTCCC

implications for the full enjoyment of human rights (Human Rights Council, 2009). This milestone report identified the intrinsic link between the environment and the realisation of human rights, before discussing the impacts on many civil, political, economic, social and cultural rights (Atapattu, 2016).

Since the 2009 report, concerns about the impact of climate change on rights have steadily risen. Social, cultural and economic rights are at risk as changes in weather patterns, sea-level rise and other environmental changes affect the ability of people to stay healthy, to make a living, and to access adequate housing and education. But there are also flow-on effects to other rights families. The anticipated rise in tensions over resources and conflict associated with climate change will affect security, due process and liberty rights. Political rights will also be impacted, particularly for people in vulnerable situations who may not have access to political power or the ability to participate in decision making. As discussed, these risks are most significant for those already vulnerable, in particular for minority and group rights which protect women, racial and ethnic minorities, Indigenous peoples, children, migrant workers and the disabled.

Those who need to migrate as a result of climate change are particularly at risk across the spectrum of rights, including the loss of land, livelihood and culture. Some face the loss of nationhood and citizenship, as sea-level rise and desertification make small islands and other vulnerable places uninhabitable. For while the majority of climate-change-induced migration is predicted to revolve around internal displacement, low-lying island states face distinct threats. This has important implications for exercising rights because firstly, when a nation's territory becomes uninhabitable, citizens may lose their right to political self-determination. Secondly, according to the Montevideo Convention, which forms the foundation for the Law of Statehood, a state is defined by having a permanent population, a government, the capacity to enter into relations with other states and, crucially, a defined territory. If island states disappear or are made permanently uninhabitable, then a key condition for being a state ceases to exist because where there is no territory there is no state, and this creates stateless population groups whose right to a nationality and national citizenship is at risk of being irrevocably lost.

As Chapters 8 and 9 highlight, Indigenous groups are particularly affected by climate change, facing the impacts outlined above, and the ongoing challenges associated with rights to self-determination and development. Key to this is the right of peoples to permanent sovereignty over their natural resources. These rights are also closely linked to the existence of a healthy environment, on which the attainment of economic, social and cultural rights is dependent. These core rights

— and, therefore, the right of peoples to self-determination — are threatened by climate change (Frere et al., 2020).

In Aotearoa, tangata whenua interests are fundamental to climate change frameworks. Te Tiriti o Waitangi provides the basis for Māori rights to land, knowledge and culture, all of which are impacted by climate change. However, it also provides the grounds for partnerships to protect the land and people, and recognises kaitiaki responsibilities of tangata whenua to care and look after the environment and natural resources, although as Kaiser and Kenney (Chapter 9) explain, it is unclear whether these provisions are sufficient.

Responding to climate change

Of all the challenges facing humanity, climate change best highlights our interdependence and the need for global action. No country can protect its citizens alone, and while the work of key institutions, groups and individuals is important, it is not sufficient in isolation. As the United Nations Human Rights Council highlighted in Resolution 26/27 (2014, p. 3), 'climate change is an urgent global problem requiring a global solution'.

The global community has begun to wake up to this challenge. The formalisation of what may be termed 'the climate change regime' began with the establishment of the United Nations Framework Convention on Climate Change (UNFCCC) in 1992. The UNFCCC, and particularly its supreme decision-making body, the Conference of the Parties (COP), is an attempt to institute a system of global governance in the context of curbing GHG concentrations. One of the most important COPs to date was the 2015 event in Paris. Here, for the first time, nations adopted a universal agreement to fight climate change — the Paris Agreement — and undertook to keep global warming to well below 2 degrees Celsius. The Paris Agreement allows each country to set its own emission-reduction targets and adopt its own strategies for reaching them. The issue, as the 2021 IPCC report makes clear, is that under existing policies we will fail to achieve any meaningful reduction in greenhouse gas emissions.

Climate action also features prominently in the Sustainable Development Goals (SDGs). Goal 13 focuses on climate change and the need to take urgent action to combat climate change and its impacts. Targets include: strengthening resilience and adaptive capacity; integrating climate change measures into national policies, strategies and planning; and improving education, awareness-raising and human and institutional capacity on climate change mitigation, adaptation, impact reduction and early warning.

However, global commitments are not sufficient on their own and require action from national and local governments. States determine if and when they comply with international resolutions and agreements. When they choose to do so, they essentially 'give up' some sovereignty, because they need to change or adjust domestic laws. One example is the 2019 Zero Carbon Bill, which constitutes Aotearoa's commitment to addressing climate change and provides a framework for meeting our obligations to the Paris Agreement and SDG 13.

While state governments exercise sovereignty, the policies that affect citizens in their everyday lives often sit within local or regional governance structures. As such, cities, municipalities and local as well as regional government can drive change. The *Renewables in Cities 2019 Global Status Report* suggests that more than half the world's population live in cities, and that urban spaces account for two-thirds of global energy demand and around 75 per cent of global CO_2 emissions (REN21, 2019). The saying 'Think global, act local' has real and important meaning, as local governments can legislate for more ambitious targets than can national governments who are trapped in partisan general election cycles.

The private sector also has a role to play, particularly those that derive revenue from the generation of GHGs. As noted previously, most emissions can be traced to a relatively small number of fossil fuel producers in the private sector. Richard Heede, head of the Climate Accountability Institute, states '[T]hese companies have significant moral, financial, and legal responsibility for the climate crisis' (Climate Accountability Institute, 2019, p. 3). While the energy-producing sector still has a long way to go, other corporations and private companies have explicitly committed to achieving the zero-carbon goal. Internet giant Google, for instance, has had a zero-carbon emission goal since 2007.

Although it is important to tackle the big carbon decisions via legislation on national and local levels, there are also important responses we can take as communities and as individuals. In recent years, we have seen expressions of discontent, frustration and anger from people across the globe, particularly youth. This movement champions ecological justice, intergenerational fairness and equity, where the production of critical spaces of engagement and inclusive decision making is central for a fairer climate future. Informal networks devoted to grassroots education on a range of subjects, such as advocacy and community gardens, are tools to build empathy across different communities, which should be seen as an 'important resource for social change' (Hayward, 2017, p. 91).

Climate change and citizenship

Climate change will affect all aspects of life on Earth and all peoples. In the face of this global challenge, a narrow view of citizenship serves us poorly. As Hayward (2017) argues:

> Just by routine actions such as getting in our cars and turning on the ignition, what we do has implications for those fellow citizens far away, in communities displaced by drought and floods as a consequence of our high-carbon lifestyles. In this context, there is another, more open and inclusive way of thinking about citizenship, as a state of being, belonging and participating in communities. . . . This more open approach to citizenship . . . allows us to consider our obligations in a world experiencing climate change. We can start to consider 'distant others'. (p. 48)

The examples explored here and in the chapters that follow show how states, communities and individuals can exercise agency, driven by the people within and/or pressure from the outside. It is, therefore, of vital importance that we understand what is being done in response to climate change, both by international institutions and governments, and by communities and people across the globe. The leadership shown by Indigenous peoples is particularly important. The next chapter (Movono & McLennan) highlights one set of responses, from an Indigenous Fijian community, showing how people who both benefit from and are put at risk by international tourism (a significant contributor to climate change) are responding to multiple crises through reconnection with traditional knowledge and practices. Chapter 9 (Kaiser & Kenney) also examines Indigenous responses, exploring the impacts of climate change on tangata whenua in Aotearoa, how they are responding at local and national levels, and the challenges posed by integrating Māori climate change knowledges, world views and approaches with mainstream strategies for climate change mitigation and adaptation. The final chapter in this section (Horrocks & Doig) explores individual responses to climate change, particularly how creative writing can help us understand and live with the climate crisis, as well as making calls to action and creating space for alternative imaginings of the world.

References

Atapattu, S. A. (2016). *Human Rights Approaches to Climate Change: Challenges and opportunities*. Routledge.

Climate Accountability Institute. (2019). *Carbon Majors: Update of top twenty companies 1965–2017* [Press release]. Retrieved from http://climateaccountability.org/pdf/CAI%20 PressRelease%20Top20%20Oct19.pdf

Frere, T., Mulalap, C. Y., & Tanielu, T. (2020). Climate change and challenges to self-determination: Case studies from French Polynesia and the Republic of Kiribati. *The Yale Law Journal Forum, 129*, 648–673.

Hayward, B. (2017). *Sea Change: Climate politics and New Zealand*. Bridget Williams Books.

Human Rights Council. (2009). *Report of the United Nations High Commissioner for Human Rights on the Relationship between Climate Change and Human Rights* [A/HRC/10/61]. www.refworld.org/docid/498811532.html

Ihimaera, W., & Hereaka, W. (2019). *Pūrākau: Māori myths retold by Māori writers*. Vintage.

IPBES. (2019). *Global Assessment Report on Biodiversity and Ecosystem Services of the Intergovernmental Science-Policy Platform on Biodiversity and Ecosystem Services*. IPBES Secretariat.

IPCC. (2021). Summary for policymakers. In *Climate Change 2021: The physical science basis summary for policymakers, Contribution of Working Group I to the Sixth Assessment Report of the Intergovernmental Panel on Climate Change*. Cambridge University Press. https://doi.org/10.1260/095830507781076194

Kartha, S., Kemp-Benedict, E., Ghosh, E., Nazareth, A., & Gore, T. (2020). *The Carbon Inequality Era*. www.oxfam.org.nz/wp-content/uploads/2020/09/Research-Report-Carbon-Inequality-Era-Embargoed-21-Sept-2020.pdf

REN21. (2019). *Renewables in Cities 2019 Global Status Report*. REN21 Secretariat. www.ren21.net/wp-content/uploads/2019/05/REC-2019-GSR_Full_Report_web.pdf

United Nations Human Rights Council. (2014). *Resolution 26/27. Human rights and climate change*. https://ap.ohchr.org/documents/dpage_e.aspx?si=A/HRC/RES/26/27

08.

Climate change, tourism and the Pacific

Apisalome Movono & Sharon McLennan

Introduction

From the epic voyages of Pacific ancestors to the planeloads of tourists arriving for island holidays, the Pacific Ocean has never been still. As Hau'ofa (1994, p. 153) poignantly describes, for the ancestors, the ocean was 'a large sea full of places to explore, to make their homes in, to breed generations of seafarers like themselves'. It is a source of physical, spiritual and economic sustenance, a connection to social and trade networks, and a place for discovery, play and adventure. While much has changed over the past couple of centuries, the ocean continues to provide sustenance, connection and fun for Pacific peoples, as well as for the outsiders who travel there, drawn by romantic notions of unspoiled paradise islands and clear blue sea.

But this ocean and its islands are at risk. Climate change threatens the capacity of the ocean to sustain the communities that depend on it. A report from the Intergovernmental Panel on Climate Change (IPCC, 2018) found that climate change has impacted the Pacific a lot sooner, and to a greater extent, than had been predicted. The ocean is heating at such a rate that its chemistry is being altered, threatening food supplies and fuelling more extreme cyclones. Sea-level rise poses a profound threat to people who live on atolls or in low-lying areas. This will have a significant impact on Pacific peoples' health, access to food and water, housing, livelihoods and freedom of movement. It will also have an impact on rights to culture, to self-determination and, ultimately, to life itself.

As discussed in Chapter 7, this threat has been created by human activity. One of those activities is travel. When people travel to and through the Pacific, they contribute to both economic development in the region and rising greenhouse gas (GHG) emissions — through air, rail and road travel, and through the consumption of goods and services, which include food, accommodation and souvenirs. One study found that between 2009 and 2013, tourism accounted for about eight per cent of global GHG emissions globally (Lenzen et al., 2018).

This chapter draws on a case study of tourism in Fiji to explore the implications of climate change for the Pacific. It focuses on Vatuolalai village on the Coral Coast of Fiji, and on the Naviti Resort, which is built on land next to the town. This case study highlights the local impacts of climate change and the complex nexus between Indigenous communities, the tourism industry and climate change. Drawing on research with the community before and during the Covid-19 pandemic, we explore how the villagers' involvement in tourism has altered their practice of *solesolevaki* or collaboration. The implications for adapting to climate change show how social solidarity and access to various forms of capital provide a means to face change and uncertainty.

Tourism in the Pacific

Close your eyes and imagine yourself in the South Pacific. What do you see? Chances are you will envisage palm trees, a clear blue ocean and soft white sand. These images draw hundreds of thousands of tourists to the Pacific each year. These tourists bring much-needed foreign exchange earnings and employment opportunities. Tourism is acknowledged as the backbone and driver of economic growth in many parts of the world. It has been widely promoted for its potential to raise living standards and increase development opportunities. In much of the South Pacific, it is a significant contributor to economies and, as a 'non-extractive industry', it is favoured by many resource-deprived states, such as Fiji, as a development tool (Ayres, 2000; Harrison & Prasad, 2013). For some countries, tourism is the only feasible option for development (Harrison, 2010; Movono & Dahles, 2018).

The number of tourists visiting the region (pre-Covid) was indeed significant. The South Pacific Tourism Organisation (SPTO) reported 2.3 million tourist arrivals in Pacific Island countries (PICs) during 2016, with arrivals increasing at an average rate of around 4.9 per cent over the preceding decade (Cheer et al.,

2018). The earnings from these tourists were significant, providing between 10 and 70 per cent of gross domestic product (GDP) in eight PICs (Scheyvens & Movono, 2018). However, as Scheyvens and Movono (2018) argue, these figures actually underestimate the overall impact of tourism, as they do not include the indirect effects on GDP and job creation through associated industries, such as construction and retailing.

While the economic benefits may be significant, tourism has the potential to cause immense ecological disturbances, from the construction stage through to daily operations, particularly in coastal systems (Bidesi et al., 2011). Coastal and island regions are acknowledged for their natural beauty, rich biodiversity and high species endemicity. At the same time, they are highly vulnerable ecosystems (Kitolelei & Sato, 2016). Tourism has been empirically linked to marine pollution, habitat degradation, disturbance of wildlife, and a loss of place and ambience in many tourist destinations (Croall, 1995; Hall, 1996). These ecosystem disturbances often become an accepted cost as resort-based development replaces a pre-existing ecological setting (Hall, 1996; Movono, 2017), leading some commentators to argue that tourism propagates its own destruction (Harrison, 2010).

The economic and social benefits have also been questioned. Tourism in the region is generally characterised by high levels of foreign investment and ownership, limited local participation and inadequate stimulation of local industries (Scheyvens & Movono, 2018). In addition, employment in the tourism industry is often precarious. The Pacific tourism industry pays some of the lowest wage rates in the world (Scheyvens & Movono, 2018), and local workers are concentrated in lower levels of employment (Hughes, 2016). This has arguably changed little since Samy (1980, p. 68) suggested that Fijian workers received only the 'crumbs from the table' in multinational resorts.

While tourism in the region can contribute to the realisation of many economic, social and cultural rights, including the right to work, to freedom of movement, and to rest and leisure, it can also present some significant challenges to human rights — particularly those of the local community. These challenges include: displacement from homes and lands to make way for tourism development; the loss of traditional livelihoods and access to natural resources, including coastal areas and freshwater; commodification of cultures as tourist attractions; and poor pay and conditions for tourism industry employees (Baum & Hai, 2020). Rights under the United Nations Declaration on the Rights of Indigenous Peoples (UNDRIP) are particularly affected. As the case study below will show, tourism triggers changes in the socio-cultural and political structures of Indigenous communities. This is significant, as changes in livelihoods, access to traditional resources and knowledge, and changes to relationships had a profound effect on Indigenous communities even before the challenges of climate change and the pandemic.

Climate change, Covid-19 and tourism adaption in the Pacific

While Pacific communities have a long history of adaption to environmental, social and economic change, the rapid pace of climate change, coupled with the sudden arrival of Covid-19, presents an unprecedented challenge. The Covid pandemic has had a profound impact, particularly on the tourism industry, but the implications of climate change are potentially more devastating in the long term. Despite this, there is a tendency within the political leadership and industry to express a desire to return to 'normal'; to reinstate tourism as usual (UNWTO, 2020). But this may not be possible. The Pacific Ocean and its islands are highly vulnerable to climate change, and the region's reliance on tourism exacerbates this. The potential losses of coastal land and infrastructure, more-intense weather patterns and storms, the failure of crops and coastal fisheries, and losses of coral reefs and mangroves, are already affecting the Pacific way of life and the sustainable development of the islands. For places that rely heavily on the arrival of tourists, these challenges could be insurmountable.

Responding to these challenges will require changes at all levels. Tourism in the region is particularly reliant on the relationship between tourism operators and the communities in which the hotels and related businesses are located. Tourism operators rely on local communities as employees, and lease land directly from them under preferential arrangements that are meant to be mutually beneficial. However, this is not always the case, as witnessed in recent developments in Malolo Islands in Fiji, where Chinese developers were found guilty of environmental breaches (Lyons, 2021). Government decisions and actions also play a significant role, by implementing the necessary frameworks that can either protect or exploit local communities and the environment. For example, the Vanuatu National Sustainable Development Plan (NSDP) provides a policy framework that includes policies around traditional medicine and healing practices, traditional knowledge, access to traditional wealth items, access to customary land, and use of Indigenous languages. These examples place the interests of local communities at the heart of climate change adaptation and resilience building in the Pacific (Nalau et al., 2018).

However, these efforts can be undermined by the reliance on international travellers and the activities of tourists. Air transport is the primary mode of transportation both to the islands and within them, and air travel is a high emitter of GHGs. The tourists themselves also have responsibilities related to climate change, which include making informed and sustainable consumer decisions and acting responsibly. The most climate-friendly options are travelling domestically, localising benefits through local consumption, and supporting sustainable tourism options. Yet, it is a difficult way forward given the global appetite for international experiences and pre-existing investments in global travel infrastructure.

Above all, adaption to climate change must respond to the needs and rights of the affected communities and be socially and culturally acceptable to them. This requires the deep involvement of the communities themselves, alongside recognition of the knowledge and connection of Indigenous people to the land and ocean. This will be explored in the remainder of this chapter through a case study of tourism in Fiji and Vatuolalai village.

Case study: Fijian tourism in crisis? Vatuolalai village

The case study for this chapter is an example of a community that is highly tourism dependent. The Coral Coast, where the case study community is situated, is also where resort-based tourism was pioneered in the 1950s, with Vatuolalai villagers among the first native Fijians to be involved in tourism. The tourism industry grew quickly and, since the late 1970s, has been the backbone of the Fijian economy. In 2019, tourism was still Fiji's largest industry, foreign exchange earner and employer, a feat attained despite four coups and numerous cyclones. However, in 2020, the onset of the global pandemic decimated the Fijian tourism industry, leaving many communities and people without any livelihood source. Particularly hard hit were coastal communities, who are also the most vulnerable to climate change.

Vatuolalai village is set along the Coral Coast of Fiji. It is an area of significant geo-cultural attributes, is home to Fiji's fourth-largest reef and has year-round summer weather (Belt et al., 1973). The Coral Coast comprises five principal administrative districts, which consist of interrelated villages, and remains one of Fiji's leading tourism regions, offering a diverse tourism experience. The region receives around 27 per cent of all visitors to the country annually (Ministry of Tourism and Trade, 2016).

In 1972, the Naviti Resort, a relatively large-scale and all-inclusive resort, was built on land next to the case study community of Vatuolalai village, ushering in a new era of change and development for villagers. Vatuolalai village comprises two clans who occupy either side of the town, separated by an invisible line indicating the upper and lower village grounds. Each clan collectively owns, and has rights and access to, land and customary marine resources commonly known as their

AHO 8.1 PACIFIC SPIRITUALITY AND CLIMATE CHANGE

'In this household, everything is interrelated and interconnected in a healthy inextricable way to benefit the whole. This household idea is central to some of the ecological programmes that Pacific Theological College currently runs such as the "Reweaving the Ecological Mat" and "Earth Justice Advocacy". This signals a shift into a kind of "neighbourly relational spirituality". . .

'For many years, many Pacific islanders have maintained this state of harmony and balance through their life-affirming value systems. That is why islanders have promoted relational principles and values such as "sautu" in Fiji, "va" or "wa" in many Polynesian cultures, "fakaaloalo" in Tuvalu, "fakaapaapa" in Tonga, "piri'anga" in Niue, "thalaba" in Kanaki New Caledonia, and "gudpela sindaum" in Papua New Guinea, to name a few. These are not just principles of life. They are principles of security and sustainability that control greed and manage adaptability and resilience.' (Lumā Vaai, 2019, p. 9)

Many Pacific Islanders have strong ties with Christianity. As climate change has become a pressing concern, Christian ideas regarding the Earth have been reworked alongside traditional knowledge and values, and innovatively engaged with by Pacific Christians to address the challenges of climate change. As Reverend Dr Upolu Lumā Vaai (2019) points out, the political and economic emphasis of Western solutions for sustainability are 'colonial approaches', which disregard the rich spiritual heritage and knowledge of Pacific peoples. As indicated in the quote above, rather than dominant development agendas of Western science and international organisations, Lumā Vaai advocates for an Indigenous holistic framework of a 'living relational household'.

Reference

Lumā Vaai, U. (2019). 'We are therefore we live': Pacific eco-relational spirituality and changing the climate change story. *Policy Brief* 56: Toda Peace Institute.

ikanakana and iqoliqoli. There are 48 households, equating to about 340 people, in the village. Most residents are aged below 38. The gender distribution is relatively balanced, with a slightly higher percentage of females (54 per cent) to males (46 per cent). A high proportion of the people in the communities are involved, or have been involved, in some form of tourism (over 92 per cent) (Movono et al., 2015). Vatuolalai village is relatively well-endowed with infrastructure, which reflects the fact that 94 per cent of households had relied primarily on the tourism sector before the pandemic struck.

Indigenous Fijian communities are, in essence, complex adaptive systems (Movono & Dahles, 2018) where people are connected socially and ecologically through traditional knowledge and customs, livelihoods, activities and specific totemic connections or links. Villages are not the simple settings often described in Western literature, but rather centres of learning and development for Indigenous peoples (Movono, 2017). Traditional Indigenous knowledge about the world is transferred orally in a communal setting, and via a practical process through observances of specific cultural and daily livelihood activities (Ravuvu, 1983, 1987; Seruvakula, 2000). Traditional livelihoods practice facilitates traditional knowledge exchange, as well as preserving particular techniques and skills unique to a specific village, which have been passed down from generation to generation (Derrick, 1957; Nayacakalou, 1975; Seruvakula, 2000). Cultural knowledge and totemic associations also govern the activities and interactions between Indigenous Fijians and nature, which are entrenched within Indigenous Fijian notions of time and place. Such practices have provided Pacific peoples with the knowledge to live and thrive, while also respecting their place within the pre-existing natural ecosystems for millennia.

The Fijian lunar calendar — the Vula Vakaviti — provides an overarching framework for livelihood activities, providing structural support for the observance of totemic connections, customs and traditions at specific stages throughout the year (Ravuvu, 1987; Seruvakula, 2000). The Fijian calendar follows a 12-month lunar system that is based on the yam cultivation cycle. Each stage in the yam cycle, from planting to harvesting, is attached to another naturally occurring phenomenon, such as fish spawning, turtle nesting and the migration of birds, which all indicate the months of the year. The Fijian calendar not only serves to inform people of what the new month brings, but also guides daily livelihood activities by providing a platform for people's continued symbiotic relationship with their natural surroundings (Scott, 1970). In essence, the cultural philosophies of Indigenous Fijians, and their rich knowledge about all creatures and plants, serve as 'socio-cultural links' that guide behaviours, connecting people and the ecological and social elements within their systems. Moreover, their togetherness as a community is precast by their associations with nature and each other (Movono, 2017).

Over their four decades of involvement in tourism, people in Vatuolalai have continued to adapt to changes that have come about from the industry (Movono et al., 2018). This has allowed them to benefit from the various opportunities that arise from tourism. Significantly, most tourism-related businesses owned by locals are run, managed and owned by female entrepreneurs. People have also become more resilient to sudden changes through their traditional customary systems (Movono et al., 2018). In recent years they have demonstrated their responsiveness to sudden shocks, including the coups and specific climate-change-related impacts.

Key to this adaption is solesolevaki, a Fijian term that refers to community togetherness or working in solidarity for a common purpose. The process of solesolevaki has many positive outcomes, including building social capital and, in some instances, spurring changes in gender dynamics and peaceful negotiations of shifts within traditional hierarchical systems (Movono & Dahles, 2018). The remainder of this chapter will explore the ways in which Vatuolalai Village is adapting to the dual challenges of climate change and the pandemic, and the role of solesolevaki in this.

Aerial photograph of Vatuolalai village and Naviti Resort. GOOGLE © 2020 CNES/ASTRIUM, MAXAR TECHNOLOGIES

Adaptivity in the face of climate change impacts

Being a coastal community, Vatuolalai is on the frontline of climate change impacts and can attest to the growing instances of voracious weather phenomena experienced in the past two decades alone. Despite being used to the annual cyclone season and the occasional five-year storm, the people of Vatuolalai have observed an increase in the frequency and intensity of natural phenomena. Elders in Vatuolalai have also described how the Fijian calendar has become out of sync with the weather and climate experience.

In 2000, Fiji's coastal communities experienced their first coral-bleaching event. Coral bleaching occurs when stressed corals expel their zooxanthellae (symbiotic algae that give corals their distinctive colours), exposing the white coral skeleton. While bleached, corals are susceptible to damage, and prolonged bleaching can result in the death of the coral. This is a significant threat to marine biodiversity and the local livelihoods that depend on the coral reef community. Each coral-bleaching event was followed by a massive loss in fish and marine life within the surrounding coral reefs, leading to depleted fish stocks, disrupting food security, and affecting visitor experiences. Tourism enterprises that depend on coral reefs as attractions were also affected, and the livelihoods of people along Fiji's Coral Coast were significantly impacted by an event that would repeat itself three times by 2020.

In response, people in Vatuolalai and other villages along the Coral Coast partnered with the Fiji Locally Managed Area Network to establish Marine Protected Areas (MPAs) to rehabilitate bleached corals. They also worked to mitigate the pressures of overfishing on already depleted stocks. Vatuolalai and Votua village established their MPA in early 2004, also as a response to the over-extraction of conch shells and other large shellfish for the souvenir trade. Fong (2006) found that the MPAs in Votua and Vatuolalai effectively restored fish populations, and further notes that the results were complemented by the encouragement by tourism in the area to increase conservation.

In 2011, the Coral Coast, including Vatuolalai, was hit for the first time with massive storm surges that reached hotel rooms and pools, and devastated communities across the western coast of Fiji's main island of Viti Levu. The surges from distant ocean storms brought large waves that breached the shoreline, spilling into hundreds of hotel rooms and homes in Vatuolalai and other Coral Coast villages. Several small handicraft businesses in Vatuolalai were utterly wiped out, giving people a taste of what climate change looks like. However, the locals did not waiver, with affected businesses rebuilding on higher and more stable structures, as well as raising funds to build seawalls. Such adaptive responses indicate that

AHO 8.2 PACIFIC PEOPLE IN ACTION

Climate change will significantly impact development in whatever form or shape, requiring strategic thinking from planning to implementation and, more importantly, in thinking about how to deal with future uncertainties. The Pacific development space is already complex, with many pre-existing challenges that will be exacerbated by climate change. It is therefore a key focus in the Pacific, with countries such as Tuvalu, New Zealand, Fiji and Kiribati leading the global call for targeted climate action for the sake of the region. These short videos from the WHO and UNDP take us to the islands where we hear from Pacific peoples on what climate change means to them and how they are acting to build resilience.

Video 1: How is climate change affecting the Pacific?

Video 2: Climate change in the Pacific: COASTS

Pacific peoples are not mere bystanders in responding to climate change.

In 2016, increasing sea surface temperatures resulted in mass fish kills, with reports of dead fish strewn along Fiji's Coral Coast. This came on the heels of observations in Vanuatu of hundreds of dead fish and invertebrates floating near Pango Village on Efate, at Emten Lagoon in Port Vila and Aneityum Island. Fish kills can occur due to several factors, ranging from the release of toxic chemicals to low concentrations of dissolved oxygen in the water; in this case, it was the latter. However, this was to be a sign of what was to come. Fiji's first category five storm, Cyclone Winston, hit only a few months after the fish kills. It affected around 57 per cent of Fiji's tourism resources and forced some operators to close indefinitely.

Just as tourism and communities in Fiji were beginning to recover from Cyclone Winston, the Covid-19 pandemic struck. People in Vatuolalai, like many Pacific Islanders, lost their jobs in the tourism industry and were left to fend for themselves. People despaired, feeling hopeless, as they no longer had the means to purchase food and essentials — something they had become accustomed to because of the income provided through tourism.

With massive job losses, uncertainty and limited economic alternatives, the people of Vatuolalai turned inwards. While some created new small businesses, many people returned to the land and the ocean and to the ancient arts of hunting and fishing, planting more diversified crops and revamping traditional food preservation techniques to get by and to ensure food security. As they did so, they reinvigorated their cultural practices and engaged in the age-old tradition of solesolevaki, working together within their communities to support each other.

This paved the way for a cultural renaissance of sorts, where people who had never held a spear or worked the land were now learning these skills to survive — in essence, turning away from their dependence on the wider world and living in a more synchronised fashion with nature and their unique cultural systems. More importantly, people were re-engaging with their roots to cope with the pandemic's challenges (Movono & Scheyvens, 2021; Scheyvens et al., 2020). Togetherness and solidarity increased as people engaged in solesolevaki, confirming the adaptive tendencies of Pacific people, but also indicating that they are active and aware of changes and are responding accordingly (Movono & Scheyvens, 2021). In facing the challenges of both the pandemic and the need to adapt to climate change, the people of Vatuolalai are doing what they needed to at the communal level, reducing their impact on nature, enriching themselves with traditional knowledge, and improving wellbeing and solidarity within the community.

Adapting to change: Not a new thing for Pacific Islanders

Much of the writing on the Pacific, both academic and popular, focuses on the smallness, poverty and isolation of PICs and their vulnerability to climate change. Like many PICs, Fiji faces immense difficulties in managing its vulnerabilities and pivoting when required. However, adapting to change is not new to Pacific Islanders. They have adapted to the challenges brought by the rapid growth of the tourism industry, successive natural disasters and political crises. They have recently faced the challenges of Covid-19 and, beyond that, the long-term impacts of climate change compounded by the inability of world powers to take necessary steps to combat these threats. Such threats have immense economic implications, especially for Fiji's key industry, tourism.

As discussed above, tourism has been the driver of development in much of the developing world, especially island states. But the future could be very different. The tourism sector is likely to change when the pandemic ends; it may not be on the same scale or form or provide the same level of economic security. However, tourism-affected communities in the Pacific have shown resilience, bouncing back from many shocks, both political and environmental, particularly in Fiji (Movono et al., 2015). In this the experience of Vatuolalai village and their responses to changes brought by the rise and fall of the tourism industry are enlightening. Communities such as Vatuolalai have successfully navigated the experiences of colonisation, religion, development and globalisation, while maintaining their culture and drawing on solesolevaki. That culture will continue to provide a way forward beyond the pandemic and through the climate change crisis.

While the contributions of Pacific peoples to climate change responses are largely invisible to the wider world, there are many encouraging ways in which their adaptivity contributes not only to locally appropriate and sustainable development, but also to global climate change responses and to the health of the ocean that sustains them. As Hau'ofa (1994, p. 35) argues, while Pacific people generally live within confined land spaces, viewed within their ocean 'the world of Oceania is neither tiny nor deficient in resources'. These communities have a wide repertoire of traditional and non-traditional knowledge and practices to draw on, and inhabit a sea that can sustain them physically, spiritually and economically, even in the midst of the profound changes accompanying climate change.

References

Ayres, R. (2000). Tourism as a passport to development in small states: Reflections on Cyprus. *International Journal of* *Social Economics, 27*(2), 114–133. https://doi.org/10.1108/03068290010308992

Baum, T., & Hai, N. T. T. (2020). Hospitality, tourism, human rights and the impact of COVID-19. *International Journal of Contemporary Hospitality Management, 32*(7), 2397–2407. https://doi.org/10.1108/IJCHM-03-2020-0242

Belt, Collins and Associates. (1973). *Tourism Development Program for Fiji.* United Nations Development Program/International Bank for Reconstruction and Development.

Bidesi, R. V., Lal, P., & Conner, N. (2011). *Economics of Coastal Zone Management in the Pacific.* Quality Print.

Cheer, J. M., Pratt, S., Tolkach, D., Bailey, A., Taumoepeau, S., & Movono, A. (2018). Tourism in Pacific island countries: A status quo round-up. *Asia and the Pacific Policy Studies, 5*(3), 442–461. https://doi.org/10.1002/app5.250

Croall, J. (1995). *Preserve or Destroy: Tourism and the environment.* Calouste Gulbenkian Foundation.

Derrick, R. A. (1957). *A History of Fiji.* Government Press.

Fong, S. (2006). Community Based Coastal Resource Management in the Fiji Islands: A case study of Korolevuiwai District, Nadroga [Unpublished MA thesis, University of the South Pacific].

Hall, M. (1996). Environmental impacts of tourism in the Pacific. In M. Hall & S. Page (Eds.), *Tourism in the Pacific: Issues and cases* (pp. 81–90). Thompson Business Press.

Harrison, D. (2010). Tourism and development: Looking back and looking ahead — more of the same? In D. Pearce & R. Butler (Eds.), *Tourism Research: A 20:20 vision* (pp. 40–52). Goodfellow Publishers.

Harrison, D., & Prasad, B. (2013). The contribution of tourism to the development of Fiji and other Pacific Island Countries. In C. A. Tisdell (Ed.), *Handbook of Tourism Economics: Analysis, new applications and case studies* (pp. 741–761). World Scientific.

Hau'ofa, E. (1994). Our sea of islands. *The Contemporary Pacific, 6*(1), 147–161.

Hughes, E. (2016). *The Tourist Resort and the Village: Local perspectives of corporate community development in Fiji.* Massey University.

IPCC. (2018). Summary for policymakers. In *Global Warming of 1.5°C. An IPCC Special Report on the impacts of global warming of 1.5°C above pre-industrial levels and related global greenhouse gas emission pathways.* www.environmentalgraphiti.org

Kitolelei, J. V., & Sato, T. (2016). Analysis of perceptions and knowledge in managing coastal resources: A case study in Fiji. *Frontiers in Marine Science, 3*(189), 1–12. https://doi.org/10.3389/fmars.2016.00189

Lenzen, M., Sun, Y. Y., Faturay, F., Ting, Y. P., Geschke, A., & Malik, A. (2018). The carbon footprint of global tourism. *Nature Climate Change, 8*(6), 522–528. https://doi.org/10.1038/s41558-018-0141-x

Lyons, K. (2021, April 9). Fiji reef battle: Judge finds China-linked developers guilty in landmark case. *The Guardian.* www.theguardian.com/world/2021/apr/09/fiji-reef-battle-judge-finds-china-linked-developers-guilty-in-landmark-case

Ministry of Tourism and Trade. (2016). *General Information on Tourism in Fiji.* Ministry of Tourism and Trade.

Movono, A. (2017). Conceptualizing destinations as a vanua: An examination of the evolution and resilience of a Fijian social and ecological system. In J. Lew & J. M. Cheer (Eds.), *Tourism Resilience and Adaptation to Environmental Change* (pp. 286–302). Routledge.

Movono, A., & Becken, S. (2018). Solesolevaki as social capital: A tale of a village, two tribes, and a resort in Fiji. *Asia Pacific Journal of Tourism Research, 23*(2), 146–157. https://doi.org/10.1080/10941665.2017.1410194

Movono, A., & Dahles, H. (2018). Female empowerment and tourism: A focus on businesses in a Fijian village. *Asia Pacific Journal of Tourism Research, 22*(6), 681–692.

Movono, A., Dahles, H., & Becken, S. (2018). Fijian culture and the environment: A focus on the ecological and social interconnectedness of tourism development. *Journal of Sustainable Tourism, 26*(3), 451–469. https://doi.org/10.1080/09669582.2017.1359280

Movono, A., Harrison, D., & Pratt, S. (2015). Adapting and reacting to tourism development: A tale of two villages on Fiji's Coral Coast. In S. Pratt & D. Harrison (Eds.), *Tourism in Pacific*

Islands: Current issues and future challenges (pp. 100–114). Routledge.

Movono, A., & Scheyvens, R. (2021). Tourism in a world of disorder: A return to the vanua and kinship with nature in Fiji. In Y. Campbell & J. Connell (Eds.), *COVID in the Islands: A comparative perspective on the Caribbean and the Pacific* (pp. 265–277). Springer Singapore. https://doi.org/10.1007/978-981-16-5285-1_15

Nalau, J., Movono, A., & Becken, S. (2018). Conceptualizing vulnerability and adaptive capacity of tourism from an indigenous Pacific Islands perspective. In J. Saarinen & A. M. Gill (Eds.), *Resilient Destinations and Tourism* (pp. 89–105). Routledge.

Nayacakalou, R. R. (1975). *Leadership in Fiji.* South Pacific Social Sciences Association in association with Institute of Pacific Studies, University of the South Pacific.

Ravuvu, A. D. (1983). *Vaka Itaukei: The Fijian way of life.* Institute for Pacific Studies, University of the South Pacific.

Ravuvu, A. D. (1987). *The Fijian Ethos.* Institute for Pacific Studies, University of the South Pacific.

Samy, J. (1980). Crumbs from the table? The workers' share in tourism. In F. Rajotte & R. Crocombe (Eds.), *Pacific Tourism as Islanders See It* (pp. 67–82). University of the South Pacific.

Scheyvens, R., & Movono, A. (2018). Development and change: Reflections on tourism in the South Pacific. *Development Bulletin, 80,* 134–139. https://mro.massey.ac.nz/handle/10179/15162

Scheyvens, R., Movono, A., Strickland, D., Bibi, P., Tasere, A., Hills, G., Rihai, N., & Teama, F. (2020). Development in a world of disorder: Tourism, COVID-19 and the adaptivity of South Pacific people. *IDS Working Paper Series, October.*

Scott, R. J. (1970). *The Development of Tourism in Fiji since 1923.* Fiji Visitors Bureau.

Seruvakula, S. B. (2000). *Bula Vakavanua.* Institute for Pacific Studies, University of the South Pacific.

UNWTO. (2020). *One Planet Vision for a Responsible Recovery of the Tourism Sector.* www.unwto.org/covid-19-oneplanet-responsible-recovery-initiatives

09.

Tangata whenua responses to climate change

Lucy Kaiser & Christine Kenney

Introduction

Māori have a long history of successfully preparing for, responding to and recovering from periods of adversity caused by natural hazard events. Yet, iwi, hapū and other Māori communities in Aotearoa have been identified as being most at risk from the impacts of climate change, because of their significant reliance on the environment as a cultural, social and economic resource (Ministry for the Environment, 2017). Moreover, tangata whenua who are already experiencing the impacts of climate change, particularly coastal communities (Manning et al., 2015), are vulnerable to ongoing environmental stressors (King et al., 2010).

Coastal inundation and sea-level rise are impacting wāhi tapu (sacred places), urupā (burial grounds), marae and mahinga kai (food-gathering sites). This has ramifications for important cultural, spiritual and social practices, as well as biodiversity and waiora (health and wellbeing) (Angeloni, 2021; Carter, 2018; Rowe, 2020). Events such as the 2020 flooding in Southland and the 2019 wildfires in the Nelson Tasman District indicate that the impacts of climate change are not limited to coastal areas (Environment Southland, 2021; Strand, 2019). Given that the scale and severity of such events are expected to increase (Lawrence et al., 2019) along with the diversity of impacts, it is timely to consider how tangata whenua are actively responding to climate change.

Māori responses to climate change are grounded in te ao Māori (Māori world views). Their approaches harness mātauranga (Māori knowledge), kaupapa (values) and tikanga (practice) to support Māori rights and responsibilities in the context of climate change. Iwi and hapū are providing significant leadership in environmental management, disaster management and nation-state level responses to the impacts of climate change. This chapter provides an overview of this political context.

Indigenous peoples and climate change

For many Indigenous peoples, climate change is exaserbating pre-existing challenges to culture and livelihoods. The impacts of colonisation, including loss of ngā ipukarea (ancestral homelands) and forced relocation (Roosvall & Tegelberg, 2013), are undermining the sovereignty of many Indigenous peoples. The erosion of Indigenous bodies of knowledge and natural resources has also exacerbated trauma associated with dispossession of land and culture (Pearce et al., 2015). Health and wellbeing outcomes are compromised for Indigenous communities, who experience high levels of job insecurity, poverty and environmental degradation (Reading & Wien, 2009). The impacts of climate change amplify existing stresses and threaten food security, access to housing and infrastructure and to opportunities for sustainable development. Indigenous people, therefore, are disproportionately affected by the impacts of climate change (Abate & Kronk, 2013; Green & Raygorodetsky, 2010). This raises issues of fairness and justice, given that the contribution of Indigenous communities to greenhouse gas (GHG) emissions is relatively low.

Yet, Indigenous peoples have been referred to as the 'advance guard' of climate change. They observe climate and environmental change first-hand and are using their traditional knowledge and survival skills — the heart of their cultural resilience — to trial adaptive responses to these changes as they occur (Galloway-McLean, 2017). Significantly, Indigenous and Māori scholars (including Awatere & Harmsworth 2014; Kenney & Phibbs, 2020; King et al., 2008; Langton et al., 2012; Saunders, 2017; Whyte, 2017; and Wildcat, 2013) are creating a body of research literature that presents Indigenous and Māori perspectives, aspirations and responses regarding climate change. However, uptake of Indigenous knowledges into mainstream climate change management practices and science has been slow, partly due to the hegemony of Western scientific discourses, generalised scepticism and cultural appropriation (Gilchrist, 2010; Huntington, 2011; Leigh Thorpe, 1994; O'Gorman et al., 2016; Pierotti & Wildcat, 2000). The latter issue is exemplified in the frequent cases of Indigenous perspectives and/or approaches to addressing climate change being presented through the lens of non-Indigenous researchers (Veland et al., 2013). Within these outsider-led research contexts, Indigenous peoples are often relegated to data points or 'local guides' instead of the primary authors and experts (Watson, 2017), while Indigenous knowledge assets are captured and rebranded for 'etic' or non-Indigenous consumers.

Discourses in Indigenous communities globally have, therefore, focused on how to reclaim or protect culture, the environment, traditional knowledges and political agendas through mitigative and adaptive responses to climate change. Indigenous peoples are utilising a range of local, regional, national and global initiatives to effectively navigate the uncertainties and impacts of climate change to better reduce risks and maintain resilient collective memories and cultures. Indigenous sovereignty remains at the forefront of climate change discussions between Indigenous collectives. For example, the International Indigenous Peoples' Forum on Climate Change (IIPFCC) was established in 2008 as a caucus for collective representation and agreement between Indigenous peoples negotiating in the United Nations Framework Convention on Climate Change (UNFCCC). The forum asserts that 'indigenous peoples' knowledge and strategies to sustain their environment should be respected and taken into account when we develop national and international approaches to climate change mitigation and adaptation' (WCIP, 2014, cited in IIPFCC, n.d., para. 9).

The wider involvement of Indigenous peoples and communities in climate change adaptation planning and response implementation has been advocated (UNISDR, 2015). Yet, UN recommendations have been variably integrated into climate-related risk mitigation policies and practices such as the 2015 Paris Agreement (Howitt et al., 2011; UN, 2015). There are ongoing tensions around recognition of Indigenous perspectives and stakeholders in government and local authority-led initiatives (Kenney & Phibbs, 2020). This is mirrored in Aotearoa, where differing policy, legislative and strategic approaches to mitigating climate change impacts have been implemented by the government, local authorities and Māori communities, highlighting issues pertaining to sovereignty, equity and collaboration.

Governing climate change in Aotearoa

In Aotearoa, climate change response and management are the responsibility of government and local authorities, in partnership with iwi, hapū and other Māori collectives. This partnership is a reflection of te Tiriti o Waitangi provisions (previously discussed in Te Take) recognising kaitiaki responsibilities of tangata whenua to care and look after the environment and natural resources (Joseph et al., 2018). Tangata whenua interests, therefore, are a fundamental attribute of Aotearoa's climate change framework, although it is unclear whether these provisions are sufficient for realising Māori goals and expectations.

Aotearoa's climate change framework includes several Acts of Parliament, policy statements, plans, reports and strategies. Several are explored here with a commentary on their capacity to realise Māori priorities and interests.

Resource Management Act 1991

The Resource Management Act (RMA) 1991 promotes the sustainable management of natural and physical resources. There are several provisions that support Māori rights and responsibilities regarding resource management, including provisions for the practice of kaitiakitanga. In theory, this creates opportunities for Māori to contribute to decision making and shape resource management policy and practice. The reality, however, is that fully realising Māori expectations has proven to be a challenge. It is hoped that revisions to the Act will address some of these issues. Early drafts indicate these provisions will be retained and strengthened.

There are also provisions within the Act to manage 'significant risks from natural hazards' (Section 6[h]) and to manage 'the effects of climate change' (Section 7[j]), although there is some contention as to whether 'natural hazards' is a broad enough term to encompass the impact of climate change (Kelman, 2017).

Despite these limitations, climate change responses as positioned within the Act require tangata whenua involvement. This is reaffirmed by national policies governing the management of coastal environments, such as the New Zealand Coastal Policy Statement.

New Zealand Coastal Policy Statement 2010

National Policy Statements (NPS) are legislative tools that can support government-led climate change mitigation and policy activities. The 1994 iteration of the New Zealand Coastal Policy Statement (NZCPS) was the first national-level tool that required local government to recognise rising sea levels (Rouse et al., 2017). The NZCPS (updated in 2010) outlines a risk-based approach to the management of coastal hazards such as flooding and water management, as well as specific considerations of the effects of climate change. Policy 24 requires that areas at high risk of being affected by coastal hazards (including sea-level rise and climate change) are identified and assessed, taking into account national guidance and best available information on the effects of climate change (Department of Conservation, 2010, Policy 24). The statement also updates policy on how planning and decision making should recognise Māori values in relation to the coast, and the relationships Māori have with certain coastal places and resources (Department of Conservation, 2010, Policy 2). This includes Māori interests in protecting special sites (such as wāhi tapu), using resources and developing places, for example, gathering kaimoana (seafood), and developing papakāinga (housing developments on Māori land) and marae. A 2017 review by the Department of Conservation found that in several cases iwi were able to use policies in the NZCPS to support their aspirations in planning processes. However, tangata whenua also reported that financial constraints limited iwi involvement in decision making, particularly 'non-settled' iwi who struggle to bear the costs of engaging with councils and applicants (Department of Conservation, 2017, p. 25).

It must be noted that while the RMA and the NZCPS provide tools for governing resource management and land use, they are not specifically targeted towards, or adequate for, responding to climate change. The Climate Change Response Act (2002) was created to address this statutory shortfall.

Climate Change Response Act 2002

Aotearoa's approach to addressing climate change is governed by the Climate Change Response Act 2002. This established a legal framework to ratify the Kyoto Protocol and to meet regulatory obligations under the UNFCCC. Its purpose was to develop and implement '(i) clear and stable climate change policies that contribute to the global effort under the Paris Agreement to limit global temperature increases to 1.5 degrees Celsius above pre-industrial levels; and (ii) allow Aotearoa to prepare for, and adapt to, the effects of climate change' (Climate Change Response Act, 2002, Section 3[aa]). It also provides for the New Zealand Emissions Trading Scheme (ETS) (Section 3[b]). While Māori businesses have participated in the ETS scheme, Māori landowners have faced difficulties, particularly negotiating the forestry components of the ETS (Johnstone, 2013), price fluctuations, access to finance and insurance issues (Mercer, 2021).

In 2017, the Labour-led Government announced that climate change would be a key priority over its first three-year term. Key initiatives included proposing a Zero Carbon Act, creating an independent climate change committee and bringing agricultural emissions into a carbon pricing scheme (Kitchin, 2017). The Climate Change Response (Zero Carbon) Amendment Act of 2019 (CCRZCAA) provides a legal and regulatory framework for meeting Aotearoa's target of net zero emissions of carbon dioxide and nitrous dioxide by 2050. Two actions stemming from this Act are the development of a National Climate Change Risk Assessment with specific risks identified as relevant to Māori (released 2020) and a National Adaptation Plan (in development in 2021). Criticism about the lack of inclusion of Māori voices in the legislation emerged following the consultation process for the CCRZCAA, as, out of 96 iwi entities nationally, only four were directly consulted. Further criticism was levelled at the wording included within amendments to the Act. Particular mention was made of the Act's failure to give appropriate and substantive weight to Māori voices, as well as the absence of both a mechanism for enabling tikanga Māori to inform issues and outcomes, and processes for tangata whenua to exercise kaitiakitanga or stewardship over the environment (Kelly, 2020).

Other legislation

Several other pieces of legislation are relevant to the climate change arena, including the Local Government Act (LGA) 2002, the Civil Defence and Emergency Management Act (CDEMA) 2002 and the Building Act 2004. These three pieces of legislation draw on holistic wellbeing and resilience frameworks and promote sustainable management and development approaches (Saunders et. al., 2020). Many of the climate adaptation measures that would be necessary to actively protect tangata whenua interests are the responsibility of, and managed by, the government, as well as subject to the regulations of local government authorities. However, there is no explicit recognition of, or provision for, Māori to take the lead in responding to climate change within the language of these three Acts. It is, therefore, unsurprising that none of these pieces of legislation refer to Māori climate change aspirations or are informed by specific Māori perspectives. Moreover, the CDEMA does not include any reference to Māori or Māori interests.

Emergency management declarations

In Aotearoa, climate change emergencies have been declared by local governments as a means of communicating the urgency of the ecological crisis, and in an attempt to spur meaningful responses and mitigation actions (Farrell et al., 2019). A 2021 study by Nissen & Cretney in Canterbury identified stakeholder concerns that little engagement had occurred with mana whenua in the lead-up to Environment Canterbury declaring a climate emergency. This is cause for concern, as emergency legislative tools have previously been used in the oppression of Indigenous and minority communities, and emergency approaches have the potential to amplify existing inequities (Bargh & Hall, 2019; Phibbs et al., 2015; Phibbs et al., 2018; Whyte, 2017).

Although Aotearoa has integrated climate change management into policy and legislation over the past few decades (Carter, 2018), it is argued that the country lacks a strong climate change framework, employs inadequate measures and lacks ambition in comparison with targets set by other developed nations (Climate Action Tracker, 2015). Māori agree, advocating for stronger inclusion in central and local government-led climate change planning and decision making (MFE, 2007; Ngāi Tahu ki Murihiku, 2008). This would prioritise partnership with tangata whenua (Kaiser et al., 2020) and more effective integration of mātauranga Māori and Māori perspectives into policy and planning processes to ensure meaningful commitment to Māori rights and responsibilities (Harmsworth & Awatere, 2014). Indigenous planning would, therefore, challenge 'Western' forms of planning that have 'been complicit in the colonial project, a weapon brandished to erase/eradicate Indigenous peoples' by prioritising 'internal community setting[s] that it can largely control, circumscribe, and define, [to challenge] an external political and planning environment' (Matunga, 2013, p. 5). Indigenous planning can influence the reform of national climate change policies (Kaiser & Saunders, 2021), and tangata whenua are implementing a range of responses.

Tangata whenua responses to climate change

Climate change related disasters are a particular concern for iwi and hapū (Kenney & Phibbs, 2020; Saunders & Kaiser, 2019). Through enacting their role as kaitiaki, iwi and hapū are often among the first responders to climate change issues. Recent Māori responses to catastrophic events have included the Ngāti Awa Volunteer Army actions following the 2017 Edgecumbe flooding event (SunLive, 2017), and the Te Arawa iwi response to the erosion of an ūrupa at Ōkurei Point in Maketū during 2019 (Neilson, 2019). The impacts of these sudden-onset events were mitigated by the ability of Māori communities to respond rapidly and effectively, due in part to strong social ties and whakapapa connections in the region. Another critical aspect is knowledge of the environment, with intergenerational mātauranga Māori *and* Western scientific information related to environmental changes informing Māori responses to climate change (King et al., 2008).

Climate change response actions (i.e. policies, planning, legislation, activism and tikanga-centred environmental management practices) are being asserted at marae, whānau, hapū and iwi levels. These actions are underpinned by Māori frameworks, values and priorities. This includes the use of cultural mechanisms such as rāhui (temporary restriction of access to protect the health and wellbeing of people and the environment). Rāhui have been used to allow the mauri (life essence of a resource) to replenish (Maxwell & Penetito, 2007) and could be used as a tool for mitigating the impacts of climate change on biodiversity. Other prominent

AHO 9.1 BRING IN THE ARMY!

Māori, like many Indigenous peoples, are not sitting around waiting for climate change to decimate their lands. They are stepping up and using their gifts, talents and community power to respond to climate change events. In 2017, the small Bay of Plenty town of Edgecumbe experienced severe flooding when the local river broke its stop banks. Many homes were totally flooded, and devastation ensued. Ngāti Awa community leaders collaborated to form NAVA — 'Ngāti Awa Volunteer Army'. Te Teko Hauora manager, and deputy chair of the Mataatua District Māori Council at the time, Winifred Geddes, took on the Māori emergency manager's role, established a Māori emergency response centre at Ruaihona marae, and coordinated around 1500 volunteers. Four surrounding marae — Kokohinau, Rautahi, Tūteao and Uiraroa — collaborated with Ruaihona to serve over 10,000 meals, hold three tangihanga and provide shelter for those in need. NAVA volunteers also led the clean-up operation and cleared flooded homes, businesses and other properties of silt in only 11 days.

Māori community-led emergency management responses can be effective throughout Aotearoa. The iwi model used in Edgecumbe, the Ngāti Hau response to the 2015 Whanganui floods and other iwi responses to climate change-related disasters are informing the National Emergency Management Agency's new approach to managing the impacts of climate change.

Further reading

Geddes, W. (2019). Ka Takatū Be Ready: Māori Emergency Management (MEM). APRU 15th Multi-hazards symposium: Building resilience through disaster risk reduction, response, recovery and reconstruction. Mexico City, 28 October–1 November.

Newstalk ZB Staff. (2017, April 15). Volunteer army helps clean up flooded Edgecumbe. www.newstalkzb.co.nz/news/national/volunteer-army-helps-clean-up-flooded-edgecumbe

Te Ao Māori News. (2017, May 2). Native Affairs — Ngāti Awa Volunteer Army. www.teaomaori.news/native-affairs-ngati-awa-volunteer-army

NAVA ia an iwi-led volunteer army formed in response to the severe flooding in Edgecumbe in 2017. W. GEDDES tools include iwi/hapū management plans (IHMPs) and iwi and hapū-led climate change-specific plans and strategies.

Iwi/Hapū Management Plans (IHMPs)

IHMPs are a key RMA mechanism that iwi and hapū can deploy to embed their planning and resource management priorities into regional plans of territorial authorities. These plans are developed and approved by collectives representing iwi or hapū and address matters of tribal resource management significance within a specific region (Saunders, 2017). IHMPs typically address issues, objectives, tasks, actions and indicators of environmental health (Nelson & Tipa, 2012). The plans both incorporate and draw on mātauranga Māori and Western scientific evidence to inform key priorities and actions. Crown Research Institutes and science organisations are partnering with Māori to provide climate change data that can inform IHMPs and Māori-led environmental management initiatives.

Climate change issues and priorities are increasingly being addressed within IHMPs (Kaiser & Saunders, 2021) and in climate change strategies developed by tangata whenua. In an analysis of North Island IHMPs, 29 out of 93 total plans mention climate change explicitly, with extreme weather events and rising sea level the most frequently anticipated impacts (Saunders, 2017). Other impacts focused on effects on biodiversity (Hauraki Māori Trust Board, 2004), infrastructure (Ngāti Rangiwewehi, 2012), transportation (Ngā Hapū o te Wahapū o te Hokianga nui a Kupe, 2008), health (Ngāti Hine, 2008) and whānau wellbeing (Passl, 2004).

Te Tangi a Tauira 2008, an IHMP developed by the four Murihiku (Southland-based) Papatipū Rūnanga of Ngāi Tahu, has a section dedicated to climate change issues. Key concerns include discharging of GHG emissions into the environment, exposure to noxious and toxic substances, and the impact of deforestation on carbon dioxide levels. This IHMP sets out recommended policies and practices for addressing iwi concerns: active engagement with local, iwi and national initiatives; supporting Māori ownership of climate change issues; advancing climate change research on seafood impacts; and supporting sustainable energy systems.

While climate change is generally embedded throughout most IHMPs as one of several different priorities for iwi and hapū, some iwi and hapū are also developing targeted strategies, including stand-alone plans for responding to climate change.

Iwi-led climate change strategies

Government policies and legislation pertaining to climate change have historically been reactive and only minimally responsive or inclusive to the needs and priorities of iwi. As iwi are already experiencing the impacts of climate change, some are choosing to develop their own climate change strategies rather than wait to be included in national, regional and local government responses. Iwi-led climate change strategies have a dual function: as focal documents for iwi, hapū and whānau issues, priorities and aspirations; as well as being public-facing documents. These strategies are underpinned by Māori frameworks, values and priorities. A prominent iwi-led strategy called *Te Tāhū o te Whāriki* has recently been released by Te Runanga o Ngāi Tahu (2019). A summary of the main points of strategy is included in Table 1, pages 152–153.

Te Tāhū o te Whāriki (Te Rūnanga o Ngāi Tahu, 2019) articulates collective issues, concerns and approaches for responding to climate change. It represents a philosophical departure from Western and quantitative approaches to measuring and understanding the impacts of climate change. The strategy is informed by mātauranga Māori and Western European science to articulate some of the physical impacts of climate change, but is framed within Ngāi Tahu values and priorities. Echoing the calls of Māori scientists, economists and planners (Harmsworth & Awatere, 2014; Matunga, 2013; Nelson & Tipa, 2012), the strategy highlights the need for impactful information to be grounded in te ao Māori, as well as strong community involvement, which will ensure approaches remain locally and culturally relevant. Resourcing implementation of these strategies is an ongoing concern. Iwi and hapū have a range of competing priorities; organisational capacity is often stretched, and funding for implementing climate change mitigation and adaptation projects limited.

Another strategy deployed by Māori is partnering with government entities and businesses to develop culturally grounded science and technology approaches that effectively address climate change impacts. Ngāi Tahu, for example, is partnering with the National Institute of Water and Atmospheric Research (NIWA) to develop initiatives that promote climate change resilience. Tribal actions include using mātauranga Māori as the basis for cultural GIS mapping and core-sampling in areas of previous coastal inundation. These areas will likely be impacted by climate change-induced sea-level rise in the future, and the current initiatives are designed to identify, and, in due course, help communicate hazard risks (Te Rūnanga o Ngāi Tahu, 2019). Te Whānau-ā-Apanui and Ngāti Porou, iwi that are situated on the East Coast lands of the North Island, constitute further exemplars, as they have successfully lobbied the government to fund their $34 million Raukūmara Pae Maunga Restoration Project. This project will restore the native forest in their regions and mitigate impacts of climate change by providing a carbon sink.

Māori are also embracing historical, activist and creative approaches for addressing climate change. For example, continuing the tradition of Tahupōtiki Wiremu Rātana petitioning King George V and the League of Nations, rangatahi

Table 1: Summary of key points within *Te Tāhū o te Whāriki* (Te Rūnanga o Ngāi Tahu, 2019)

WHAKATAUKĪ

Mō tātou, ā, mō kā uri ā muri ake nei — For us and our children after us.

PURPOSE

To create Ngāi Tahu responses to the risks and opportunities presented by climate change, referencing the entire tribal structure, so that iwi, hapū and whānau aspirations can be met in a changing world.

NGĀI TAHU VISION

Te kaitiakitanga me te tāhuhu Organisational development and governance	Te Rūnanga o Ngāi Tahu will take appropriate action to adapt all areas of tribal interests and activity to withstand the compounding effects of our changing climate, to ensure Ngāi Tahu activities are aligned to the best projected climate change outcomes, and to make the most of opportunities, so that Ngāi Tahu whānui have every chance to thrive even in the most extreme scenarios.
Tō tātou Ngāi Tahutanga Culture and identity	We will face the challenges of a changing climate in our takiwā/area with the courage, resilience, and wisdom of our tūpuna/ancestors, strengthened by all that makes us Ngāi Tahu, as we create a cultural legacy for those to come who must live in a changed world.
Te ao tūroa Environment	We will manage tribal resources wisely, continuing to protect wāhi tapu, mahinga kai, and other taonga tuku iho (treasures) handed down, where possible, focusing on strategic restoration activities, while actively investing in places and species of likely future abundance.
Ko ngā whakapāpātanga Tribal communications	Ngāi Tahu whānui are well informed about all aspects of climate change relevant to their interests and wellbeing. They know how the tribe as a whole is responding to the risks, challenges, and opportunities, and can act with confidence within their whānau and hapū.
Te whakaariki Influence	Te Rūnanga o Ngāi Tahu and Papatipū Rūnanga are embedded within key climate change response structures and programmes, working with central and local governments and others. These programmes support desired outcomes for Ngāi Tahu whānui as a result of tribal influence and leadership.

Te whakatipu Growing the future	Papatipū Rūnanga has the resources and information necessary to generate and implement marae and community-centred climate change response strategies that are designed to meet the needs of whānau and hapū, aligned with tribal direction.
Whānau Family	Whānau needs and aspirations are central to tribal climate change response, with tribal resources targeted towards addressing fundamental challenges to kāinga (settlements) within the takiwā, maximising opportunities for whānau, and assisting whānau facing climate change impacts in other parts of the country and the world.
Mātauranga Knowledge	Tribal investment in the future, focused on education and training supports Ngāi Tahu whānui to generate and take up opportunities related to climate change response.
Te pūtea Investment planning	The economic base of Te Rūnanga o Ngāi Tahu is built on leading, climate-responsible, innovative and adaptive businesses and partnerships, meeting the needs and aspirations of Ngāi Tahu whānui while applying Ngāi Tahu values to address the business risks, challenges and opportunities associated with climate change.

(youth) from Te Ara Whatu, Aotearoa's first Indigenous youth delegation to the United Nations, attended the COP25 talks in Madrid in 2019 to advocate for climate justice and Indigenous sovereignty (Huffadine, 2019). Another example is Māori-led climate change activism that draws on a range of art forms, including film, photography, dance and the visual arts (Tyson, 2020). Then there are mainstream avenues such as the Waitangi Tribunal claims process, where Māori can lobby the Crown to address breaches of te Tiriti o Waitangi that relate to climate change.

Conclusion

Climate change research and policy sectors are beginning to acknowledge the value of Indigenous knowledges for informing adaptive planning and mitigation practices (Whyte, 2017). Yet, globally, policy issues persist relating to government and/or institutional recognition of Indigenous autonomy and rights to sovereignty (Ramos-Castillo et al., 2017).

AHO 9.2 MANA MOANA PROJECT

In 2019, a group of Māori and Pasifika artists came together to curate the Mana Moana Project. Mana Moana is a digital interactive experience consisting of multimedia, immersive imagery that was shown in Wellington Harbour on a background of moving water. The central theme is how climate change is affecting the ocean, and how this has devastating implications for islands in the Pacific, including Aotearoa. The project release was timed to coincide with Matariki, which is traditionally a time for renewal for Māori.

To experience the Mana Moana exhibition online, scan the QR code.

Further reading

MacGibbon, A. (2020, July 10). Māori and Pasifika creatives weave art and tech together for new Mana Moana Digital Ocean. *The Big Idea*. www.thebigidea.nz/stories/media-releases/227498-maori-and-pasifika-creatives-weave-art-and-tech-together-for-new-mana-moana-digital-ocean

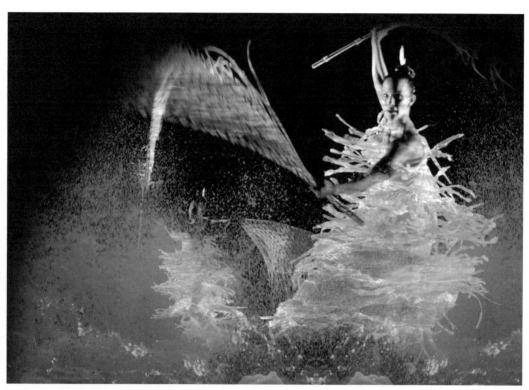

Still from the film *Tūātea*, by Louise Pōtiki Bryant, featuring dancer Bianca Hyslop, with music by Paddy Free and taonga puoro by Horomona Horo. COURTESY OF LOUISE POTIKI BRYANT

Within an Aotearoa context, climate change is a high priority for tangata whenua, and a range of actions and mechanisms are being implemented to advance tangata whenua interests, rights and responsibilities. For example, climate change adaptation and mitigation recommendations are being integrated into planning documents such as IHMPs, and some iwi and hapū are releasing climate change strategies that articulate locale-specific priorities and objectives. Yet, there are concerns that these efforts could be derailed by a planning sector that has a long history of ignoring Māori values, priorities, strategies and aspirations (Carter, 2018; Matunga, 2017) and by persistent challenges related to integrating Māori climate change knowledges, world views and approaches with mainstream Aotearoa strategies for mitigation and adaptation (MFE, 2007). A concern is that this political setting could ignore or under-utilise Māori resources that facilitate community resilience to climate change. Enhanced engagement with Māori communities and resources is, therefore, essential, particularly recognition of the right and responsibility of tangata whenua to practise kaitiakitanga when responding to climate change. A comprehensive and effective adaptation response to climate change, therefore, requires substantive provisions for tangata whenua climate change aspirations, knowledges and responses.

References

Abate, R. S., & Kronk, E. A. (2013). Commonality among unique Indigenous communities: An introduction to climate change and its impacts on Indigenous peoples. In R. S. Abate & E. A. Kronk (Eds.), *Climate Change and Indigenous Peoples: The search for legal remedies* (pp. 3–18). Edward Elgar Publishing.

Angeloni, A. (2021, January 28). Historical Māori kōiwi bones unearthed by erosion in Nūhaka. *Radio New Zealand.* www.rnz.co.nz/news/ldr/435375/historical-maori-koiwi-bones-unearthed-by-erosion-in-nuhaka

Awatere, S., & Harmsworth, G. (2014). *Ngā Aroturukitanga Tika mō ngā Kaitiaki: Summary review of mātauranga Māori frameworks, approaches, and culturally appropriate monitoring tools for management of mahinga kai* (Contract Report LC1774). Landcare Research.

Bargh, M., & Hall, D. (2019). Maria Bargh and David Hall on the low-emissions transition. *The Policy Fix.* https://thepolicyobservatory. aut.ac.nz/__data/assets/pdf_file/0016/322342/Maria-Bargh-and-David-Hall-on-the-low-emissions-transition-edited-transcript.pdf

Carter, L. (2018). *Indigenous Pacific Approaches to Climate Change: Aotearoa/New Zealand.* Springer.

Climate Action Tracker. (2015). Climate change tracker report: New Zealand deploys creative accounting to allow emissions rise. https://climateactiontracker.org/publications/new-zealand-deploys-creative-accounting-allow-emissions-rise

Climate Change Response Act 2002. www.legislation.govt.nz/act/public/2002/0040/latest/DLM158590.html

Department of Conservation. (2010). *New Zealand Coastal Policy Statement.* www.doc.govt.nz/about-us/science-publications/conservation-publications/marine-and-coastal/new-zealand-coastal-policy-statement/new-zealand-coastal-policy-statement-2010

Department of Conservation. (2017). *Review of the Effect of the NZCPS 2010 on RMA Decision-making. Part 1 — Overview and key findings.* www.coastalrestorationtrust.org.nz/site/assets/files/1189/review-of-effect-of-nzcps-2010-on-rma-part-one.pdf

Environment Southland. (2021). *Climate Change.* www.es.govt.nz/environment/climate-change

Farrell, C, Green, A, Knights, S, & Skeaping, W. (Eds.). (2019). *This Is not a Drill: The extinction rebellion handbook.* Penguin Random House.

Galloway-McLean, K. (2017). *Advance Guard: Climate change impacts, adaptation, mitigation and Indigenous peoples: A compendium of case studies.* United Nations University.

Gilchrist, K. (2010). 'Newsworthy' victims? Exploring differences in Canadian local press coverage of missing/murdered Aboriginal and white women. *Feminist Media Studies, 10*(4), 373–390. https://doi.org/10.1080/14680777.20 10.514110

Green, D., & Raygorodetsky, G. (2010). Indigenous knowledge of a changing climate. *Climatic Change, 100*(2), 239–242. https://doi.org/10.1007/s10584-010-9804-y

Harmsworth, G. R., & Awatere, S. (2014). Indigenous Māori knowledge and perspectives of ecosystems. In J. Dymond (Ed.), *Ecosystem Services in New Zealand: Conditions and trends* (pp. 274–286). Manaaki Whenua Press.

Hauraki Māori Trust Board. (2004). *Hauraki Iwi Environmental Plan.* www.waikatoregion.govt.nz/assets/WRC/Community/Iwi/Hauraki-Iwi-EMP-March-2004.pdf

Howitt, R., Havnen, O., & Veland, S. (2011). Natural and unnatural disasters: Responding with respect for Indigenous rights and knowledges. *Geographical Research, 50*(1), 47–59. https://doi.org/10.1111/j.1745-5871.2011.00709.x

Huffadine, L. (2019, December 21). A youth perspective on climate talks: Time for Indigenous leadership. *Radio New Zealand.* www.rnz.co.nz/news/te-manu-korihi/406000/a-youth-perspective-on-climate-talks-time-for-indigenous-leadership

Huntington, H. P. (2011). Arctic science: The local perspective. *Nature, 478,* 182–183. https://doi.org/10.1038/478182a

International Indigenous Peoples' Forum on Climate Change (IIPFCC). (n.d.). www.iipfcc.org/key-issues

Johnstone, N. (2013). Negotiating climate change: Māori, the Crown and New Zealand's emission trading scheme. In R. S. Abate & E. A. Kronk (Eds.), *Climate Change and Indigenous Peoples: The search for legal remedies* (pp. 508–533). Edward Elgar Publishing.

Joseph, R., Rakena, M., Te Kuini Jones, M., Sterling, R., & Rakena, C. (2018). The Treaty, tikanga Māori, ecosystem-based management, mainstream law and power sharing for environmental integrity in Aotearoa New Zealand — Possible ways forward. Te Mata Hautū Taketake.

Kaiser, L. H., & Saunders, W. S. (2021). Vision mātauranga research directions: Opportunities for iwi and hapū management plans. *Kōtuitui: New Zealand journal of social sciences online,* 1–13. https://doi.org/10.1080/117708 3X.2021.1884099

Kaiser, L., Thomas, K. L., & Campbell, E. (2020). Wāhine tapuhi ō te Parawhenuamea kia mataara: Wāhine-led, community-based research on earthquake resilience. In New Zealand Society for Earthquake Engineering (Eds.), *Proceedings of the 2020 New Zealand Society for Earthquake Engineering Annual Technical Conference.* https://repo.nzsee.org.nz/handle/nzsee/1713

Kelly, H. (2020). *Frustration and Failure: The Zero Carbon Bill and the Treaty of Waitangi* (Legal Research Paper 27). Victoria University of Wellington.

Kelman, I. (2017). Linking disaster reduction, climate change, and the sustainable development goals. *Disaster Prevention and Management, 26*(3), 254–258. https://doi.org/10.1108/DPM-02-2017-0043

Kenney C., & Phibbs, S. (2020). Indigenous peoples and climate change: Situating culture, identity, and place in climate change risk mitigation and resilience. In W. Leal Filho, J. Luetz, & D. Ayal (Eds.), *Handbook of Climate Change Management.* Springer. https://doi.org/10.1007/978-3-030-22759-3_113-1

King, D. N. T., Penny, G., & Severne, C. (2010). The climate change matrix facing Māori society. In R. A. C. Nottage, D. S. Wratt, J. F. Bornman, & K. Jones (Eds.), *Climate Change Adaptation in New Zealand: Future scenarios and some sectoral perspectives* (pp. 100–111). New Zealand Climate Change Centre.

King, D. N. T., Skipper, A., & Tawhai, W. B. (2008). Māori environmental knowledge of local weather and climate change in Aotearoa-New Zealand. *Climatic Change, 90*(4), 385. https://doi.org/10.1007/s10584-007-9372-y

Kitchin, R. (2017, October 20). Jacinda Ardern discusses climate change. *Stuff.* https://stuff.liveblog.pro/stuff/blogs/59e8ee9606c6fec30eb9d385/index.html?liveblog._id=urn:newsml:localhost:2017-10-20T06:30:42.311071:19dddf98-ff28-4785-901d-c6eca61173f5-%3Eeditorial

Langton, M., Parsons, M., Leonard, S., Auty, K., Bell, D., Burgess, P., Edwards, S., Howitt, R., Jackson, S., McGrath, V., & Morrison, J. (2012). *National Climate Change Adaptation Research Plan for Indigenous Communities.* National Climate Change Adaptation Research Facility.

Lawrence, J., Bell, R., & Stroombergen, A. (2019). A hybrid process to address uncertainty and changing climate risk in coastal areas using dynamic adaptive pathways planning, multi-criteria decision analysis & real options analysis: A New Zealand application. *Sustainability, 11*(2), 406. https://doi.org/10.3390/su11020406

Leigh Thorpe, N. (1994). Contributions of Inuit Ecological Knowledge to Understanding the Impacts of Climate Change on the Bathurst Caribou Herd in the Kitikmeot Region, Nunavut [Unpublished master's dissertation, University of Toronto].

Manning, M., Lawrence, J., King, D N., & Chapman, R. (2015). Dealing with changing risks: A New Zealand perspective on climate change adaptation. *Regional Environmental Change, 15*(4), 581–594. https://doi.org/10.1007/s10113-014-0673-1

Matunga, H. (2013). Theorizing Indigenous planning. In R. C. Walker, T. S. Jojola, & D. C. Natcher (Eds.), *Reclaiming Indigenous Planning* (pp. 3–33). McGill-Queen's University Press.

Matunga, H. (2017). A revolutionary pedagogy of/for Indigenous planning. *Planning Theory and Practice, 18*(4), 640–644. https://doi.org/10.1080/14649357.2017.1380961

Maxwell, K. H., & Penetito, W. (2007). How the use of rāhui for protecting taonga has evolved over time. *MAI Review, 1*(3), 15. www.review.mai.ac.nz/mrindex/MR/article/download/58/58-69-1-PB.pdf

Mercer, L. W. L. (2021). Beyond the Dollar: Carbon farming and its alternatives for Tairāwhiti Māori landowners [Unpublished doctoral dissertation, Victoria University of Wellington].

Ministry for the Environment (MFE). (2007). *Consultation with Māori in Climate Change: Hui report.* https://environment.govt.nz/assets/Publications/Files/consultation-maori-hui-report-nov07.pdf

Ministry for the Environment (MFE). (2017). *Adapting to Climate Change Stocktake.* https://environment.govt.nz/publications/adapting-to-climate-change-in-new-zealand-stocktake-report-from-the-climate-change-adaptation-technical-working-group

Neilson M. (2019, January 28). Māori burial grounds under threat from rising seas increasing storm events. *New Zealand Herald.* www.nzherald.co.nz/nz/maori-burial-grounds-under-threat-from-rising-seas-increasing-storm-events/5XCN72RZH6OKH7CX2BOWDSUF7I

Nelson, K., & Tipa, G. (2012). Cultural indicators, monitoring frameworks & assessment tools. *Report for the Wheel of Water Project.*

Ngā Hapū o te Wahapū o te Hokianga nui a Kupe (2008). *Ngā Hapū o te Wahapū o te Hokianga nui a Kupe Iwi Management Plan.* https://docplayer.net/34341609-Hapu-environmental-management-plan.html

Ngāti Hine. (2008). *Ngā Tikanga mō te Taiao o Ngāti Hine Iwi Environmental Management Plan.* http://old.wdc.govt.nz/PlansPoliciesandBylaws/Plans/DistrictPlan/Documents/Iwi-Management-Plan-Ngati-Hine-Iwi-Environmental-Management-Plan-2008.pdf

Ngāti Rangiwewehi. (2012). *Ngāti Rangiwewehi Iwi Environmental Management Plan.* https://cdn.boprc.govt.nz/media/270922/ngati_rangiwewehi_iwi_environmental__management_plan__2012__part_1_smallest.pdf

Ngāi Tahu ki Murihiku. (2008). *Te Tangi a Tauira*. www.es.govt.nz/repository/libraries/id:26gi9ay0517q9stt81sd/hierarchy/about-us/plans-and-strategies/regional-plans/iwi-management-plan/documents/Te%20Tangi%20a%20Tauira%20-%20The%20Cry%20of%20the%20People.pdf

Nissen, S., & Cretney, R. (2021). Retrofitting an emergency approach to the climate crisis: A study of two climate emergency declarations in Aotearoa New Zealand. *Environment and Planning C: Politics and space*. https://doi.org/10.1177%2F23996544211028901

O'Gorman, E., Beattie, J., & Henry, M. (2016). Histories of climate, science, and colonization in Australia and New Zealand, 1800–1945. *Wiley Interdisciplinary Reviews: Climate change, 7*(6), 893–909. https://doi.org/10.1002/wcc.426

Passl, U. (2004). *Ngā Taonga Tuku Iho ki Whakatū Management Plan*. www.nelson.govt.nz/assets/Our-council/Downloads/Iwi-Management-Plans/Iwi-Management-Plan-2004-A142958.PDF

Pearce, T., Ford, J., Willox, A. C., & Smit, B. (2015). Inuit traditional ecological knowledge (TEK), subsistence hunting and adaptation to climate change in the Canadian Arctic. *Arctic, 68*(2), 233–245. http://dx.doi.org/10.14430/artic4475

Phibbs, S., Kenney, C., Rivera-Munoz, G., Huggins, T., Severinsen, C., & Curtis B. (2018). The inverse response law and relevance to the aftermath of disasters. *International Journal of Environmental Research and Public Health, 15*(5), 916. https://doi.org/10.3390/ijerph15050916

Phibbs, S., Kenney, C., & Solomon M. (2015). Ngā Mōwaho: An analysis of Māori responses to the Christchurch earthquakes. *Kotuitui: New Zealand journal of social sciences online, 10*(2), 72–82, https://doi.org/10.1080/1177083X.2015.1066401

Pierotti, R., & Wildcat, D. (2000). Traditional ecological knowledge: The third alternative (commentary). *Ecological Applications, 10*(5), 1333–1340. https://doi.org/10.1890/1051-0761(2000)010[1333:TEKTTA]2.0.CO;2

Ramos-Castillo, A., Castellanos, E. J., & McLean, K. G. (2017). Indigenous peoples, local communities and climate change mitigation. *Climatic Change, 140*(1), 1–4. https://doi.org/10.1007/s10584-016-1873-0

Reading, C. L., & Wien, F. (2009). *Health Inequalities and Social Determinants of Aboriginal Peoples' Health*. National Collaborating Centre for Aboriginal Health.

Resource Management Act 1991. www.legislation.govt.nz/act/public/1991/0069/latest/DLM230265.html

Roosvall, A., & Tegelberg, M. (2013). Framing climate change and Indigenous peoples. *International Communication Gazette, 75*(4), 392–409. https://doi.org/10.1177%2F1748048513482265

Rouse, H. L., Bell, R. G., Lundquist, C. J., Blackett, P. E., Hicks, D. M., & King, D. N. (2017). Coastal adaptation to climate change in Aotearoa-New Zealand. *New Zealand Journal of Marine and Freshwater Research, 51*(2), 183–222. https://doi.org/10.1080/00288330.2016.1185736

Rowe, D. (2020, September 14). Takutai o Te Tītī Marae faces erosion challenges in Colac Bay. *Stuff*. www.stuff.co.nz/pou-tiaki/te-reo-maori/122726772/takutai-o-te-tt-marae-faces-erosion-challenges-in-colac-bay

Saunders, W. (2017). *Setting the Scene: The role of iwi management plans in natural hazard management*. GNS Science, Te Pū Ao.

Saunders, W. S., & Kaiser, L. H. (2019, April 1). Investigating the role of iwi management plans in natural hazard management [Paper presentation]. *New Zealand Planning Institute Annual Conference. Napier.*

Saunders, W. S., Kelly, S., Paisley, S., & Clarke, L. B. (2020). Progress toward implementing the Sendai Framework, the Paris Agreement, and the Sustainable Development Goals: Policy from Aotearoa New Zealand. *International Journal of Disaster Risk Science, 11*(2), 190–205. https://doi.org/10.1007/s13753-020-00269-8

Strand, T. (2019, March 31). Fire danger. *Scion Connections*. www.scionresearch.com/about-us/about-scion/corporate-publications/scion-connections/past-issues-list/scion-connections-issue-31,-march-2019/fire-danger

SunLive. (2017, April 16). Ngati Awa Volunteer Army cleans up. https://sunlive.co.nz/news/152029-ngati-awa-volunteer-army-cleans-up.html

Te Rūnanga o Ngāi Tahu. (2019). Te Tāhū o te Whāriki. https://taituara.org.nz/Attachment?Action=Download&Attachment_id=1990

Tyson, J. (2020, July 11). 'Art as activism' new art collection to explore climate change and Indigenous voices. *Te Ao Māori News*. www.teaomaori.news/art-activism-new-art-collection-explore-climate-change-and-indigenous-voices

United Nations (UN). (2015). *Paris Agreement*. https://unfccc.int/sites/default/files/english_paris_agreement.pdf

United Nations Strategy for Disaster Reduction (UNISDR). (2015). *The Sendai Framework for Disaster Risk Reduction 2015–2030*. UNISDR.

Veland, S., Howitt, R., Dominey-Howes, D., Thomalla, F., & Houston, D. (2013). Procedural vulnerability: Understanding environmental change in a remote Indigenous community. *Global Environmental Change*, *23*(1), 314–326. https://doi.org/10.1016/j.gloenvcha.2012.10.009

Watson, I. (2017). Resilience and disaster risk reduction: Reclassifying diversity and national identity in post-earthquake Nepal. *Third World Quarterly*, *38*(2), 483–504. https://doi.org/10.1080/01436597.2016.1159913

Whyte, K. (2017). Indigenous climate change studies: Indigenizing futures, decolonizing the anthropocene. *English Language Notes*, *55*(1–2), 153–162. https://doi.org/10.1215/00138282-55.1-2.153

Wildcat, D. R. (2013). Introduction: Climate change and Indigenous peoples of the USA. In J. K. Maldonado, B. Colombi, & R. Pandya (Eds.), *Climate Change and Indigenous Peoples in the United States* (pp. 1–7). Springer.

10.
Writing the climate crisis

Ingrid Horrocks & Tom Doig

Introduction

Nau mai haere mai — a warm welcome to this chapter on creative writing and the climate crisis. We have broken our discussion into three approaches to how creative writing about the climate crisis contributes to global citizenship: first, by helping us understand and live with the climate crisis; second, as climate activism; and third, as forging a space for creating alternate imaginings of the world we inhabit.

Living with the climate crisis

fact / david attenborough will soon be dead / and that man knows his shit / about the importance of diversity / fact / my son is 12 / and he knows his shit too / about what he's set to inherit / fact / the look on his face when he realised / crushed / eyes cracked / under the weight / of how the earth might turn / of what tomorrow might do / burnfloodstarve / fact / this knowledge did not deter him / we saved the whales from extinction / he said / we can save ourselves too

— 'extinction', Meagan France (2022)

AHO 10.1
HĪKOITIA TE AO

Art can also be a powerful way to bear witness, and to help us understand the experience of global citizenship and its shared anxieties. As Huhana Smith (2020, pp. 187–189) (Ngāti Tukorehe), an artist-kaitiaki located in Kuku, Horowhenua, Aotearoa, explains in relation to this work, Hīkoitia te Ao:

'Through our work, we note environmental decline, biodiversity loss, climate change and all the effects on the human condition from a Māori perspective . . . My paintings highlight multifaceted agency as acts of healing . . .

The constrained, pruned, potted and controlled trees in Hīkoitia te Ao were selected from [my travels around the world]. Each tree radiates the experiences and conversations I had while I was away from Aotearoa . . . They highlight my concerns about the inadequate global, political, social, economic and cultural agency to accelerate the change we need to make.'

Reference

Smith, H. (2020). E tata tope e roa whakatipu. In S. Goldsmith (Ed.), *Tree Sense: Ways of thinking about trees* (pp. 169–190). Massey University Press.

Huhana Smith, Hīkoitia te Ao | Walk the World, 2020 COURTESY OF THE ARTIST

Climate change is everywhere; it affects the whole world and everything living on it. It's also nowhere; you can't directly see, hear or touch climate change. It's a slippery, overwhelming idea, as well as a hard-to-measure scientific reality. Auckland-based writer Meagan France's poem 'extinction' captures some of this complexity, as it explores how most people (not scientists, politicians or policymakers) experience climate change. There are many emotions being expressed simultaneously: fear, outrage, grief, tenderness, fierce determination. But at the same time, France's poem, like all poems, remains open to interpretation. Some people might find it depressing ('burnfloodstarve'); others will find it inspiring ('we can save ourselves too'). Poetry's ability to mean different things to different people — and even different things to the same person on different days — isn't a weakness. Quite the opposite: poetry's focus on metaphor, symbol, image and abstraction helps people express their feelings of confusion and ambivalence (experiencing conflicting emotions at the same time), while honouring the enduring complexity and mystery of life on this planet.

In the case of the climate crisis, many people use creative writing as a form of self-expression, to make sense of their everyday experiences. Around the world, people are writing millions of climate change-themed poems, short stories, scripts, rants, and unclassifiable textual experiments. Some of this writing is published in books or literary journals; some is shared in oral form within communities; some is self-published on the internet; an unknown amount (probably a huge amount) remains on people's laptops, in their private diaries, or even just in their heads.

All these words have value to their creators, firstly as a form of art therapy or narrative therapy. In addition to this, the right to express oneself creatively is a vital element of cultural citizenship. Cultural studies scholar Jo Caust (2020) has argued that 'all citizens should have access to and be able to participate in the artistic and cultural practices of their choosing' (p. 1). Education theorist Paul J. Kuttner (2015) pushes this idea further, suggesting that 'engagement in cultural production and consumption includes a vital political dimension. The visual art [and creative writing] we create, the music we listen to, and the online media we share can all serve to reinforce and challenge existing social systems' (p. 70). In other words, writing creatively about climate change — and sharing your writing with the world, whether virtually or in real life — is a form of politics, an expression of your global and national citizenship. It reflects fears, aspirations and demands for the future, no matter how unclear they may be.

Works of creative writing also represent a form of *bearing witness* to life lived in a time of climate crisis, evoking the uncanny daily experience of being a suffering human in this eerie moment in the Earth's history. While, as North American non-fiction writer Rebecca Solnit (2021) puts it, 'the scale and danger of the crisis still seems to challenge human psychology' (para. 15), we all still have our ongoing individual lives as daughters and sons, parents, siblings, workers, sportspeople and so on. Creative writing can help us understand the intense dissonance of this shared experience of global citizenship, and its attendant anxieties, which brings global collapse and mass extinctions to our smartphones and breakfast tables and commutes to uni.

A good example of this is North American writer Jenny Offill's novel *Weather* (2020). *Weather* interweaves the daily experience of motherhood and work with the narrator's growing concern about the global climate. It is made up of everyday scenes like this one, as the narrator Lizzie drives home at the end of the day, and listens to a podcast in that short interlude between work and family:

> I listen to *Hell and High Water* on the way home. This one is about Deep Time. The geologist being interviewed speaks quickly, sweeping through millions and millions of years in a moment. The Age of Birds has passed, he says. Also of Reptiles. Also of Flowering Plants. (Offill, 2020, pp. 30–31)

In another chapter, Lizzie has a party where she gets very drunk and talks to everyone, 'Because the fact that there are six thousand miles of New York sewers and all of them lie well below sea level has become my go-to conversational gambit' (Offill, 2020, p. 66). And she wonders how to live with all this knowledge.

If a novel like *Weather* is a call to action — which it is — it is also a call of consolation. It allows readers to enter an imagined global community: there are other people, all over the globe, feeling this way (Horrocks, 2021). It suggests some ways of mapping this complex mess that we encounter every day. Offill's writing shows us a mind constantly making connections between the intimate and the global, the emotional and the factual, the present and the future. The book ends with the narrator in bed with her partner, and this line: 'The core delusion is that I am here and you are there' (Offill, 2020, p. 201). To experience the climate crisis as a global citizen is not just to work out how to act; it is to understand the extent we are all connected to one another. Creative writing can help us see — and so understand — that better. Perhaps as a result we will act differently.

Writing as climate activism, writing about climate activism

Climate crisis writing can also make direct, powerful calls to action. At its most direct and politically motivated, some people use creative writing with the aim of effecting immediate, tangible change in the present. This includes writing poems, songs, short stories, slogans, tweets and memes that encourage people to vote for certain political parties, or boycott certain products or demand certain policy changes. For an inspiring example, let's turn to Kathy Jetñil-Kijiner, a 26-year-old poet from the Marshall Islands, 5000 kilometres due north of Aotearoa. In 2014, Jetñil-Kijiner performed her poem 'Dear Matafele Peinam' at the United Nations Climate Summit. Jetñil-Kijiner wanted to move people, but she had a clear message, too. (For the full effect of her words, and for the full poem, search on YouTube for 'UN Climate Summit Poem Dear Matafele Peinem'.)

> [...]
>
> dear matafele peinam,
>
> i want to tell you about that lagoon
> that lucid, sleepy lagoon lounging against the sunrise
>
> men say that one day
> that lagoon will devour you
>
> they say it will gnaw at the shoreline
> chew at the roots of your breadfruit trees
> gulp down rows of your seawalls
> and crunch your island's shattered bones
>
> they say you, your daughter
> and your granddaughter, too
> will wander rootless
> with only a passport to call home
>
> dear matafele peinam,
>
> don't cry
>
> [...]
>
> no one's drowning, baby
> no one's moving

no one's losing
their homeland
no one's gonna become
a climate change refugee

or should i say
no one else

[...]

[we are]
hands reaching out
fists raising up
banners unfurling
megaphones booming
and we are
canoes blocking coal ships
we are
the radiance of solar villages
we are
the rich clean soil of the farmer's past
we are
petitions blooming from teenage fingertips
we are
families biking, recycling, reusing,
engineers dreaming, designing, building,
artists painting, dancing, writing
and we are spreading the word

and there are thousands out on the street
marching with signs
hand in hand
chanting for change NOW

and they're marching for you, baby
they're marching for us . . .

(Jetñil-Kijiner, 2014)

AHO 10.2 MOANA AND CLIMATE CHANGE

Environmental advocate Brianna Fruean has spoken at numerous international summits to push for greater action on climate change. In this extract, she argues that movies like *Moana* have the power to inspire further climate activism among Pacific Islanders.

'Almost everything in [the movie] MOANA gave me chills, from the Tatau on Chief Tui to the familiar beats of Te Vaka. Although, there was one scene that stood out the most to me, the scene where Grandma Tala's spirit appears to reinsure MOANA of her purpose and MOANA sings *"I am a girl who loves my island, I'm the girl who loves the sea, it calls me"*. At the sound of those lyrics, images of Pacific climate change warriors and activists started appearing in my head. I saw Jacynta Fuamatu leading rallies, I saw Raedena Solomona blocking coal ships, I saw Kathy Jetnil-Kijiner reading poetry and I saw 11-year-old me planting trees while annoying everyone in my family with big talk about saving the world. At this moment in the movie it clicked, MOANA in part, is a huge metaphor about climate change and man's relationship with Mother Nature . . .

'This is a reality of Pacific people today, our fish stocks are declining, crops are dying and the ocean our ancestors taught us to love is now something we fear. Now our weather patterns are unpredictable, tides growing stronger and sea-level rising is becoming a real-life villain. Nothing stands to be the same as it once did when our great-grandparents roamed our lands. In the Disney film, even though the reality was sad, there was a silver lining and a beacon of hope. This was MOANA. She knew the problem was bigger than her, but her love for her island was bigger than her fear of Te Ka. There are so many real life MOANAs out there in the world today, fighting for their islands and not backing down to climate change, nor the hands that feed it.'

Scan the QR code to read the full article.

Brianna Fruean is a climate change activist and the youth representative of the Pacific Climate Warriors council of elders. STUFF LIMITED

Reference

Fruean, B. (n.d.). Moana and climate change.
 The Coconet.tv. www.thecoconet.tv/coco-learning/climate-change/moana-and-climate-change-1

Jetñil-Kijiner's poetry — the words of a young mother from a tiny Pacific Island, which is at risk of disappearing between the rising seas — is a clear invocation of national and global citizenship. She is declaring her rights, and the rights of her child: to live in their homeland; more to the point, for that homeland not to be destroyed by the carbon dioxide emissions of wealthy industrial nations. Jetñil-Kijiner also articulates some of the responsibilities that come with being a citizen of this Earth: to speak out against environmental destruction (like she is doing), and to take action, in the form of protest and activism. 'Canoes blocking coal ships'; 'thousands out on the streets / Marching with signs'; and — significantly, in the context of this chapter — 'Artists painting, dancing, writing'. Jetñil-Kijiner clearly identifies creative writing as an act of citizenship, and (potentially) an act of activism.

For some people, Jetñil-Kijiner's overtly political mode of expression will seem too obvious, too preachy; not subtle or sophisticated (or creative) enough. Critics of this didactic style might describe it as agitprop — short for agitation propaganda, a form of expression that tells people what to think and/or do, and is arguably closer to attempted brainwashing than art. But others would argue that creative writing that is unapologetically political, even activist, is exactly what the world needs right now. It's up to you to make up your own mind about how political you think creative writing should be, and how political you want your own writing to be.

Closer to home, last year Maia Ingoe, a 19-year-old from Tairāwhiti (Gisborne), wrote about her experiences as one of the organisers of the School Strike 4 Climate movement. Ingoe's (2020) personal essay, 'School Strike 4 Climate: A Fight for Future', is non-fiction, so it's not creative in the sense that she made things up. What makes Ingoe's essay creative is the care she takes in describing events, the effort made to evoke the *feeling* of being at a climate protest. This makes it different (better, some would say) than journalism, which tells us what happened, but not what it was like to be there.

> The main street of Tairāwhiti is small, and usually quiet: dotted with cafés, two-dollar shops and the odd retail store, brought to life by people who smile when you walk past. It begins just past the Pak'nSave carpark, where palm trees line the edges of the terracotta sidewalk, framing the road and its parked cars on either side. The grey town clock in the middle of the road holds tight to its art-deco style. Chain stores outnumber locally owned — but empty storefronts, gathering dust, are something we're used to. The road widens at a set of traffic lights, one of only two in the entire city. The street might seem bare or out of date, but if you look up on a good day, you'll see the bluer-than-blue sky that Tairāwhiti is known for.

One Friday afternoon in September 2019, a cacophony of voices bounced between buildings. Traffic was stopped as a protest a few hundred strong filled the street. Teenagers still in school uniform were joined by parents with young children, grandparents, workers having left the office for the day, a few local councillors but no MPs.

'What do we want?'

'Climate justice!'

'When do we want it?'

'Now!'

At the front of the crowd, four young protest organisers held a hand-painted light-blue banner, the same one that had been in use since our first strike. The misty rain made the paint run, distorting the letters that spelled WE DEMAND CLIMATE JUSTICE. The crowd marched on, holding cardboard protest signs bearing slogans written in colourful paint and vivid an hour earlier, trying to describe our anger. YOU'LL DIE OF OLD AGE, WE'LL DIE OF CLIMATE CHANGE. DON'T BE A FOSSIL FOOL. WHEN LEADERS ACT LIKE KIDS, KIDS BECOME LEADERS.

I was caught in the middle: wearing a too-big hi-vis vest our team had borrowed from a local company, holding a massive (but not really effective) megaphone we'd wrangled from the rowing club. My friend and I led chants through the crowd, running from middle to front to back, trying to keep the pace steady and the chants strong. We eventually handed the megaphone off to one of our team, finding our raw voices more effective; he yelled chants of climate action while holding his skateboard, painted with the letters 'SS4C', above his head . . .

(Ingoe, 2020, pp. 29–31)

Ingoe's account of the 2019 School Strike 4 Climate protests is a classic example of why 'show, don't tell' is excellent advice for early-career writers. She doesn't just *tell* us she was inTairāwhiti Gisborne; she *shows* us the place, painting a vivid picture of palm trees, empty shops and art-deco clock. Then she evokes the protest itself with carefully chosen details: 'a too-big hi-vis vest', 'a hand-painted light-blue banner', 'misty rain [that] made the paint run'. She also captures the excitement — the fun — of marching in the streets, in a way that has the potential to recruit just as many people to the climate movement as Jetñil-Kijiner's more earnest approach.

In both cases, it's clear that activist creative writing can be effectively used to articulate our rights and responsibilities as citizens of nations and members of the human race. At the same time, and unlike other forms of writing, *creative* writing has a unique ability to foreground complex emotions and thoughts, and to etch images into readers' minds, through the creation and selection of powerful, striking images, from seawater 'chew[ing] at the roots of . . . breadfruit trees', to excited high-school students clutching useless megaphones, homemade banners . . . and skateboards.

Radical hope: Imagining alternative worlds

Finally, a key value of creative writing is the potential for *imagination.* From the vantage point of the twenty-first century, it seems that simply telling human-centred stories, without much regard for nature, has not served any of us especially well. Stories that only have human protagonists have helped us forget a lot of important stuff. Some exciting new creative writing that has the climate crisis in the background is asking: What if we told stories radically differently? How would that work? How might we better see that the non-human world is as important as the human world, and inextricably interconnected?

In Massey lecturer Laura Jean McKay's wildly inventive novel *The Animals in that Country* (2020), which won the 2021 Arthur C. Clarke Award for best science fiction novel, McKay presents us with a vision of an Australia in which humans can suddenly understand animals — evoking a mad, cacophonous, scary and often hilarious world. We are invited to imagine what the non-human animals we live alongside might be thinking and saying. In the scene below, the novel's protagonist, Jean Bennett, lets a truckful of battery hogs out onto the road; the pig's communication is represented by **bold text**. (If you're wondering what pigs have to do with climate change, remember that livestock accounts for 18 per cent of the world's carbon dioxide emissions, and that contemporary industrialised farming practices have made this problem much worse [Goodland & Anhang, 2009]).

> . . . I wrench the big metal door open and pull down the gangway.
> **It was here**
> **before.**

There's around thirty of them, crammed ear to tail in the hay- and shit-strewn bed of the truck. The smell seeps into my scarf — sweet, like they're already dead and cooking. One squints at me, a thick crust of infection in both her eyes. Her tail calls to the pig beside her, an ear for the outside and her snout for my left armpit. I squint, try to see the whole pig.

Got a

light.

'What?' A ripple through the darkness, like laughter.

It brings the

sun.

Another one pushes forward.

Is there

more.

I clear my throat. 'I don't know. You better get out of this truck.' Those that are facing me peer up.

Is it

good.

At first, I think she means me . . .

. . . I breathe through my nose again with the last of them. Out over the bitumen on uncertain hooves. A hurt sow sits on her haunches, then lies down on the verge, panting unevenly under the slathering sun. Another weaves blindly over the asphalt toward her, flies spinning around her head. They push their noses into each other.

Send me

a postcard,

the sick one says. Postcard, indeed. What the fuck. I watch more closely. The meaning bright off that tight skin. All the little bits saying,

Leave me,

and,

I'll hear about it,

and,

Don't you see

it. Move on. There's

more.

The ones that can walk stretch their legs, for,

More,

more, more.

I stand at the top of the truck ramp watching them break into a group trot

WRITING THE CLIMATE CRISIS 173

toward the next paddock. Skin rippling. Hooves carolling. I know that heart-in-your-mouth run. Know exactly what 'more' is. I've seen it in my son Lee and I've had it too, at times. These pigs are half dead, they're stumbling around, blind, mad, and fucking *hopeful*.

(McKay, 2020, pp. 127–130)

Such writing can help us more fully imagine our kinship, our shared citizenship, with the non-human world. McKay raises powerful questions about what rights other members of the non-human world have — or should have.

Creative writing raises other profound and disorienting questions, such as what might happen if the lives of water or trees, rather than human needs, dictated story structure? What if trees could talk, as in the queer love story between a woman and a talking tree told by Mununjali Yugambeh writer Ellen van Neerven (2014) in *Heat and Light?* Such stories can help us radically change our perspective, which in turn alters what seems important in the world.

To truly confront the climate crisis, we need to be able to understand that non-human creatures and other citizens of the non-human world, such as awa and whenua, have stories of their own. Indigenous creative works are replete with these types of narratives. If it is hard for us to conceive of this, creative writing can help. Sometimes, it can come down to something as simple as verb choice to grant a non-human animal agency within a story. Or it might extend to imaginative leaps, such as considering what an animal, or a river, might want and need. The section in Chapter 6 on Māori notions of responsibility demonstrated a fully living non-human world, not distinct from but intimately related to human experience. In a powerful forthcoming anthology of climate change poetry from Aotearoa (Hamel et al., 2022), Papatūānuku appears as a recurring figure, vitally re-conceived in this new moment by poets like Tayi Tibble. In embracing such approaches, the hierarchies and structures we live so much of our lives by can seem to dissolve. And we can imagine the world anew.

Creative writing can also help us imagine *alternative futures*. In recent years, a whole genre of creative writing in Aotearoa and elsewhere has been dedicated to imagining possible futures in a world impacted by climate collapse. In a sense, these are stories of warning, allowing us to fully imagine how bad things could get if we do not act collectively. But they are also much more than that: they are bold thought-experiments that allow us to take the nebulous idea of the future more seriously.

A striking recent example is Wellington-based writer Clare Moleta's eco-thriller *Unsheltered* (2021b), which tells the story of a woman looking for her lost child in a barren future afflicted by destructive weather and social breakdown. *Unsheltered* allows us to enter an imagined scenario of how people might act when faced, for instance, with chronic water shortages. Moleta's account of how she came to find the focus for her novel is helpful for seeing how creative writing works. She writes, 'If I'd had to articulate my reasons, I might have said I was looking for a way to write about things I couldn't stop thinking about: the loss of home, the search for refuge, the unavoidable consequences of the way we persist in living on this planet. But what I was actually writing about was a woman searching for a missing child roughly the same age as my own child' (2021a, para. 3). What might have felt overwhelming and numbing, finds story in the loss of one child. The focus on the specific — which is where the power of much creative writing lies — can also provide room for hope. Even in the worst circumstances, individuals continue to find joy, to love, and to try to make things better. As Moleta (2021a) puts it of her imagined future world, 'In the midst of a long unfolding climate and human catastrophe, strangers do what they can to build communities and help each other' (para. 9).

Importantly, creative writing isn't constrained by the facts in the way that much science writing or journalism is. Science fiction, speculative fiction, magic realism, fantasy, horror, myth, visionary poetry (and other styles besides) all offer ways to imagine a world very different from the one we are currently living in. This includes (re)connecting with older ways of living, such as Indigenous and pre-capitalist lifestyles. This kind of writing may or may not have immediate practical or political value, leading to changes in the real world. But regardless of this, the act of imagining different worlds is an emancipatory act. Environmental geographer Ruth Machen (2019) claims that some forms of imaginative work 'construct, circulate, or otherwise enable, possible alternative imaginaries, courses of action, or future states' (p. 337). Creative writing in this vein might be explicitly *normative* — that is, making claims about how things are or ought to be. It also might 'provocatively or subversively carve out space for others to imagine and construct' alternative ways of thinking about future societies (Machen, 2019, p. 338).

Wellington novelist Elizabeth Knox (2020), in her opening address to the New Zealand Festival's Writers Week, noted that the current limits of our collective imagination in relation to climate — our failure to imagine how we could do things differently — 'might be the death of us all' (para. 63). Creative writing is one place where we can imagine differently. Imagining future worlds need not be dystopian, or at least not purely so; they might instead be founded in *radical hope.* Australian climate-change fiction writer James Bradley (2020) draws on the work of philosopher Jonathan Lear to describe radical hope this way:

AHO 10.3
PACIFIC POETRY AND CULTURE

The Poetry Foundation, publisher of *Poetry* magazine, is an independent literary organisation that exists to discover and celebrate the best poetry and present it to a wide audience. Included on their website is an introduction to contemporary poets, poems and articles exploring the history and the aesthetics of the Pacific, including poetry that comments on the ongoing legacies of colonialism, and which explores decolonisation and the revitalisation of Pacific cultures.

'In the 1960s and 1970s, students and faculty at the newly established University of Papua New Guinea and the University of the South Pacific in Fiji begin to study, write, and publish poetry and stories in broadsides, chapbooks, zines, anthologies, and full-length collections. Other centers of Pacific poetry soon emerged across the Pacific, including Aotearoa (New Zealand), Samoa, Tonga, Hawai'i, Tahiti, and Guam. Today, several Pacific writers have become internationally renowned, and their work has been translated into multiple languages and media, including film. Pacific literature courses are now taught in high schools and colleges throughout Oceania, and there are publishers and literary journals dedicated wholly to Pacific writing. Several dissertations, theses, essays, and monographs have focused on the history, theory, and aesthetics of Pacific literature. Book festivals, reading series, open mics, spoken word slams, writing workshops, humanities councils, author retreats, and literary conferences have created a dynamic and vibrant Pacific literary scene.

'On one hand, a major thread of Pacific poetry documents, critiques, and laments the legacy and ongoing impacts of colonialism. Poems address issues related to social injustice, economic dispossession, militarization, nuclearism, plantationism, disease, tourism, urbanization, racism, migration, homophobia, and environmental degradation. Conversely, another thread of Pacific poetry explores decolonization and revitalization of native Pacific cultures, nations, customs, languages, kinship networks, histories, politics, and identities. In terms of form, Pacific poetry draws from a range of styles, including formalism, free verse, projectivism, ecopoetics, documentary, avant-garde, postmodernism, beat, confessionalism, surrealism, vis-po, vid-po, protest poetics, spoken word, performance, conceptualism, queer poetics, multicultural poetics, multilingualism, and more. Pacific poetry is as diverse as the cultures of Oceania.' (Poetry Foundation, 2021)

To discover some of these Pacific poets, scan the QR code.

Reference

Poetry Foundation. (2021). Pacific Islander poetry and culture. www.poetryfoundation.org/collections/142017/pacific-islander-poetry-and-culture-5913874061754

Radical hope is not simple optimism, or the opposite of despair. Instead it involves accepting the fears so many of us [are] grappling with and using them as the basis for a new set of priorities. Or, as Lear writes, 'What makes . . . hope radical is that it is directed toward a future goodness that transcends the current ability to understand what it is. Radical hope anticipates a good for which those who have the hope as yet lack the appropriate concepts with which to understand it.'

[. . .] radical hope is a psychological practice as well as a political position. It requires us to accept the past is gone, and that the political and cultural assumptions that once shaped our world no longer hold true. It demands we learn to live with uncertainty and grief, and to face up to the reality of loss. But it also demands what Lear describes as 'imaginative excellence', a deliberate fostering of the flexibility and courage necessary to 'facilitate a creative and appropriate response to the world's challenges' that will enable us to envision new alliances and open up new possibilities, even in the face of catastrophe. (para. 47)

Creative writing might help us do this. It is one tool for trying to imagine this Earth we need to inhabit anew.

And in case that sounds like too daunting a challenge for one person, let's close this chapter with the inspiring, bittersweet words of Craig Santos Perez, in 'Love in a Time of Climate Change' (recycling Pablo Neruda's 'Sonnet XVII'; 2020):

I don't love you as if you were rare earth metals,
conflict diamonds, or reserves of crude oil that cause
war. I love you as one loves the most vulnerable
species: urgently, between the habitat and its loss.

I love you as one loves the last seed saved
within a vault, gestating the heritage of our roots,
and thanks to your body, the taste that ripens
from its fruit still lives sweetly on my tongue.

I love you without knowing how or when this world
will end. I love you organically, without pesticides.
I love you like this because we'll only survive

in the nitrogen rich compost of our embrace,

so close that your emissions of carbon are mine,

so close that your sea rises with my heat.

References

Bradley, J. (2020, October 13). The library at the end of the world. *Sydney Review of Books.* https://sydneyreviewofbooks.com/essay/library-end-world-bradley

Caust, J. (2020). Cultural rights as human rights and the impact on the expression of arts practices. *Journal of Citizenship and Globalisation Studies, 31*(1), 1–14. https://doi.org/10.2478/jcgs-2019-0004

France, M. (forthcoming, 2022). Extinction. In J. Hamel, R. Hawkes, E. Kennedy & E. Ranapiri (Eds.), *No Other Place to Stand: An anthology of climate change poetry from Aotearoa.* Auckland University Press.

Goodland, R., & Anhang, J. (2009, November/December). Livestock and climate change: What if the key actors in climate change are . . . cows, pigs, and chickens? *World Watch,* 10–19.

Hamel, J., Hawkes, R, Kennedy, E., & Ranapiri, E. (Eds.). (2022). *No Other Place to Stand: An anthology of climate change poetry from Aotearoa.* Auckland University Press.

Horrocks, I. (2021, March 28). The climate crisis is seeping into books and making them really, really weird. *The Spinoff.* https://thespinoff.co.nz/books/28-03-2021/the-climate-crisis-is-seeping-into-books-and-making-them-really-really-weird

Ingoe, M. (2020). School Strike 4 Climate: A fight for future. In T. Doig (Ed.), *Living with the Climate Crisis: Voices from Aotearoa* (pp. 29–46). Bridget Williams Books.

Jetñil-Kijiner, K. (2014, September 24). *UN Climate Summit Poem 'Dear Matafele Peinem'.* YouTube. www.youtube.com/watch?v=DJuRjy9k7GA

Knox, E. (2020, February 22). Useless grasses: On imagination. *New Zealand Festival of the Arts Writers' Week Opening Address.* https://elizabethknox.com/useless-grasses-on-imagination

Kuttner, P. J. (2015). Educating for cultural citizenship: Reframing the goals of arts education. *Curriculum Inquiry, 45*(1), 69–92. https://doi.org/10.1080/03626784.2014.980940

Machen, R. (2019). Critical research impact: On making space for alternatives. *Area, 52*(2), 329–341. https://doi.org/10.1111/area.12574

McKay, L. J. (2020). *The Animals in that Country.* Scribe Publications.

Moleta, C. (2021a, May 19). I wrote my worst nightmare. *The Spinoff.* https://thespinoff.co.nz/books/19-05-2021/i-wrote-my-worst-nightmare

Moleta, C. (2021b). *Unsheltered.* Scribner.

Offill, J. (2020). *Weather.* Granta Publications.

Santos Perez, C. (forthcoming, 2022). Love in a time of climate change. In J. Hamel, R. Hawkes, E. Kennedy & E. Ranapiri (Eds.), *No Other Place to Stand: An anthology of climate change poetry from Aotearoa and the Pacific.* Auckland University Press.

Solnit, R. (2021, July 20). Our climate change turning point is right here, right now. *The Guardian.* www.theguardian.com/commentisfree/2021/jul/12/our-climate-change-turning-point-is-right-here-right-now

van Neerven, E. (2014). *Heat and Light.* University of Queensland Press.

11.
Encountering conflict

David Littlewood

Introduction

Living in Aotearoa, it is tempting to regard violent conflict between separate groups of people as an issue of little direct significance, or as something that is relegated to our distant past. After all, this country possesses a highly democratic institutional structure and always features near the top when measures such as political stability, peacefulness and happiness are ranked.

Yet the global interconnections that have exerted such a profound influence on Aotearoa have not only led to its frequent involvement in international conflict, but also meant that the impacts of past domestic conflicts are still being felt today. European colonisation witnessed innumerable acts of violence against Māori, not least during the costly and divisive New Zealand Wars, which undermined Māori self-determination and sovereignty as Pākehā rights were privileged (Walker, 2004).

This country then spent one-third of the twentieth century participating in overseas conflicts, including imperial wars alongside Britain, wars of alliance alongside the United States, and peacekeeping operations (Rabel, 2009); with its military personnel currently (at the time of writing) being deployed in South Korea, South Sudan and several countries in the Middle East. Even before the tragic events of the Christchurch Mosque attack shattered any illusions that domestic terrorism

IHO ATUA

Margaret Forster (Rongomaiwāhine, Ngāti Kahungunu)

Conflict is an enduring condition of encounters. It stems from uncertainty, sometimes disagreement and the need for change:

> In New Zealand, where Earth and Sky were the first parents, one of their sons — the mighty Tānemahuta — did nothing less than raise the sky so that life and light could flood the world between. This act might have freed the sons, but it also led to aeons-long battles between them. (Ihimaera & Hereaka, 2019, p. 11)

In this narrative, conflict presents as a battle that yields both positive and negative outcomes. The battle between the sons produced change and freedom, creating space to transform and for the pursuit of potentiality. However, the divergence in opinion and associated action was also destructive and harmful, leading to a violent and traumatic event. And because te ao Māori is an ethical world, there are always consequences associated with actions. Aroha, acts of love and protection, and manaaki, acts of generosity, must eventually prevail. Conflict must give way to responsibility and reciprocity, moving towards acts of recovery and healing. Conflict, therefore, is part of a dynamic cycle, a continuous struggle between discord and harmony to achieve a state of wellness and wellbeing, as exemplified by the phrase tihei mauri ora — let there be life!

could not happen here, it was clear that the relative geographical isolation of Aotearoa had not granted it any immunity from conflict.

This summary chapter examines the repercussions of conflict in Aotearoa and elsewhere, as well as their relevance for ideas of global citizenship. It begins by describing the frequency of conflict in the early twenty-first century, before outlining the most persistent causes. Attention then turns to the multifaceted links between conflict and human rights violations, an area that is further analysed by Bramwell, Banks, Holm and Taffel in their chapter on conflict commodities (Chapter 13). A final part covers responses to conflict, with two of these — the Responsibility to Protect concept (Rogers) and arts responses (Hazou) — being the focus of the other chapters in this section.

Frequency of conflict

Conflict remains a ubiquitous global challenge. There were hopes that the catastrophic events of the Second World War, combined with the establishment of the United Nations (UN) and the drawing-up of wide-ranging human rights instruments, would see a reduction in conflict over the second half of the twentieth century. Other commentators viewed the end of the Cold War in the early 1990s as a pivotal moment, given the apparent triumph of Western liberal democracy and a presumption that that form of government would become increasingly prevalent (Fukuyama, 1992). Yet while there has been no third world war, and while set-piece military engagements are much rarer than they used to be, there has still been a vast amount of conflict over the past 80 years, and even over the past 30 years. Indeed, looking beyond formally declared wars reveals a proliferation of other types of conflict, such as civil wars, revolutions, proxy wars, insurgencies, genocides and campaigns of terrorism. At the time of writing, the Global Conflict Tracker, maintained by the Center for Preventive Action (2021), lists more than 25 ongoing situations. These range from Mexico in the west to the South China Sea in the east, and from the Democratic Republic of the Congo in the south to Ukraine in the north.

There are reasons to think conflict will become even more common over the next few decades. Political and social divisions around matters of race, gender and national identity are already causing heightened tensions in many countries, with this being just as evident in the more economically developed parts of the world as it is in poorer nations. One only needs to look at the debates surrounding the 2020 United States presidential election, or Brexit, or public health responses to the Covid-19 pandemic, to see that populations are becoming increasingly polarised over fundamental issues. These frictions are likely to be exacerbated by other challenges. As climate change leads to increased global temperatures, the resulting disruption to weather patterns and reduced access to essential resources will compromise food security, health and sanitation in large parts of the world. Moreover, rising sea levels and growing desertification will make many areas less inhabitable, and render some coastal areas and low-lying islands totally uninhabitable. Such eventualities will not only heighten the probability of conflict over increasingly scarce resources, but also result in mass displacement and forced migration (Bretthauer, 2017). Given that the admission and resettlement of refugees is already a point of significant controversy, any rise in numbers is likely to provoke further conflict (Alvarez, 2017). Linked to the risks posed by climate change are those arising from inequality. The widening gap between the haves and the have-nots, both within and between different countries, is already a frequent source of unrest. As the unequal impacts of climate change combine with the unequal economic burdens of the Covid-19 pandemic, the resentment and distrust that stem from increased inequalities will almost certainly foster additional conflict (Wilkinson & Pickett, 2009).

Causes of conflict

Three causes of conflict have persisted across different times, places and scales. First, whether arising from a desire for revenge or a perception of unreasonable outcomes, the legacies of one conflict have often sown the seeds of further disputes. An obvious example is the Treaty of Versailles that was imposed on Germany by the Allies following the First World War. During the 1920s and 1930s, German politicians were able to generate support by arguing that Versailles had enacted intolerable economic burdens and an unjustifiable loss of territory and prestige. Overturning Versailles was a key motivator of Germany's aggressive foreign policy once Hitler came to power (Neiberg, 2019).

A second perennial driver of conflict, discussed in detail in Chapter 13, has been the competition for, or desire to obtain, resources. These resources have often been coveted at a national level, such as the quest for precious metals that prompted Spain and Portugal's brutal conquest of central and southern America, or the desire to safeguard oil supplies that motivated much twentieth-century imperialism in the Middle East. Other disputes have centred on an unequal distribution of resources, and therefore power, within a particular society. A leading cause of the Russian Revolution was the concentration of wealth and privileges in the hands of elite groups, to the virtual exclusion of the majority (McMeekin, 2017).

The third ubiquitous cause of conflict are notions of superiority and inferiority. Whether these revolve around religion, race, nationality, or a combination of factors, groups of people have often acted on a belief that it is their right, or even their responsibility, to dominate others. European colonialism and imperialism frequently stemmed from an assumption of racial superiority and a perception that Indigenous peoples needed to be assimilated or swept aside as part of the natural order of things. As discussed in Chapter 2, the primary motivation behind Britain's colonisation of Aotearoa was a sense that European dominance of an Indigenous people was necessary, preordained and in the best interests of Māori. Similarly, the Thirty Years War began as a contest between the adherents of Catholicism and Protestantism, while the decades preceding the First World War were a time of virulent nationalism, with the citizens of many nations holding themselves to be inherently superior to the citizens of rival nations (Mombauer, 2013). Ultimately, conflict occurs when strong ideas of 'us' and 'them' take hold. The people of one group decide it is in their best interests to fight the people of another group, who are held to be different, and therefore opposed, at some fundamental level.

Conflict and human rights

Every conflict carries potentially devastating implications for human rights. Most obviously, the right to life of those involved in the fighting comes under significant threat. Yet even during the vast military campaigns of the Second World War, the highest number of deaths and injuries occurred among civilians. Widespread destruction threatens rights to property and health, thereby seriously undermining people's capacity to enjoy a decent standard of living. Violence and persecution have also left tens of millions of people displaced in their own countries or forced them to flee across national borders in the hope of achieving official recognition as refugees. Even if such recognition is granted, refugees frequently face practical limitations on their rights due to discrimination, intolerance and the need to meet restrictive criteria to qualify for support and assistance in their host countries (Bourbeau, 2015; New Zealand Human Rights Commission, 2010).

Other rights violations tend to feature prominently among the causes and consequences of conflict. Discrimination against certain groups through differing access to health care and education, or denial of political participation, is often a precursor to violence and resistance. Likewise, groups who find themselves on the losing side of a conflict frequently suffer a reduction in their rights and privileges vis-à-vis the victors, and sometimes become the victims of mass atrocities.

As Sriram and colleagues (2017) assert, human rights violations are 'also potentially transformative of conflict and may make their resolution a greater challenge' (p. 6). Fighting that begins at a local level, or that is motivated by access to resources or territorial claims, can be increased in scale and ferocity if one or both sides commit human rights violations. Indeed, leaders are much better able to mobilise their citizens to participate in conflict if they can portray the struggle as one for basic human survival and freedoms. Systematic human rights violations also make it much more difficult to bring a conflict to an end and achieve a lasting peace, as trust between the parties is eroded (Mertus & Helsing, 2006).

Responding to conflict

While the harmful impacts of conflict are beyond doubt, how best to respond remains a matter of debate. Conflict responses tend to be determined more at an international level than at national, local or individual levels. Much soul-searching took place following the Rwandan Genocide of 1994 and the massacre of Bosnian Muslims at Srebrenica in 1995. Both these events occurred despite the presence of UN peacekeeping forces, and without any major attempts to halt the killings by the international community. As discussed in Chapter 12, the resulting sense of failure was a key motivator behind the UN General Assembly's adoption, in 2005, of the Responsibility to Protect (R2P) concept. The R2P seeks to impose a universal obligation on states to protect their populations from four mass atrocity crimes, as well as requiring the wider international community to intervene if a state is manifestly failing to meet that obligation (Bellamy, 2014). However, reactions to, and the implementation of, the R2P have been decidedly patchy. Nations still tend to act, or not act, according to their own interests and strategic goals, rather than according to the universalist notions embodied in the R2P. Moreover, the R2P, and particularly its provisions for military intervention, have been portrayed as a tool of Western neo-colonialism and forced regime change, rather than as a means of safeguarding human rights (Thakur, 2019).

Another way of responding to conflict at the international level is through war crimes trials. These first occurred with the Nuremburg and Tokyo trials following the Second World War, before being reinstituted with the International Criminal Tribunal for the former Yugoslavia and the International Criminal Tribunal for Rwanda in the 1990s. Following criticism of these later bodies as ad hoc and disorganised, the International Criminal Court (ICC) was opened in 2002 as a permanent venue for trying alleged war criminals. Yet much like the R2P, war crimes trials have been the subject of considerable debate. Some argue they represent a form of victors' justice and a means of deflecting from the multi-

AHO 11.1 ACKNOWLEDGING AND LEARNING ABOUT THE NEW ZEALAND WARS

The New Zealand Wars have had a chequered history in the New Zealand psyche, often being skirted around or ignored in the classroom. This has undergone a radical change in 2022, with Aotearoa history becoming a compulsory subject for school students from Years 1 to 10. The New Zealand Wars, and Māori experiences of colonisation more broadly, occupy a central place in the new curriculum.

The decision to make Aotearoa history a compulsory subject was largely due to the success of a 2015 petition to Parliament led by Otorohanga College students, who were incensed that public knowledge of the New Zealand Wars, and the devastating impacts they had on Māori, was decidedly limited. In their September 2019 announcement about the curriculum change, Prime Minister Jacinda Ardern and Minister of Education Chris Hipkins argued that knowing about the past and understanding its lasting effects on Aotearoa would help build better connectedness across this country's diverse communities.

From the time of the curriculum announcement, much work has been done to create resources that schools can use in teaching the history of Aotearoa. One of these is the Radio New Zealand-developed The New Zealand Wars Collection, which tells the stories of these conflicts across the country. Scan the QR code to explore these stories.

The one hundred and fiftieth commemoration of the Battle of Gate pā, Tauranga, 2014.
CHRIS WEISSENBORN, COURTESY OF THE NEW ZEALAND DEFENCE FORCE, CC BY-ND 2.0

ENCOUNTERING CONFLICT   187

sided causes of conflict. Others have attacked the perceived Western orientation of the ICC by noting that it has almost exclusively indicted black Africans and focused on establishing the responsibility of individuals rather than collectives (Cassese, 2008).

Conflict and citizenship

Other responses to conflict occur beyond the more formal international and national structures. As Nigel Dower (2002) puts it, 'global peace is in large measure constituted by local peace or rather many local peaces' (p. 245). Some groups organise boycotts or lobbying campaigns against parties they accuse of fostering conflict — such as the BDS campaign against Israel discussed in Chapter 14 — while others utilise films, plays or artworks to put their message across. Given that conflict is always instigated and conducted by people, every person who can be persuaded to renounce violence and speak out against human rights abuses makes conflict that little bit less likely to occur. Arguably the greatest role that global citizenship can play in this regard comes with increasing awareness and understanding. If people can embrace difference and work as part of collectives, rather than dividing themselves along national or other lines, then perhaps the continuance of conflict need not be as likely as it seems at present.

References

Alvarez, A. (2017). *Climate Change, Conflict, and Genocide.* Rowman & Littlefield.

Bellamy, A. J. (2014). *Responsibility to Protect: A defense.* Oxford University Press.

Bourbeau, P. (2015). Migration, resilience and security: Responses to new inflows of asylum seekers and migrants. *Journal of Ethnic and Migration Studies, 41*(2), 1958–1977. https://doi.org/10.1080/1369183X.2015.1047331

Bretthauer, J. M. (2017). *Climate Change and Resource Conflict: The role of scarcity.* Routledge.

Cassese, A. (2008). *International Criminal Law.* Oxford University Press.

Center for Preventive Action. (2021). *Global Conflict Tracker.* www.cfr.org/global-conflict-tracker/?category=us

Dower, N. (2002). Global citizenship and peace. In N. Dower & J. Williams (Eds.), *Global Citizenship: A critical introduction* (pp. 224–252). Routledge.

Fukuyama, F. (1992). *The End of History and the Last Man.* Penguin.

Ihimaera, W., & Hereaka, W. (2019). Introduction. In W. Ihimaera & W. Hereaka (Eds.), *Pūrākau: Māori myths retold by Māori writers* (pp. 11–21). Vintage.

McMeekin, S. (2017). *The Russian Revolution: A new history.* Profile Books.

Mertus, J. A., & Helsing, J. W. (2006). Introduction: Exploring the intersection between human rights and conflict. In J. A. Mertus & J. W. Helsing, (Eds.). *Human Rights and Conflict: Exploring the links between rights, law, and peacebuilding.* US Institute of Peace Press.

Mombauer, A. (2013). *The Origins of the First World War: Controversies and consensus* (Rev. ed.). Routledge.

Neiberg, M. (2019). *The Treaty of Versailles: A very short introduction.* Oxford University Press.

New Zealand Human Rights Commission. (2010). *Human Rights in New Zealand 2010: Ngā tika tangata o Aotearoa.* www.hrc.co.nz/files/7014/2388/0544/Human_Rights_Review_2010_Full.pdf

Rabel, R. (2009). New Zealand's wars. In G. Byrnes (Ed.), *The New Oxford History of New Zealand* (pp. 245–262). Oxford University Press.

Sriram, C. L., Martin-Ortega, O., & Herman, J. (2017). *War, Conflict and Human Rights: Theory and practice.* Routledge.

Thakur, R. (2019). *Reviewing the Responsibility to Protect: Origins, implementation and controversies.* Routledge.

Walker, R. (2004). *Ka Whawhai Tonu Matou — Struggle without end.* Penguin.

Wilkinson, R. G., & Pickett, K. (2009). *The Spirit Level: Why more equal societies almost always do better.* Allen Lane.

12.

Responsibility to Protect
Using armed force to counter atrocity crimes

Damien Rogers

Introduction

What are atrocity crimes? Why do these phenomena concern members of the wider international community, including the society of states and those individuals who claim global citizenship? How does the Responsibility to Protect (R2P) concept feature in the collective response to this grisly and recurring problem in contemporary world affairs? After answering those preliminary questions, this chapter traces the emergence of R2P through various official reports, before locating the concept's roots amidst the horror of mass atrocity committed as part of the civil wars in Rwanda and the Former Republic of Yugoslavia during the 1990s. The next section considers the United Nations (UN) Security Council's use of R2P to frame its authorisation of armed force countering atrocity crimes committed in Libya, before speculating why the council did not subsequently authorise armed force in response to atrocity crimes occurring in Syria. Finally, there are some reflections on what the potential use of armed force in the future implies for Aotearoa, particularly regarding the various efforts of the UN to maintain peace and international security.

Atrocity crimes

The use of especially cruel forms of violence for political purposes is a distinctly human phenomenon, with a macabre history dating back to Antiquity (Kiernan, 2007). Europe's religious wars of the seventeenth century were fuelled by such atrocities (Wilson, 2009), before the Westphalian settlement of 1648 ushered in a states-based system that was subsequently exported to other parts of the world and used by Europeans as a means of domination and exploitation (Anghie, 2004). Mass atrocity remains an important factor in the making of modernist world affairs (Bauman, 1989) and contemporary history is littered with the human debris left in the wake of atrocities committed by authoritarian regimes in the Soviet Union, the People's Republic of China and South America (Lutz & Reiger, 2009) — to name just a few examples.

Atrocity crimes usually involve acts of violence that deliberately inflict pain and suffering on others, as social groups struggle against one another to establish, maintain or augment a collective sense of self. More than antagonising others by casting them in the reductive terms of their national, racial, ethnic, class, religious or tribal affiliations, those who commit atrocity crimes seek to tear apart the social fabric that binds collective identity together. The brutalising methods by which social groups target others for serious harm and, in some cases, annihilation, are so vile that the commission of such acts concerns us all, because they diminish our status as human beings (Robertson, 1999). Breaches of individual human rights cause alarm, but the link between discrimination and the destruction of communities and groups threatens to reduce human diversity, rendering the phenomena of atrocity crimes a serious concern for the wider international community.

The catch-all term 'atrocity crimes' refers to war crimes, crimes against humanity and crimes of genocide. A war crime is a serious violation of international humanitarian law (Cassese, 2008), which involves the mistreatment of prisoners of war or wounded combatants, the targeting of civilians or the use of prohibited weapons on the battlefield (Schabas, 2012). A link to an underlying situation of armed conflict must exist for an act to be considered a war crime. United States (US) President Truman's decision to drop an atomic bomb on Hiroshima and a nuclear bomb on Nagasaki in early August 1945, while the Japanese were negotiating their own surrender, is, perhaps, the most spectacular and far-reaching war crime ever committed. Those two cities were civilian objects and thereby supposedly protected from the fury of war (Blix, 2000; Goldhagen, 2009).

War crimes tend to exclude crimes committed by a government against its own citizens. Filling this gap, a crime against humanity is an inhumane or odious act committed within the context of a widespread and systemic attack against a civilian population. The act must be committed, knowingly, as part of an attack against a civilian population (Slye & Schaack, 2009). If the acts of murder, extermination and torture are isolated acts, then they fall short of the threshold needed to become a crime against humanity. Unlike war crimes, crimes against humanity do not require a link to an underlying situation of armed conflict. Pol Pot's regime killed over a million Cambodians, many of whose corpses were left to rot in so-called killing fields, making this one of the twentieth century's most egregious crimes against humanity (Shawcross, 2002; Short, 2004).

Unlike war crimes, but like crimes against humanity, crimes of genocide can occur irrespective of any underlying situation of armed conflict. Genocide's mens rea ('guilty mind') element lies in those acts being committed with the intent to destroy, in whole or in part, national, ethnic, racial or religious groups. Acts constituting the crime of genocide were first enunciated in Article 2 of the Convention on the Prevention and Punishment of the Crime of Genocide (1948) and have remained largely unchanged since then. These are as follows: killing members of the group; causing serious bodily or mental harm to members of the group; deliberately inflicting on the group conditions of life calculated to bring about its physical destruction, in whole or in part; imposing measures intended to prevent births within the group; and forcibly transferring children of the group to another group. The Holocaust stands as an exemplar of genocide, while the scale of its destructiveness renders it without precedent and exceeds all comparisons (Bauer, 2001; Tatz, 2003).

Atrocity crimes are best understood as a politico-social problem in contemporary world affairs, even though this challenges the conventional view of international politics as something done by states and state leaders. Nevertheless, this problem is one that demands a collective response from the society of states, a response that, for some individuals and groups, helps constitute a global citizenship. The wider international community responds to atrocity crimes through the UN Security Council, which has the primary responsibility for maintaining or restoring international peace and security under Article 24 of the UN Charter. Firstly, the council can remind specific governments of their responsibility to protect their own populations (for instance, United Nations Security Council, 2006; United Nations Security Council, 2011). Secondly, it can establish sanction regimes that target those who are responsible for atrocity crimes, seeking to coerce a change of behaviour rather than to punish (Farrall, 2016). Thirdly, it can authorise peacekeeping operations that include mandates for the use of armed force to counter mass atrocity (Williams, 2016). Fourthly, it can establish ad hoc international criminal tribunals to prosecute individuals — such as the International Criminal Tribunal for the Former Republic of Yugoslavia and the International Criminal Tribunal for Rwanda, as well as 'hybrid' institutions in the form of the Special Court for Sierra Leone, the Extraordinary Chambers of the Courts of Cambodia and the Special Tribunal for Lebanon — or refer situations to the International Criminal Court for further investigation.

What follows focuses on the use of armed force, because this is the most controversial among the collective responses to atrocity crimes. It is controversial, in part, because the use of armed force in international affairs is prohibited by Article 2(4) of the UN Charter, except where it is used in self-defence by a UN member-state or where it has been authorised by the UN Security Council. The use of armed force is also controversial because it tends to generate unforeseen consequences that can increase human suffering. Those in favour of armed force tend to assume that violence can remedy violence, whereas those against its use tend to believe that violence begets violence. Any consensus here is, of course, illusory.

R2P's emergence

The term Responsibility to Protect was first used by the International Commission on Intervention and State Sovereignty (ICISS), featuring as the title for its 2001 report. The Canadian government established the commission in late 2000 to answer the vexing question 'when, if ever, is it appropriate for states to take coercive — and in particular military — action, against another state for the purpose of protecting people at risk in that other state?' (ICISS, 2001, p. vii). According to Gareth Evans (2008), co-chair of ICISS, 'we very much had in mind the power of new ideas, or old ideas newly expressed, to actually change the behavior of key policy actors. And the model we looked to in this respect was the Brundtland Commission, which a few years earlier had introduced the concept of "sustainable development" to bridge the huge gap that existed between developers and environmentalists' (p. 42).

To bridge the gap between the norm of non-interference in the affairs of state and the desire to intervene with military force to protect human beings, the report drew on the logic of human security. People were to be the objects of protection, rather than states, and they were to be protected from an array of harms associated with armed conflict, insurgency and internal repression, and other human-made miseries involving hunger, disease and climate change. The promotion of internationally recognised human rights, especially where those rights are precarious, lay at the heart of their report. Although it was not expressed

AHO 12.1 SLOBODAN MILOŠEVIĆ AND THE INTERNATIONAL CRIMINAL TRIBUNAL FOR THE FORMER YUGOSLAVIA

Slobodan Milošević was the leader of Yugoslavia and its successor state Serbia from the late 1980s to the late 1990s. He became infamous for his actions during the Balkan Wars of the 1990s and was charged with war crimes in 1999.

The International Criminal Tribunal for the former Yugoslavia (ICTY) was established by the United Nations (UN) in 1993. Following the Balkan Wars, it became a 'Court' with 'jurisdiction to prosecute individuals who, in the territory of the former Yugoslavia, commit grave breaches of the Geneva Conventions (Article 2), violations of the laws or customs of war (Article 3), genocide (Article 4), and crimes against humanity (Article 5)' (Scharf, 1999, para. 1).

Milošević was accused of ordering and facilitating violence against, and ethnic cleansing of, Albanians in Kosovo (at the time an autonomous province of Serbia), Croatians and several other non-Serbian peoples. A particularly violent episode was the massacre of up to 8000 Bosnian Muslim men and boys at Srebrenica in 1995. This incident was especially shocking for NATO and Western European states, as Dutch peacekeeping forces, who had been sent by the UN to protect the enclave and had declared it a 'safe area', stood aside and let the killings happen. Milošević denied any part in the massacre at Srebrenica, instead blaming General Ratko Mladić. He was still on trial at the ICTY when he died of a heart attack in 2006, which meant no verdict was given on the war crimes charges laid against him.

Reference

Scharf, M. P. (1999). The indictment of Slobodan Milosevic. *American Society of International Law Insights, 4*(3). www.asil.org/insights/volume/4/issue/3/indictment-slobodan-milosevic

Protestors against the regime of President Slobodan Milošević clash with participants in an anti-NATO rally in Belgrade, 29 March 1999. SHUTTERSTOCK

in these terms, the objective was to create conditions ensuring people enjoyed a freedom from fear and a freedom from want. Moreover, any use of military force to protect people in harm's way would draw on the criteria of Just War and be based on precautionary principles.

The R2P concept attracted considerable attention at the UN. It featured in the report of the UN Secretary-General's High-Level Panel on Threats, Challenges, and Change, entitled *A More Secure World: Our shared responsibility* (Panyarachun, 2004). The then-UN Secretary-General, Kofi Annan (2005), urged UN member-states to embrace R2P as a basis for collective action against genocide, ethnic cleansing and crimes against humanity in his own report, *In Larger Freedom: Towards development, security and human rights for all.* Adopted in September 2005 by the UN General Assembly, the UN World Summit's Outcome Document had a subsection dealing with the responsibility to protect populations from genocide, war crimes, ethnic cleansing and crimes against humanity. Given it has strong international support, the relevant passage deserves to be cited in full:

> Each individual State has the responsibility to protect its populations from genocide, war crimes, ethnic cleansing and crimes against humanity. This responsibility entails the prevention of such crimes, including their incitement, through appropriate and necessary means. We accept that responsibility and will act in accordance with it. The international community should, as appropriate, encourage and help States to exercise this responsibility and support the United Nations in establishing an early warning capability.

> The international community, through the United Nations, also has the responsibility to use appropriate diplomatic, humanitarian and other peaceful means, in accordance with Chapters VI and VIII of the Charter, to help protect populations from genocide, war crimes, ethnic cleansing and crimes against humanity. In this context, we are prepared to take collective action, in a timely and decisive manner, through the Security Council, in accordance with the Charter, including Chapter VII, on a case-by-case basis and in cooperation with relevant regional organizations as appropriate, should peaceful means be inadequate and national authorities manifestly fail to protect their populations from genocide, war crimes, ethnic cleansing and crimes against humanity. We stress the need for the General Assembly to continue consideration of the responsibility to protect populations from genocide, war crimes, ethnic cleansing and crimes against humanity and its

> implications, bearing in mind the principles of the Charter and international law. We also intend to commit ourselves, as necessary and appropriate, to helping States build capacity to protect their populations from genocide, war crimes, ethnic cleansing and crimes against humanity and to assisting those which are under stress before crises and conflicts break out. (United Nations General Assembly, 2005, paras. 138–139)

This text shows that the scope of R2P has narrowed from a very broad range of human-made harms to a particular type of political violence; that is, atrocity crimes. It also signals that the use of armed force would not necessarily be justified in terms of criteria derived from theories of Just War.

Today, there is consensus on R2P's meaning. Firstly, R2P recognises the international community's responsibility not only to react to atrocity crimes, but also to help prevent those atrocities from occurring in the first place, as well as to help rebuild governments, economies and societies in the aftermath of atrocity crime. Secondly, three interrelated presumptions, or so-called pillars, underpin R2P: first, that the state bears primary responsibility for protecting its own population from atrocity crime; second, that the international community is responsible for assisting states to meet these duties; and third, that the UN Security Council is also responsible for taking collective action that protects at-risk populations when the host state fails to provide the necessary measures.

R2P, then, is a concept that can inform the collective use of armed force to counter atrocity crime, without envisaging the creation of new international organisations or the development of new instruments of international law. To assist UN member-states as they build capacity to discharge their collective responsibilities, the UN Secretary-General established two positions, one on the prevention of genocide, the other on R2P. In 2009, the UN Secretary-General also released a report on the UN's implementation of R2P, urging member-states to use the General Assembly as the forum in which to consider a more strategic approach that includes 'strengthening the United Nations early warning capacity . . . [and] bolstering the Office of the Special Adviser on the Prevention of Genocide' (United Nations General Assembly, 2009, p. 29). Without seeking to enlarge the plethora of relevant treaties, R2P similarly relies on existing instruments of human rights law, international humanitarian law and international criminal law.

While the 1648 Treaty of Westphalia gave rise to the state's right to protect its own territory and population from external interference, it also recognised the state's responsibility to protect certain rights held by its citizens. In fact, the origins of human rights can be traced back through the Westphalian settlement, which offered protections to members of religious minorities (Reus-Smit, 2013). In this respect, states bear the primary responsibility to ensure human rights are respected and upheld. The enduring importance of human rights is illustrated in the first paragraph of the Charter of the United Nations (United Nations, 1945):

> *We the peoples* of the united nations determined to save succeeding generations from the scourge of war, which twice in our lifetime has brought untold sorrow to mankind, and to *reaffirm faith in fundamental human rights*, in the *dignity and worth of the human person*, in the *equal rights of men and women* and of nations large and small, and to establish conditions under which justice and respect for the obligations arising from treaties and other sources of international law can be maintained, and to promote social progress and better standards of life in larger freedom . . . (emphasis added).

Drafted in 1948 after the UN Charter became law, the Universal Declaration of Human Rights (United Nations, 2015) is now a cornerstone of human rights doctrine, law and practice, though some claim it is a product of Enlightenment thinking and promulgates an Anglo-American world view. However, the drafters of the declaration had a broad range of religious, cultural, social and political backgrounds and views, which meant the declaration was heavily influenced by rights traditions other than the individualist Anglo-American one (Kaplan, 2018). Here, then, R2P emerged from within the international architecture governing the politics of contemporary world affairs, which is underpinned by a form of collective security among states, as well as a collective responsibility for the protection of human beings from harm, including various forms of political violence.

R2P's roots

The roots of R2P lie in the early 1990s when the ending of the Cold War stimulated hopes for a revitalised UN Security Council (the council had been stymied for much of the Cold War by the veto power held by the five permanent members). Rising to the challenge posed by Saddam Hussein's unlawful attack against Kuwait in 1990, US President George Bush set about building a 'coalition of the willing' that ejected Iraqi armed forces from the small emirate in just 43 days. In his subsequent speech to the UN General Assembly, Bush (1992) proclaimed, enthusiastically, as follows:

> The U.N. was all too often paralyzed by cruel ideological divisions and the struggle to contain Soviet expansion. And today, all that's changed. And the collapse of imperial communism and the end of the cold war breathe new life into the United Nations. It was just one year ago that the world saw this new, invigorated United Nations in action as this Council stood fast against aggression and stood for the sacred principles enshrined in the U.N. Charter. (para. 4)

The Security Council authorised the coalition to use armed force (Resolution 678) in a way that restored the status-quo arrangements within the international order established by the victors of the Second World War (Zolo, 2009), while regulating the conduct of what Gerry Simpson (2004) would describe as an 'outlaw state'.

The 1990s also saw a sharp increase in the outbreak of civil wars (Wallensteen & Sollenberg, 2001). Mary Kaldor (2001) describes these as 'new wars' shaped by the forces of globalisation that intensify interconnectedness across the economic, social and cultural dimensions of international political life, and are increasingly fought over claims to exercise power based on traditional concepts of identity — nationalism, tribalism, ethnicity and religion. These new wars are brutal, targeting civilians for mass killing and forcible resettlement. The UN Security Council responded to some of these wars by authorising peacekeeping operations under Chapter VI of the UN Charter. Typically, these operations supported extant peace agreements and required permission from the host state. Any armed force used by peacekeepers was only for their own self-defence, and not for the defence of the mandate or to protect local civilians found in harm's way.

Despite the deployment of a UN peacekeeping operation, the Rwandan civil war descended into genocide. Beginning in 1990, the civil war in Rwanda was fought for control of the government. The warring parties were divided by social cleavages created by former colonial authorities, and the animosity between Hutu and Tutsi was intensified by the opening of Rwanda's economy to international competition. The death of President Habyarimana in a plane crash on 6 April 1994 sparked a mass killing spree, which was well-planned and meticulously organised by senior members of the Rwandan army and saw Hutu groups murder 900,000 Tutsi and moderate Hutu in about 90 days (Paris, 2004). A fierce nationalism, based on strict distinctions between ethnic identity, lay at the heart of the Rwandan genocide.

The wars of dissolution in the Former Republic of Yugoslavia also provided conditions for atrocity crime, despite the deployment of peacekeepers there. The war, beginning in mid-1991, was fought mostly over who would control the machinery of government following the collapse of the Soviet Union, though

AHO 12.2 WHO IS MOST CULPABLE IN CONFLICT SITUATIONS?

It can be difficult to figure out who is responsible for war crimes and crimes against humanity in the messy arena of conflicts. If we take the 1994 Rwandan Genocide as an example, there are several actors who could be held up for blame. One is Colonel Bagosora, a high-ranking member of the Rwandan armed forces. Another is Omar Serushago, who belonged to the Interahamwe paramilitary units that slaughtered civilians.

A particularly complicated case is that of Major-General Roméo Dallaire, who commanded the United Nations Assistance Mission for Rwanda. His mandate was to supervise the implementation of a peace agreement between the Hutu-led government of Rwanda and the Tutsi-led Rwandan Patriot Front, a non-state armed group. Dallaire was aware that the Rwandan government's armed forces were re-arming and preparing to attack Tutsi civilians. He sent a telegram to his superiors at the United Nations Headquarters in New York, but they replied that he was not authorised to seize the weapons, which had been imported from France and the United Kingdom, among others.

Dallaire was also aware that the government's armed forces were checking identity cards which identified individuals as Hutus or Tutsis. Following the murder of 10 Belgium peacekeepers, Dallaire used his remaining forces to provide a few protected areas where Tutsis were hiding, but his forces did not fight the soldiers who were committing the genocide. They were, in effect, bystanders. The events in Rwanda subsequently led Dallaire to suffer from severe post-traumatic stress and to attempt suicide. He recovered and went on to establish the Dallaire Institute, which rehabilitates child soldiers and works for the rights of children in conflict zones.

To learn more about the Dallaire Institute, scan the QR code.

200   TŪ RANGARANGA

Major-General Roméo Dallaire in Kigali, Rwanda, 1994. RYAN REMIORZ/CP PHOTO

the opening of the Yugoslav economy to the flows of goods, services and currencies from the Global North contributed to deepening socio-economic inequalities that fuelled hostility (Krever, 2013). Nationalism was fused here with ethnic and religious dimensions, giving rise to the hideous practice of 'ethnic cleansing', the forcible removal of Muslims who had resided in Serbian-controlled areas (Paris, 2004). The UN peacekeeping operation created 'safe zones', though the safe zone protecting the inhabitants of Srebrenica was overrun in 1995 by Bosnian-Serb forces who massacred about 8000 military-aged males (Orford, 2003). Like the genocide in Rwanda, the fall of Srebrenica shocked the conscience of humanity, especially as the meagre UN forces on the ground became bystanders to atrocity crimes.

At the close of the millennium, the UN released two important reviews into these tragedies (Annan, 1999a; Annan, 1999b). While painting these episodes as dark chapters in the UN's history, both reports noted that the operational mandates were crafted to keep the peace in times of civil strife but were never designed to confront atrocity crimes; the UN Security Council should have, nevertheless, responded with more assertive measures. Yet neither report settled the vexing question of when the international community should use armed force in the territory of a sovereign state.

NATO's 1999 intervention in Kosovo, without UN Security Council authorisation, brought the controversy to its head. British Prime Minister Tony Blair waxed lyrical on the need to defend cherished values, including human rights, and advance humanity's progress through military means as NATO forces dropped over 25,000 bombs from high-altitude sorties, killing 500 Yugoslav civilians (Orford, 2003).

R2P's application

So far, R2P has been referred to 92 times in UN Security Council Resolutions and 21 times in UN Security Council Presidential Statements — and with respect to 13 situations around the world (Global Centre for the Responsibility to Protect, 2021). In 2011, the UN Security Council used R2P to frame its authorisation of NATO's use of armed force in Libya (Resolution 1973), even though Muammar Gaddafi's use of especially cruel violence against what was, in practice, a rebellion did not approach the gravity of the Rwanda genocide or reach the scale of ethnic cleansing in the Former Republic of Yugoslavia. More than just enforce a no-fly zone to protect civilians, NATO attacked and destroyed Libya's air force, then targeted other elements of Gaddafi's war-making machine, enabling Gaddafi's capture and his killing. R2P's use to justify military action that resulted in regime change has produced a chilling effect for Russia and China, among others. Russia continues to veto resolutions authorising R2P-framed use of force in Syria, for instance. The lack of UN Security Council action on Syria might also reflect President Assad's support among Syrians and other members of the wider international community (Doyle, 2016).

Since R2P is a concept that can inform the collective use of armed force to counter atrocity crime, it represents a radical departure from the highly controversial muscular humanitarian interventions of the 1990s that used armed force to protect human rights in times of war. Nevertheless, the common ways in which the UN Security Council responds to both atrocity crimes and armed conflict, and seeks to protect both humanity's social diversity and human rights, are subject to, and limited by, the same configurations of power informing contemporary world affairs. In other words, the politics informing this use of armed force in international affairs, which largely takes place within international organisations and in accordance with the rule of international law, is still held hostage by the geopolitical concerns of the UN Security Council. As the Syrian case demonstrates, R2P might well be counterproductive in some situations, as it precludes the unauthorised use of armed force by states, or coalitions of states, and requires a high threshold of human suffering before any action is undertaken to discharge the UN Security Council's responsibilities.

Conclusion: Implications for Aotearoa

When the fury of war slips the restraints of international humanitarian law or when governments no longer protect their citizens from human-made harm, but predate on targeted groups instead, atrocity crimes become possible. As demonstrated by the horrors unleashed in Rwanda and Yugoslavia during the 1990s, the intensifying pressures of economic globalisation and the manipulation of identity politics by partisans to civil war can spur on especially cruel forms of violence. This grisly type of political violence, and the global forces informing, shaping and sustaining that violence, should concern, if not disturb, New Zealanders, because it gives succour to the unchecked rule of tooth and claw while reducing the shape and contours of human diversity.

Yet the emergence of R2P as a concept framing the use of armed force in international affairs, and its application or otherwise, also raises important implications for Aotearoa, particularly in relation to the United Nations' efforts to maintain peace and international security. A founding member of the United Nations, Aotearoa has served on the Security Council four times (1954–55, 1966,

1993–94 and 2015–16) and has regularly contributed to UN peacekeeping operations. Aotearoa remains a strong supporter of multilateral diplomacy, especially within international organisations and in accordance with the rule of international law. Moreover, Aotearoa has an array of state responsibilities and international duties relating to human rights, derived from international human rights, humanitarian and criminal law. Yet a commitment to collective security seems at odds with the logic underpinning this country's close defence relationship with the United States, when its armed forces attack, invade and occupy sovereign states (Afghanistan in 2001, Iraq in 2003) and use torture during the so-called War on Terror (US Senate Select Committee on Intelligence, 2014; see also Guild et al., 2018; Sanders, 2018). The government of Aotearoa must fully participate in international organisations and abide by international rules if it is to be recognised as a good international citizen, alongside those individuals who claim global citizenship based upon a notion of a common humanity.

References

Anghie, A. (2004). *Imperialism, Sovereignty and the Making of International Law*. Cambridge University Press.

Annan, K. (1999a). *Report of the Independent Inquiry into the Actions of the United Nations during the 1994 Genocide in Rwanda* (S/1999/1257). www.securitycouncilreport. org/atf/cf/%7B65BFCF9B-6D27-4E9C-8CD3-CF6E4FF96FF9%7D/POC%20S19991257.pdf

Annan, K. (1999b). *Report of the Secretary-General Pursuant to General Assembly Resolution 53/35: The fall of Srebrenica* (A/54/519). https://peacekeeping.un.org/en/report-of-secretary-general-pursuant-to-general-assembly-resolution-5335-fall-of-srebrenica-a54549

Annan, K. (2005). *In Larger Freedom: Towards development, security and human rights for all*. www.un.org/en/events/pastevents/in_larger_freedom.shtml

Bauer, Y. (2001). *Rethinking the Holocaust*. Yale University Press.

Bauman, Z. (1989). *Modernity and the Holocaust*. Cornell University Press.

Blix, H. P. (2000). *Hirohito and the Making of Modern Japan*. HarperCollins.

Bush, G. (1992). Partial text of president's Security Council remarks. www.latimes.com/archives/la-xpm-1992-02-01-mn-1002-story.html

Cassese, A. (2008). *International Criminal Law* (2nd ed.). Oxford University Press.

Doyle, M. W. (2016). The politics of global humanitarianism: R2P before and after Libya. In A. J. Bellamy & T. Dunne (Eds.), *The Oxford Handbook of the Responsibility to Protect* (pp. 673–690). Oxford University Press.

Evans, G. (2008). *The Responsibility to Protect: Ending mass atrocity crimes once and for all*. Brookings Institution Press.

Farrall, J. (2016). The use of UN sanctions to address mass atrocities. In A. J. Bellamy & T. Dunne (Eds.), *The Oxford Handbook of the Responsibility to Protect* (pp. 655–672). Oxford University Press.

Global Centre for the Responsibility to Protect. (2021). *R2P References in United Nations Security Council Resolutions and Presidential Statements*. www.globalr2p.org/resources/un-security-council-resolutions-and-presidential-statements-referencing-r2p

Goldhagen, D. J. (2009). *Worse than War: Genocide, eliminationism and the ongoing assault on humanity*. Little, Brown.

Guild, E., Bigo, D., & Gibney, M. (Eds.). (2018). *Extraordinary Rendition: Addressing the challenges of accountability*. Routledge.

International Commission on Intervention and State Sovereignty. (2001). *The Responsibility to Protect*. www.un.org/en/genocideprevention/key-documents.shtml

Kaldor, M. (2001). *New and Old Wars: Organized violence in a global era*. Polity.

Kaplan, S. D. (2018). *Human Rights in Thick and Thin Societies: Universality without uniformity*. Cambridge University Press.

Kiernan, B. (2007). *Blood and Soil: A world of genocide and extermination from Sparta to Darfur*. Yale University Press.

Krever, T. (2013). International criminal law: An ideology critique. *Leiden Journal of International Law, 26*(3), 701–723. https://doi.org/10.1017/S0922156513000307

Lutz, E. L., & Reiger, C. (Eds.). (2009). *Prosecuting Heads of States*. Cambridge University Press.

Orford, A. (2003). *Reading Humanitarian Intervention: Human rights and the use of force in international law*. Cambridge University Press.

Panyarachun, A. (2004). *A More Secure World: Our shared responsibility*. www.un.org/en/events/pastevents/a_more_secure_world.shtml

Paris, R. (2004). *At War's End: Building peace after civil conflict*. Cambridge University Press.

Reus-Smit, C. (2013). *Individual Rights and the Making of the International System*. Cambridge University Press.

Robertson, G. (1999). *Crimes Against Humanity: The struggle for global justice*. Penguin.

Sanders, R. (2018). *Plausible Legality: Legal culture and political imperative in the global war on terror*. Oxford University Press.

Schabas, W. (2012). *Unimaginable Atrocities: Justice, politics and rights at war crimes tribunals*. Oxford University Press.

Shawcross, W. (2002). Lessons of Cambodia. In N. Mills & K. Brunner (Eds.), *The New Killing Fields: Massacre and the politics of intervention* (pp. 37–49). Basic Books.

Short, P. (2004). *Pol Pot: The history of a nightmare*. John Murray.

Simpson, G. (2004). *Great Powers and Outlaw States: Unequal sovereigns in the international legal order*. Cambridge University Press.

Slye, R. C., & Shaack, B. V. (2009). *International Criminal Law: The essentials*. Aspen Publishers.

Tatz, C. (2003). *With Intent to Destroy: Reflecting on genocide*. Verso.

United Nations. (1945). *Charter of the United Nations and Statute of the International Court of Justice*. https://treaties.un.org/doc/publication/ctc/uncharter.pdf

United Nations. (2015). *Universal Declaration of Human Rights*. www.un.org/en/udhrbook/pdf/udhr_booklet_en_web.pdf

United Nations General Assembly. (2005). *UN World Summit's Outcome Document*.

United Nations General Assembly. (2009). *Implementing the Responsibility to Protect: Report of the Secretary-General (A/63/677)*.

United Nations Security Council. (2006). *Resolution 1653 (S/RES/1653)*.

United Nations Security Council. (2011). *Resolution 1975 (S/RES/1975)*.

United States Senate Select Committee on Intelligence. (2014). *Study of the Central Intelligence Agency's Detention and Interrogation Program: Executive summary*.

Wallensteen, P., & Sollenberg, M. (2001). Armed conflict, 1989–2000. *Journal of Peace Research, 38*(5), 629–644. https://doi.org/10.1177/0022343301038005008

Williams, P. D. (2016). The R2P, protection of civilians, and UN peacekeeping operations. In A. J. Bellamy & T. Dunne (Eds.), *The Oxford Handbook of the Responsibility to Protect* (pp. 524–544). Oxford University Press.

Wilson, P. H. (2009). *The Thirty Years War: Europe's tragedy*. Belknap Press of Harvard University Press.

Zolo, D. (2009). *Victors' Justice: From Nuremberg to Baghdad*. Verso.

13.
Conflict commodities, rights and responsibilities

Vanessa Bramwell, Glenn Banks, Nicholas Holm & Sy Taffel

Introduction

In this chapter, we invite you to reflect on the connections and processes that shape the ways in which your material (and virtual and social) life is entangled in numerous other usually unseen worlds and conflicts. What might this mean for your rights and responsibilities as global citizens, in parallel with the rights and responsibilities of other key actors, such as corporations, NGOs and nation-states?

We explore the complexity of commodities, conflict, rights and responsibilities through three main themes. The chapter first introduces the idea of 'commodity thinking' as a central tenet of the capitalist society in which we live. This opens up the possibility of exploring alternative ways of understanding our relationship with the 'things' that our lives are surrounded by and dependent upon. The notion of political ecology is then introduced to think through connections between our lives and those of people involved in other stages of the production of the goods that we encounter every day, such as mobile technologies. In the third section, we explore how an understanding of the ways in which matter and energy are moved and transformed through multiple systems in contemporary commodity production can produce novel approaches to the transformation of those systems.

Throughout the chapter, we ask you to reflect on the extent to which national regulation, individual consumer decisions and power, and global forms of power (corporate and supranational regulation) affect commodity cycles. We examine the role these forces play in mediating the relations of consumption and production that define our relationships to the commodities that are so central to our modern lives.

Commodity thinking

When we encounter a product in a store — be it online or in real life — most of us do not stop to think about how it got there. Instead, we tend to be more concerned with things like price, features and style. What can it do for us? How will it improve our lives? Perhaps the most emblematic product in this regard is the Apple iPhone. Apple stores are the pinnacle of retail minimalism: all white surfaces and smooth teak. They can seem like science fiction spaces, from which consumable objects materialise fully formed from behind the front counter. In this sense, Apple stores are physical extensions of online shopping — a process where, with a few taps and swipes of a finger, we can conjure up almost any good we can imagine to be delivered (hopefully) efficiently to our front door. Such ways of encountering products do not encourage us to think about where they come from, or the ways in which their cycles of production may be connected to rights and responsibilities.

One way of referring to this orientation towards products and consumption is 'commodity thinking'. Commodity is a term that describes not just a certain type of object, but a certain way of relating to objects that favours relationships of the market — of buying and selling — over an understanding of how and why it was made and how it got to you (Jhally, 2006; Marx, 2000). Given that we inhabit a capitalist society, where we meet most of our basic needs and wants through a market, the overwhelming quantity of products, services and ideas that we encounter function as commodities. When we identify an object as a commodity, we are acknowledging that we tend to think about it in terms of how we encounter it in a shop (online or in 'real life'), rather than as something that was made from raw materials. The idea of the commodity is, therefore, a spur to remember that most of the things that surround us come from somewhere else, and to begin to learn about what that means. Behind the familiar appearance of commodities, there lurk surprising stories and complicated networks of economic, ecological and political connections that usually remain hidden from our view. Consequently, the impact of these networks on the rights of others also remains obscured.

When we encounter a commodity, most of what we know and feel about it is a result of various levels of marketing and advertising. In a technical sense, these can be referred to as 'relations of consumption': a set of socially shared beliefs about what a commodity says about us as its (potential) owner, and the social and cultural meanings that are inscribed upon that object (Holm, 2017). For example, if you have ever seen an Apple ad, you know that buying an iPhone tells the world that you are a sophisticated, hip, creative person (congratulations!). These meanings are primarily created by advertising messages, which attribute feelings, emotions, narratives, images and aspirations to the wealth of products around us. Everything — from phones to breakfast cereal, and from beverage of choice to preferred bank — apparently says something about you (Goldman & Papson, 2006).

What these 'relations of consumption' prevent us from thinking about are the 'relations of production'. The 'relations of production' are not shared dreams, though: they are the complicated economic and political systems that shape our world. For example, when you buy milk at the supermarket, what you know about it is a result of how it is displayed and positioned in the store, along with how it has been advertised in ways that seek to construct a certain set of values and ideas to associate with it. A bottle of milk in a supermarket provides little indication of where it has come from; for all intents and purposes, we encounter it as if it emerged out of thin air.

This is a commodity understanding of milk. What this leaves out, however, is any sense of the conditions of production of the milk. This involves not only the cows, but also the farmers, their relationship to their commercial context through Fonterra say, as well as the transit costs, the supermarket structure and employees, and, even more broadly, the climactic conditions that produced the rain that produced the grass that fed the cows that made the milk (not to mention the plastic bottle itself!). All this is absent when we encounter a commodity. So, if we want to understand our connection to the world around us, we need to start unpacking the different relations of people, money and materials that go into producing a given commodity.

And milk is a relatively straightforward example. What happens when we turn our attention to something more complicated, like a smartphone? Someone made your phone, someone dug up the minerals inside it, and someone crewed the ship that transported the components around the world. The story of your phone connects you to all those people, often in ways that are not always as fun as the advertising suggests. Advertising and commodity thinking distracts us from considering how products are made by people (Lefebvre, 2008). In fact, it turns out that even before the marketing messages, most commodities already had meanings and histories that connect us to hundreds, if not thousands, of people around the world. However, whereas the 'relations of consumption' tend to focus on good times, the 'relations of production' are often structured by different forms of conflict. On one level, this is the structural conflict between those whose living conditions make it seem undesirable to work in an iPhone factory, versus those shareholders and managers who reap massive profits from their labour. These conflicts are inseparable from the ethical problem of human rights protection. Commodities may be sold in localities in which a minimum standard of human rights protection is considered a given, but they may be produced in places where labour rights, for example, are only minimally respected. On a deeper level, then, we can discover how our smartphones link us to more immediate ecological and political conflicts.

The political ecology of extraction

The point of extraction of commodities is often also the starting point for examination of the effects of our material usage. However, the distance of our own lives in Aotearoa from the origins of many source products complicates considerations of responsibility for these effects. There are approximately 60 minerals that are used in the production of a smartphone (it depends on the make and model) that all come from somewhere. Many of the minerals have a limited or tightly defined geographical distribution. Tantalum, for example, is found only in a small number of countries, and the largest, most accessible, resource is in Central Africa, with the Democratic Republic of the Congo (DRC) and Rwanda the source of around 70 per cent of global supply in 2014 (Bleiwas et al., 2015). Nickel is another — in our region, New Caledonia is the fifth largest producer and around 10 per cent of world nickel reserves are located there (Plaza-Toledo, 2016).

In this context, the *political ecology* of the mineral access and extraction is critical. A political ecology lens forces us to recognise that the extraction of minerals is not simple or neutral, and that the impacts of mineral extraction interact with the pre-existing social, political, cultural and economic conditions in various places. In the context of the DRC, the tantalum (in the form of a raw mineral sand known as coltan) has fed a massive, destructive and brutal civil conflict over the past three decades.

The impact of said conflict is acknowledged as severe in the international humanitarian community, which uses internationally acknowledged human rights instruments such as the Universal Declaration of Human Rights (UDHR) (United Nations, 1948) and Convention on the Rights of the Child (CRC, 1989) as benchmarks for rights protections. The most basic rights included in the UDHR are heavily impacted by conflict. For example, Article 3 — the right to 'life, liberty and security of person' — is impacted for obvious reasons by warfare, and Article 4 — the right not to be held in 'slavery or servitude' — is impacted by forced recruitment by armed forces.

Commodity conflict adds extra complexities to these impacts. One may also technically be held in 'slavery or servitude' if one is extracting minerals from a mine, for example, without any or adequate pay; and may also be at risk of loss of life in a dangerous forced labour environment. Children are recruited for work in commodity conflict areas, which contravenes rights laid out in the CRC, including Article 32 prohibiting unregulated child labour. Reliable estimates put the casualties of this conflict in DRC — overwhelmingly civilian — at up to 6 million people (DR Congo country profile, 2021). Revenues from the sale of tantalum have provided the resources for the two sides (and forces from neighbouring countries) to obtain the supplies of weaponry necessary to keep the deadly conflict going for as long as it has. And, although the civil conflict was sparked by other historical factors internal to the country, control over the eastern DRC, rich in coltan, cobalt and other minerals, is a primary driver of the current fighting. In this sense, it is clear how commodity conflict, fuelled in places by resource extraction, has an undeniable impact on human rights.

To divert from mineral commodities for a moment, and return to our daily glass of milk, agriculture is increasingly seen as another form of extractive industry. Agricultural production not only depends on a range of extensive and intensive inputs, but it also *extracts*— from soils and water primarily. The extensive literature on the effects of over-extraction of agriculture cites increasing desertification of grasslands in Africa, infertile soils in North America and the effective destruction of the Murray–Darling River in Australia. While we have already examined the rights impacts of conflict in extractive industries, let us also think about rights impacts of things like desertification — ecological impacts. These impacts may certainly lead to conflict as resources become scarcer, but even before that point there will be impacts on access to food, clean water and shelter; and on access to income (which may, in turn, lead to exploitation).

Significant cultural sites may even disappear, which has impacts on the rights of Indigenous peoples. The United Nations Declaration on the Rights of Indigenous Peoples outlines certain rights that require access to these sites. Article 3 preserves the right of Indigenous peoples to self-determination, including economic self-determination; the loss of traditional cultural sites can impact ancient heritages of food-gathering. Article 10 protects Indigenous peoples from being relocated without consent and appropriate recompense. The question of who should be responsible for such recompense is a question of responsibilities. Even in Aotearoa, the dairy industry is under increasing scrutiny for its dual impacts on water — over-extraction in places, and contamination and pollution of waterways in others (Joy, 2015, 2019). This has complex impacts on the rights of Māori as Indigenous people of Aotearoa. The links here between commodities, political ecology and conflict (environmental and political) are closer to home, but rarely expressed in these terms (and it is worthwhile reflecting on why this is the case).

Some raw materials feed more 'luxury' forms of consumption. 'Blood diamonds' — a mineral that has become embedded in popular culture through a Hollywood movie of the same name — became the subject of campaigns that exposed the links between high-street jewellery stores and forced labour and child soldiers in parts of southern Africa. Public pressure from consumers in the West led to the development of protocols around traceability within the industry, and to changes in corporate behaviour in relation to their activities. This became something of a model for thinking about how to drive change in commodity extraction.

The effects of mining for other minerals — the copper and gold that is also used in smartphones, along with myriad other uses that infuse our daily lives — can have many different social, economic and environmental effects in other places, depending on the geography, history and nature of the mineral itself. Large-scale copper and gold mining in various parts of the world — from Papua New Guinea to Colombia — has had massive detrimental environmental and social effects on local communities, and even on nation-states (Banks, 2006). A key point to make is that *context* — people, place, history and geography — is centrally important in shaping the effects of minerals extraction. Mining of the same minerals in different settings does not necessarily produce the same effects or conflicts.

One of the key factors that shapes the outcomes of mining in a particular place is the institutional and regulatory setting of the country. Those countries with clear legislation, limited corruption and effective regulatory agencies tend to be able to leverage positive outcomes from mining — economic growth, improvements in physical and social infrastructure, and broad-based improvements across society — all with more constrained and better managed social and environmental effects (Christensen et al., 2020). Others, such as the DRC, along with some of our Pacific neighbours, such as Papua New Guinea, have not had the benefit of this sort of institutional and governance setting. In these locations, conflict can be generated or intensified, and governance undermined, by the revenues that minerals generate. This means that rather than being 'blessed' by a bounty of natural resources, communities and countries are actually 'resource cursed', as the literature refers to it, by violence, corruption and poor social and economic outcomes (Mahdavi, 2019; Ross, 1999).

In these debates, the *political* in the political economy framework comes to the fore, and it brings home the ways in which there are deliberately constructed and deeply embedded structures that shape and, in large part, determine the forms of effect of extraction and commodity cultures that we are part of. The mineral extraction — like other forms of 'extraction' — that fuels the commodity chains that make the devices that allow you to craft lifestyles and forms of self-expression and identity, certainly does not always benefit all the people whose lives form part of the links along the 'chain', and raises questions of whose responsibility it may be to remedy these situations.

Life cycles and infrastructure

Another way of thinking ecologically about the relations of production involves mapping how matter and energy are moved and transformed through multiple systems that are necessary for them to be present and functional as commodities. Ecology here has a slightly different definition to the colloquial use of being analogous to an environment — a term which is etymologically derived from the French word *environ*, meaning to surround or encircle, which gestures towards the non-human systems that surround human society. Unlike biology, which, as the science of life, focuses on organisms at molecular, cellular, chemical and evolutionary levels, ecology, whose literal translation is the science of the household, examines the relationships between organisms or, put another way, how matter and energy circulate through ecosystems. Ecology, then, is not about things in or by themselves, but about the ways that things are always inherently interconnected and relate to one another.

Political ecology emphasises that many of these relationships are affected or structured by human activities, which means that they are also inherently political (Robbins, 2011). For example, consider the circulation of nitrogen that is extracted from the atmosphere using the Haber-Bosch process (Erisman et al., 2008). This nitrogen is then employed in fertilisers and used in vast quantities to grow grass in Aotearoa, which is eaten by cows, who subsequently excrete the excess nitrogen, a significant volume of which then enters waterways and contributes to algal blooms that kill the native fish in those waterways (Foote et al., 2015). This series of relationships is in no way inevitable and is not politically neutral. Some entities, such as the agribusiness corporations selling the fertiliser, and the farmers who own the cows, benefit, while other entities are harmed, such as the dead fish or the communities who can no longer fish or swim in their polluted rivers.

Returning to the example of Apple's iPhone, making two types of life cycles visible helps to get a sense of the enormously complex web of relationships and decisions that surround contemporary digital devices. The first of these is the life cycle of the device itself. While the previous section outlined some of the key issues and conflicts that surround the extraction of specific materials from specific places, this is only the first step in producing a smartphone. While we might imagine mines to produce the specific materials that are needed, such as silicon, copper, aluminium or tantalum, extracted ores are rarely a single substance. Instead, elements exist entangled with one another. To be useable for high-performance contemporary microelectronics, another form of extraction must occur to separate and purify materials (Starosielski, 2016). To give you an idea of the level of purity required for digital devices, consider the silicon used in microprocessors. This requires 'nine nines' purity (99.999999999 per cent), meaning that for every billion atoms of silicon, one non-silicon atom is acceptable (Vince, 2018). Achieving such an elevated level of purity typically requires a series of energy-intensive industrial processes that often involve toxic chemicals or produce toxic waste.

After mining and refinement, materials are transformed through a further series of industrial processes into components, which are eventually manufactured into devices. Today, this manufacturing predominantly occurs within gargantuan factories located in China and other parts of Southeast Asia, where wages are low and environmental and labour rights regulation is lax. Until this work was outsourced as part of the wave of neoliberal globalisation during the 1980s, microprocessor fabrication largely occurred within Silicon Valley, the area now famous for housing the corporate headquarters of multibillion-dollar tech corporations such as Apple, Google and Facebook, but whose name references the silicon chips that used to be produced there.

The environmental legacy of this industrial activity is that Silicon Valley has the United States's highest concentration of severely polluted locations, which the Environmental Protection Agency has designated as 'Superfund' sites (Gabrys, 2013), largely because of highly toxic chemicals used in microprocessor manufacture seeping out of underground storage tanks. As with many other elements of the digital supply chain, these environmental harms now largely take place outside the Global North. While this does bring employment opportunities to workers in the Global South, there is a steady stream of stories detailing how lax health and safety regulations have led to microelectronics workers being poisoned (Barboza, 2011; Branigan, 2010; France-Presse, 2014). Additionally, the extremely long hours, compulsory overtime, strict disciplinary regime and poor

AHO 13.1 THE DODD-FRANK ACT

The Dodd-Frank Act (DFA), signed into being by United States (US) President Barack Obama in 2010, sought to make financial institutions on Wall Street more accountable for their actions and investments. 'Dodd-Frank', as it became known, resulted from the 2008 financial crisis that nearly broke the global financial system, and was supposed to introduce stricter government regulation and oversight. It had a significant impact on all aspects of the US financial system, as well as consequences for many financial institutions outside the US.

Section 1502 of the DFA deals specifically with 'conflict minerals', that is, minerals mined in the conflict zone of the Democratic Republic of the Congo. It requires US companies to find out and disclose whether their finances or products are associated with conflict minerals. This affects not only US companies, but also the supply chains of non-US entities, as most mineral merchants have US clients or financial links.

These US requirements have had a ripple effect throughout the world and forced global institutions to develop their own guidelines for conflict minerals to meet US reporting requirements. The OECD, for example, enacted the 'Due Diligence Guidelines', which are 'recommendations for global responsible supply chains of minerals to help companies respect human rights and avoid contributing to conflict through their mineral or metal purchasing decisions and practices' (OECD, 2011). Elements of the DFA were weakened under the Trump Administration, but it still sets a precedent for tracing and declaring conflict minerals.

Reference

OECD. (2011). OECD work on responsible mineral supply chains and the U.S. Dodd-Frank Act. www.oecd.org/daf/inv/mne/OECD-Guidance-and-Dodd-Frank-Act.pdf

Gold miners near Iga Barrière, Democratic Republic of the Congo. ALAMY

living conditions for workers have seen them described as iSlaves (Qiu, 2017). These conditions were highlighted by a spate of suicides among microelectronics workers who produce iPhones and other digital devices at the Foxconn-owned factory in Shenzhen during 2010.

The average duration a smartphone remains in use is just three years (Ercan et al., 2016). After this, their lithium-ion batteries are usually significantly degraded, many corporations stop providing software updates for operating systems and some brands deliberately reduce the performance of old devices, all of which prompt consumers to purchase replacements (Vonk, 2018). While we often think of waste as being inert and something that goes 'away' (or, more precisely, goes away from us), electronic waste continues to have a range of impacts on the environments in which it accumulates and on the workers who reclaim valuable materials, such as copper and gold from old digital devices in places such as Guiyu, China and Agbogbloshie, Ghana. When environmental NGOs and academics have examined these places, they have found children with elevated levels of toxicants such as lead and bisphenol A in their blood and significant DNA damage (Guo et al., 2014; Liu et al., 2009; Zhang et al., 2020).

Every step of the complex process that produces iPhones is laden with these conflicts in which certain parties benefit and others are harmed. The corporations who produce devices typically outsource manufacturing, mining, refining and all the logistics that move matter between these stages of production. Their priority is driving down costs to increase profit margins, and those reductions in costs also benefit the consumers who purchase iPhones. On the other hand, reducing costs often means reducing wages that are paid to workers throughout the supply chain, increasing health and safety risks to workers and externalising costs by polluting environments.

Considering the life cycle of an iPhone demonstrates a range of conflicts that primarily take place far from Aotearoa. However, solely focusing on the life cycle of the device in some ways repeats the issue of commodity fetishism; it effectively severs the relationships between the device and the socio-technical infrastructures it is functionally dependent upon (Taffel, 2019). Alongside considering the life cycle of the device itself, a political ecology of an iPhone requires the infrastructural relationships that allow the device to function to be made visible. Unlike the glamorous technologies that have enormous sums spent on advertising campaigns, infrastructure tends to be rather boring. It is the collection of back-end hardware, software, protocols and standards that are designed not to be visible or thought about. However, as science and technology studies scholar Susan Leigh-Star (1999, p. 377) argues, 'Study an information system and neglect its standards, wires, and settings, and you miss equally essential aspects of aesthetics, justice, and change.'

By itself, an iPhone cannot fulfil most of the activities we associate with it. Without a connection to a cellular network, you could not make calls or send text messages. Without a Wi-Fi or 3/4/5G Internet connection, you would not be able to browse or search the web, use social media, stream audio or video, or access an app store. This connection is what enables a huge amount of the functionality we associate with smartphones. It wirelessly connects our devices to the vast (mainly wired) network infrastructure of the Internet, which contains millions of kilometres of undersea and underground fibre-optic cable, alongside gigantic data centres which store exabytes of data and perform most of the heavy computational processing that enables contemporary 'AI' systems. Without a network of global-positioning satellites, you would not be able to access locational services, such as Google Maps, or locative games like Pokémon Go. Much of this infrastructure has similar social, environmental and labour justice issues to an iPhone in terms of extracting raw materials, refining and manufacturing those materials, and the waste that this generates. Further problems include the enormous volume of energy and water that is required to operate a data centre (Hogan, 2015). Indeed, it is estimated that 7 per cent of global electricity and 5 per cent of global greenhouse gases (GHGs) are associated with digital technology, and that this is likely to double by 2030 (Andrae, 2020), making digital technology a major contributor to climate change.

Considering the life cycle of a device and the infrastructure that is required for a device to function helps us begin to grasp the enormity of the planetary assemblage that is required for an iPhone to function. Of course, it is not just matter and energy that are needed. The sum of thousands of years of human knowledge of how to work with materials and the labour of thousands of humans, from artisanal tin miners in DRC to Silicon Valley CEOs, are also key components. While a detailed examination of these issues would require hundreds of pages of text, hopefully this brief introduction to thinking about life cycles and infrastructure provides a way of seeing and thinking about the multiplicity of relations that surround a smartphone, and how a range of conflicts surrounding class, race, gender and environment present significant social and environmental justice issues.

Conclusions and ways forward

To conclude, we have travelled from the notion of commodity that underpins the materially focused neoliberal society of which we are a part, to the complex intermediate steps that transform mineral resources into these desired objects, and finally to their origins — the complex and often socially violent, environmentally

AHO 13.2 THE COCHABAMBA WATER WAR

Is water a commodity? In 2021, the United Nations' special rapporteur on the human rights to safe drinking water and sanitation, Pedro Arrojo-Agudo, was clear:

'You can't put a value on water as you do with other traded commodities. Water belongs to everyone and is a public good. It is closely tied to all of our lives and livelihoods, and is an essential component to public health.' (Anselm, 2021, paras. 16–17)

However, water is increasingly being traded as a commodity, and this is leading to a growing number of conflicts. An example of this was the so-called 'Cochabamba Water War' that took place in Bolivia in 2000. Cochabamba is a city of around 800,000. In the late 1990s, the city's water supply was privatised and sold to a multinational consortium led by US company, Bechtel. As a result, water prices in the city skyrocketed. When citizens came out in large groups to protest, the Bolivian government declared martial law and sent in the military. Victor Daza, a young student, was killed in the melee, which came to be called the guerra del agua — the Water War. This enraged Bolivians even more and led to bigger and bigger protests.

Bolivia had been forced into selling their public services to private investors to obtain loans and funding from the World Bank, placing limitations on the rights of Bolivians to their own clean water. The 'water warriors' argued that water is a human right before it is a consumable commodity to be sold to the highest bidder. Ultimately, the protestors won, with the private firm withdrawing from the country. The fight for drinkable water is not just playing out in Bolivia. China and parts of south-western United States, for example, are experiencing severe droughts due to climate change and overuse of water sources for agriculture, which are making water an increasingly rare and precious entity.

Reference

Anselm, M. (2021, January 18). Water becomes a commodity. *New Zealand Herald*. www.nzherald.co.nz/business/analysis-water-becomes-a-commodity/XH5DP4NOFGZBRWNTNIRFPTXZPA

'The agony of water'. Poster from the International Water Fair commemorating the ten-year anniversary of the Cochabamba Water War. KRIS KRÜG

destructive and politically fraught processes tied up with mineral extraction. Alongside making the social and environmental costs associated with the production, circulation and disposal of commodities visible, there are a range of strategies that can, and have been, enacted to mitigate, reduce or alleviate these issues with regard to the case study of smartphones and microelectronics. These include actions that have been taken by governments, by civil society, by NGOs, and by consumers and corporations, such as the Basel Convention, the Eropean Union's RoHS directive, the Dodd-Frank legislation, New Zealand's E-Day initiative, the Dell Computer Takeback Campaign, the 'Fairphone', and Apple's code of corporate conduct.

Viewing commodities through the lens of rights and responsibilities, we can distinguish different 'scales' of action. Individual rights may be severely impacted by resource extraction and commodity life cycles, but so might the collective rights of Indigenous peoples. Given increasing regulatory acknowledgement in Aotearoa about the spiritual and cultural importance of awa (rivers) to tangata whenua, for example, what implications might things like corporate water-bottling rights have for Māori rights to cultural self-determination?

Responsibilities, too, can be conceptualised at the different scales of individual and collective. Consumer power is enormously influential; while corporations are always going to be thinking of their customer base as collective, all of us can make purchasing decisions as individuals that are informed by an awareness of commodity life cycles. Our support or distaste for certain products — expressed through, for example, reviews left online or product endorsements by social media influencers — can sometimes have a significant impact on corporate decisions in terms of adjusting these life cycles.

However, there are also collective responsibilities to address these issues from the other end, involving 'elite' actors like states and global governance organisations. This was the aim in creating mechanisms like the Dodd-Frank Wall Street Reform and Consumer Protection Act (which was altered and 'softened' under the Trump Administration in 2018). In January of 2021, the Conflict Minerals Regulation came into effect in the EU — this aims to heavily regulate the trade of tin, tantalum, tungsten and gold (minerals associated with the kind of resource extraction conflict described earlier in this chapter). The utility of this regulation will need to be assessed over time. However, it is noteworthy that such an example of regional, supranational responsibility-taking has succeeded, despite the potential problems with political will that industry regulation can face. It is also encouraging to see corporations like Apple publicising a corporate code of conduct. This may have the function of engendering a new influence mechanism on other corporations.

The collective responsibility of global civil society — NGOs — is a tricky thing to define, as NGOs all work within budgetary and access constraints and generally do not contribute to the problem of commodity harm themselves. However, part of exercising our individual responsibility may be donating funds to such organisations, in which case we would have an expectation of accountability. Intergovernmental organisations like the United Nations and World Health Organization, which generally enjoy a precedent of legitimacy as authorities, would surely be considered responsible for directing efforts at consensus-based change in commodity life cycles to reduce harm.

We hope that this exploration of conflict commodities, their life cycles, and their association with rights and responsibilities has provided an opportunity to think more deeply about their relevance to global citizenship. While the enormity of this problem can threaten to be overwhelming, it is important to remember the various scales of action available to those who recognise the responsibility, as global citizens, to consider rights. The crucial point is to engage critically with these issues, and to think about your own position on these complex global challenges.

References

Andrae, A. S. (2020). Hypotheses for primary energy use, electricity use and CO_2 emissions of global computing and its shares of the total between 2020 and 2030. *WSEAS Transactions on Power Systems, 15*, 50–59. https://doi.org/10.37394/232016.2020.15.6

Banks, G. (2006). Mining, social change and corporate social responsibility: Drawing lines in the Papua New Guinea mud. In S. Firth (Ed.), *Globalization and Governance in the Pacific Islands* (pp. 259–274). ANU Press.

Barboza, D. (2011, February 22). Workers sickened at Apple supplier in China. *The New York Times.* www.nytimes.com/2011/02/23/technology/23apple.html

Bleiwas D. I., Papp, J. F., & Yager, T. R. (2015). *Shift in Global Tantalum Mine Production, 2000–2014* (Fact Sheet 2015–3097). USGS. https://doi.org/10.3133/fs20153079

Branigan, T. (2010, May 7). Chinese workers link sickness to N-Hexane and Apple iPhone screens. *The Guardian.* www.theguardian.com/world/2010/may/07/chinese-workers-sickness-hexane-apple-iphone

Christensen, H. B., Maffett, M., & Rauter, T. (2020). Reversing the resource curse: Foreign corruption regulation and economic development. https://doi.org/10.2139/ssrn.3712693

Convention on the Rights of the Child. (1989). Treaty no. 27531. *United Nations Treaty Series,* 1577, pp. 3178. https://treaties.un.org/doc/Treaties/1990/09/19900902%2003-14%20AM/Ch_IV_11p.pdf.

DR Congo country profile. (2021, February 4). *BBC News.* www.bbc.com/news/world-africa-13283212

Ercan, M., Malmodin, J., Bergmark, P., Kimfalk, E., & Nilsson, E. (2016). Life Cycle Assessment of a Smartphone. Proceedings of the ICT for Sustainability, Amsterdam, The Netherlands. https://doi.org/10.2991/ict4s-16.2016.15

Erisman, J. W., Sutton, M. A., Galloway, J., Klimont, Z., & Winiwarter, W. (2008). How a century of ammonia synthesis changed the world. *Nature Geoscience, 1*(10), 636–639. https://doi.org/10.1038/ngeo325

Foote, K. J., Joy, M. K., & Death, R. G. (2015). New Zealand dairy farming: Milking our environment for all its worth. *Environmental Management, 56*(3), 709–720. https://doi.org/10.1007/s00267-015-0517-x

France-Presse, A. (2014, December 19). Apple under fire again for working conditions at Chinese factories. *The Guardian.* www.theguardian.com/technology/2014/dec/19/apple-under-fire-again-for-working-conditions-at-chinese-factories

Gabrys, J. (2013). *Digital Rubbish: A natural history of electronics.* University of Michigan Press.

Goldman, R., & Papson, P. (2006). Capital's brandscapes. *Journal of Consumer Culture, 6*(3), 327–353. https://doi.org/10.1177/1469540506068682

Guo, P., Xu. X., Huang, B., Sun, D., Zhang, J., Chen, X., Zhang, Q., Huo, X., & Hao, Y. (2014). Blood lead levels and associated factors among children in Guiyu of China: A population-based study. *PLoS ONE, 9*(8) https://doi.org/10.1371/journal.pone.0105470

Hogan, M. (2015). Facebook data storage centers as the archive's underbelly. *Television and New Media, 16*(1), 3–18. https://doi.org/10.1177/1527476413509415

Holm, N. (2017). *Advertising and Consumer Society: A critical introduction.* Palgrave Macmillan.

Jhally, S. (2006). *The Spectacle of Accumulation.* Peter Lang.

Joy, M. (2015). *Polluted Inheritance: New Zealand's freshwater crisis.* Bridget Williams Books.

Joy, M. (2019). The environmental and human health impacts of dairy intensification: A case study — Canterbury, *Vetscript,* September. https://openaccess.wgtn.ac.nz/articles/journal_contribution/The_environmental_and_human_health_impacts_of_dairy_intensification_a_Canterbury_case_study/12469994/files/23092580.pdf

Lefebvre, H. [1947] (2008). *Critique of Everyday Life: Volume one.* Trans. John Moore. Verso.

Leigh-Star, S. (1999). The ethnography of infrastructure. *American Behavioral Scientist, 43*(3), 377–391. https://doi.org/10.1177/00027649921955326

Liu, Q., Cao. J., Li, K. Q., Miao, X. H., Li, G., Fan, F. Y., & Zhao, Y. C. (2009). Chromosomal aberrations and DNA damage in human populations exposed to the processing of electronics waste. *Environmental Science and Pollution Research, 16*(3), 329–338. https://doi.org/10.1007/s11356-008-0087-z

Mahdavi, P. (2019). Institutions and the 'resource curse': Evidence from cases of oil-related bribery. *Comparative Political Studies, 53*(1), 3–39. https://doi.org/10.1177/0010414019830727

Marx. K. (2000). The fetishism of the commodity and its secret. In J. B. Schor & D. B. Holt (Eds.), *The Consumer Society Reader.* New Press. (Original work published 1867)

Plaza-Toledo, M. (2016). The mineral industry of New Caledonia. *USGS 2016 Minerals Yearbook.* https://prd-wret.s3-us-west-2.amazonaws.com/assets/palladium/production/atoms/files/myb3-2016-nc.pdf

Qiu, J. L. (2017). *Goodbye iSlave: A manifesto for digital abolition.* University of Illinois Press.

Robbins, P. (2011). *Political Ecology: A critical introduction.* Blackwell.

Ross, M. L. (1999). The political economy of the resource curse. *World Politics, 51*(2), 297–322. https://doi.org/10.1017/S0043887100008200

Starosielski, N. (2016). Thermocultures of geological media. *Cultural Politics, 12*(3), 293–309. https://doi.org/10.1215/17432197-3648858

Taffel, S. (2019). *Digital Media Ecologies.* Bloomsbury.

United Nations. (1948). Universal Declaration of Human Rights. www.un.org/en/about-us/universal-declaration-of-human-rights

Vince, B. (2018). *The World in a Grain: The story of sand and how it transformed civilization.* Riverhead Books.

Vonk, L. (2018). Paying attention to waste: Apple's circular economy. *Continuum, 32*(6), 745–757. https://doi.org/10.1080/10304312.2018.1525923

Zhang, B., He, Y., Zhu, H., Huang, X., Bai, X., Kannan, K., & Zhang, T. (2020). Concentrations of bisphenol A and its alternatives in paired maternal–fetal urine, serum and amniotic fluid from an e-waste dismantling area in China. *Environment International, 136.* https://doi.org/10.1016/j.envint.2019.105407

14.
Arts and conflict
Banksy, art and Palestinian solidarity

Rand Hazou

Introduction

In August 2005, the United Kingdom (UK) street artist Banksy travelled to the occupied Palestinian territories where he created nine stencilled images on the Israeli Separation Wall that divides Israel from the West Bank.[1] One of Banksy's nine images, the 'Floating Balloon Girl', provides satirical and subversive commentary on how the Israeli barrier violates the rights of Palestinians, such as their freedom of movement. However, Banksy also reported that while he was painting the image, an old Palestinian man said his painting made the wall look beautiful. When Banksy thanked the Palestinian man for what he took to be a compliment, he was told: 'We don't want it to be beautiful, we hate this wall. Go home' (Jones, 2005, para. 10). For this Palestinian man, Banksy's work may have inadvertently made the Separation Wall an object of beauty, rather than reinforcing its ugly reality as an instrument of control that violates Palestinian rights. By making the wall less of an eyesore and more aesthetically appealing, the 'Floating Balloon Girl' might have been perceived as normalising, rather than resisting, the Israeli occupation.

---

1   Banksy's engagement with Palestine for over a decade has also sparked a burgeoning of street art in the wider Middle East and North Africa. Sabrina DeTurk (2015) argues that the 'Banksy Effect' and the influence of the artist prompted the emergence of street art as a means of popular political expression during the revolution in Egypt and Tahrir Square.

I begin with reference to this Banksy artwork because it is a good example of the kind of complexities that can emerge when we consider arts interventions within sites of conflict, the role of the arts in highlighting rights abuses, and the responsibilities of artists as global citizens. As outlined in this book, global citizenship articulates a sense of belonging to an imagined global community, and an engagement with rights and responsibilities beyond a narrow or legalistic notion of citizenship defined in relation to the nation-state. Mansouri and colleagues (2017) define global citizenship as 'one's identity as a social, cultural, and economic being, with rights and responsibilities to act locally, nationally, and globally' (p. 3). In some ways, global citizenship might be a useful concept to explain the motivations of a street artist from Bristol in the UK and his ongoing engagement with the Palestinian struggle.

In this chapter, I explore Banksy's creative engagements in Palestine to interrogate the extent to which his interventions can be considered acts of global citizenship. I begin with a brief history of the Palestinian–Israeli conflict to contextualise Banksy's most recent venture, which has involved establishing a boutique art hotel in Bethlehem. I then explore the issue of rights by highlighting how the hotel draws attention to the impact of the Israeli Separation Wall on Palestinian rights, as well as the impact of the hotel on tourism in Bethlehem. I then explore the notion of responsibility by highlighting how the hotel and Banksy's work might reinforce or resist the normalisation of the occupation, and how these considerations might help bring about a more nuanced and critical understanding of solidarity as an expression of global citizenship.

The Palestinian–Israeli conflict: A very brief history

One of the biggest myths about the Israel–Palestine conflict is that it is a centuries-old conflict fuelled by religious hatred. While religious differences have exacerbated tensions, the conflict essentially concerns two groups of people who claim the same land, with the dispute stretching back about a century to the early 1900s and the development of Zionism in Europe. Zionism is a political doctrine and movement that aims to gather Jews together in Palestine in their own state. It was first elaborated politically in 1896 in *The Jewish State* by Theodor Herzl and received its first coherent expression in 1897 with the Zionist World Congress (Gresh & Vidal, 2004). After centuries of persecution, many believed that establishing a Jewish state in the Middle East was the only way to secure the safety of the Jewish people. After the First World War and the collapse of the Ottoman Empire, the British assumed control of the area and allowed Jewish migrants to settle in what they called the British mandate for Palestine. The influx of Jewish migrants from Europe eventually created tensions with local Arab populations, who had been promised independence for helping to fight against the Ottoman forces. The increasing tensions led to acts of violence on both sides, and by the 1930s Britain began limiting Jewish immigration. The advent of the Holocaust led many more Jews to leave Europe for British Palestine and galvanised international support for a Jewish state.

In 1947, with increasing sectarian violence between Jews and Arabs, the United Nations approved a plan to divide British Palestine into two separate states: a Jewish state called Israel, and a state for Arabs called Palestine. The city of Jerusalem, where Jews, Muslims and Christians all have holy sites, was to become a special international zone. The plan caused outrage in the Arab world, where the imposition of Israel by Western powers was seen as a form of imperialism in the Middle East. Tensions continued to escalate, eventually leading to the withdrawal of British forces and the establishment of the state of Israel in 1948. This led to a war between the newly self-declared Israeli state and its Arab neighbours. Israel, with backing from the United States, won the war and expelled large numbers of Palestinians from their homes, creating a massive refugee population whose descendants today number more than seven million. At the end of the war, Israel controlled all of the territory except for Gaza and the West Bank of the Jordan River. This marked the beginning of the decades-long Arab–Israeli conflict. During this period, many Jews living in Arab countries fled to Israel (Vox, 2016).

Although Israelis celebrate 1948 as the birth of the Jewish nation, for Palestinians this date is referred to as the Nakba, or catastrophe, when 'two thirds of the population — were driven out, our property taken, hundreds of villages destroyed, an entire society obliterated' (Said, 2000, p. 185). Fleeing villagers had their houses blown up or bulldozed, the main objective being to prevent the return of refugees and to help perpetuate the Zionist myth that Palestine was 'a land without a people for a people without a land' (Masalha, 2008, p. 130).

In 1967, Israel and the neighbouring Arab states fought another war. In its aftermath, Israel occupied the remaining Palestinian lands — the West Bank, East Jerusalem and the Gaza Strip. Palestinians in these territories live under occupation and military law that severely restricts their freedom and rights. Under military rule, Palestinians are subjected to policies of discrimination and segregation, as well as military brutality and repression. As Human Rights Watch (2010) has stated, 'Palestinians face systematic discrimination merely because of their race, ethnicity, and national origin, depriving them of electricity, water, schools, and access to roads, while nearby Jewish settlers enjoy all of these state-provided benefits' (para. 3).

AHO 14.1 ISRAEL'S WALL: SECURITY OR APARTHEID?

Israel's Separation Wall is a controversial and imposing structure. It stands at 8 metres high and is around 450 kilometres long. Israel says it built the wall for security reasons, to keep Palestinians from the occupied West Bank out of Israel. Palestinians say its placement in the West Bank effectively allows Israel to annex more territory and make life difficult for them. They even call it the apartheid wall. On 4 July 2004, the Separation Wall was condemned as illegal by the International Court of Justice. Nevertheless, the wall remains in place and is defended by Israel as a security measure. Find out more about Israel's Seperation Wall by watching Dena Takruri's 2015 report for AJ+.

To watch AJ+ *Israel's Wall: Security or Apartheid?* visit www.youtube.com/watch?v=PecEVGStsNw or scan the QR code.

SHUTTERSTOCK

Israel's construction of the Separation Wall in 2002 exacerbated the division of rights between Jewish Israelis and Arab Palestinians. The Israeli authorities justified the construction of the Separation Wall, which is connected by a system of observation towers, as a security measure to prevent would-be suicide bombers from entering Israel. However, the wall penetrates deep into areas beyond the 'Green Line' — the internationally recognised border separating Israel from the Occupied Palestinian Territories — annexing Palestinian land, denying Palestinian farmers access to fruit orchards and olive groves, and severely restricting the rights of movement of local Palestinians.

In 2004, Special Rapporteur to the United Nations Commission on Human Rights, Professor John Dugard, reported that the construction of the massive Separation Wall:

> violates important norms of international humanitarian law prohibiting the annexation of occupied territory, the establishment of settlements, the confiscation of private land and the forcible transfer of people. Human rights norms are likewise violated, particularly those affirming freedom of movement, the right to family life and the right to education and health care. (United Nations Commission on Human Rights, 2004)

The Walled Off Hotel: The worst view in the world

In March 2007, Banksy was back in Palestine and back causing controversy when he opened The Walled Off Hotel in Bethlehem. The boutique hotel's 10 rooms all face the Israeli Separation Wall, with the hotel boasting that it offers guests 'the worst view in the world' (McKernan, 2017). The hotel also includes a gallery space featuring work of prominent Palestinian artists, who are often restricted from travelling abroad to exhibit their art, as well as a small museum that offers information about life under occupation, including details about the Israeli Separation Wall. The Israeli activist and journalist Haggai Matar (2017) provides a useful description of visiting the hotel, describing it as 'a business, art show and protest project rolled into one', which has 'the feel of a haunted house, at once terrible and magical' (para. 3). Visitors to the hotel are welcomed at the entrance by a monkey-porter, one of whose suitcases has fallen open, its contents spilling onto the street opposite the Separation Wall (see Figure 1).

The hotel lobby is styled like a gentlemen's club. The western wall of the lobby is adorned with CCTV cameras mounted on the wall to resemble trophies, a collection of slingshots, and two criss-crossed sledgehammers (Figure 2). The actual Separation Wall can be seen from every room, and, in addition to having to deal with the fake security cameras dotted throughout the hotel, guests must contend with real Israeli security cameras stationed along the barrier, which can swivel and observe them even when they are indoors. Some of the rooms feature Banksy artworks, including a mural that depicts a pillow fight between an Israeli soldier in full military gear and a Palestinian youth in civilian clothes with a Keffiyeh (black-and-white scarf) covering his face. Some critics of the hotel point to this mural and suggest that Banksy is reinforcing the language of moral equivalency popular in Western liberal media and public discourse, which frames the Israeli–Palestinian conflict as a struggle between two equal and equally legitimate narratives. But as Jamil Khader (2017) explains, the Palestinian youth cannot possibly indulge in a pillow fight with his Israeli persecutor, unless he is forced to do so:

> The homosocial and intimate subtext of the pillow fight between an Israeli soldier and a Palestinian youth betrays the dialectic of involuntary participation and forced identification in such power games between persecutors and their victims. (para. 18)

FIGURE 1: The entrance to the Walled Off Hotel in Bethlehem. The Israeli Separation Wall can be seen on the right topped by barbed wire. ILYA VARLAMOV, WIKIMEDIA, CC-B7-SA 4.0

Importantly, the hotel lounge features a remote-controlled mechanical baby grand piano, which is programmed with bespoke scores of contemporary arrangements recorded exclusively for the hotel. The piano has allowed international artists to feature their work in the hotel; remotely, but nevertheless connected by an international network. Musicians who have contributed arrangements and compositions for the Walled Off Hotel include Tom Waits, Trent Reznor and Atticus Ross from Nine Inch Nails, Massive Attack's 3D, Flea and Hans Zimmer (Blistein, 2017).

Next door to the Walled Off Hotel is 'Wall Mart', which allows guests to buy paint, as well as rent ladders and any other materials necessary, to deface the wall with art. Here the hotel offers visitors a chance to perform their support for the Palestinian cause on the ground. The art does not have to be political, though most spray 'Free Palestine' and/or the country they are from to show their solidarity (Davis, 2018). In this way, the hotel can be considered an important node in an international solidarity network of artists, performers, activists and everyday travellers, who can lend their support to the Palestinian cause.

FIGURE 2: Inside the lobby of the Walled Off Hotel in Bethlehem. ILYA VARLAMOV, WIKIMEDIA, CC-B7-SA 4.0

Educational vs occupation tourism

The Israeli occupation and the Separation Wall have had a debilitating effect on the local Palestinian economy. Bethlehem is a town that has traditionally been highly dependent on tourism, catering mainly for international tourists who visit key religious sites, such as the Church of the Nativity where Jesus is said to have been born. Banksy's hotel has had a meaningful impact on the local economy, encouraging a younger and not necessarily religious demographic to visit Bethlehem to see the Separation Wall up close and visit the small museum, which offers an alternative Palestinian narrative about the creation of the state of Israel. In an article in the *Jerusalem Post*, Davis reports that an Israeli-American tourist was told by friends to visit the hotel. The article details the impact this visit had on the visitor, who stated: 'The museum is really impactful, it's heart-breaking. I grew up with one view on this, and to hear another view is really important' (Davis, 2018, para. 23). What this points to is the educating impact that the hotel can have on tourists who might normally visit Israel but never see the 'other side' of the conflict or have their perspective challenged. As Davis (2018) suggests, 'when tourists exit the Walled Off Hotel, they leave with a new, more developed view of the conflict. The Walled Off Hotel, Wall Mart, and local street artists encourage visitors to be more active and informed about the situation in the West Bank' (para. 32). Moreover, the local Palestinian economy benefits from the Walled Off Hotel with taxi businesses, restaurants and shops taking advantage of the new tourists flocking to the area.

Despite this impact on the local economy, some have criticised the hotel venture saying that it trivialises the Israel–Palestinian conflict by making it a tourist attraction. Banksy seems to have responded explicitly to these concerns on the Walled Off Hotel's website. On the 'questions' page, he has provided answers to some frequently asked questions, including travel advice, information on whether the hotel is a prank, and whether the hotel and its artwork is anti-Semitic.

> **Are you just making a profit from other people's misery?**
> The hotel is now an independent local business. The aim is to break even and put any profits back into local projects.
>
> **Painting the wall — Is it legal?**
> It's not 'not' legal. The wall itself remains illegal under international law.
>
> **Is it ethical?**
> Some people don't agree with painting the wall and argue anything that

trivialises or normalises its existence is a mistake. Then again, others welcome any attention brought to it and the ongoing situation. So in essence — you can paint it, but avoid anything normal or trivial.

(A sample of questions from the Walled Off Hotel website: www.walledoffhotel.com)

Two friends of mine from Melbourne, Sary Zananiri (Palestinian) and Idan Ben-Barak (Israeli), wrote an article in the *Sydney Morning Herald* linking Banksy's hotel venture to the long history of tourism in the Middle East. Specifically, they linked the hotel to the development of 'occupation-tourism'. Zananiri and Ben-Barak point to the fact that Israel/Palestine has long occupied a special place in Western imagination, with Christian pilgrims visiting the Holy Land over centuries to connect to its biblical history. The authors argue that:

> In recent decades a new brand of tourism has emerged: solidarity tourism. Progressive, left-leaning Westerners travel to Palestine to identify with the struggle and get an authentic 'occupation experience'. British artist Banksy's new 'Walled Off Hotel' offering a view of the West Bank barrier wall in Bethlehem is the latest example of this trend. (Zananiri & Ben-Barak, 2017, paras. 6–7)

The authors suggest that occupation or solidarity tourism, like any form of tourism, is an income generator, which can be seen as helping people who are suffering under occupation. But when well-meaning tourists come to witness the struggle, they also unwittingly create 'an economic demand for maintaining the status quo' (Zananiri & Ben-Barak, 2017, para. 9).

BDS and anti-normalisation

One consistent criticism of Banksy work is that it seems to be normalising the occupation. Although anti-normalisation with Israel has a long history, in recent years the strategy has become part of an international solidarity movement of Boycott, Divestment and Sanctions (BDS) against Israel.

The BDS campaign began as an academic and cultural boycott following the decision of the International Court of Justice (ICJ) to condemn as illegal Israel's Separation Wall (Abu-Laban & Bakan, 2009, p. 40). Coinciding with the ICJ ruling, the Palestinian Campaign for the Academic and Cultural Boycott of Israel (PACBI) issued a call urging the international community to boycott all Israeli academic and cultural institutions as a 'contribution to the struggle to end Israel's occupation, colonisation and system of apartheid' (Barghouti, 2011, pp. 55–56). A year later, more than 170 Palestinian civil society organisations and unions, including the main political parties, issued the Call for BDS against Israel until it fully complied with international law (Barghouti, 2011).

Inspired by the anti-apartheid struggle in South Africa, BDS adopts a rights-based and non-violent approach to pressure the Israeli state to comply with international law and respect the rights of Palestinians by:

1. ending its occupation and colonisation of all Arab lands (occupied in 1967) and dismantling the Separation Wall;
2. recognising the fundamental rights of the Arab-Palestinian citizens of Israel to full equality; and
3. especting, protecting and promoting the rights of Palestinian refugees to return to their homes and properties, as stipulated in UN Resolution 194 (BDS, n.d.)

These calls have resulted in a transnational social movement supporting BDS initiatives. Best-selling authors like Iain Banks and Alice Walker have endorsed the boycott, and musicians like Elvis Costello, Gil Scott-Heron and Carlos Santana have cancelled concerts in Israel. Renowned authors and cultural figures such as John Berger, Naomi Klein, Arundhati Roy, Ken Loach and Judith Butler have also supported BDS (Barghouti, 2011).

The impact of BDS has been felt here in Aotearoa. In December 2017, Justine Sachs, a member of Dayenu, which is a group of young New Zealand Jews against the occupation of Palestine, and Nadia Abu-Shanab, a teacher, unionist and Palestinian activist, wrote an open letter published by the *Spinoff* urging Lorde to cancel a planned concert in Tel Aviv (Abu-Shanab & Sachs, 2017). The article argued that playing in Tel Aviv will be seen as tacit support of Israeli policies. A few days later Lorde announced that she had cancelled the concert in Tel Aviv, with the singer citing an 'overwhelming number of messages and letters' she had received as having led to her decision (Beaumont, 2017, para. 2).[2]

---

2   This support reflects the distinctive position New Zealand (through the United Nations) has taken on Palestine over the years. These instances include New Zealand's vote in 1974 in favour of issuing an invitation to the Palestine Liberation Organization's (PLO's) chairman Yasser Arafat to address the UN General Assembly (UNGA). New Zealand's position can also be traced in its 2012 UNGA vote to upgrade the status of Palestine to non-member observer state. As Parsons and Watson note, in both these instances, New Zealand voted in favour of Palestine, which 'contrasted directly with all four of the country's traditional Anglosphere allies in Australia, the United States, Canada and the United Kingdom' (2018, p. 457). The New Zealand state and its people have historically maintained an even-handed, diplomatic, and consistent approach to the Palestinian–Israeli Conflict.

In terms of criticism of Banksy's work as normalising the occupation, PACBI provides a useful definition of normalisation, describing it as:

> a colonization of the mind, whereby the oppressed subject comes to believe that the oppressor's reality is the only 'normal' reality that must be subscribed to, and that the oppression is a fact of life that must be coped with. Those who engage in normalization either ignore this oppression, or accept it as the status quo that can be lived with. (Jadaliyya, 2011, para. 2)

Banksy's hotel and artwork are potentially problematic in that they offer mainly Western tourists an engagement with the Israeli Separation Wall, which is predicated on a series of transactions that ultimately depends on the Wall's existence. This ultimately contributes to the acceptance of the Israeli Separation Wall and occupation as 'normal' facets of Palestinian life.

Conclusion: Creative interventions and global solidarity

So, how can we make sense of Banksy's creative intervention? Is Banksy's hotel and creative work profiteering from Palestinian suffering, as some have described it? Or is it using creativity and art to draw attention to the violation of Palestinian rights? And how might this creative intervention give us a more nuanced and critical understanding of solidarity as an expression of global citizenship?

In some ways, the hotel functions as a locus for a network of international solidarity that encourages and facilitates engagement with Palestine, either remotely, through the remote piano, or locally on the ground through the Wall Mart. This helps promote the visibility of Palestine and recognition of the Palestinian experience globally.

However, there are many ways to conceptualise solidarity. Olesen identifies that 'inequality' is a key feature of many forms of solidarity. He argues that these forms of solidarity 'denote a one-way relationship between those who offer solidarity and those who benefit from it' (Olesen, 2004, p. 258). Informing this understanding is also a critique of the 'politics of recognition', which Coulthard (2014) describes as something that is 'granted' or 'accorded' to underprivileged groups by dominant groups or individuals (p. 30). Instead of a 'provider' and 'beneficiary' relationship, Olesen (2004) argues for the importance of what he calls 'global solidarity', which he describes as 'a form of solidarity that emphasises similarities between physically, socially, and culturally distant people, while at the same time respecting and acknowledging local and national differences' (p. 259).

Activist and scholar Harsha Walia calls for replacing a 'politics of solidarity' with a 'practice of decolonisation'. She argues that this involves creating 'a radical terrain for struggle where our common visions for justice do not erase our different social locations, and similarly, that our differing identities do not prevent us from walking together towards transformation and mutual respect' (Walia, 2012, p. 254). For Boudreau Morris (2017), decolonising solidarity involves 'ways of seeing the other that are distinct from the politics of recognition' (p. 461). She suggests that as a strategy and a process, decolonising solidarity can 'help amplify action, reorient our approaches to recognition, and help people and communities to cope with the legacies and current realities of settler colonialism' (Boudreau Morris, 2017, p. 457).

One way to work through these complexities is to consider how local Palestinians engage with Banksy's creative work and the hotel. It is important to note that the hotel does feature a gallery that exhibits the work of local Palestinian artists, who often might not be able to exhibit overseas. While there are also undoubtedly other local benefits that are generated by tourists visiting the hotel, in some ways Palestinians are subordinate beneficiaries. While it is staffed by Palestinian workers, the hotel itself caters for a particular type of fairly wealthy Western tourist. The rooms are too expensive for most Palestinians to enjoy. Similarly, Banksy's artworks and the remote musical performances are also aimed at a 'hip' international tourist audience, rather than at local Palestinian residents.

Banksy's hotel and the artwork are very much pitched at a global (Western) audience, even though it is located and attempts to speak to the local experience of Palestinians living under Israeli occupation. A key point here when thinking about art interventions and where they sit as forms of global citizenship and solidarity is that this is not a creative dialogue *with* Palestinians. It is a dialogue that a Western artist is having with the West *about* Palestinians or, more specifically, about the Israeli occupation. This is a crucial point to consider as we try to understand the responsibilities of artists as global citizens and how they might engage with local rights issues. Rights responses must engage and empower local communities most affected by abuses so that they can be empowered to take control and assert their rights and their vision for self-determination and liberation. When cultural and artistic production intersects with notions of global citizenship, it is important to consider hierarchies of power in order to privilege participation of local communities so that cultural interventions speak *with* rather than *for* those whose rights have been violated.

References

Abu-Laban, Y., & Bakan, A. (2009). Palestinian resistance and international solidarity: The BDS Campaign. *Race and Class, 51*(1), 29–54. https://doi.org/10.1177/0306396809106162

Abu-Shanab, N., & Sachs, J. (2017, December 21). Dear Lorde, here's why we're urging you not to play Israel. *The Spinoff*. https://thespinoff.co.nz/politics/21-12-2017/dear-lorde-heres-why-were-urging-you-not-to-play-israel

Barghouti, O. (2011). *BDS: Boycott, Divestment, Sanctions — The global struggle for Palestinian rights*. Haymarket Books.

BDS. (n.d.). *What is BDS?* https://bdsmovement.net/what-is-bds

Beaumont, P. (2017, December 25). Lorde cancels Israel concert after pro-Palestinian campaign. *The Guardian*. www.theguardian.com/music/2017/dec/25/lorde-cancels-israel-concert-after-pro-palestinian-campaign

Blistein, J. (2017, October 31). Tom Waits lends instrumental 'Innocent When You Dream' to Banksy hotel. *Rolling Stone*. www.rollingstone.com/music/music-news/tom-waits-lends-instrumental-innocent-when-you-dream-to-banksy-hotel-121218

Boudreau Morris, K. (2017). Decolonizing solidarity: Cultivating relationships of discomfort. *Settler Colonial Studies, 7*(4), 456–473. https://doi.org/10.1080/220147 3X.2016.1241210

Coulthard, G. S. (2014). *Red Skin, White Masks: Rejecting the colonial politics of recognition*. University of Minnesota Press.

Davis, T. (2018, March 17). Welcome to the Walled Off: A visit to Banky's hotel in Bethlehem. *The Jerusalem Post*. www.jpost.com/Jerusalem-Report/Welcome-to-the-Walled-Off-A-visit-to-Banksys-hotel-in-Bethlehem-544463

DeTurk, S. (2015). The 'Banksy Effect' and street art in the Middle East. *SAUC — Street Art and Urban Creativity, 1*(2), 22–30. https://doi.org/10.25765/sauc.v1i2.25

Gresh, A., & Vidal, D. (2004). *The New A–Z of the Middle East*. I. B. Tauris.

Human Rights Watch. (2010). Israel/West Bank: Separate and unequal. www.hrw.org/news/2010/12/19/israel/west-bank-separate-and-unequal

Jadaliyya. (2011, November 3). Israel's exceptionalism: Normalizing the abnormal. www.jadaliyya.com/Details/24583

Jones, S. (2005, August 5). Spray can prankster tackles Israel's security barrier. *The Guardian Online*. www.theguardian.com/world/2005/aug/05/israel.artsnews

Khader, J. (2017, March 13). The Walled Off Hotel: The struggle for decolonisation. *Al Jazeera*. www.aljazeera.com/indepth/opinion/2017/03/walled-hotel-struggle-decolonisation-170312143224959.html

Mansouri, F., Johns, A., & Marotta, V. (2017). Critical global citizenship: Contextualising globalisation. *Journal of Citizenship and Globalisation Studies, 1*(1), 1–9. https://doi.org/10.1515/jcgs-2017-0001

Masalha, N. (2008). Remembering the Palestinian Nakba: Commemoration, oral history and narratives of memory. *Holy Land Studies: A multidisciplinary journal, 7*(2), 123–156. https://doi.org/10.3366/E147494750800019X

Matar, H. (2017). Exit through the checkpoint: Inside Banksy's new Bethlehem hotel. *+972 Magazine*. https://972mag.com/exit-through-the-checkpoint-inside-banksys-new-bethlehem-hotel/125588/

McKernan, B. (2017, March 15). Banksy hotel in Palestinian West Bank with 'worst view in the world' divides locals. *The Independent*. www.independent.co.uk/news/world/middle-east/banksy-hotel-west-bank-palestinian-territory-israel-worst-view-world-local-residents-barrier-fence-a7631556.html

Olesen, T. (2004). Globalizing the Zapatistas: From third world solidarity to global solidarity? *Third World Quarterly, 25*(1), 255–267. https://doi.org/10.1080/0143659042000185435

Parsons, N., & Watson, J. (2018). New Zealand, the Palestine Liberation Organization and the United Nations: 2012 and 1974 in comparative perspective. In R. Patman, R. I. Iati, & B. Kiglics (Eds.), *New Zealand and the World: Past, present and future* (pp. 457–469). World Scientific.

Said, E. (2000). Invention, memory, and place. *Critical Inquiry, 2*(Winter), 175–192. https://doi.org/10.1086/448963

United Nations Commission on Human Rights. (2004). Report of the Special Rapporteur of the Commission on Human Rights, John Dugard, on the situation of human rights in the Palestinian Territories occupied by Israel since 1967. https://unispal.un.org/DPA/DPR/unispal.nsf/0/631C8DEB907650E985256E6000520F3B

Vox. (2016). The Israel–Palestine conflict: A brief, simple history [Video]. www.youtube.com/watch?v=iRYZjOuUnlU

Walia, H. (2012). Moving beyond a politics of solidarity toward a practice of decolonization. In E. Shragge, J. Hanley, & A. Choudry (Eds.), *Organize!: Building from the local for global justice* (pp. 240–253). PM Press.

Zananiri, S., & Ben-Barak, I. (2017, March 17). Banksy's Walled Off Hotel: Palestinians under occupation reduced to a spectacle. *The Sydney Morning Herald*. www.smh.com.au/world/banksys-walled-off-hotel-palestinians-under-occupation-reduced-to-a-spectacle-20170311-guvw6h.html

15.
Encountering inequality and poverty

Carol Neill & Samantha Gardyne

What gets in the way of equity, justice and all people reaching their full potential? Why is there such a divide between those who thrive and those who suffer? Inequality is a persistent theme throughout this book. As previously examined, inequality is a driver of conflict and an amplifier of the challenges brought by climate change. Inequality refers to disparate and/or unfair sharing of opportunities and resources between people, with overlapping spatial, economic and social dimensions (MacNaughton et al., 2021; Wilkinson & Pickett, 2010). It has multiple intersections across issues of human rights, responsibilities, power, advantage and disadvantage in our modern, globalised world. Despite the Global North's tendency to view inequality and poverty as features of 'underdeveloped' societies, almost all wealthy countries and regions also maintain inequalities within them.

Often poverty — rather than inequality — is highlighted as the big challenge in our contemporary world, where material wellbeing is a core measure of success. Certainly, those with fewer resources are disproportionately impacted by the negative aspects of globalisation. However, focusing on people's material deprivation implies deficiencies on those people's part, which in turn provides justifications for discrimination and exclusion. In contrast, an equity perspective

IHO ATUA

Margaret Forster (Rongomaiwāhine, Ngāti Kahungunu)

Harmony and restoring balance are recurring themes in the origin narratives.

> Father-Sky and Mother-Earth were first division from the universal mauri. They are Tapu and Noa — the two energies who balance themselves. They did so in the beginning by holding tight to each other . . . Together Sky and Earth produced over 70 sons and an existence of imbalance . . . After the separation of their parents the sons set about creating their own dreams. They mated with elements of the universe producing flora, fauna and life everywhere to clothe, bejewel and nurture their parents. All of their offspring developed methods of co-existing within the universe to become part of the whole. The sons of Sky and Earth loved these offspring wholeheartedly and were content, except for one son who had a final desire to create his own physical image. Tāne confided this thought with his mother. Earth realised the request of her first-born would be the final path to restoring balance to the universe . . . Eventually the human cycle, the last of all living beings, was completed. Tapu and Noa were finally restored to harmony. The universal balance returned, and it has been the duty of all living creatures to maintain it as their creation-songs remind them. (How, 2017, pp. 7–8)

Maintaining balance involves the pursuit of equality by responding to inequities and injustices. One way to achieve this is through enacting practices that elevate the mana and presence of others — including the environment. This is manaaki in action — acts of kindness, generosity and respect for others. At its core, manaaki recognises the connectedness of our lives and the experiences that we share by virtue of being human and being part of the world. Connectedness establishes responsibility and reciprocity to empower and support people to reach their full potential.

shines a light on the systematic imbalances in and across societies, and the interconnectedness of wealth and poverty. As Max Rashbrooke (2015) highlights, the problem in our contemporary world is not so much poverty, but the severe imbalances in wealth across economic systems. This summary chapter provides a platform for considering how contexts of inequality and poverty emerge and are responded to, as a platform for closer examinations in the following chapters. Gardyne and Malecki (Chapter 16) take a global perspective in considering the role of the Sustainable Development Goals, while the other two chapters are located within Aotearoa, and focus on Māori Covid responses (Forster et al., Chapter 17) and Pacific peoples' community work towards sustainable livelihoods (Alefaio-Tugia et al., Chapter 18).

Causes and extent of inequality and poverty

Today's inequalities have long historical roots, driven by factors such as gender, ethnicity, race and class, which in turn reflect the ongoing legacies wrought by colonialism, globalisation and uncompromising prescriptions for capitalist economic progress. Centuries of Western, human-centred development that have advanced technologies, industries, communications and interactions have touted scientific advancement and industrial production as the drivers of equal opportunities and democratisation for all people. However, the reality that colonisation and neoliberal globalisation have fed off the unequal treatment of peoples — especially Indigenous peoples — needs to be recognised as such (Rist, 2014).

Colonial economies like that of Aotearoa were built on natural resource exploitation and land acquisition — and confiscation — from Indigenous peoples that not only removed their means of livelihood, but also their spiritual and cultural bases. The colonial political and social institutions that were established, especially in education, privileged the colonisers over the colonised, further marginalising those who should have been respected as hosts, rather than treated as obstacles to colonial endeavour (Walker, 2004). These historical processes caused the important components of a good life for Indigenous peoples to be de-emphasised, diminishing their capabilities to live the kinds of lives they value. As such, the burden of inequity falls all too frequently on Indigenous peoples and minority groups, who are marginalised by today's systems of lopsided privilege and disadvantage (Watene, 2016). The ongoing implications of these issues for Māori are highlighted by Forster and others in Chapter 17, and for Pacific peoples by Alefaio-Tugia and colleagues in Chapter 18.

The historical injustices that globally embedded deep-rooted and pervasive class, gender and ethnic inequalities have not decreased in the past century. Indeed, despite an extensive and long-running development agenda led by the United Nations (UN) and powerful Western states like the United States (US) since the end of the Second World War, poverty and inequality have grown rather than diminished. There are more billionaires than ever before, while the world's poorest have grown poorer. Currently, the richest one per cent have more than twice as much wealth as the remaining 6.9 billion people, and almost half of humanity lives on less than US$5.50 a day (UNDP, 2020). Furthermore, patterns of inequality remain tied to historical imbalances in power. Inequality maps highlight regions in Africa and Central/South Asia as having the most poverty, while Western Europe and North America show the highest average wealth. Sub-Saharan Africa is often cited as the lowest-income region, with average incomes there being 11 times less than those across European Union countries, and 16 times less than the average incomes of North Americans (UNDESA, 2020, p. 22). Behind these statistics lie substantial differences in quality of life, health outcomes, life expectancies and opportunities for improvement.

Inequality has grown globally and within countries under the neoliberal economic policies that have been pursued across the world since the 1980s. Neoliberal beliefs, promoted globally by United Kingdom Prime Minister Margaret Thatcher and US President Ronald Reagan, held that by promoting rapid, unregulated economic growth, economic surplus would 'trickle down' through increased employment generation and service demand, thereby reducing inequality and poverty. Neoliberal thinking informed Structural Adjustment Programmes[1] in international development that encouraged developing countries to roll back government responsibility for the provision of basic needs and services, and to promote a free market approach as a catalyst for boosting economic growth. However, despite the widespread adoption of neoliberal policies, inequality and poverty have grown within both developed and developing countries (Rist, 2014).

Ironically, neoliberal thinking embraces inequality as a good thing, arguing that inequalities provide an incentive for people to work hard to pursue 'better' lives for themselves and their families (Robertson, 2020). However, the labour market has been shaped under neoliberalism to support precarity rather than a promise of security, even when a job is secured. Over the past 30 years, labour legislation

---

1   Structural Adjustment Programmes have been led by international organisations such as the World Bank and International Monetary Fund, providing lending to countries for development while also imposing conditions for those countries to restructure and liberalise their economies.

has enabled the increase of work arrangements that give no guarantees for set hours or long-term stability, meaning that many jobs come with inherent risks over how much work is promised, or how long it may last. Shocks, such as economic recessions and, more immediately, the global Covid-19 pandemic, have exacerbated that precarity.

As Esposito (2016) notes, neoliberalism also encourages and normalises structural violence.[2] As patterns of injustice and exploitation are built into the economic system, enormous wealth is generated for the elite, alongside massive exploitation of those who are obliged to fulfil roles at the most basic levels of the supply chain. We are all interconnected with those injustices. Across the world, the increasingly complex supply and production chains that create our everyday consumer goods have been facilitated by a 'race to the bottom' in terms of labour and production costs. This means those who are mining the raw resources or doing the production work experience poor, hazardous working conditions with low remuneration. Examples abound, from child mining for cobalt and lithium for cellphone components in the Congo (Kara, 2018), through to Uyghur people making sports shoes in prison-like conditions in China (Hannigan, 2020). The cheapness of their labour makes goods more accessible in the global marketplace, but with ethical implications for all who consume them (see Chapter 13 for how these challenges extend to conflict contexts as well).

Inequality, poverty and human rights

With human rights being based on notions of justice for and equality of all humans, it is easy to see why inequality of any type constitutes a violation. There is a paradox in the fact that recent decades have seen the human rights agenda become central to ethical language, informing frameworks for justice across the world, while at the same time economic inequalities that violate those rights have risen (MacNaughton et al., 2021). Human rights declarations and agreements were developed to give hope and justice to all peoples across the world, but persistent inequality and poverty, more than anything else, stifle that hope.

The privilege for those with material wealth and associated social status in the modern capitalist world means that human rights can be more or less taken

---

2   Structural violence is a term used to describe the systematic ways in which social structures (political and economic systems and institutions), inequities in power, wealth and overall life cause harm to certain groups and individuals. It includes racism, sexism, ableism, homophobia and income inequality, and results in risk and increased mortality and morbidity. Structural violence is subtle, frequently invisible, and often has no one specific person who can (or will) be held responsible.

AHO 15.1 MAPPING POVERTY AND INEQUALITY

When trying to assess the extent of inequality and poverty across the world, multiple types of measures are used.

Absolute measures of poverty use simple global income lines, whereas relative measures take the local or national context into account. Multidimensional measures are more complex, incorporating a range of factors (such as access to education and health) and indicators (such as security of housing). The top map opposite uses the absolute measure of $1.90 per day to show the proportion of people living in extreme poverty within countries, thereby highlighting the stark differences across continents.

Inequality indexes measure wealth differentiations across the world and within countries. One commonly used method is Gini-coefficient calculations, which measure distributions of income within populations. The higher the number, the greater the inequality — shown in lighter colours on the income inequality map opposite. As you can see, this map highlights how even countries that have less extreme poverty can still have high levels of inequality.

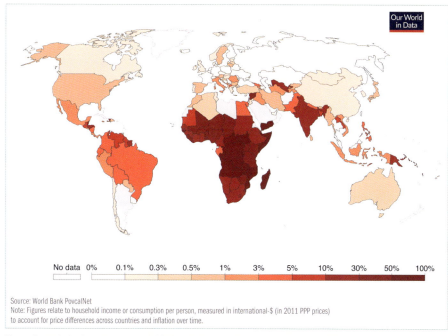

Share of population in extreme poverty, 2019, showing the share of inidivduals living below the International Poverty Line of 1.90 international-$ per day. OURWORLDINDATA.ORG/EXTREME POVERTY, CC BY

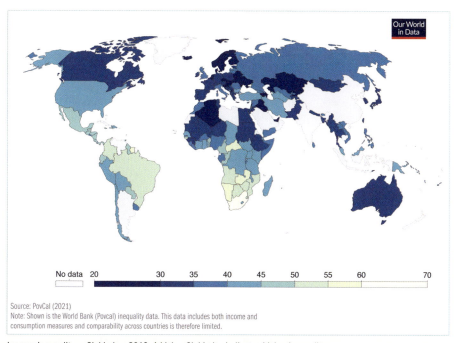

Income Inequality — Gini Index, 2019. A higher Gini index indicates higher inequality.
OURWORLDINDATA.ORG/INCOME-INEQUALITY, CC BY

ENCOUNTERING INEQUALITY AND POVERTY

for granted. The lived experience of poverty, on the other hand, requires the negotiating of rights rather than fulfilment of them all. For example, Jackson and Graham's (2017) research in Aotearoa highlighted the difficult trade-offs for struggling families, when unexpected costs arise:

> As Ginny puts it, 'everything comes out of the food budget'. Carys, who has two school-aged boys, can only pay for compulsory school stationery items by reducing her already low fruit and vegetable spend. Sophie was faced with urgent dental treatment, necessitating debt that she must now pay out of her food money each week. When the food money becomes squeezed through routine costs of unexpected events, there can be very little money left to feed the family. In response, purchases of non-food items are regularly delayed. (p. 79)

From these observations, we can see multiple violations of rights, particularly social and economic rights, including the security of food and health care. They also impinge on housing security and extend to affect children's engagement with education. A UNICEF report in 2018 highlighted how inequality was affecting educational outcomes in Aotearoa, placing this country thirty-third out of 38 countries for inequality in the classroom (RNZ, 2018). Such analyses are particularly worrying when education is commonly considered a vehicle for social mobility and higher living standards.

Inequalities are also wrought across human rights impacts by gender. In sub-Saharan Africa, for example, research has shown that 'women in this region are more likely to be undernourished than men, and that undernourished women and children are found in non-poor households' (Brown et al., as cited in UNDESA, 2020, p. 39). The intersecting factors of inequality, like gender, race and disability, create overlapping barriers to individuals being able to do anything to change their impoverished circumstances. How intersectionality has developed as a concept to inform understanding and responses to inequality and poverty is expanded upon by Gardyne and Malecki in Chapter 16.

Responses to inequality and poverty

So, what can be done to address global inequality and poverty? Inequality has come to be recognised as bad for everyone, not just the poor (Wilkinson & Pickett, 2010). Societies in which inequality is rampant experience more insecurity and disconnection across all peoples, as well as using resources trying to 'mop up' the effects of inequality — for example, poor education, health and crime outcomes

— that would otherwise be directed to more positive development. As Gardyne and Malecki argue in their chapter, extreme poverty will only be addressed by tackling global inequality. Structural change that goes to the root of those deeply embedded causes brought about by history needs to be part of the agenda for the lofty goals of eliminating poverty and inequality, and increasing living standards, around the world.

While global-level goals, such as the Sustainable Development Goals, are now agreed upon and are on the United Nations' agenda, the fact remains that state governments hold the ultimate power in addressing inequality and poverty within their societies. Gaining agreement within countries on what should be done, and how, is not easy, however. While most agree that growing inequality is a pressing issue, 'as soon as you drill down to questions of why and how, it opens a Pandora's box of competing frameworks and value systems that are used to make sense of it' (Beausoleil, 2017, para. 6). Political expediency often dictates that governments want to do something, usually through 'welfare' policies, but balance how far they go with voter interests. Often, the more privileged middle classes are assuaged by political tinkering with welfare measures, rather than the government making any substantial change that may meaningfully address advantage/disadvantage imbalances.

It has become increasingly clear that state-level responses can only do so much. Government policies alone will not solve the problems of inequality and poverty within and across societies, because those long historical causes are hard to shift. Power needs to be dispersed across different actors and groups so that the root causes of inequality and poverty can be addressed from multiple angles, necessitating work across and between the public, civil society and private sectors, at all levels. However, although specialised agencies, governments, NGOs and corporations may hold the money and power to create change, the most important actors in poverty alleviation are the people themselves. They are not passive or helpless; they have often already found creative and innovative ways to exist that many of us would never think or feel capable of.

Recognising the capabilities of people to find their own solutions, and supporting them to do so, is crucial. Often, local communities and groups — and especially Indigenous peoples — are side-lined in big strategies for change. However, when community action is unlocked and enabled, then this is where the magic can happen, as two of our chapters prove in the Aotearoa context. In Chapter 17, Forster and colleagues highlight how Indigenous-led responses can effectively address gaps left by government responses, as was shown through iwi, hapū and whānau responses to Covid-19. Alefaio-Tugia and her colleagues show in Chapter 18 how

Pacific communities have employed traditional engagement practices to find new ways of working, addressing contemporary challenges and thriving, Pasifika-style.

Equity and citizenship

Inequality impacts — and implicates — us all. For many people, inequality and poverty are things they feel uncomfortable about, perhaps because they feel helpless to do something about it, or believe they only have the resources and energy to 'get by' themselves. But we are all affected by inequality and there are multiple ways that people can enact their citizenship to address disparity and work towards equity. The past decades have proved that expecting governments to enact policies that will 'save' people from poverty, or curb aggressive, exploitative wealth accumulation, is naïve optimism. Real, substantive, equitable change needs to be sought by all actors in the system. Our chapters in this section provide a rich variety of thinking about how that may be achieved.

What is possible for human flourishing; for people to be able to reach their own measures of success? The answer lies in each of our own senses of what a good life is, and what impedes that good life. Solutions to poverty and inequality need to be led by those who know the challenges best. Rather than being passive recipients of charity or aid, people in poverty around the world address their own situations through local initiatives, grassroots community organisations and support programmes. Protest and resistance are expressions of local agency that highlight the barriers to wellbeing, and direct energy towards new forms of solutions. These could be manifestations of 'imaginative excellence' (Lear, 2006, as cited in Smith, 2013, p. 235) that provide radical hope for change towards a more equitable, just, global future.

References

Beausoleil, E. (2017, August 28). Let them eat cake: Inequality is growing, so how can we fix it? *Stuff*. www.stuff.co.nz/national/politics/opinion/96213793/let-them-eat-cake-inequality-is-growing-so-how-can-we-fix-it

Esposito, L. (2016). Neoliberalism and the transformation of work. In V. Berdayes & J. W. Murphy (Eds.), *Neoliberalism, Economic Radicalism, and the Normalisation of Violence* (pp. 87–106). Springer.

Hannigan, D. (2020, December 10). America at large: Nike must wake up to human rights.

Irish Times. www.irishtimes.com/sport/other-sports/america-at-large-nike-must-wake-up-to-human-rights-1.4431905

How, N. (2017). *Tangata Whenua Worldviews for Wastewater Management in Wairoa*. A report prepared for Wairoa District Council, Wairoa, New Zealand.

Jackson, K., & Graham, R. (2017). When dollar loaves are all you have: Experiences of food insecurity in Hamilton, New Zealand. In S. Groot, C. Van Ommen, B. Masters-Awatere, & N. Tassell-Matamua (Eds.), *Precarity:*

Uncertain, insecure and unequal lives in Aotearoa New Zealand (pp. 76–86). Massey University Press.

Kara, S. (2018, October 12). Is your phone tainted by the misery of the 35,000 children in Congo's mines? *The Guardian*. www.theguardian.com/global-development/2018/oct/12/phone-misery-children-congo-cobalt-mines-drc

MacNaughton, G., Frey, D. F., & Porter, C. (Eds.). (2021). *Human Rights and Economic Inequalities*. University of Cambridge ESOL Examinations.

Rashbrooke, M. (2015). *Wealth and New Zealand*. Bridget Williams Books.

Rist, G. (2014). *The History of Development: From Western origins to global faith*. Zed Books.

RNZ. (2018, October. 30). NZ among worst ranked for inequality in education — report. *RNZ*. www.rnz.co.nz/news/national/369779/nz-among-worst-ranked-for-inequality-in-education-report

Robertson, N. (2020, December 7). Why inequality matters for growth. *BERL*. https://berl.co.nz/our-probono-inequality-and-new-zealand

Smith, L. T. (2013). The future is now. In M. Rashbrooke (Ed.), *Inequality: A New Zealand crisis* (pp. 228–235). Bridget Williams Books.

United Nations Department of Economic and Social Affairs (UNDESA). (2020). *Inequality in a Rapidly Changing World: World social report 2020*. www.un.org/development/desa/dspd/wp-content/uploads/sites/22/2020/01/World-Social-Report-2020-FullReport.pdf

United Nations Development Programme (UNDP). (2020). Human development report 2020. The next frontier: Human development and the Anthropocene. http://hdr.undp.org/en/2020-report

Walker, R. (2004). *Ka Whawhai Tonu Matou — Struggle without end*. Penguin.

Watene, K. (2016). Valuing nature: Māori philosophy and the capability approach. *Oxford Development Studies, 44*(3), 287–296. http://dx.doi.org/10.1080/13600818.2015.1124077

Wilkinson, R., & Pickett, K. (2010). *The Spirit Level: Why greater equality makes societies stronger*. Bloomsbury Press.

16.
Poverty, inequality and the SDGs
Transforming our world for whom?

Samantha Gardyne & Axel Malecki

Introduction

Is inequality inevitable — a natural law like gravity that we cannot change? Or is inequality a political choice — something which governments and the international community have the resources and capabilities to change if they wanted to? The world has made significant strides in reducing global poverty, but in recent years progress has slowed. The main obstacle is that eliminating extreme poverty requires tackling inequality, which often leads us to ask questions such as:

> Do I have a right to be rich? And do I have a right to be content living in a world with so much poverty and inequality? These questions motivate us to view the issue of inequality as central to human living. (Sen, 2004, p. 67)

In 1949, after the end of the Second World War, President Harry Truman gave an inaugural address that outlined the United States' plan to ensure greater peace, equity and justice between countries across the world. Truman's speech triggered the global project of development, which aimed to reduce inequality and poverty through the sharing of technical knowledge and expertise by those countries considered developed with those considered underdeveloped or developing (Rist, 2014). However, 70 years later we find ourselves in an opposite situation, where poverty and inequality have been exacerbated rather than eradicated.

The year 2015 marked the beginning of a new phase in international development conversations about sustainability, poverty and inequality. The United Nations (UN) 2030 Agenda launched a global plan of action that aims to be 'genuinely transformative by placing people and their inherent dignity at the heart of all development efforts' (UN, 2015, p. 3). This is to be achieved through the 17 Sustainable Development Goals (SDGs), which have been informed by broader understandings of development embracing integration and diversity. These are reflected in the three universal principles which drive the SDGs: a human rights-based approach, leave no one behind and gender equality and empowerment. The UN believes that the principles underscoring the SDGs will address discrimination, confront the root causes of poverty and inequality, and empower all people to become active partners in their own development. Through the lens of these three principles, we reflect on the SDGs as an integrated and internationally collective response to the challenges of poverty and inequality.

This chapter first explores the concept of sustainability, before delving into the importance of a human rights-based approach to poverty and inequality and how that differs from mainstream definitions of poverty. Building on the idea that everyone has a right to a full life, we introduce the notion of intersectionality as a powerful concept to explore how conditions of inequality can be exacerbated by aspects of geography, socio-economic status and discrimination, among others. Engaging further with the call to genuinely challenge current systems of power and discrimination, we conclude with a critique of the SDGs' approach to gender equality and empowerment.

Sustainability: Origins and implications

In 1987, at the World Conference on Environment and Development, global leaders began talking about sustainability as an integrated concept, recognising the need to progress towards 'Development that meets the needs of the present, without compromising the ability of future generations to meet their own needs' (WCED, 1987, p. 6). For the first time, the international community recognised that 'our common future' depended on meeting people's needs, specifically the essential needs of the poor, and that the mass consumption and production patterns of industrialised countries, primarily in the Global North, were unsustainable. Why is this important? For one, it signalled sustainable development as an endeavour to create a balance between ecological concerns, social equity and economic development, without prioritising one over the other. Secondly, the concept of

AHO 16.1 A CRITICAL LENS ON DEVELOPMENT

Gilbert Rist has critically examined the history of development discourse and argues that it has been shaped as a seductive, yet unattainable, idea: 'The strength of the "development" discourse comes of its power to seduce, in every sense of the term: to charm, to please, to fascinate, to set dreaming, but also to abuse, to turn away from the truth, to deceive. How could one possibly resist the idea that there is a way of eliminating the poverty by which one is so troubled? How dare one think at the same time, that the cure might worsen the ill which one wishes to combat? . . . How could it have been thought necessary and urgent to do everything to speed up the process of development . . . after all, for centuries no one — or virtually no one — took it into their head to relieve the misery of others by structural measures, especially when they lived on different continents . . .

'What sense can we make of the numerous debates which . . . have offered a solution to the problem that majority destitution poses in the face of minority opulence? How are we to explain this whole phenomenon, which mobilises not only the hopes of millions but also sizeable financial resources, while appearing to recede like the horizon just as you think you are approaching it?' (Rist, 2014, p. 1)

Reference

Rist, G. (2014). *The History of Development: From Western origins to global faith.* Zed Books.

sustainability highlighted the limitations of the Earth's resources and the need to consider the future implications of our actions. Thirdly, defining development in terms of sustainability placed the provision of human needs at the very centre of conversations about sustainable development.

The shift to sustainability constituted a significant departure from conventional meanings of 'development', which is often equated with economic growth that pays little regard to ecological concerns or a fair redistribution of wealth. Nevertheless, the concept of sustainable development has not gained the attention and priority given to the continued international drive for economic growth (Korten, 2018).

The launch of the SDGs achieved what previous UN attempts had failed miserably to do — move issues of sustainability to the centre of the conversation and policy making at international, national and local levels. The goals are based on the imperative that we recognise that there are limits to growth and that the planet's natural resources are not infinite. In addition, there is a price to be paid for the growth-orientated goal of mass consumption and, for the most part, this is not paid by consumers within developed nations. For example, the Oxfam study *Confronting Carbon Inequality* (2020) illustrated the significantly disproportionate responsibility between the richest and the poorest for rising carbon emissions (see Figure 1).

Addressing poverty and inequality, including its various expressions such as

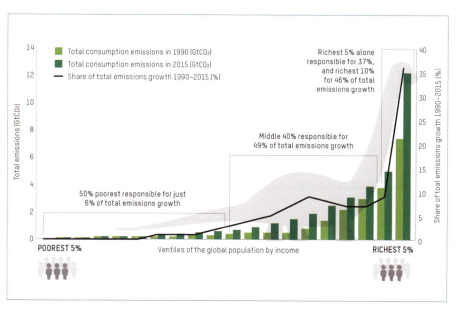

FIGURE 1: The dinosaur graph of unequal carbon emissions growth 1990-2015. OXFAM

food poverty, energy poverty and inequality of opportunity, take centre place within conversations about sustainability. However, while few would disagree with the idea of a world without poverty and inequality, where climate change and environmental damage have been reversed and where peace and justice reign for all, there is much debate about if, and how, we can achieve this.

Human rights-based approach

> We envisage a world of universal respect for human rights and human dignity, the rule of law, justice, equality and non-discrimination; of respect for race, ethnicity and cultural diversity . . . A just, equitable, tolerant, open and socially inclusive world in which the needs of the most vulnerable are met. (UN, 2015, p. 7)

Chapter 5 introduced the Universal Declaration of Human Rights (UDHR) and highlighted how international law and norms such as the UDHR may be seen as central components that structure the international human rights system within which countries operate. The notions of obligation, accountability and compliance that are associated with the UDHR have deeply layered implications in relation to poverty and inequality. Using a human rights-based approach (HRBA) to frame inequality and poverty conjures a legal dimension that, in theory, compels governments to eliminate conditions that create and perpetuate particular forms of deprivation and disparity. More specifically, a rights-based approach to development seeks to empower people to understand and claim their fundamental rights. Such an approach recognises that empowerment must develop in conjunction with the accountability of individuals and institutions who are responsible for respecting, protecting and fulfilling these rights. In particular, it is about giving those who are most often excluded or marginalised greater opportunities to participate in defining and making the decisions that impact their human rights, and their ability to defend and assert these (Saiz & Donald, 2017).

Approaching poverty and inequality through the prism of human rights shifts the frame of reference from the historical focus on addressing *the basic needs* of marginalised population groups, to *fulfilling and safeguarding their intrinsic human rights*. The distinction between addressing *needs* and fulfilling *rights* is crucial, for it allows people to hold governments and other duty bearers of rights to account. Indeed, framing the relationship between poverty and inequality as an issue of rights explicitly conjures the notion of obligation, because it shifts the focus from *beneficiaries with needs* to *citizens with rights*. By extension, then, HRBAs and associated principles, such as participation, accountability, non-discrimination, dignity and empowerment, may be seen as stepping stones towards building capacity in order to claim rights, seek recognition and demand justice, particularly for population groups who have been historically deprived of access to equal opportunities (Dunne & Wheeler, 2016).

Unlike political and civil rights (see Chapter 5), poverty and inequality are considered progressive rights and fall under the umbrella of social and economic rights, such as the right to housing, food, health, education and work. However, any inability to exercise basic social and economic rights implicates political and civil rights, too, because extreme inequality causes declines in access to justice, political participation and, therefore, representation of marginalised population groups. Like understanding the different expressions of inequality, recognising the multidimensionality of poverty entails an understanding that goes beyond income poverty to encapsulate multiple deprivations, including poor health, disempowerment and lack of education. Moreover, reducing inequality between population groups is likely to decrease the probability of conflict (Landman & Larizza, 2009). Key to understanding these links between the multidimensionality of poverty and inequality is the recognition that economic inequality may be seen as both a cause and a consequence in the deprivation of human rights (Saiz & Donald, 2017).

The utility of rights-based approaches lies in their potentiality to achieve societies characterised by more parity, equity and social inclusion of traditionally disenfranchised groups. What do we mean by this? When we address poverty and inequality from this perspective, efforts need to redress discriminatory practices and unjust distributions of power that often lead to the exclusion of many groups of people. From a holistic perspective, the interlinked nature of the SDGs further reflects the rights-based approach to development, because it acknowledges the intersecting and dynamic nature of poverty and inequality.

The adoption of the 2030 Agenda for Sustainable Development was accompanied by the candid commitment to 'leave no one behind' (Stuart, 2018). With specific goals dedicated to particular issues, such as SDG1 focusing on poverty, and SDG10 focusing on inequality, the SDGs are not only universal in scope, but also compel all countries, including high-income countries, to address domestic socio-economic inequalities that have soared in recent years. For example, SDG10 aims to 'reduce inequalities of outcome, including by eliminating discriminatory laws, policies and practices', which underscores how the SDGs may reach into both domestic policy arrangements and policy directions (UN, 2015). SDG10 also highlights how high-income countries contribute to the perpetuation of inequality in lower-income countries, for example through trade protectionism or international migration. Essentially, then, SDG10 is informed by concerns that current levels of inequality, if left unaddressed, will not only continue to undermine related rights such as access to health and education domestically, but also exacerbate disparities between countries (Stuart, 2018).

The SDGs advocate that all people deserve to exercise their right to a sustainable, equitable and just world, so an inseparable and integrated approach to all 17 goals is required. Eradicating, or even reducing, poverty and inequality requires a united approach, predicated on comprehensive understandings of the complex, dynamic and intersecting root causes of poverty and inequality (Stuart, 2018; Van Niekerk, 2020). It is not okay just to know who is being left behind — we also need to know why and what to do about it.

Leave no one behind

> As we embark on this great collective journey, we pledge that no one will be left behind. Recognizing that the dignity of the human person is fundamental, we wish to see the Goals met for all nations and peoples, and for all segments of society. And we will endeavor to reach the furthest behind first. (UN, 2015, p. 6)

Building on the HRBA approach, the SDGs commitment to leave no one behind (LNOB) is predicated on the premise that central to overcoming poverty and inequality is the identification of persistent and interconnected, or intersecting, forms of discrimination. Those differing forms cause disparities by undermining marginalised peoples' ability to make their own choices and decisions. Poverty is not just about insufficient money. It is significantly more complex than that, involving a range of inequalities that shape people's experiences of poverty, and which overlap and intersect with each other. Through the 17 goals, the SDGs aim to identify how those diverse discriminatory factors intersect with each other, allowing some people to flourish and causing others to remain excluded and marginalised (Ryder & Boone, 2019).

Intersectionality was first coined by the African-American feminist Kimberlé Williams Crenshaw in 1989. The term considers how an individual or community's social and political realities coalesce to cause either discrimination or privilege.

AHO 16.2 INDIGENOUS PEOPLES AND THE SDGS

This excerpt from Krushil Watene and Mandy Yap's 2015 article summarises their argument that Indigenous perspectives have much to contribute to the articulation of the SDGs.

'As the international community turns its focus to the Post15 Agenda and the Sustainable Development Goals, indigenous communities look to sustainable development as a vehicle for change. To the disappointment of the indigenous community, the Sustainable Development Goals (much like the Millennium Development Goals) sideline culture as a dimension of development. Culture is absent from the broad aims of sustainable development and the sustainable development goals, and mentioned (a mere five times) only in the targets, which fall under the goals. In other words, culture is useful merely as a means to achieve sustainable development in its economic, social and environmental dimensions. Culture (and the survival of indigenous cultures, for instance) is not valued for its own sake . . .

'. . . when we say that indigenous peoples can contribute to sustainable development, what we ought to mean is not merely that indigenous cultures (traditional knowledge and practices) support the pursuit and achievement of sustainable development goals. What we also ought to mean is that indigenous values are able to provide us with different foundations for, and perspectives of, sustainable development. Indigenous peoples help to shape conversations about development and sustainability, for instance, by extending the foundations of sustainable development to include relationships and culture. The inclusion of relationships and culture reframes how well-being and poverty might be understood. Poverty includes not just material wealth, but also the content and quality of our relationships with other people, and our connections to and expressions of culture. Indigenous perspectives are, in other words, important contributions to a shared understanding of how sustainable development ought to be conceived, and the goals that ought to be pursued.' (Watene & Yap, 2015, pp. 51–52)

Reference

Watene, K., & Yap, M. (2015). Culture and sustainable development: Indigenous contributions. *Journal of Global Ethics, 11*(1), 51–55.

Crenshaw found that social characteristics such as race, class and gender are important categorisations for understanding how racism, discrimination and marginalisation reside in a range of hierarchies of power. For instance, black women experience forms of misogyny and racism, but at the same time their experience of misogyny will be different from that of white women, and their experience of racial discrimination will be different from that of black men. Therefore, intersectionality compels us to consider how women's overlapping identities render them subject to a range of social justice and human rights issues, which are experienced in combination rather than in isolation. Achieving gender equality and women's rights requires going beyond representing the experience of women through a white, middle class, heterosexual, able-bodied lens, to account more clearly for structural inequality at the core of, for instance, the experience of Indigenous women (Crenshaw, 2017).

When utilising this concept of intersectionality as a framework for analysing poverty and inequality, we recognise that people experience oppression or deprivation in overlapping ways and not as separate and distinct entities that can be easily separated or dealt with individually. Furthermore, intersectionality directs us to identify how interconnected systems of power affect those who are most marginalised in society; and how these systems make it extremely difficult for people to break free from poverty or to overcome inequality (Ryder & Boone, 2019; UNSDG, 2019).

The SDGs implicitly recognise that the experience of multiple oppressions must be dealt with from a holistic and integrated perspective. Those most likely to be left behind by development are those facing intersecting inequalities, leading to discrimination and exclusion on the grounds of identity and locational disadvantage (UNSDG, 2019).

An intersectional approach solicits widespread collaboration and cooperation between government, the private sector and civil society. However, implementing the SDGs in a cross-cutting, interconnected manner will mean facing a broad range of challenges, not least an extensive reframing of how countries and organisations work that shifts from the traditional 'silo' or sectoral approach (where each department or organisation works separately on its own) towards collaboration across a range of sectors (Stuart, 2018). It is important to point out that the SDGs are an aspirational framework existing within a weak global accountability mechanism that privileges self-regulation and state-centrism, which is further complicated by intrinsic conflicts of interest that lead to disagreement about trade-offs when implementing the SDGs. This ultimately leads to conflicts between goals, such as striking a balance between SDG8 (Decent Work and Economic Growth) and

AHO 16.3 INTERSECTION OF INFLUENCES REINFORCING DEPRIVATION

At the intersection of factors, people face multiple, reinforcing sources of deprivation and inequalities, making them more likely to be left behind.

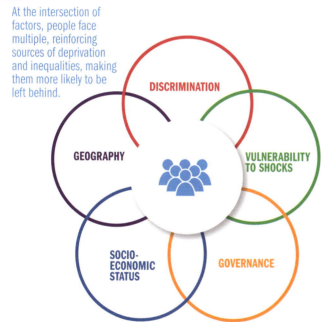

DISCRIMINATION
On the basis of assumed or ascribed identity or status

Consider: SDG outcomes and opportunities by sex, age, disability and social groups (as specified in the 2030 Agenda); evidence and recommendations from international human rights mechanisms, national human rights institutions.

GEOGRAPHY
Isolation, risk or exclusion due to location; includes environmental degradation, transport, technology

Consider: SDG outcomes and opportunities broken down by sub-national locality; inequities in mobility related to transport and internet access.

VULNERABILITY TO SHOCKS
Includes conflict, climate and environmental

Consider: Places or populations that endure more frequent and/or severe setbacks due to natural or environmental disasters, violence, crime or conflict, economic or other shocks

GOVERNANCE
Laws, policies, institutions, voice and participation (includes informal and traditional governing systems)

Consider: Impact of laws, policies, taxes, budgets, formal and traditional practices by sub-population and locality (distribution impacts); ability to participate in government and decision-making; civic space

SOCIO-ECONOMIC STATUS
Multidimensional poverty, inequalities

Consider: Multidimensional poverty of women, men and children; Gini coefficient; Inequalities-weighted Human Development Index; SDG outcomes and opportunities by income (and/or Multidimensional Poverty Index) quintile; sources on informal and vulnerable employment

Adapted from UNSDG, *Leaving no one behind: A UNSDG operation guide for UN country teams — Interim draft, 2019.* HTTPS://UNSDG.UN.ORG/SITES/DEFAULT/FILES/INTERIM-DRAFT-OPERATIONAL-GUIDE-ON-LNOB-FOR-UNCTS.PDF

preserving biodiversity for SDG15 (Life on Land) and SDG14 (Life Below Water). For example, while we recognise the need for SDG9 (Industry, Innovation and Infrastructure) and creating Sustainable Cities and Communities (SDG11), these need to be achieved in a manner that does not impede our actions towards SDG13 (Climate Action).

In particular, there is reason for caution about achieving transformative change through an approach that continues to champion export-led economic growth and trade policies driving industrial expansion and consumption (Van Niekerk, 2020). While the SDGs are articulated around themes of responsibility, there is broad consensus that they do not effectively challenge and critique the extent to which countries of the Global North are deeply involved in perpetuating ongoing forms of inequality. However, the SDGs do raise more general questions about persisting poverty and inequality, and how these are intrinsically intertwined within power relationships, which inhibit many marginalised groups from achieving the SDGs (Esquivel, 2016). This is a significant shift towards a more global view that acknowledges the role and responsibility of the Global North in progressing towards a more sustainable and resilient world for all.

Considering that a substantial number of the world's poorest and most excluded people are women and girls, it is not surprising that the third universal value guiding the design and implementation of the SDGs is gender equality and women's empowerment. As with the intersectional approach of LNOB, what is required to achieve gender equality is a transformative approach that moves beyond dealing with the symptoms of gender inequality, and towards addressing social norms, attitudes, behaviours and social systems that serve to replicate discrimination and exclusion (Esquivel, 2016).

Gender equality and women's empowerment

> The achievement of full human potential and of sustainable development is not possible if one half of humanity continues to be denied its full human rights and opportunities. Women and girls must enjoy equal access to quality education, economic resources and political participation as well as equal opportunities with men and boys for employment, leadership and decision making at all levels. (UN, 2015, p. 10)

While widely renowned for their synergetic effect on the eradication of poverty and inequality, to date no country has fully achieved gender equality and empowerment of women and girls. Consider, for a moment, that in Saudi Arabia, women were finally allowed to vote in their 2015 elections, and as of 2019, only six countries in the world have granted women equal legal and economic rights. Across the globe, women experience exclusion due to legal discrimination, harmful beliefs, limited education opportunities, lack of access to sexual and reproductive health care, and low or unequal levels of economic and political participation. Furthermore, discriminatory laws still exist which lead to low participation rates in employment, politics and education, while there are still 104 countries with laws that prevent women from working in certain industries purely based on their gender (Picheta & Mirchandani, 2019). This often means that women and girls experience poverty differently and face different barriers in accessing services, economic resources and political opportunities. For example, women and girls face specific obstacles to gaining employment, due to lesser opportunities for employment, and to social and cultural norms, including occupational segregation and unpaid care work that prevent them from accepting employment opportunities (Esquivel, 2016).

The UN has demonstrated its commitment to working towards system-wide gender parity through legislative and institutional frameworks, such as the Commission on the Status of Women (CSW), the Convention on the Elimination of All Forms of Discrimination Against Women (CEDAW) and the Beijing Declaration and Platform for the Action of the Fourth World Conference on Women. More recently, this commitment is evident in the inclusion of a gender-specific goal and the third universal principle, gender equality and women's empowerment (Stuart & Woodroffe, 2016). Many women's rights activists were relieved that gender equality gained prominence within the SDG Framework through Goal 5 (to achieve gender equality and empower all women and girls), which was applauded for its broad and diverse approach. As with all of the goals, SDG5 has specific targets, which include removing discriminatory practices, eliminating violence and harmful practices, recognising and ascribing value to unpaid work, ensuring women's full and effective participation in decision-making processes, and ensuring universal access to sexual and reproductive health rights (Ryder & Boone, 2019).

Gender inequality is one of the most pervasive forms of inequality, because it places women and girls at a disadvantage regardless of their social position (Stuart, 2018). Genuine empowerment demands action established with an understanding of how social norms and power structures differentially impact the lives and opportunities of women and, in many cases, gender minorities. This requires actions such as promoting the position of women in leadership positions, challenging resource distribution and addressing the power relationships between men and women in communities (Morgan et al., 2020). For example, work is progressing in Aotearoa to eliminate the gender pay gap, specifically in the public service. This is in response to the recognition that 'ensuring women's pay reflects their skills, efforts and responsibilities, and is not negatively affected by their gender, is about fundamental human rights' (Te Kawa Mataaho, 2020, p. 2).

Achieving gender equality is, therefore, about both *empowering* individual women, girls and gender minorities and *transforming* the power dynamics and structures that serve to reinforce gendered equities. This necessitates a genuine and proactive questioning and changing of rigid gender-based social norms and power imbalances. However, it is also important to point out that interpreting 'gender equality' along narrow binaries of men and women, or boys and girls, is problematic, too, because it not only reproduces heteronormative assumptions, but also exclusionary policies and practices that underpin structural inequalities. Therefore, achieving true and inclusive gender equality also requires going beyond binary categories and rigid social constructions to both account for the lived experiences of population groups identifying with non-binary expressions of gender and avoid ignoring differences within 'women' and other identities (Ongsupankul, 2019).

Progression towards genuine participation and acknowledgement of the

SDG 4 aims to ensure that women and girls have an equal right, and are given equal access and opportunity, to quality education throughout all phases of their lives. This is of vital significance because education increases prospects for employment, health and well-being.

SDG 8 seeks to ensure inclusive growth is achieved by making decent work equally accessible to women and men. This includes promoting equal pay for equal work, equal access to economic assets and opportunities and the fair distribution of unpaid care work.

SDG 9 aims to close the gender gap in research and innovation, as well as in the construction, manufacturing and energy sectors. This involves creating equal access for job opportunities, including leadership positions allowing women to become decision-makers.

FIGURE 2: Examples of cross-cutting goals for gender. UN, 2015

diversity of girls, women and gender minorities ensures that the most marginalised are included in decision-making processes at all levels. Many argue that the 2030 Agenda should be used as an advocacy tool to initiate action and to ensure that member states are held accountable for implementing policies, processes and practices to accelerate progress towards gender equality and empowerment. Gender equality and empowerment-related targets are embedded in 11 of the 17 goals (to different degrees), alongside Goal 5's explicit focus on gender equality. Figure 2 illustrates how the SDGs provide avenues to deal with gender-related challenges through cross-cutting goals.

However, despite the specific reference to gender in many of the SDGs, there is often insufficient regard given to gender equality by practitioners, policymakers and researchers, meaning that gender is regularly not prioritised or is missed altogether. Unfortunately, it is often the case that without explicit consideration gender-related challenges are ignored. It is essential that attention is continually paid not only to the stand-alone gender equality goal, but also to integrating gender equality throughout the SDGs. Without full integration, gender equality will remain a separate issue and be relegated to gender specialists or advocates, rather than being holistically addressed within all areas of sustainable development. In the era of the SDGs, recognising the interconnectedness of sustainable development and gender equality is vital if we are to make progress on and achieve the goals.

Conclusion

In this chapter, we began with the idea that inequality is a political choice and that, within this context, the SDGs have the potential to motivate and inspire genuine change on a global scale. The SDGs advocate this transformative approach to tackling poverty and inequality through the lens of their three universal principles, which dictated the design and delivery of the 2030 Agenda. We explained the human rights-based approach and emphasised the foundational idea that every person has value, and therefore universal rights, purely because they are human. If we value every person individually and believe in everyone's right to live a full life, then we recognise that development is only meaningful if it is enjoyed by all, and none are excluded. If development is about increased wellbeing for all, then we cannot claim success or progress if more than half the world is being left behind. When we start to genuinely engage in challenges of power and discrimination, then we must prioritise those who experience the most discrimination and particularly those who are marginalised due to their gender. The SDGs aim to achieve sustainable wellbeing for all by prioritising those most excluded and by challenging the structures and systems that replicate these unjust and unequal patterns of society. While this endeavour faces complex challenges, we believe that the relatively quick changes in the understanding of, approaches to and conversations about how to achieve the goals reflect some significant shifts in development thinking that offer hope for the future.

References

Crenshaw, K. W. (2017). *On Intersectionality: Essential writings.* Columbia Law.

Dunne, T., & Wheeler, N. J. (2016). 'We the Peoples': Contending discourses of security in human rights theory and practice. *International Relations, 18*(1), 9–23. https://doi.org/10.1177/0047117804041738

Esquivel, V. (2016). Power and the Sustainable Development Goals: A feminist analysis. *Gender and Development, 24*(1), 9–23. https://doi.org/10.1080/13552074.2016.1147872

Korten, D. (2018). *When Corporations Rule the World* (2nd ed.). Routledge.

Landman, T., & Larizza, M. (2009). Inequality and human rights: Who controls what, when, and how. *International Studies Quarterly, 53*(3), 715–736. https://doi.org/10.1111/j.1468-2478.2009.00553.x

Morgan, R., Dhatt, R., Kharel. C., & Muraya, K. (2020). A patchwork approach to gender equality weakens the SDGs: Time for cross-cutting action. *Global Health Promotion, 27*(3), 3–5. https://doi.org/10.1177/1757975920949735

Ongsupankul, W. (2019). Finding sexual minorities in United Nations Sustainable Development Goals: Towards the deconstruction of gender binary in international development policies. *LSE Law Review, 5*, 1–30.

Oxfam. (2020). Confronting Carbon Inequality: Putting climate justice at the heart of the COVID-19 recovery. Oxfam Media Briefing. www.oxfam.org/en/research/confronting-carbon-inequality

Picheta, R., & Mirchandani, K. (2019, March 2). Only 6 countries have equal rights for men and women, World Bank finds. *CNN.* https://edition.cnn.com/2019/03/02/europe/world-bank-gender-equality-report-intl/index.html

Rist, G. (2014). *The History of Development: From Western origins to global faith.* Zed Books.

Ryder, S., & Boone, K. (2019). Intersectionality and sustainable development. In W. Leal Filho, L. Brandli, P. Özuyar, & T. Wall (Eds.), *Gender Equality. Encyclopedia of the UN Sustainable Development Goals.* Springer. https://doi.org/10.1007/978-3-319-70060-1_51-1

Saiz, I., & Donald, K. (2017). Tackling inequality through the Sustainable Development Goals: Human rights in practice. *The International Journal of Human Rights, 21*(8), 1029–1049. https://doi.org/10.1080/13642987.2017.1348696

Sen, A. (2004). Amartya Sen. In D. Barsamian (Ed.), *Louder than Bombs: Interviews from The Progressive Magazine* (pp. 57–68). South End Press.

Stuart, E. (2018). Why leaving no one behind matters. In OECD (Ed.), *Development Co-operation Report: Joining forces to leave no one behind.* OECD Publishing.

Stuart, E., & Woodroffe, J. (2016). Leaving no-one behind: Can the Sustainable Development Goals succeed where the Millennium Development Goals lacked? *Gender and Development, 24*(1), 69–81. https://doi.org/10.1080/13552074.2016.1142206

Te Kawa Mataaho. (2020). *Eliminating the Public Service Gender Pay Gap: 2018–2020 action plan, version 2.* www.publicservice.govt.nz/assets/SSC-Site-Assets/Workforce-and-Talent-Management/The-Gender-Pay-Gap-Action-Plan.pdf

United Nations (UN). (2015). *Transforming Our World: The 2030 Agenda for Sustainable Development.* United Nations. https://sustainabledevelopment.un.org/content/documents/21252030%20Agenda%20for%20Sustainable%20Development%20web.pdf

United Nations Sustainable Development Goals (UNSDG). (2019). *Leaving No One Behind: A UNSDG operational guide for UN country teams — Interim draft.* https://unsdg.un.org/sites/default/files/Interim-Draft-Operational-Guide-on-LNOB-for-UNCTs.pdf

Van Niekerk, A. (2020). Inclusive economic sustainability: SDGs and global inequality. *Sustainability, 12*(5427), 1–19. https://doi.org/10.3390/su12135427

World Commission on Environment and Development (WCED). (1987). *Report of the World Commission on Environment and Development: Our common future.* UN Documents: Gathering a Body of Global Agreements.

17.
Covid-19 and inequality in Aotearoa

Margaret Forster, Sharon McLennan & Catherine Rivera

> Historically, pandemics have forced humans to break with the past and imagine their world anew. This one is no different. It is a portal, a gateway between one world and the next. (Arundhati Roy, 2020)

In 2021, Māori Television aired *Ka Puta Ka Ora*, a documentary showcasing activities across the mid-central region of Aotearoa during the 2020 Covid-19 lockdown. The documentary featured stories from whānau members, kaimahi or social service workers, iwi leaders and government agencies that highlighted how the region flourished during that time:

> When Covid-19 hit the shores of Aotearoa, and as fear started to take hold across the country, iwi and Māori communities mobilised. Relationships that had been forged across generations were able to move and activate resources with urgency. The realisation [grew] that iwi and Māori had the capability to move together to ensure communities were well-equipped to provide for their whānau, hapori [community], hapū and iwi. (Te Tihi o Ruahine, 2020)

In this chapter, we highlight Māori community responses to Covid-19 as a powerful display of rangatiratanga in action — one that saw the duty to protect and manaaki, or take care of others, prioritised over other rights, such as freedom of movement and economic security. While the Covid-19 pandemic both highlighted and exacerbated pre-existing inequality and precarity, we argue that Māori responses, through expressions of manaaki, agency, capacity and solidarity, disrupted this precariousness. These responses provide insight into how health and social systems can be reimagined in ways that reduce inequality and ensure resilience and sustainability for the future.

As recent writers (for example, Khosla et al., 2020; Leotti, 2021; Roy, 2020) have noted, the pandemic has created an opportunity for societies to break from past patterns and beliefs, and to imagine and step towards a new future. Leotti (2021) remarks that a pandemic provides 'a tremendous opportunity to (re)consider and (re)formulate the kind of world we want to live in' (p. 200). In the health context, Wahlberg and others (2021) see this as a portal to rethink the structures, systems and ideologies that shape health and wellbeing. We argue that Indigenous approaches in their various forms provide an insight into the possibilities of the world beyond the pandemic, as well as having a greater potential than the nation-state to disrupt and dismantle systems of inequality.

Colonialism, globalisation and health inequalities

In Aotearoa, we generally enjoy a high standard of living, and the country ranks highly on measures such as life expectancy and mortality rates. However, beneath gross measures of health and high OECD rankings lie deeply entrenched, longstanding inequalities. Gaps in health outcomes can be seen between rich and poor, between different ethnic groups and across genders. One example is the worldwide trend of gross disparities in morbidity and mortality between Indigenous and non-Indigenous people (Paradies, 2016; Reid & Robson, 2007; United Nations, 2009). This is linked to compromised socio-economic status, racial discrimination and inappropriate, and consequently ineffective, health-care systems (Zambas & Wright, 2016) — those 'unfair and avoidable' (Guise, 2014, p. 16) factors that adversely affect health and maintain health injustices. The resulting inequalities in health outcomes indicate that the right to good health as declared in several international instruments[1] is not a reality for all citizens.

1   These instruments include the Universal Declaration of Human Rights (UDHR), the United Nations Declaration on the Rights of Indigenous People (UNDRIP) and the Sustainable Development Goals (SDGs).

Consequently, when a pandemic strikes it does not affect all populations or individuals equally.

Colonisation forced Māori communities into 'prolonged and extreme levels of poverty' (Reid et al., 2016, pp. 39–40) as connections to whenua and to each other were severed. The deliberate dismantling of tribal structures such as whānau, hapū and iwi through colonial processes led to increasingly compromised cultural, social, economic and political wellbeing. Communities were devastated by the corresponding impact of the loss of culture, identity and sense of belonging. The lived experiences of Māori became synonymous with insecure housing, employment, education and/or access to health care (see, for example, Moewaka Barnes & McCreanor, 2019; Reid et al., 2014, 2016; Robson & Harris, 2007). As King et al. (2020) note:

> Even without a pandemic, we already experience significant inequities in accessing healthcare, have higher hospitalisation rates for avoidable and/ or amenable conditions and receive lower quality care. In addition, racism within the health and disability system drives inequities and poorer health for Māori. Such drivers of inequitable access to high quality healthcare for Māori will be intensified if the health and disability system becomes overloaded. This can occur from factors relating to broader determinants of health (such as unemployment and loss of income) or increasing racism against Māori within the context of pressured decision-making by health professionals. It can also occur through severe restrictions to a range of health services for non-COVID conditions. (para. 8)

Nation-state responses to these inequalities have been limited, and gains, while arguably steady, are slow to emerge (see Moewaka Barnes & McCreanor, 2019). The government has been aware of significant socio-economic disparities between Māori and non-Māori since the 1960s (Hunn, 1961), yet successive attempts to close the gaps have had minimal impact on the overall socio-economic trends. For example, in addition to higher rates of health conditions, chronic disease and disability rates, higher proportions of Māori still live in more deprived areas, and Māori are still more likely to have 'lower rates of school completion, higher rates of unemployment, less personal income and live in more crowded households than Pākehā' (Ministry of Health, 2015). In part, this reflects a failure to decolonise social structures and institutions that were designed to reproduce non-Māori cultural values and interests (Te Rōpū Whāriki, 2014). The system that has been created does not benefit everyone equally and, therefore, requires 'people to be treated differently to achieve equal outcomes' (Te Rōpū Whāriki, 2014, p. 3). Globalisation has further exacerbated the situation, leading to the rise of the Māori precariat (Groot et al., 2017) — people who experience a precarious existence *and* identify as Māori. Precarity is a common experience for Indigenous peoples across the globe (United Nations, 2009).

Responding to the Covid-19 crisis

Globally, Covid-19 'pushed all health systems to their limits, exposing severe gaps in public health infrastructure' (Lal et al., 2021, p. 61) and amplifying disadvantage by increasing the severity of socio-economic inequalities, racism and uneven access to health care. Globally, nation-states instituted curfews and lockdowns, closed borders, and tested and quarantined people in sometimes coercive and authoritarian ways. Within six months, 'over half the world's population was affected by restrictions of movement, checking both global and local flows of goods and populations' (Wahlberg et al., 2021, p. 4). These restrictions were experienced in racially, socio-economically and globally uneven ways, with the precariat at high risk of exposure to the virus, and equally vulnerable to the resulting severe symptoms, sequelae and death (Wahlberg et al., 2021). Their vulnerability was due in part to the high demand for essential workers, a perilous opportunity that many were not able to refuse. The outcome, as Wahlberg and colleagues (2021) note, was that 'at the societal level, everywhere, viral loads [were] disproportionately shouldered by the disadvantaged and discriminated' (p. 12).

Aotearoa experienced some of the toughest restrictions on movement globally, as the government implemented a clear elimination strategy. This strategy was considered exemplary, resulting in one of the lowest cumulative case counts, incidence and mortality among higher-income countries in 2020 (Jefferies et al., 2020). However, from the outset of the pandemic, health experts and Māori leaders were worried about an inadequate focus on Māori health equity in pandemic planning (King et al., 2020). The whole-of-government 'one-size-fits-all' approach had not involved local Māori organisations (McClintock & Boulton, 2020). Moreover, Te Rōpū Whakakaupapa Urutā (the Māori national pandemic response group) criticised the government's Māori Covid-19 Plan for its use of 'feel-good aspirational statements' without substantial detail as to how inequality within the health system could be addressed (Barber & Naepi, 2020, p. 695). Further, Māori considered it risky to rely on the national health policy and mainstream health services given the government's long and poor track record in delivering satisfactory health outcomes to Māori communities.

AHO 17.1 PANDEMICS AND INDIGENEITY

Pandemics have been particularly lethal for Indigenous people (King et al., 2020). For example, Māori death rates during the 1918 influenza pandemic were seven times higher than those for Pākehā, and during the 2009 H1N1 influenza pandemic, Māori rates of influenza were twice as high as those of Pākehā (Espiner, 2020; McMeeking & Savage, 2020; Wilson et al., 2012). As Barber and Naepi (2020) note: 'Covid-19 can be joined by a single thread to both the virulent diseases that arrived with Europeans as well as the subsequent influenza pandemic of 1918 and more recently the measles epidemic in Samoa in 2019. What connects these pandemics is that they exacerbate and intensify existing conditions of colonial inequality and injustice.' (pp. 693–694)

In this part of the world, we have a very clear example of the link between colonialism and pandemics. So clear in fact, that in 2002 Prime Minister Helen Clark formally apologised for New Zealand's 'inept and incompetent' administration of what was then a colony under New Zealand control. That colony was Western Sāmoa.

In November 1918, the New Zealand passenger and cargo ship *Talune* arrived at Apia from Auckland. Passengers from the ship were allowed ashore, despite several being seriously ill from pneumonic influenza, a highly infectious disease already responsible for hundreds of thousands of deaths around the world.

The consequences were catastrophic, as the disease spread rapidly throughout the islands. Sāmoa's local health facilities were unable to cope, and the death toll rose with terrifying speed. Within a week, the disease had devastated the main Samoan island of Upolu and spread to neighboring Savai'i.

Approximately 8500 people died in the outbreak, 22 per cent of the population. According to a 1947 United Nations report, it ranked as 'one of the most disastrous epidemics recorded anywhere in the world during the present century, so far as the proportion of deaths to the population is concerned'.

Survivors blamed the New Zealand Administrator, Lieutenant-Colonel Robert Logan, for failing to quarantine the *Talune* and for rejecting an offer of medical assistance from American Sāmoa. In comparison with the 8500 deaths in Western Sāmoa, there were no deaths in

The steamship *Talune*, photographed in Wellington Harbour between 1890 and 1925.
ALEXANDER TURNBULL LIBRARY, 1/1-002436-G

American Sāmoa as the governor, J. M. Poyer, had promptly quarantined vessels arriving at the islands and so avoided any outbreak.

References

Barber, S., & Naepi, S. (2020). Sociology in crisis: COVID-19 and the colonial politics of knowledge production in Aotearoa New Zealand. *Journal of Sociology, 56*(4), 693–703. https://doi.org/0.1177/1440783320939679

Espiner, E. (2020, March 25). New Zealand must learn lessons of 1918 pandemic and protect Māori from Covid-19. *The Guardian.* www.theguardian.com/commentisfree/2020/mar/26/new-zealand-must-learn-lessons-of-1918-pandemic-and-protect-maori-from-covid-19

King, P., Cormack, D., McLeod, M., Harris, R., & Gurney, J. (2020, April 10). COVID-19 and Māori health — When equity is more than a word [Blog]. Public Health Expert. https://blogs.otago.ac.nz/pubhealthexpert/covid-19-and-maori-health-when-equity-is-more-than-a-word/

McMeeking, S., & Savage, C. (2020). Māori responses to COVID-19. *Policy Quarterly 16*(3), 36–41.

Wilson, N., Barnard, L. T., Summers, J. A., Shanks, G. D., & Baker, M. G. (2012). Differential mortality rates by ethnicity in 3 influenza pandemics over a century, New Zealand. *Emerging Infectious Diseases, 18*(1), 71–77. https://doi.org/10.3201/eid1801.110035

The Māori Covid-19 response

A key reason for the lack of trust in the ability of the government and mainstream health services is the vivid memories many Māori have of the 1918 influenza pandemic that caused many deaths and decimated whakapapa connections. A visit to any urupā reveals how much Māori suffered and were disproportionately affected compared with their Pākehā neighbours. For this reason, when the Covid-19 pandemic struck in 2020, Māori quickly stepped up to protect their communities from the outbreak.

Māori community responses to the Covid-19 lockdown, as documented in the film *Ka Puta Ka Ora* (Te Tihi o Ruahine, 2020) and the report *Ko Tōku Ara rā Aotearoa* (McClintock & Boulton, 2020), included the provision of community based assessment centres (CBAC), mobile health teams and virtual consultations by Māori health providers. The emphasis was placed on physical, not social, distancing (i.e. remaining apart while still maintaining social contact and relationships). Iwi and Māori social services organised visits, distributed food and care packages, and regularly contacted members of the community — the elderly, those living alone and families, Māori and non-Māori. The right of communities to protect themselves was expressed through iwi-led checkpoints, which prevented unnecessary travel into isolated communities. The intent was to halt the spread of the disease and conserve local resources, including the capacity of health services.

Emphasis was also placed on social cohesion, which is critical for maintaining the collective, developing and transmitting culture, and maintaining identity and a sense of belonging. However, in a Covid-19 world, some cultural practices were considered to place Māori communities at risk. For example, it is difficult to physically isolate at large social gatherings, such as hui or tangi. Early in the pandemic, health and iwi leaders advised marae to modify social engagement practices (Dawes et al., 2021). As a result, many marae suspended the hongi, where people share breath by the act of pressing noses, as well as kihi (kisses) and harirū (handshakes). When the state restricted the practice of tangihanga during lockdown, Te Rōpū Whakakaupapa Urutā strongly advocated for maintaining the right to farewell the dead according to custom. New ways to navigate restrictions over freedom of movement and the exercise of cultural rights were devised by tikanga experts, whānau and the funeral industry.

These community responses were a powerful display of rangatiratanga — Māori sovereignty and self-determination in action. They were characterised by 'innovative, decisive, and robust decision making' (Te One & Clifford, 2021, p. 9) by Māori communities, driven by tikanga. The result was an unexpected outcome for Māori. Māori had been expected to have double the infection and mortality rates of non-Māori. However, in 2020, Māori collectively had a lower Covid-19 infection rate than the population as a whole — the first time Māori had better health and social outcomes than non-Māori (McMeeking & Savage, 2020). The remarkable achievement of Māori communities and leadership in 2020 spared many from suffering and emphasised the potential of Indigenous-led solutions to global crises.

In 2021, the Delta variant of Covid-19 arrived in Aotearoa and Māori once again went into action caring for communities. However, Delta was quite a different beast. At the time of writing, Māori comprised 28 per cent of all cases since Covid-19 first arrived in Aotearoa, and over 45 per cent of active cases (Taonui, 2021). The rapid spread of Delta was attributed to low vaccination rates among Māori — when lockdown restrictions were eased in the Auckland outbreak, Māori communities were severely under-vaccinated. In part, this is linked to the way in which the vaccination strategy was planned and rolled out through the mainstream health sector without the prioritisation of Māori. But it was also due to longstanding Māori mistrust of the health sector (linked to a legacy of systemic racism and discrimination), meaning that vaccination clinics were not well attended by Māori and Pasifika peoples. It was evident that one size definitely did not fit all.

Iwi Covid-19 checkpoint at Waitangi, September 2020. PETER DE GRAAF, *NORTHERN ADVOCATE*

AHO 17.2 PASIFIKA RESPONSES

While the Covid-19 pandemic was ongoing, there were already signs of adaptation and resilience in the ways in which people around the globe coped with and responded to the first year of the pandemic. This was the focus of the book *COVID in the Islands: A comparitive perspective on the Caribbean and the Pacific* (2021). In the book, Colin Tukuitonga disusses the pandemic in New Zealand, with a focus on Pacific Islands people living in New Zealand.

'With encouragement and support from public health officials and Pacific health professionals, the Pacific Islands communities affected by the outbreak responded by working together to limit the spread of the virus. Pacific social support agencies and Pacific personalities responded in a coordinated way to support case identification and isolation, contact tracing and public health measures provided by the national health services. Pacific community activities were strongly supported by Pacific Members of Parliament with support from national leaders. The Pacific MPs were also able to secure dedicated additional resources to support activities by and for Pacific communities. A Pacific Expert Group was established to provide technical and policy advice to Pacific Ministers. All government agencies provided specific and additional support for Pacific communities.

'Despite socio-economic disadvantages and difficulties accessing health services, the response to the Auckland August cluster by Pacific communities proved a triumph over adversity. In response to the threat of COVID-19 Pacific Islands families and communities, church and community leaders, health care providers and media came together to inform and support their communities to prevent the spread of COVID-19. Churches became focal points for the distribution of food parcels and social support and centres for COVID-19 testing. Church leaders became important and visible champions for public health measures such as hand washing, social distancing and limitations on mass gatherings. Churches rapidly transitioned to online services and congregations advised to remain at home. Pacific media were responsible for the dissemination of information on radio, TV, print and social media, including information translated into several Pacific languages.

'Pacific Islands primary health care providers were able to respond promptly to the needs of their communities. For example, community COVID-19 testing

K'aute Pasifika Trust staff give away vouchers as part of an incentive scheme at a drive-through vaccination clinic in Kirikiriroa Hamilton in October 2021. STUFF LIMITED

centres, including mobile clinics, were set up in strategic locations throughout the community which allowed Pacific Islands people to get tested without the traditional geographical barriers that existed in accessing health care. As a result, testing rates for COVID-19 were highest among Pacific Islands people.

The Auckland Regional Public Health Service established a 'Pacific Team' to support the national contact tracing efforts with staff able to speak one of the Pacific languages.
This improved the efficiency and reliability of contact tracing activities.' (Tukuitonga, 2021, pp. 64–65)

Reference

Tukuitonga, C. (2021). COVID-19 in Pacific Islands people of Aotearoa / New Zealand: Communities taking control. In Y. Campbell & J. Connell (Eds.), *COVID in the Islands: A comparative perspective on the Caribbean and the Pacific* (pp. 55–69). Palgrave Macmillan.

Disrupting precariousness

The responses showcased in the previous section are just a snapshot. While distinct and often bespoke to people and place, several interconnected threads are evident — the right to transform Māori futures, ensuring Māori prosper and flourish as Māori, and the responsibility to care for the community during a health crisis. These goals can be achieved through two key Māori cultural concepts — manaaki and rangatiratanga — and by leveraging international rights movements and instruments, such as the World Health Organization (WHO) and UNDRIP. This section explores how these concepts, movements and instruments are brought together in Aotearoa to prioritise wellbeing.

Enacting manaaki

A Māori response to precarity is to enact manaaki — the duty to care. This is a strengths-based, long-term protective strategy derived from actions set by atua (see iho atua in Chapter 4) and a collective sense of responsibility. Māori responses to Covid-19 have centred around the power of whānau, hapū, iwi and pan-tribal organisations to reach their members and connect with each other, as well as their ability to connect with government agencies, particularly health and social services. These whānau, hapū, iwi and pan-tribal organisations are the same entities that, pre-Covid-19, were advocating for the marginalised, the ill and those at risk by leveraging Māori culture as a foundation to strengthen, build resilience and fight for social justice.

The examples showcased in the previous section demonstrate manaaki in action. Culture and tribal networks are leveraged proactively to keep the community safe and well, with actions often being linked to the recognition of mana, the authority and power of the collective and the individual, as well as focusing on mana-enhancing practices.

'Mana-enhancing practice' is a phrase attributed to Māori social worker Leland Ruwhiu (2008) that advocates for respectful and empowering engagement. In his experience, these types of interactions are the key to building resilience to the consequences of colonisation (Munford & Sanders, 2011) and a positive step towards disrupting and countering precariousness. Mana-enhancing practices mobilise rangatiratanga, culture, identity and belonging as protective mechanisms against crises like the Covid-19 pandemic.

Enacting rangatiratanga

Rangatiratanga involves taking control of Māori futures through acts of Māori self-determination and authority. In a contemporary context, it is closely linked to Māori development. Māori development first emerged in the 1980s (Fitzgerald, 2004) to ensure that Māori prosper and flourish as Māori (Durie, 1998). It introduced a new agenda for development based on potentiality, driven by Māori, with a renewed commitment to Māori self-reliance for realising Māori aspirations. This movement continued the work started by early Māori leaders, including Sir Apirana Ngata, Sir Maui Pomare and Princess Te Puea, who were strong advocates for addressing poverty to support the health and wellbeing of Māori communities (see, for example, Durie, 1994; King, 2003).

Māori development today presents in various ways. There are pan-tribal national political collectives, such as the New Zealand Māori Council, Māori Women's Welfare League and the Iwi Leaders Forum, that advocate on matters of importance to all Māori. There are also collectives that represent the interests of the iwi, hapū and whānau — the rūnanga (tribal council), trust boards, marae committees and incorporated societies. While tribal interests are wide and varied, these collectives engage in activities that reaffirm local tribal authority and culture. Priorities centre around supporting cultural identity and belonging, and include te reo revitalisation, strengthening of culture and marae and community development. Several innovative initiatives have emerged from this space, including pā wars (tribal sporting events), tribal housing projects and tribal saving schemes such as Whai Rawa — a Ngāi Tahu savings and investment scheme that can be used to purchase a home or fund retirement. Many of the tribal collectives also work with Māori businesses, who are engaged in building the Māori economy and economic asset base, and kaupapa Māori services.

Kaupapa Māori services is a generic term that refers to a wide range of social, cultural and environmental activities designed by Māori for Māori. Some examples include Māori health and social service providers, Māori resource management units and Māori research units. They also include urban authorities that have emerged to advocate for those living in the cities and engage in many of the same Māori-focused activities. All of these collectives interact with the nation-state, NGOs and communities in various ways to advance Māori interests, particularly towards reducing inequalities and disadvantages and advocating for positive Māori development. They were also at the centre of the Māori response to Covid-19.

Māori development focuses on ensuring that Māori people can live as Māori, can participate as citizens of the world, and can enjoy good health and a high standard of living (Durie, 1998). It emphasises Māori rights as Indigenous people in Aotearoa, as humans and as local and global citizens. Māori development supporters demand that the government recognise and address our colonial past by honouring the spirit of te Tiriti o Waitangi and providing greater opportunities for Māori self-determination. Towards this end, the Māori social structures and organisations outlined above support Māori capability and capacity building and resilience.

Enacting whānau ora

Māori responses to Covid-19 provide a great exemplar of mana-enhancing practices and whānau ora in action. Whānau ora as a state policy builds on the power of whānau to enhance the wellbeing of individuals and families. It involves placing the interests of the family at the centre of any interventions, as well as wrapping around services and support structures to address crises and work towards realising potential and aspirations.

Whānau ora as a cultural concept draws on Māori world views and knowledge that recognises the importance of family connectedness for responding to precarity. It is understood that a functional whānau can protect and support its members to be productive citizens, thereby contributing to the prosperity and vibrancy of the community. A functional whānau, therefore, has the potential to care for its members — culturally, socially and economically.

Enacting kāwanatanga

Māori concepts such as manaaki have the potential to protect against uncertain, insecure and unequal lives for all who live in Aotearoa. We can consider manaaki as a precursor of good governance and, therefore, as a citizenship right. Good governance is a principle derived from Article One of te Tiriti o Waitangi. It requires government to design and manage relevant and equitable systems (i.e. health or education systems) that enable Māori self-determination, equity, social justice and active protection (see, for example, Ministry of Health, 2020a, 2020b). This means that government can support Māori self-determination through the allocation of resources to Māori sovereign entities and Māori health and social providers.

Unfortunately, the aspiration is not reflected in reality. This was especially noticeable during the Covid-19 vaccine roll-out, when initial advice from Māori leaders and Māori health experts was ignored and the government failed to capitalise on the early success of Māori health providers in protecting the community. This may be seen as predictable, given that this country's primary health-care system has continually failed Māori and the precariat, and has been unable to achieve any equity of health outcomes (Waitangi Tribunal, 2019). Entrenched and longstanding resourcing issues also became more visible during the vaccination roll-out, as Māori health and social service providers struggled to secure resources from government and its agencies to protect and support Māori communities (see for example, Tahana, 2021). The gains made in 2020 were slowly eroded in Covid's Delta wave, as many of the earlier successes had been reliant on the efforts of Māori communities and Māori health and social services. While government funds were finally released to support these efforts, questions were raised as to whether this was sufficient or timely.

How do we ensure the lived experiences of the precariat are not exacerbated by events such as a global pandemic? One response is supporting rangatiratanga through international rights-based instruments. The government is a signatory to UNDRIP and has committed to achieving the aims of the WHO and the Sustainable Development Goals (see Chapter 16). All of these instruments strongly support Indigenous sovereignty and social justice. However, they are aspirational, and it is unclear how the government will meet these responsibilities.

Some clarity was sought by the New Zealand government when a working group was established to devise a plan to realise the intent of UNDRIP. The group's report, *He Puapua* (Charters et al., 2019), assumed that wellbeing is a key government priority and te Tiriti o Waitangi is a central part of the constitutional foundation of Aotearoa (Charters et al., 2019). The report acknowledged that 'Aotearoa is comparatively advanced globally in providing for Māori inclusion in Kāwanatanga Karauna (state governance) and cultural rights, although there remains room for improvement' (Charters et al., 2019, p. iii). Further, it criticised the lack of government support for 'Māori self-determination, which we understand to be Māori control over Māori destinies. Based on the evidence, we would expect Māori well-being to improve as our authority over our lives increases' (Charters et al., 2019, p. iii). Consequently, the working group recommended a 'refocus [and] restructure of governance to realise rangatiratanga' (Charters et al., 2019, p. iii) and provided a roadmap for achieving this by 2040 — the bicentenary of the signing of te Tiriti o Waitangi.

It is noteworthy that the government is taking these steps, with the report's authors observing that 'New Zealand is the first state to embark on a process for a Declaration plan, and has the capacity to be a world-leader in realising Indigenous people's rights, especially if it is ambitious' (Charters et al., 2019, p. iv). If adopted, the vision outlined in *He Puapua* has the potential to make a significant shift towards equality, and to dismantle the systems that maintain precariousness.

The vision is based on a future where 'Māori and the Crown enjoy a harmonious and constructive relationship and work together to restore and uphold the wellbeing of ngā tangata [people], Papatūānuku and the natural environment' (Charters et al., 2019, p. iv). The roadmap is not prescriptive, as it needs to accommodate local tribal-level aspirations and respond to future developments and challenges, such as climate change. Equality would be achieved through a range of strategies and measurable outcomes, which are based on at least three priorities. The first revolves around exercising authority over, and building the resilience of, culture and Māori governance and social structures to support Māori identity and belonging, to grow the tribal estate (tangible and intangible assets) and to ensure Māori people and communities prosper and flourish. The second priority is involvement in meaningful decision making in matters of importance to Māori, including decision making at the nation-state governance level. The final priority is centred around the notion of biculturalism, where distinctiveness and wellbeing, including Māori perspectives, are valued. Success will be evident when Māori culture is an integral part of national identity and heritage, embraced and respected by all New Zealanders. This will require citizenship education that builds awareness of responsibilities regarding te Tiriti o Waitangi and the UNDRIP (Tawhai, 2020). Glimpses of this vision are already evident through a recent announcement by the New Zealand government to establish a Māori Health Authority to work alongside Health New Zealand to grow Māori-specific services and ensure better health outcomes for Māori.

Conclusion

In this chapter, we have argued that Māori security, protection and wellbeing are dependent on enacting rangatiratanga as a critical response to the Covid-19 pandemic, and to inequality in general. Māori collectives in their various forms are a central part of this response and have a greater potential than the nation-state to disrupt and dismantle systems of precariousness. This includes reimagining our rights regimes to develop more inclusive policies and practices for realising Indigenous rights and achieving equality for all.

The rapid spread of the Delta variant of Covid-19 in Māori communities in late 2021 is evidence of the impacts of colonialism, entrenched socio-economic disadvantage, overcrowded housing and higher prevalence of underlying health conditions (Tukuitonga, 2021). It also highlights the results of decision making that did not include Māori, health structures that do not respond adequately to Māori communities, and a deep lack of trust in mainstream health services. This raises the question of what responsibility we have as a society to dismantle the ongoing impacts of inequality and precarity. If social structures and policies of the nation-state play a substantive role in the maintenance of precariousness, how do we disrupt and liberate? Part of the answer lies in addressing the social conditions that adversely affect health — including 'the impact of neoliberal globalisation on the fundamental causes of health injustice' (Flynn, 2021, p. 1) — while also advocating for the fair and just distribution of nation-state health resources. This approach acknowledges the importance of social structures for realising the universal right to good health and wellbeing.

While the prognosis might be grim if left to rely on nation-state-level responses, hope lies in the ability of Indigenous peoples to act and respond to global crises like Covid-19. This means moving away from those aspects of globalisation that privilege private property rights and economic competitiveness towards 'new systems suited to the more open, flexible economies' (Standing, 2017, p. 9) that prioritise and centre wellbeing. In Aotearoa, this means returning to Indigenous systems in order to enact rangatiratanga as a response to precarity. The power of rangatiratanga to disrupt precarity and ensure a more just, sustainable and equitable future is rendered visible through Māori responses to Covid-19.

References

Barber, S., & Naepi, S. (2020). Sociology in crisis: COVID-19 and the colonial politics of knowledge production in Aotearoa New Zealand. *Journal of Sociology 56*(4), 693–703. https://doi.org/0.1177/1440783320939679

Charters, C., Kingdon-Bebb, K., Olsen, T., Ormsby, W., Owen, E., Pryor, J., Ruru, J., Solomon, N., & Williams, G. (2019). *He Puapua*. Report of the working group on a plan to realise the UN Declaration of the Rights of Indigenous Peoples in Aotearoa/New Zealand. Te Puni Kōkiri. www.tpk.govt.nz/docs/undrip/tpk-undrip-he-puapua.pdf

Dawes, T., Muru-Lanning, M., Lapsley, H., Hopa, N., Dixon, N., Moore, C., Tukiri, C., Jones, N., Muru-Lanning, C., & Oh, M. (2021). Hongi, Harirū and Hau: Kaumātua in the time of COVID-19. *Journal of the Royal Society of New Zealand, 51*(S1), S23–S36. https://doi.org/10.1080/03036758.2020.1853182

de Graaf, P. (2020, September 4). Covid 19 coronavirus: Māori more likely to die from the virus, says new study. *New Zealand Herald*. www.nzherald.co.nz/kahu/covid-19-coronavirus-maori-more-likely-to-die-from-the-virus-says-new-study/WA4UUOBSMKQ33DG4N5AS5TUWNU/

Durie, M. H. (1994). *Whaiora: Māori health development*. Oxford University Press.

Durie, M. H. (1998). *Te Mana te Kawanatanga — The politics of Māori self-determination*. Oxford University Press.

Fitzgerald. E. (2004). Development since 1984 Hui Taumata. In P. Spoonley, C. MacPherson, & D. Pearson (Eds.), *Tangata Tangata: The changing ethnic contours of New Zealand* (pp. 43–58). Dunmore Press.

Flynn, M. B. (2021). Global capitalism as a societal determinant of health: A conceptual framework. *Social Science and Medicine, 268* (November 2020), 113530. https://doi.org/10.1016/j.socscimed.2020.113530

Groot, S., Van Ommen, C., Masters-Awatere, B., & Tassell-Matamua, T. (Eds.). (2017). *Precarity: Uncertain, insecure and unequal lives in Aotearoa New Zealand*. Massey University Press.

Guise, A. (2014). Globalization, social change and health. In J. Hanefeld (Ed.), *Globalization and Health* (pp. 14–25). McGraw-Hill Education.

Hunn, H. K. (1961). *Report on Department of Māori Affairs*. Government Printer.

Jefferies, S., French, N., Gilkison, C., Graham, G., Hope, V., Marshall, J., McElnay, C., McNeill, A., Muellner, P., Paine, S., Prasad, N., Scott, J., Sherwood, J., Yang, L., & Priest, P. (2020). COVID-19 in New Zealand and the impact of the national response: A descriptive epidemiological study. *The Lancet Public Health, 5*(11), e612–e623. https://doi.org/10.1016/S2468-2667(20)30225-5

Khosla, R., Allotey, P., & Gruskin, S. (2020). Global health and human rights for a postpandemic world. *BMJ Global Health, 5*(8), e003548. https://doi.org/10.1136/bmjgh-2020-003548

King, M. (2003). *Te Puea: A life*. Reed.

King, P., Cormack, D., McLeod, M., Harris, R., & Gurney, J. (2020, April 10). COVID-19 and Māori Health — When equity is more than a word [Blog]. Public Health Expert. https://blogs.otago.ac.nz/pubhealthexpert/covid-19-and-maori-health-when-equity-is-more-than-a-word/

Lal, A., Erondu, N. A., Heymann, D. L., Gitahi, G., & Yates, R. (2021). Fragmented health systems in COVID-19: Rectifying the misalignment between global health security and universal health coverage. *The Lancet, 397*(10268), 61–67. https://doi.org/10.1016/S0140-6736(20)32228-5

Leotti, S. M. (2021). The imaginative failure of normal: Considerations for a post-pandemic future. *Qualitative Social Work, 20*(1–2), 200–205. https://doi.org/10.1177/1473325020973338

McClintock, K., & Boulton, A. (Eds.). (2020). *Ko Tōku Ara rā Aotearoa, Our Journey, New Zealand COVID19 2020*. Te Kīwai Rangahau, Te Rau Ora & Whakauae Research Centre. https://terauora.com/wp-content/uploads/2020/11/Ko_toku_ara_ra_18_11_20_FINAL_Interactive.pdf

McMeeking, S., & Savage, C. (2020) Māori responses to COVID-19. *Policy Quarterly 16*(3) 36–41.

Ministry of Health. (2015). *Tatau Kahukura: Maori health chart book 2015* (3rd ed.). Ministry of Health.

Ministry of Health. (2020a). *Te Titiri o Waitangi Framework*. www.health.govt.nz/system/files/documents/pages/whakamaua-tiriti-o-waitangi-framework-a3-aug20.pdf

Ministry of Health. (2020b). *Whakamaua. Māori health action plan 2020–2025*. www.health.govt.nz/system/files/documents/publications/whakamaua-maori-health-action-plan-2020-2025-2.pdf

Moewaka Barnes, H., & McCreanor, T., (2019). Colonisation, hauora and whenua in Aotearoa. *Journal of the Royal Society of New Zealand. 49*(1), 19–33. https://doi.org/10.1080/03036758.2019.1668439

Munford, R., & Sanders, J. (2011). Embracing the diversity of practice: Indigenous knowledge and mainstream social work practice. *Journal of Social Work Practice, 25*(1), 63–77. www.tandfonline.com/doi/pdf/10.1080/02650533.2010.532867?needAccess=true

Paradies, Y. (2016). Colonisation, racism and indigenous health. *Journal of Population Research, 33*(1), 83–96. https://doi.org/10.1007/s12546-016-9159-y

Reid, J., Taylor-Moore, K., Varona, G. (2014). Towards a social-structural model for understanding current disparities in Maori health and well-being. *Journal of Loss and Trauma, 19*, 514–536. https://doi.org/10.1080/15325024.2013.809295

Reid, J., Varona, G., Fisher, M., & Smith, C. (2016). Understanding Māori 'lived' culture to determine cultural connectedness and wellbeing. *Journal of Population Research, 33*(1), 31–49. https://doi.org/10.1007/s12546-016-9165-0

Reid, P., & Robson, B. (2007). Understanding health inequities. In B. Robson & R. Harris (Eds.), *Hauora: Māori standards of health IV: A study of the years 2000–2005* (pp. 3–10). Te Rōpū Rangahau Hauora a Eru Pōmare.

Robson, B., & Harris, R. (Eds.). (2007). *Hauora: Māori standards of health IV. A study of the years 2000–2005*. Te Rōpū Rangahau Hauora a Eru Pōmare.

Roy, A. (2020, April 4). The pandemic is a portal. *Financial Times*. www.ft.com/content/10d8f5e8-74eb-11ea-95fe-fcd274e920ca

Ruwhiu, L. (2008). Indigenous issues in Aotearoa New Zealand. In M. Connolly & L. Harms (Eds), *Social Work Contexts and Practice* (pp. 107–120). Oxford University Press.

Standing, G. (2017). Foreword. In S. Groot, C. Van Ommen, B. Masters-Awatere, & T. Tassell-Matamua (Eds.), *Precarity: Uncertain, insecure and unequal lives in Aotearoa New Zealand* (pp. 9–11). Massey University Press.

Tahana, J. (2021, September 23). Government denies it has failed Māori on Covid. RNZ. www.rnz.co.nz/news/te-manu-korihi/452174/government-denies-it-has-failed-maori-on-covid

Taonui, R. (2021, November 14). Continuous exposure to virus risk for vaccinated Māori isolating at home. *Waatea News*. https://waateanews.com/2021/11/14/dr-rawiri-taonui-continuous-exposure-to-virus-risk-for-vaccinated-maori-isolating-at-home/

Tawhai, V. M. H. (2020). A red-tipped dawn: Teaching and learning about indigeneity and the implications for citizenship education [Doctoral Dissertation, Massey University]. http://hdl.handle.net/10179/16332

Te One, A., & Clifford, C. (2021) Tino rangatiratanga and well-being: Māori self determination in the face of Covid-19. *Frontiers in Sociology, 6*, 1–10.

Te Rōpū Whāriki. (2014). Alternatives to anti-Māori themes in news media. Massey University. https://trc.org.nz/sites/trc.org.nz/files/AlternativesA4-booklet.pdf

Te Tihi o Ruahine. (Producer). (2020). *Ka puta, Ka Ora* [Video documentary]. www.maoritelevision.com/docos/ka-puta-ka-ora

Tukuitonga, C. (2021, September 21). New Zealand cannot abandon its COVID elimination strategy while Māori and Pasifika vaccination rates are too low. *The Conversation*. https://theconversation.com/new-zealand-cannot-abandon-its-covid-elimination-strategy-while-maori-and-pasifika-vaccination-rates-are-too-low-168278

United Nations. (2009). *State of the World's Indigenous Peoples.* Department of Economic and Social Affairs. www.un.org/esa/socdev/unpfii/documents/SOWIP/en/SOWIP_web.pdf

Waitangi Tribunal. (2019). *Hauora. Report on stage one of the Health Services and Outcomes Kaupapa Inquiry.* https://forms.justice.govt.nz/search/Documents/WT/wt_DOC_152801817/Hauora%20W.pdf

Wahlberg, A., Burke, N. J., & Manderson, L. (2021). Introduction: Stratified livability and pandemic effects. In L. Manderson, N. J. Burke, & A. Wahlberg (Eds.), *Viral Loads* (pp. 1–23). UCL Press.

Zambas, S. I., & Wright, J. (2016). Impact of colonialism on Māori and Aboriginal healthcare access: A discussion paper. *Contemporary Nurse, 52*(4), 398–409. https://doi.org/10.1080/10376178.2016.1195238

18.

Shifting the poverty lens for sustainable livelihoods
Pasifika perspectives on better quality of life

Siautu Alefaio-Tugia, Malcolm Andrews, Emeline Afeaki-Mafile'o, Petra Satele, Stuart Carr, Jarrod Haar, Darrin Hodgetts, Jane Parker, James Arrowsmith, Amanda Young-Hauser & Harvey Jones

While every individual should have the freedom to a better quality of life and the opportunity to thrive in the community they live in, for the Pacific diaspora in Aotearoa the journey has been marred by socio-political impacts. Between the 1950s and 1970s, the New Zealand government encouraged immigration from Pacific nations with the promise of employment and good wages. Migration flows increased from Pacific countries over this time to meet the demands of a booming economy. As a result, Auckland city became affectionately known as the Polynesian capital of the world.

This was short-lived due to an economic recession in the 1970s. In an about-face, the New Zealand government targeted Pacific migrants, mainly from Samoa and Tonga, with racial denigration through what is now infamously referred to as the 'Dawn Raids'. This is a blighted period in Aotearoa's history where Pacific migrants were targeted and chased down by police for overstaying when the majority of overstayers at the time were from Europe. In the early hours of the morning while still asleep, Pacific families were raided and, if overstayers found, were herded like animals into police vans for deportation back to their islands of origin. The bitter taste of betrayal by government authorities remains for many Pacific generations now citizens of Aotearoa. Over 40 years on, Pacific migrants still pay the harsh price of blue-collar abuse, where on average they are the lowest paid in comparison with other ethnic groups. This chapter focuses on poverty and income inequality among Pasifika in Aotearoa, focusing the issue of the 'living wage' through a Pasifika-lens, and exploring examples of community-led initiatives that move beyond questions of employment and income, to reflect community aspirations for a thriving and flourishing future.

Pasifika diaspora in Aotearoa and the reality of impoverishment

Generally, Pacific peoples in Aotearoa consist of a youthful and growing population with a higher percentage residing in urban areas. For most Pacific peoples, quality of life is centred around community. Churches as village-contexts are what Pacific diaspora build and invest in economically to uphold cultural-faith values and beliefs, at the same time maintaining language, identity and social-cohesiveness. It is a diasporic village where quality of living is sustained through hopes and dreams for flourishing and thriving generations. However, life in Aotearoa is not easy. Although evidence has shown an increase in their level of employment, Pacific peoples remain relatively low paid when compared with other ethnic groups. Further, the stark reality is that despite the years of Pacific peoples labouring in employment to build the economic infrastructure of New Zealand through its formative years of development as a nation, the majority of Pacific diaspora are the 'working poor'.

For more clarification, it is important to begin by defining the Pasifika[1] population in Aotearoa. According to a profile of Pacific families (Ministry of Pacific Peoples, 2020), Pacific people make up 8.1 per cent (381,642) of the total population of Aotearoa, and are the fourth largest ethnic group following New Zealand European (70.2 per cent), Māori (16.5 per cent) and Asian (15.1 per cent) (Statistics New Zealand, 2019). Pacific peoples are a growing population and have increased by 29 per cent in just over a decade since the census of 2013. Pacific peoples have a median age of 23.4 years, 14 years younger than the median age of the New Zealand population (Statistics New Zealand, 2019). With this growth rate,

---

1   Pasifika (also spelt Pasefika) is a transliteration of the term Pacific. It is localised in the context of Aotearoa by Pacific reseachers and academics as a homogenous term, used to describe various Pacific ethnic groups born in their Island homelands or Aotearoa. It should not be misunderstood as a singular culture.

the Pacific population is predicted to reach over half a million (590,100) by the year 2028 (Statistics New Zealand, 2019).

The Pacific diaspora living within Aotearoa is diverse, with almost half being of Samoan descent (47.9 per cent, or 182,721). This is followed by Tongan (21.6 per cent, or 82,389), Cook Islands Māori (21.1 per cent, or 80,532), Niuean (8.1 per cent, or 30,867) and Fijian (5.2 per cent, or 19,722) (Ministry of Pacific Peoples, 2020). Further, Pacific families have on average more children than any other ethnic group in Aotearoa, contributing to Pacific children comprising the highest proportion of children under 14 of all ethnic groups (Statistics New Zealand, 2018). Although the Pacific population is relatively youthful when compared with other ethnic groups, it is important to highlight that the largest percentage increase in the age categories was in the 65 years and over age group, signalling the rise of an ageing Pacific population as the diaspora are now living longer (Statistics New Zealand, 2018).

Data shows that the mainly youthful Pacific population is located in urban settings. Records show that over 90 per cent (91.7 per cent) of Pacific peoples live in the North Island and two-thirds (243,966) of that population reside in Auckland (Statistics New Zealand, 2018). When explored within the context of Auckland, the majority of Pacific people live in South and West Auckland. The highest growth rate of Pacific peoples has been in Auckland's southern suburbs, especially in Papakura where there was a 57.2 per cent increase of Pacific peoples from the 2013 to 2018 census (Auckland Council, 2020).

Second to Auckland, the Wellington region has the next largest population of Pacific people at 11.2 per cent, then Waikato at 5.4 per cent (Statistics New Zealand, 2019). The data showing where Pacific peoples reside is critical as the vast majority reside in urban areas where there is a direct link to employment as it is a primary source of income. While Pacific employment rates have been increasing in recent years, it is still sobering to realise that Pacific peoples continue to have high rates of unemployment in comparison to other ethnic groups. For example, a recent labour force survey of Auckland unemployment rates across ethnic groups revealed Pacific had the highest at 9.2 per cent, followed by Māori (8.6 per cent), Asians (5.2 per cent) and Europeans (3.9 per cent) (Auckland Council, 2021).

Pacific peoples on average are the lowest wage earners despite a median income increase of 23 per cent from $19,700 in 2013 to $24,300 in the 2018 census (Statistics New Zealand, 2018). Although these slight increases look promising on paper, it is still implausible to consider the income levels as adequate when compared with the European population ($34,300) and total overall ($31,800). This poor state of wage-earning for Pacific peoples is also reflected in the median weekly income from wages and salaries, which on average is $959 compared with

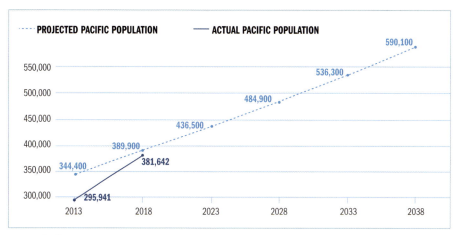

FIGURE 1: Pacific People's Actual and Projected Population 2013-2038 (Adapted from Statistics New Zealand, 2017).

AGE GROUP	POPULATION CHANGE 2013-2018	2018 % OF TOTAL POPULATION	PERCENTAGE INCREASE
65 years and over	13,944 → 20,232	5.3%	45%
15-19 years	76,563 → 103,752	27.7%	36%
30-64 years	99,918 → 129,504	33.9%	30%
Under 15 years	105,519 → 128,154	33.6%	21%
Total	295,955 → 381,642	**100%**	**29%**

FIGURE 2: The Pacific Population Increase by Age Categories (Adapted from Statistics New Zealand, 2018).

AUCKLAND LOCAL BOARD AREA	2013 CENSUS POPULATION	2018 CENSUS POPULATION	PERCENTAGE INCREASE (2013-2018)
Papakura	6201	9750	57.2%
Manurewa	25,020	34,707	38.7%
Henderson-Massey	19,698	24,771	25.8%
Ōtara-Papatoetoe	31,671	39,198	23.8%
Māngere-Ōtāhuhu	39,045	46,578	19.3%

FIGURE 3: Auckland Local Board Area Pacific Population Growth (Adapted from Auckland Council, 2019).

$1000 for Māori and $1120 for Europeans (Statistics New Zealand, 2021).

Understanding of the inequities Pacific people face is further supported by findings released by the Human Rights Commission (2020) that revealed 7 per cent of working households (almost 60,000 families) were living in poverty (March 2013), with an overall poverty rate of 17.1 per cent for households both in work and out of work (Plum et al., 2019). The most vulnerable were identified as Pacific and Māori peoples, single parents, ethnic minorities, households with low education attainment, disabled people and renters (Plum et al., 2019). Further, Pacific peoples, alongside Middle Eastern, Latin American and African (MELAA), had the highest in-work poverty rate at 9.5 per cent, well above the 7 per cent national average (Plum et al., 2019). This ongoing disparity for Pacific peoples is disconcerting given employment has long been viewed as the antidote for poverty. As such, the concept of a living wage can potentially ameliorate poverty, but for this to be effective a Pacific perspective on the living wage requires exploration.

Understanding the living wage as social activism for poverty reduction

Better quality of life and sustainable livelihoods can be achieved by reducing poverty and investing in decent jobs that pay fairly. This lies at the heart of the 'living wage' debate, which has been consistently campaigned for by the International Labour Organization (ILO) in countries like Aotearoa, Cambodia, the United States and the United Kingdom as a means to promote 'decent work' (Alefaio et al., 2015). The word 'living' addresses the core of active participation in society and sustainable provisions for dependants and caters for unforeseen financial strains (Arrowsmith et al., 2020). In other words, a living wage enables participation in society above sustenance through, for example, the enhancement of family, active contribution to societal activities, savings and overall wellbeing (Yao et al., 2017).

The concept of a living wage seeks to shift workers from subsisting and just 'surviving' towards a thriving livelihood with greater emphasis on the wellbeing of employees. It is profoundly shaped by morality due to its focus on *quality of life*. The ultimate goal of a living wage is to shift the inequity of those working yet still in poverty through decent wages that have an impact on quality of living, which aligns with the Pacific people's aspirations for a flourishing and thriving community for future generations.

The living wage campaign has escalated since the 1990s to counter the growing failure of the legal minimum wage to prevent working poverty (Carr et al., 2019).

The living wage has become a highly contested issue due to ongoing increases in inequality, living costs and draconian welfare reforms (Yao et al., 2017). Breaking free from poverty is a significant goal for all nations, indicating the need to identify a wage threshold that would enable a subjective sense of wage justice and quality of work (Hu & Carr, 2020). For instance, Carr (2021) explains that anti-poverty initiatives are determined by policymakers who make, evaluate and improve policies based on a threshold.

Hypothetically, the process of anti-poverty initiatives would be aligned to the United Nations top priority Sustainable Development Goal (SDG) 1 of 'eradicating poverty in all its forms'. However, the challenge with defining the goal in this way suggests a deficit approach, as poverty in literature is only referred to as a range of restricted opportunities. It lacks the holistic lens of quality of life, which includes the cultural, historical, social, relocation and generational impacts of colonisation as a starting point. These are contributing factors that require immediate attention and add weight to the importance of a living wage.

A counterargument would be a shift from the wage threshold approach towards a maximum wage. The International Labour Organization confirmed that addressing working poverty cannot be separated from addressing maximum wage (ILO, 2013). A common challenge in political debates over the living wage is deciding who should take responsibility. Living wage debates are often politically charged, with arguments attributing the costs for a living wage as either the responsibility of employers or the government (Alefaio et al., 2015).

As highlighted earlier, Auckland is home to approximately two out of every three people who identify as Pasifika, where low workforce participation rates and underemployment are prevalent (Alefaio et al., 2015). Consequently, with high youth unemployment and low rates for workforce participation (56.2 per cent) compared with European migrants (80 per cent), Pasifika voices should be prominent and present when tackling issues related to poverty and inequality in Aotearoa.

Pasifika scholars, researchers and practitioners are often absent from co-creating solutions such as the living wage (Allpress, 2013; Alefaio et al., 2015). Up until recently, Pacific engagement in living wage discussions has been minimal. The Living Wage Movement Aotearoa New Zealand (LWMANZ) was formed in 2013 as a coalition of faith-based, union and community groups (Arrowsmith et al., 2020; LWMANZ, 2015). The movement aimed to enable workers to live with dignity and participate fully in society. The core of living wage literature continues to highlight certain wage thresholds at which life becomes more than bearable (Carr et al., 2016). Trying to identify a wage threshold can become a challenge as it does not

AHO 18.1 THE PACIFIC PAY GAP

Toby Morris, 'The Side Eye's Two New Zealands: The Pacific pay gap'. FIRST PUBLISHED ON THE SPINOFF

As Equal Employment Opportunities Commissioner Saunoamaali'i Dr Karanina Sumeo points out, there are large pay gaps in Aotearoa between Pākehā and Pasifika peoples. Research shows that the average Pākehā man earns around $1442 a week, while the average Pasifika woman earns around $1049. While some of this can be put down to lower education levels and a young population, a large role in this discrepancy is played by being offered less pay for the same role (the horizontal pay gap), and being offered different opportunities, such as a role as a cleaner rather than as an administrator (the vertical pay gap).

Reference

Morris, T. (2021, October 15). The Side Eye's two New Zealands: The Pacific pay gap. *The Spinoff*. https://thespinoff.co.nz/society/the-side-eye/15-10-2021/the-side-eyes-two-new-zealands-the-pacific-pay-gap

take account of everyday human capabilities (Carr et al., 2017). This highlights the situation for Pasifika families in Aotearoa, because if shifting from the minimum wage to a living wage contributes to eradicating poverty for Pasifika peoples, then advocacy for a living wage by Pasifika should be high. However, given the variation of individual, household and regional circumstances and abatement rules whereby an increase in income means the reduction of benefit transfers, the living wage is often viewed as lumbering or clumsy (Arrowsmith et al., 2020; The Treasury, 2013).

Escaping poverty requires a greater focus on the deeper and more systemic components of Aotearoa's social and economic reality (Adato et al., 2006). Given that 'much of the work against poverty takes place in organisations' (Berry et al., 2009, p. 241), it is vital that Pasifika organisations, such as diasporic church-village communities, are involved in addressing economic inequities. It is paramount that sustainable methods of poverty reduction enable Pasifika peoples to engage, participate in and ultimately lead understandings of a living wage so that they are explored within their socio-cultural environments. TalanoaHUBBS, explained below, is an innovative initiative that has sought to bring together Pacific community groups, practitioners and academics for that necessary community-led engagement. In doing so, it became a vehicle for Pasifika community engagement with academic activism behind the living wage, and helped to create shifts towards sustainable livelihoods led by Pasifika social agents of change.

Engaging Pasifika: TalanoaHUBBS

Pacific peoples are deeply rooted in oral traditions. For generations, they have safeguarded their language and identity through the concept of talanoa. It is widely recognised in many Pacific nations such as Tonga, Sāmoa, Fiji, Niue, Hawai'i, Solomon Islands and the Cook Islands (Farrelly & Nabobo-Baba, 2014; Prescott, 2008). Talanoa is a concept that allows people to offload freely (Nabobo-Baba, 2007) and engage openly through telling of stories and experiences without any hidden emotional restrictions (Halapua, 2008). It can be based around a purposed plan or through casual conversation with no set agendas. Talanoa, translated into English, can be unpacked through the two originating words tala — meaning to 'inform, relate or tell', and noa — meaning 'nothing in particular' (Vaioleti 2006, p. 23). Tala can also mean 'to inform, tell, relate and command, as well as to ask or apply. Noa means of any kind, ordinary, nothing, purely imaginary or void' (Vaioleti, 2006, p. 23).

The idea of noa is sensitive and should be interpreted with caution. The phrase 'nothing in particular' for Pacific peoples may mean anything and everything.

The conversation would include external factors such as talking about one's experience during the day or week, sports, current affairs, and other topics of interest. An example would be asking a non-Pacific person about what they had for lunch. The response would likely focus solely on the meal, i.e. 'I had fish for lunch'. On the contrary, it is common for a Pacific person to answer by explaining how they got to the café and who they had lunch with, before specifying the meal. In a nutshell, talanoa is more than just a roundabout conversation or dialogue, it is a Pacific way of connecting and forming relationships through understanding family, village and community.

In the initiative TalanoaHUBBS (Humans United Beyond Borders Symposium), talanoa is used innovatively as a Pacific way of connecting diverse perspectives, from community, practitioners and academia, for a better understanding of how to support the needs of Pacific communities. TalanoaHUBBS is hosted and organised by NIUPATCH (Navigate In Unity: Pacific Approaches to Community-Humanitarianism), a research collective shining a light on community-led resilience, which operates within Massey University's School of Psychology. Its purpose is to connect community groups, practitioners and academia for talanoa on issues, and share research and ideas. NIUPATCH created TalanoaHUBBS as a way to help strengthen and mobilise diverse communities by bridging the cultural divide through talanoa (Alefaio-Tugia et al., 2019).

Community-led talanoa bring together Pacific communities and bridge the gap that often exists between research and practice. This action of bridging the gap and promoting relationships between community groups and academics (research and practice) provides a notable example of two systems working together. TalanoaHUBBS provides an insight into different Pacific communities; the work happening within these communities, as well as their strengths, concerns and challenges. TalanoaHUBBS helps to diversify the perspective of those involved, as participants are not only people representing different community groups, such as churches and non-governmental organisations (NGOs), but also those from academia and government.

The first TalanoaHUBBS was held in Tonga in 2017 (see Figure 4), through a partnership with the Joint Centre for Disaster Research (JCDR), School of Psychology, Massey University, and Tupu'anga Coffee Tonga. Hosted in the premises of social enterprise Tupu'anga coffee, and with its own onsite community café, a strategic TalanoaHUBBS in Tonga focused on disaster preparedness (see Figure 5, which showcases participants in full-talanoa mode). Previously, in 2016, a strategic gathering was hosted by Emeline and Alipate of Tupu'anga Coffee in Tonga which included staff from JCDR. As a result, TalanoaHUBBS was created by Dr Siautu

Alefaio to capture the forum and collaborating process in which diverse peoples were gathering to find new ways forward in community resilience.

Since then, there have been over 10 talanoa symposiums held in Tonga, Sāmoa, Auckland and, more recently due to Covid-19 restrictions, on Zoom, and Facebook-live. Each TalanoaHUBBS focuses on an issue relevant to Pacific communities. The extensive range of topics have included: community resilience; disaster risk resilience and humanitarian response; justice, faith and injustice; faith-based initiatives for violence prevention; Samoan pastoral counselling and trauma recovery; Covid recovery; family and sexual violence; Pacific-diasporic psychosocial recovery; and the living wage.

Each TalanoaHUBBS is always run along similar lines, although the location and topic may vary. A panel of approximately four is selected, which may consist of community leaders, academics and experts in a field relevant to the specified topic. A TalanoaHUBBS is generally limited to one hour, with time before and after to mingle and eat together. NIUPATCH provides a facilitator who guides the talanoa throughout the allotted time. Each member of the panel is given time to present their work and ideas and answer questions from the facilitator. After each panel member has spoken all are welcome to engage in talanoa; this is not specifically a question and answer session, but a time for anyone to express their thoughts, questions and concerns with all present as well as listen to others. Each TalanoaHUBBS has produced important outcomes in bringing localised solutions for addressing poverty to the fore.

Poverty solutions from localised communities

Going beyond a living wage to a sustainable quality of life is the trailblazing example of the Affirming Works social enterprise in South Auckland, a localised community-led solution to poverty, engaging Pacific youth as active citizens within their own communities for sustainable change. A Massey University alumni, Emeline Afeaki-Mafile'o is a social worker and entrepreneur who founded Affirming Works (AW) in 2001 as a company, after she had graduated with her degree in social work with honours. Born and raised in South Auckland (specifically Māngere), Emeline's original name for AW was Affirming Women, as it began as a mentoring service for young Pacific women who were referred for prostitution and high-risk needs. As work continued, the organisation evolved into Affirming Works to meet the rapid and rising diverse needs across all Pacific youth regardless of gender. As a faith-based organisation, Pacific mentors were employed to deliver the Tupu'anga mentoring programme based on a collective model of mentoring that Emeline developed. Through these entrepreneurial endeavours, Emeline furthered her education and graduated with a Masters of Social Policy, and through social innovation developed AW further into a social enterprise.

Almost a decade later, in 2010, together with her husband Alipate Mafile'o, Emeline set up Community Café based in Auckland. It morphed into a social enterprise that organically became a hub for people in local communities to gather to break down silos between services in the community and provide a citizen-centric access point for all communities. The heartbeat of Community Café became improving access to existing services and encouraging a collaborative and cooperative response to community needs.

In the same year, Emeline and Alipate were presented with an opportunity to purchase a coffee business in the Kingdom of Tonga. This enabled an enterprising opportunity for the Tongan diaspora living in Aotearoa to work together with Tongans living in the island kingdom to provide culturally sustainable ways of living. As such, they created Tupu'anga Coffee, named after the AW flagship mentoring programme, which provided the connection to the Pacific diaspora, enabling a sustainable approach for resiliency. Ultimately, setting up businesses in Tonga utilised entrepreneurial opportunities to provide social work services to Pacific communities. Using Tongan-grown coffee manufactured in the homeland (Kingdom of Tonga) for both the domestic market in Tonga and the international market of Aotearoa created a new Pacific-Indigenous model of development that empowers locally owned and sustainable solutions. Further, the coffee grown in Tonga is used exclusively in community cafés creating an intervention for poverty that comes from within the Pacific itself. Proceeds from the Community Café are then generated to fund social service programmes that AW develops and delivers across Auckland for Pacific youth and families. These include Kainga Tu'umalie (family violence prevention programmes), Tupu'anga mentoring, Young Free & Pacific, and now during the Covid-19 pandemic a local food hub distributing food packages for families most in need.

Conclusion

Overall, while reduction of poverty will contribute to the achievement of a better quality of life and sustainable livelihoods for Pasifika peoples, the road to get there is long and full of hurdles. Good intentions from outside the community are well-meaning but often fall short of sustainable change because they do not engage the very people at the heart of the issue, in this case —

TALANOA HUBBS

Humans United Beyond Borders Symposium

is a conference for practitioners, researchers, and local community to present and discuss their work. Since 2017 together with local partner Tupu'anga Coffee this Talanoa opportunity is an important channel for exchange of information between ALL Pacific with a heart for humanity.

FIGURE 4: Vision of the first TalanoaHUBBS forum held in Tonga in 2017. COURTESY OF SIAUTU ALEFAIO

FIGURE 5: TalanoaHUBBS showcases participants in full Talanoa-mode. Pictured are leaders of Tonga's humanitarian, community and church groups; the National Emergency Management Office (NEMO); and MET (Meteorological services) office. COURTESY OF SIAUTU ALEFAIO

FIGURE 6: TalanoaHUBBS in Sāmoa in 2019 focused on recovery and healing 10 years on from the Sāmoa tsunami of 2009. The keynote speaker was Hon. Fiamē Naomi Mata'afa, Sāmoa's first female prime minister. COURTESY OF SIAUTU ALEFAIO

the Pacific diaspora who have their own solutions to poverty reduction. This chapter highlights the issue of a living wage for Pacific peoples in Aotearoa and the need to understand that Pasifika livelihoods and quality of life are not just an income threshold but holistic — cultural, social, migratory, and impacted by colonisation, which in turn have shaped the Pacific diaspora as global citizens. The TalanoaHUBBS initiative shines a light on Pacific-led forums of knowledge exchange that bridge the gap between community groups, academics (research) and practice. In doing so, localised solutions for addressing poverty such as the trailblazing social enterprise Affirming Works based in South Auckland are brought to the fore. Their cultural innovations engage Pacific families across all generations as active citizens within their own communities for sustainable change, creating hope for a greater quality of life.

References

Adato, M., Carter, M. R., & May, J. (2006). Exploring poverty traps and social exclusion in South Africa using qualitative and quantitative data. *The Journal of Development Studies, 42*(2), 226–247. https://doi.org/10.1080/00220380500405345

Allpress, J. A. (2013). *The Labour Market and Skills in Auckland* (Technical Report TR2013/005). Auckland Council.

Alefaio, S., Carr, S. C., Hodgetts, D., & Mattson, T. (2015). Ending poverty and inequality? Towards psychologies of sustainable development. *Psychology Aotearoa, 7*(1), 31–37.

Alefaio-Tugia, S., Afeaki-Mafile'o, E., & Satele, P. (2019). Pacific-Indigenous community-village resilience in disasters. In J. Ravulo, T. Mafile'o, & D. B. Yeates (Eds.), *Pacific Social Work* (pp. 68–78). Routledge.

Arrowsmith, J., Parker, J., Carr, S., Haar, J., Young-Hauser, A., Hodgetts, D., & Alefaio, S. (2020). Moving the minimum wage towards a 'Living Wage': Evidence from New Zealand. In A. Forsyth, E. Dagnino, & M. Roiatti (Eds.), *The Value of Work and Its Rules between Innovation and Tradition: 'Labour is not a commodity today'* (pp. 147–170). Cambridge Scholars.

Auckland Council. (2019). *2018 Census Results: Local board and special area information sheets.* https://knowledgeauckland.org.nz/media/1181/auckland-area-2018-census-info-sheets-all-local-boards.pdf

Auckland Council. (2020). *Local Board View.* Auckland counts: Auckland census data. https://cloud.statsilk.com/l/acouncil/local-board-data-viewer/StatPlanet_Cloud.html

Auckland Council. (2021). *Auckland Regional Household Labour Force Survey: Quarterly overview — June 2021.* https://knowledgeauckland.org.nz/media/2154/auckland-hlfs-06june-2021.pdf

Berry, M. O. N., Reichman, W., Klobas, J., MacLachlan, M., Hui, H. C., & Carr, S. C. (2009). Humanitarian work psychology: The contributions of organizational psychology to poverty reduction. *Journal of Economic Psychology, 32*(2), 240–247. https://doi.org/10.1016/j.joep.2009.10.009

Carr, S. C. (2021). Setting 'poverty thresholds': Whose experience counts? *Sustainability Science, 16*, 31–36. https://doi.org/10.1007/s11625-020-00859-x

Carr, S. C., Haar, J., Hodgetts, D., Arrowsmith, J., Parker, J., Young-Hauser, A., Alefaio-Tugia, S., & Jones, H. (2019). An employee's living wage and their quality of work life: How important are household size and household income? *Journal of Sustainability Research, 1*, 190007. https://doi.org/10.20900/jsr20190007

Carr, S. C., Parker, J., Arrowsmith, J., Haar, J., & Jones, H. (2017). Humanistic management and living wages: A case of compelling connections? *Humanistic Management Journal, 1*(2), 215–236. https://doi.org/10.1007/s41463-016-0018-y

Carr, S. C., Parker, J., Arrowsmith, J., & Watters, P. A. (2016). The living wage: Theoretical integration and an applied research agenda. *International Labour Review, 155*(1), 1–24. https://doi.org/10.1111/j.1564-913X.2015.00029.x

Farrelly, T., & Nabobo-Baba, U. (2014). Talanoa as empathic apprenticeship. *Asia Pacific Viewpoint, 55*(3), 319–330.

Halapua, S. (2008). *Talanoa Process: The case of Fiji*. www.researchgate.net/publication/265273895_Talanoa_process_The_case_of_Fiji

Hu, Y., & Carr, S. C. (2020). Living wages across the Pacific Rim: A localised replication study from China. *Journal of Pacific Rim Psychology, 14*, 1–9. https://doi.org/10.1017/prp.2020.11

Human Rights Commission. (2020). *Talanoa: Human rights issues for Pacific peoples in Aotearoa New Zealand*. www.hrc.co.nz/files/3016/0728/5509/Talanoa_-_Human_Rights_for_Pacific_Peoples_in_Aotearoa_New_Zealand.pdf

ILO (International Labour Organization). (2013). *World of Work Report 2013: Repairing the economic and social fabric*. International Institute for Labour Studies.

Living Wage Movement of Aotearoa New Zealand (LWMANZ). (2015). *Accredited Living Wage Employers of New Zealand*.

Ministry of Pacific Peoples. (2020). Pacific Aotearoa Status Report: A snapshot 2020. www.mpp.govt.nz/assets/Reports/Pacific-Peoples-in-Aotearoa-Report.pdf

Nabobo-Baba, U. (2007). *Vanua Research Framework. In paper presented to the Sustainable Livelihood and Education in the Pacific Project*. Suva: Institute of Education, University of the South Pacific.

Plum, A., Pacheco, G., & Hick, R. (2019). *In-work Poverty in New Zealand*. New Zealand Work Research Institute.

Prescott, S. M. (2008). Using talanoa in Pacific business research in New Zealand: Experiences with Tongan entrepreneurs. *AlterNative: An International Journal of Indigenous Scholarship, 4*(1), 127–148.

Statistics New Zealand. (2017). National ethnic population projections: 2013(base)–2038 (update). www.stats.govt.nz/information-releases/national-ethnic-population-projections-2013base2038-update

Statistics New Zealand. (2018). *2018 Census Ethnic Group Summaries: Middle Eastern/Latin American/African*. www.stats.govt.nz/tools/2018-census-ethnic-group-summaries/middle-eastern-latin-american-african

Statistics New Zealand. (2019). *2018 Census Population and Dwelling Counts*. www.stats.govt.nz/information-releases/2018-census-population-and-dwelling-counts

Statistics New Zealand. (2021). Income tables. http://nzdotstat.stats.govt.nz/wbos/Index.aspx?_ga=2.121108744.1030851186.1638911606-1729141.1638911606#

The Treasury. (2013). *Analysis of the Proposed $18.40 Living Wage* (Report T2013/2346). www.treasury.govt.nz/sites/default/files/2013-10/lw-2726820.pdf

Vaioleti, T. M. (2006). Talanoa research methodology: A developing position on Pacific research. *Waikato Journal of Education, 12*, 21–24.

Yao, C., Parker, J., Arrowsmith, J., & Carr, S. C. (2017). The living wage as an income range for decent work and life. *Employee Relations, 39*(6), 875–887. https://doi.org/10.1108/ER-03-2017-0071

PART THREE:

TE PUĀWAI, THE FLOWERS

19.
Agency and action

Margaret Forster & David Belgrave

Global issues are messy and complicated. In planning and policymaking, the term 'wicked problems' signals challenges that are complex and difficult or seemingly impossible to resolve, and climate change has even been referred to as a 'super wicked problem' (Levin et al., 2012). De Almeida Kumlien and Coughlan (2018) liken wicked problems to a tangled mess of threads — it is hard to know which to untangle first. So, how can we respond to global issues such as climate change, conflict, poverty and inequality? What are our responsibilities to these issues and other rights abuses around the world, not just as New Zealanders or as residents in Aotearoa, but as global citizens and members of a global community? How can we exercise agency and engage in social action that makes a difference? Is it even possible to 'make a difference'?

As citizens of Aotearoa, we live in a globalised world. We have always been global citizens with strong connections to the Pacific and to Europe. Globalisation has drawn Aotearoa closer to the rest of the world, and we feel the impacts of wicked problems locally and globally. Our choices — both collective and individual — have impacts that go far beyond our shores. What we consume in Aotearoa has an impact on conflicts in Africa. The carbon we expel at home has an impact on the climate everywhere. How we spend our national income has an impact on poverty and

IHO ATUA

Margaret Forster (Rongomaiwāhine, Ngāti Kahungunu)

All action has a whakapapa or genealogy — nā te kukune, te pupuke, nā te pupuke, te hihiri, nā te hihiri, te mahara, nā te mahara, te hinengaro, nā te hinengaro, te wānanga (Best, 1924). This whakapapa sequence is a reminder that ideally action is the product of an initial thought shaped into a consciousness that evolves into wisdom.

> Māui was first. Māui hauled this land from depths at the place where his hook foul-snared . . . His hook fell and fused with the land . . . His blood smeared on the barb of his hook . . . The bare flesh of Māui's trophy was populated by mokopuna of Sky and Earth in a heartbeat; such is the nature of gods who create action through thought alone. (How, 2017, p. 3)

Action is, therefore, deliberate and purposeful, ideally upholding or strengthening mana as authority and influence and mauri or lifeforce to secure good health and wellbeing and realise full human potential. These ideas are encapsulated in the following saying: Ko te pae tawhiti, whāia kia tata. Ko te pae tata, whakamaua kia tīna. Seek out the distant horizons, while cherishing those achievements at hand. Or, in other words, grasp hold of the goals within your reach, but always strive towards realising a greater vision.

inequality. We acknowledge that from an individual perspective the issues that we face can be overwhelming, leading to indecision and frequently to entrenchment of the status quo. Nevertheless, we argue that there is potential to meet challenges through engagement with rights and responsibilities that are globally informed, collective in orientation and that facilitate structural transformation. This is where the metaphor of weaving becomes useful. Raranga is a plaiting technique where flax blades are woven together to produce a variety of products such as mats and baskets. *Tū Rangaranga* builds on this metaphor, asking that we explore the various strands — the connections and impacts associated with global encounters — and consider how we can reconstruct them into something cohesive and useful. This metaphor assumes that a single blade can be weak and isolated. When woven together, stronger and more enduring pathways or responses can come to fruition. This is the puāwai, the flowers or the agency and actions, that can emerge when we engage collectively on messy and complicated global issues.

Global rights, responsibilities and action

Responding to issues of global concern is challenging and complex, requiring thoughtful, reflective engagement with the notion of citizenship. Regardless of how we understand our rights — be it individual or collective, liberal or Indigenous, customary or constitutional — we nevertheless must exert those rights in order for them to have meaning. Citizenship is not just a status; it is also a set of practices that turn rights into action and responsibilities into solutions. 'Active citizenship' involves 'activities undertaken in public by individuals and groups to improve the life of the community' (Belgrave & Dodson, 2021, p. 10). Yet being an active citizen is not easy. It requires effort and skills that are not innate or automatic to everyone.

Negative freedoms — the liberal freedoms that allow for free speech, free thought, assembly and religious expression — are simply a right to non-interference by the state. The state in Aotearoa will not lock you up for criticising the government, but the state does not necessarily give you all the tools to be heard by the powerful either. Utilising your rights requires agency to turn ideas into action. Agency, in the simplest sense, is the feeling that one has the power to act; but more than confidence is required. Real civic action utilises skills, knowledge, time and energy to act effectively and ethically. Therefore, effectively exercising your rights requires multiple resources that, like all resources, are unevenly distributed across society. Those privileged with more of these resources find it easier to be active citizens, but this does not mean active citizenship is only available to an elite few.

Regardless of privilege, agency must be built up through experience. The practice of being an active citizen helps builds skills that generate confidence and greater agency.

The state asks relatively little from all its citizens in terms of official responsibilities; pay taxes and occasionally sit on a jury. Even voting is optional in Aotearoa. While our legal responsibilities to the state are limited, our responsibilities to one another and to the rest of the world are more complex and depend on varying ethical considerations (Schouten, 2021). It is up to citizens to ensure the state acts responsibly towards all its citizens and in the world. Accepting that it is our collective responsibility to protect others from humanitarian disaster, or to reduce our carbon footprint, is also accepting that we must try to utilise our rights to fulfil our responsibilities.

Being responsible means not just changing our own behaviour, but also demanding change from the powerful. Political, business and community leaders need to be convinced to act by those less powerful. Leaders can be made answerable to the public. Politicians require votes and public support to govern, and business and community leaders have brands and reputations that need to be protected. Active citizenship involves organising with others to utilise your rights collectively so those more powerful must not just listen, but also act. Politicians must answer to large numbers of voters speaking with one voice, employers need to negotiate when all workers are willing to strike, and businesses must adapt when customers are willing to switch products. By practising active citizenship, ordinary people turn rights and responsibilities from abstract concepts into visible positive change.

Active citizenship is both an individual and a collective effort, as there are limits on what an individual can achieve alone. Equally, problems do not exist in isolation. Action on the problems discussed in this book overlap, and so do solutions and trade-offs. Protecting the Pacific from the effects of climate change can complement decolonisation. Improving housing, creating walkable communities and improving public transport are simultaneously solutions to the climate crisis and social inequality. Decolonising the state in Aotearoa will reduce inequality between Māori and non-Māori, while also demanding greater environmental sustainability to protect the mauri (lifeforce) of our whenua, awa and moana (sea).

Trade-offs must also be made. Acting on the climate crisis could well reduce New Zealanders' ability to travel by air and private car. Reducing social inequality is likely to require higher taxes, especially on the wealthy (Belgrave & Dodson, 2021). The actions required to make these changes and trade-offs will be personal and collective. We must change our own behaviour, while also demanding that the powerful change the structures that create problems like environmental degradation and inequality. Accepting individual responsibility is crucial to making change, but demanding change to the structures that make it difficult to make responsible choices is equally important. We cannot stop using our cars if there are no practical alternatives. We cannot stop buying goods produced unsustainably by underpaid workers if we cannot afford those from responsible companies. Non-Māori cannot assist in the decolonisation of Aotearoa if the public education system continues to take a tokenistic approach to te ao Māori. Individual responsibility, therefore, has structural limits that only significant active citizenship can change.

Collective action inevitably requires engaging with different people with different views. Fulfilling your responsibilities to others involves a degree of ethical care to those you are trying to help (Alcoff, 1991–1992; Schouten, 2021). Engaging and sharing power with stakeholders is a vital part of collective action. Stakeholder engagement builds alliances, shares useful information and helps dispel opposition to positive change (Belgrave, 2021). The trade-offs required to fulfil the responsibilities of the twenty-first century will involve costs on some more than others. Difficult conversations need to be had to share the costs as equitably as possible. For instance, combating climate change in Aotearoa will have a significant impact on farming practices. If the interests of farmers were to be ignored by policymakers, then the significant opposition by farmers would be understandable. If farmers are made part of the policymaking process, then their interests can be better protected, and their opposition lessened. Of course, perfect solutions that suit everyone are rare, but stakeholder engagement can improve and ease efforts to make positive change.

As with wider stakeholders, engagement with Māori is a practical necessity, but it is also a constitutional responsibility for the state through several acts of Parliament and decisions of the courts. Mana whenua must be consulted on issues that affect them. Consultation needs to be undertaken separately from stakeholder engagement, as mana whenua have relationships with the whenua, awa and moana that go back generations. Stakeholder interests tend to be relatively ephemeral, relating to location, profession or hobby rather than whakapapa (Belgrave, 2021). Engagement can be a challenge for Māori and non-Māori alike. Non-Māori, as outsiders, can find it difficult to navigate interwoven tribal relationships to find those with the mana to make decisions in a given rohe (region). Yet Māori have this problem every day operating in a Western-dominated political and social culture. Māori active citizens must simultaneously act according to the norms of Western liberalism and those of te ao Māori (Te Momo, 2021). The difficult conversations that can emerge from engagement between Māori and non-Maori are not something that we should avoid, as they are part of the process of decolonisation.

Difficult conversations are vital for all kinds of engagement as they are an important precursor to positive change. It is easy to become despondent at the enormity of the challenges facing the world, but positive impacts can be generated locally for global problems. Colonisation, the climate crisis, inequality and conflict are problems that need to be tackled at home, as well as in the wider world. So, what does active citizenship on global concerns in Aotearoa look like in action? The remainder of this chapter will attempt to answer this question.

Disrupting colonisation in Aotearoa

Colonisation is a messy and complicated global issue. While the empire may have gone, colonial structures remain deeply rooted within the various systems, processes and thinking of modern nation-states. Colonisation might be over, but its impacts continue. It is difficult to dismantle the structures and the inherent power and privilege that emerged to benefit some citizens over others. Globalisation was built on this foundation and is complicit by association in maintaining modern-day power imbalances that become evident through conflict, poverty and climate change. Local responses in Aotearoa to disrupt the impacts of colonisation have the potential to provide global leadership, particularly in relation to Indigenous rights. So how do we dismantle these structures and exercise both individual and collective agency?

Tuia 250

> Tuia 250 commemorated a significant event in our history. The commemoration revealed the power of connections — our connection to our past; our connection to our land, our whenua; our connection to our oceans, our moana; and most of all our connection to each other. (Manatū Taonga, 2019)

The starting point for this reflection is the national commemorations in 2019, known as Tuia 250. This marked the two hundred and fiftieth anniversary of the first landfall by Europeans in Aotearoa. These celebrations are useful for exploring civic action that responds to the legacy and continued impact of colonisation in Aotearoa. It involved a range of social actions from individuals and collectives that challenged us as a nation to confront our colonial past and imagine a shared and more just future. A key consideration is how, as a nation, we confront our colonial past, and how we decolonise our systems and our minds with the intent of moving towards a more just and inclusive future.

In 2019, the New Zealand government invested $23 million towards commemorations that recognised 250 years since the first onshore encounters between Māori and Europeans. There was a highly controversial 10-week voyage of waka hourua (double-hulled deep-sea vessels) and tall ships to significant historical and cultural sites around Aotearoa (see Figure 1). This took place alongside museum and art exhibitions, the development of educational resources for schools and communities, and the creation of sculptures such as pou to commemorate significant sites and events.

Five key themes underpinned the celebrations:

1. **Heritage — shared future**. Presenting a balanced and honest historical narrative to better understand our relationships and build a strong foundation for a richer shared future.
2. **Voyaging**. Increasing awareness about Pacific, Māori and European voyaging and navigation techniques.
3. **First meetings, migration and settlement**. Considering their impact on contemporary society.
4. **The arts, science, technology and mātauranga of two great voyaging traditions (Pacific and European)**. Understanding the innovation and skill that existed in 1769 and before that time, and
5. **Whakapapa and identity**. Exploring our own stories and our common bond as voyagers to Aotearoa New Zealand (Manatū Taonga, n.d.a, para. 5).

The vision for commemorations was reflected in the whakataukī: tuia te muka tangata ki uta, weaving people together for a shared future. The intent was to encourage conversations about encounters (Manatū Taonga, 2020) in the past and the present, both good and bad, acknowledging that 'all New Zealanders are bound together, precious and different but part of our nation with a shared responsibility to build a future together' (Manatū Taonga, 2020, para. 6). Such conversations are critical for healing and encouraging people to 'embrace the country's bicultural history' (RNZ, 2019b, para. 1) and ultimately find creative solutions to our shared legacy of colonisation and failing to honour te Tiriti o Waitangi.

For many Māori communities, the notion of being 'discovered' by Abel Tasman and celebrating the arrival of Captain Cook and the *Endeavour* was highly contentious. While this event marked the arrival of Europeans to these shores and the first Māori–European encounters, Aotearoa had been 'discovered' many centuries prior. As lawyer and te Tiriti o Waitangi specialist Moana Jackson (Ngāti

Kahungunu, Ngāti Porou, Rongomaiwāhine) pointed out, the navigational feat of crossing the Pacific was not novel (Dudding, 2019; Jackson, 2021).

Conversations that count

On 16 December 2019, the local iwi Rongomaiwāhine welcomed into Māhia Beach a flotilla of ships — two waka hourua (see Figure 2) from Aotearoa, three tall ships (one a replica of the *Endeavour*) and the va'a tipaerua Fa'afaite from Tahiti. The Tahitian vessel represented Pacific connections, navigational knowledge from the Pacific and the role of Tahitian tohunga and navigator Tupaia who guided the *Endeavour* through the Pacific. Later that afternoon, the crews, the prime minister and the organisers of Tuia 250 were welcomed onto Tuahuru marae for a celebratory feast. Māhia was the final stop of the voyage around Aotearoa where communities shared their stories about encounters.

Encounters between Māori and Europeans have ranged from courteous, to friendly and mutually beneficial, to outright contentious and violent. Many of these relationships have been explored in this book. These experiences are not unique to Māori, as they are shared by other Indigenous peoples worldwide in response to imperialism. Navigating the multitude of consequences of these encounters is a key focus of global citizenship and a first step towards responding to pressing global issues, such as conflict, climate change, poverty and inequalities.

While the scenes at Māhia were welcoming and pleasant, some iwi refused to be involved when the flotilla visited other locations, arguing that the arrival of the *Endeavour* marked the beginning of Māori dispossession and marginalisation. Māori communities used the Tuia 250 event to raise a critical awareness of our tumultuous past, to demand social justice and to boycott events (McLachlan, 2019). Statues celebrating our colonial past were defaced, Indigenous rights advocate Tina Ngata (Ngāti Porou) led a campaign to scuttle the building of the *Endeavour* replica — which had been dubbed by Waikato University academic Arama Rata (Ngāruahine, Taranaki, Ngāti Maniapoto) a 'replica death ship' arriving to 're-enact the invasion of Māori whenua' (Matthews, 2019) — while Moana Jackson noted the absurdity of commemorating an event that continues to disadvantage and stifle attempts to reclaim Indigenous independence and self-determination (Dudding, 2019; Jackson, 2021).

In response, other commentators, often of non-Māori heritage, focused instead on the navigation feats and progress that accompanied colonisation (see, for example, Point of Order, 2019). The point is 'honest' conversations about the past are seldom congenial — they are heated, passionate, uncomfortable and messy — and are difficult to resolve as consensus is elusive. But these conversations

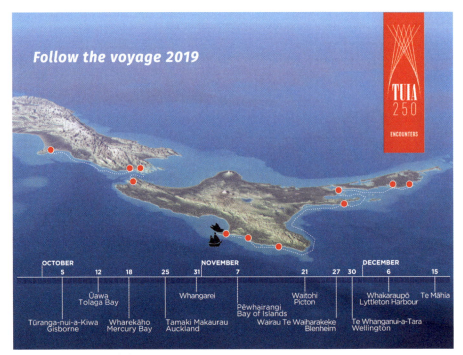

FIGURE 1: A map of the Tuia 250 voyage. MINISTRY FOR CULTURE AND HERITAGE

FIGURE 2: Waka hourua *Hinemoana* arriving in Mercury Bay, Coromandel, in October 2019. STUFF LIMITED

are a prerequisite to reimagining a new socially just future. We can deliberately choose a course of inaction or to become actively involved. Active citizenship might mean revitalising and supporting indigeneity, or it might mean disrupting apathy, paralysis and white privilege. The solutions are endless, but the first step is engaging in conversations that count, so conviviality, collaboration and healing can begin.

Navigating contested histories

During the Tuia 250 commemorations, the country's museums and art galleries also became sites of uncomfortable conversations. A challenge for many of these public institutions was to provide a space for the views of artists and communities to be expressed that simultaneously and respectfully confronted and celebrated our colonial past. *Here: Kupe to Cook* (Figure 3) was one such exhibition at Pātaka Art+Museum in Porirua that challenged 'the discovery narrative that's the cornerstone of Pākehā national history' (Friend, 2019, para. 1). While the exhibition was opened to coincide with Tuia 250, the gallery made a deliberate decision to distance itself from the commemorations. This decision enabled the expression of 'differing — and occasionally conflicting' stories with the intent of challenging interpretations of the past (Friend, 2019, para. 7). The exhibition explored 'the mistakes, misconceptions and malign effects of various arrivals' (Friend, 2019, para. 11).

Knowing and understanding the past is an important step towards finding a pathway forward. This is encapsulated in the whakataukī, ka mua, ka muri, often translated as moving backwards into the future, or know the past as a way to map out the future and move forward. However, we must be mindful that 'When we look at the past . . . we reinterpret it with all of our own contemporary thoughts and feelings cast over it' (Friend, 2019, para. 15). So, the way forward is very likely to have multiple paths that require the navigation of contests, as well as consideration of the myriad connections and responsibilities we have to each other.

Confronting our past

A key objective of the Tuia 250 commemorations was to raise awareness and reflection on the history of encounters in Aotearoa as a precursor towards making change. How did encounters that introduced new technologies, new knowledge, new economies and new peoples shape this nation and the way we engage with the rest of the world? One way to consider these questions is by exploring connections that are an intrinsic part of the tangata whenua–tangata tiriti relationship. These terms are a contemporary rendering of the two partners that signed te Tiriti o

Waitangi. Tangata whenua acknowledges the various Māori tribes as sovereign Indigenous nations. Tangata tiriti, meaning people of the Treaty, acknowledges non-Indigenous New Zealanders whose rights to citizenship or residency are derived from te Tiriti o Waitangi. These labels are a reminder of the obligations of tangata whenua and tangata tiriti to uphold the spirit and intent of te Tiriti o Waitangi and emphasise the joint responsibility to be a good Treaty partner. Being a good Treaty partner means acknowledging our tumultuous past and the legacy of colonisation that oppressed tangata whenua and privileged tangata tiriti. It also means committing to a joint future that decolonises our past and strives for a nation that is inclusive, future-focused, just and fair.

What does this look like in practice? Meng Foon is probably one of the most well-known tangata tiriti allies and champions. He is a New Zealander of Chinese descent and a fluent speaker of te reo Māori. For 24 years he served as a councillor and mayor on the Gisborne District Council, where he was well respected by the Māori community and supported Ngāti Porou engagement in council decision making. He was appointed Race Relations Commissioner in 2019 and is outspoken on issues related to hate speech, and has become a strong advocate to 'educate, expose and eradicate racism' (RNZ, 2019a, para. 2). He supports more 'local, place-based history' (Husband, 2019, para. 35) in schools — 'from wars, land confiscations

FIGURE 3: To mark 250 years since Captain Cook's arrival in Aotearoa, Pātaka Art+Museum's exhibition *Here: Kupe to Cook* explored the first voyagers to come to Aotearoa — Māori, Polynesian and European navigators. PĀTAKA ART+MUSEUM

and cultural suppression endured by Māori to the poll tax and discrimination suffered by Chinese immigrants' (MacDonald, 2019 para. 8) — as a way to 'break down barriers to racial and ethnic equality' (Little, 2019, para. 5). Tangata tiriti allies and champions make a difference every day across a range of settings.

Conclusion

Solving the world's wicked problems is a challenge closely connected to global and active citizenship, as we strive to achieve social justice through engagement with our rights and responsibilities. The goal of social justice, as expressed in this chapter through revisiting the impact of colonisation and developing strong connections between tangata whenua and tangata tiriti, is a useful foundation for considering our obligations and responsibilities. In this regard, being a good Treaty partner can be extended to include being a good global citizen. How can we as a nation advocate for an agenda that condemns and responds to ongoing conflict, climate change, poverty and other inequalities? One approach is highlighted in the whakataukī: matua whakapai i tōhou marae, ka whakapai ai i te marae o ētahi; get your own house in order before you clean up another's (Alsop & Kupenga, 2016 p. 106). This position strongly advocates for local responses that walk the talk. Global issues exist locally, and citizens of Aotearoa can utilise their rights to meet their responsibilities through active engagement with one another and with the wider world. Through unity and engagement in shared goals, we can reimagine a future — at home and abroad — that is grounded in an ethic of care and responsibility. This is global citizenship in action.

References

Alcoff, L. (1991–1992). The problem of speaking for others. *Cultural Critique, 20*, 5–32. https://doi.org/10.2307/1354221

Alsop, P., & Kupenga, T. R. (2016). *Mauri Ora: Wisdom from the Māori world*. Potton & Burton.

Belgrave, D. (2021). Sustaining democracy: The state, stakeholders and civil society. In D. Belgrave & G. Dodson (Eds.), *Tūtira Mai: Making change in Aotearoa New Zealand* (pp. 30–51). Massey University Press.

Belgrave, D., & Dodson, G. (2021). Introduction: The complexities of active citizenship. In D. Belgrave & G. Dodson (Eds.), *Tūtira Mai: Making change in Aotearoa New Zealand* (pp. 10–29). Massey University Press.

Best, E. (1924). *Māori Religion and Mythology, Part 2*. Hasselberg. http://nzetc.victoria.ac.nz/tm/scholarly/tei-Bes02Reli.html

de Almeida Kumlien A. C. M., & Coughlan, P. (2018, October 18). Wicked problems and how to solve them. *The Conversation*. https://theconversation.com/wicked-problems-and-how-to-solve-them-100047

Dudding, A. (2019, October 10). Tuia 250: I spent five days in a squeaky boat. *Stuff*. www.stuff.co.nz/national/116350298/tuia-250-i-spent-five-days-in-a-squeaky-boat

Friend, R. (2019, September 11). Calling out Cook: Porirua's Pataka gallery confronts the complexities of Tuia 250. *The Spinoff*. https://thespinoff.co.nz/art/11-09-2019/calling-out-cook-poriruas-pataka-gallery-confronts-the-complexities-of-tuia250/

How, N. (2017). Tangata whenua worldviews for wastewater management in Wairoa. A report prepared for Wairoa District Council, Wairoa, New Zealand. www.wairoadc.govt.nz/assets/Document-Library/wastewater-consenting-project/technical-reports/tangata-whenua/Technical-Report-Tangata-Whenua-Worldviews.pdf

Husband, D. (2019, September 8). Meng Foon: A journey in te ao Māori. *E-tangata*. https://e-tangata.co.nz/korero/meng-foon-a-journey-in-te-ao-maori/

Jackson, M. (2021, May 9). Decolonisation and the stories in the land. *E-tangata*. https://e-tangata.co.nz/comment-and-analysis/moana-jackson-decolonisation-and-the-stories-in-the-land/

Levin, K., Cashore, B., Berstein, S., & Auld, G. (2012). Overcoming the tragedy of super wicked problems: Constraining our future selves to ameliorate global climate change. *Policy Sciences, 45*, 123–152. https://doi.org/10.1007/s11077-012-9151-0

Little, A. (2019, July 11). Race Relations Commissioner appointed [Press release] www.beehive.govt.nz/release/race-relations-commissioner-appointed

MacDonald, N. (2019, August 3). National Portrait: Meng Foon, te reo speaker, Race Relations Commissioner. *Stuff*. www.stuff.co.nz/national/114576796/national-portrait-meng-foon-te-reo-mori-speaker-race-relations-commissioner

Manatū Taonga, Ministry for Culture and Heritage. (2019). *Tuia 250 Report*. https://mch.govt.nz/sites/default/files/projects/TUIA_250_Report_English_Digital.pdf

Manatū Taonga, Ministry for Culture and Heritage. (2020, January 28). *Accept the 'Tuia Challenge' this Waitangi Day* [Media release]. https://mch.govt.nz/accept-%E2%80%98tuia-challenge%E2%80%99-waitangi-day

Manatū Taonga, Ministry for Culture and Heritage. (n.d.a). Mō Tuia 250: About Tuia 250. Tuia 250 Encounters. https://mch.govt.nz/tuia250/about-tuia-250

Manatū Taonga, Ministry for Culture and Heritage. (n.d.b). Whakarereatanga. Legacy. Tuia 250 Encounters. https://mch.govt.nz/tuia250/legacy

Matthews, P. (2019, October 14). Tuia 250: the return of the 'death ship.' *Stuff*. www.stuff.co.nz/national/politics/116374482/tuia-250-the-return-of-the-death-ship

McLachlan, L. (2019, May 10). Critics say the $20 million Cook landing commemorations ignore Māori pain. *The Spinoff*. https://thespinoff.co.nz/atea/10-05-2019/critics-say-the-20-million-cook-landing-commemorations-ignore-maori-pain

Point of Order. (2019, October 12). The discounting of Cook's claims to a famous first — but who drew the first map of NZ? [Opinion piece]. https://pointofordernz.wordpress.com/2019/10/12/the-discounting-of-cooks-claims-to-a-famous-first-but-who-drew-the-first-map-of-nz

RNZ. (2019a, August 27). New Race Relations Commissioner Meng Foon wants to target 'hate speech, phobias and isms.' *RNZ*. www.rnz.co.nz/news/political/397572/new-race-relations-commissioner-meng-foon-wants-to-target-hate-speech-phobias-and-isms

RNZ. (2019b, December 13). Tuia 250 has created 'an unstoppable shift' — Shipley. *RNZ*. www.rnz.co.nz/news/national/405453/tuia-250-has-created-an-unstoppable-shift-shipley

Schouten, V. (2021). Practising ethics: Everyday morality and the active citizen. In D. Belgrave & G. Dodson (Eds.), *Tūtira Mai: Making change in Aotearoa New Zealand* (pp. 77–93). Massey University Press.

Te Momo, F. (2021). Tukanga whakawhanaketanga o te tangata Māori: Developmental processes of citizenship for Māori. In D. Belgrave & G. Dodson (Eds.), *Tūtira Mai: Making change in Aotearoa New Zealand* (pp. 55–76). Massey University Press.

20.
Reflections on global citizenship

Sharon McLennan

This book began with a mihimihi or greeting composed by Hone Morris (Ngāti Kahungunu, Rangitāne) that used the metaphor of birds and birdsong to represent connections between peoples, our collective wealth, and the myriad encounters that have created and continue to recreate our world. These connections were also visualised through the metaphor of raranga, the customary practice of weaving using the harakeke or flax plant, which is synonymous with unity, togetherness and strength. We asked how the multiple strands that connect peoples around the globe can be brought together to create enduring connections, the implications of these for rights and responsibilities, and what could be done about stitches that have been dropped.

As you read this book you may have noticed the range of voices represented in the chapters and aho, speaking with different tones and from different perspectives, which may at times have seemed like the birdsong of the opening mihimihi — a mixture of sounds from solo arias to harmonious compositions to a cacophony of seemingly disconnected noises. This is not unintentional. Our world is diverse, and there are as many perspectives on the challenges we face, and our rights and responsibilities in relation to these, as there are people on the planet. So, putting together a book about global citizenship was a process of weaving together a few

311

of these strands to create something new, a picture of global citizenship as it looks like from Aotearoa.

In this process, we acknowledged our tūrangawaewae, the place we stand and from where we start any journey, in Aotearoa. In doing so we emphasised Māori perspectives and knowledge as a vital strand in any discussion of citizenship, rights and responsibilities that comes from this place. Our conceptions of global citizenship are grounded in the Aotearoa context, and specifically the presence of Māori as first peoples of this land and our collective colonial history. From this tūrangawaewae we are connected to the rest of the globe through myriad threads and encounters. Some of those connections are explored in this book, in particular the global challenges of climate change, conflict, and poverty and inequality. These connections are two-way. We are impacted by these challenges, and we have an impact on them.

As we come to the end of this book, we reflect on a key thread, the concept of global citizenship. We introduced the idea in Chapter 4 as a response to globalisation and the inadequacy of legal and nation-state-based conceptions of citizenship and introduced some key questions about the nature and usage of the concept. Following from this, the chapters in the Rito section engaged with the concept in a variety of ways, with some focusing on global citizenship at the global level and/or institutional responses to local and global challenges (Rogers in Chapter 12, Bramwell et al. in Chapter 13 and Gardyne & Malecki in Chapter 16), while others focused on local and Indigenous responses to the challenges presented by globalisation (Movono & McLennan in Chapter 8, Kaiser & Kenney in Chapter 9, Forster et al. in Chapter 17 and Alefaio-Tugia et al. in Chapter 18). Other authors explored more creative and individual responses (Horrocks & Doig in Chapter 10 and Hazou in Chapter 14).

While the scales at which authors engaged with global citizenship was varied, some, particularly Bramwell et al. and Hazou, drew our attention to the interactions between individuals, groups and institutions within and across those 'scales of action'. Each chapter in the book sheds light on important components of global citizenship and the connections between Aotearoa and the rest of the world, while also highlighting the complexity and contestation that accompanies the idea that we (as individuals, Indigenous and ethnic groups, civil and corporate entities, local and national governments) can be global citizens.

To draw these threads back together, this final chapter reflects on citizenship and global citizenship as articulated in this book and answers the question of why we don't give a clear definition of global citizenship, explaining why our conception of global citizenship is messy and uncertain, critical yet hopeful, and perhaps at times reminiscent of the noisy, cacophony of birds that inhabit the forests of Aotearoa.

Complicating citizenship

The foundation of this book is the idea of citizenship. As a concept, citizenship is a very useful way to understand membership of communities, both in the formal, legal sense of the nation-state, and membership of communities and interest groups that operate at the sub-state level (Kahu, 2022). Whether in the legal sense or in the sense of belonging to a community, citizenship is important because it has consequences. As Kahu (2022) notes, it determines material benefits, fosters a sense of belonging (or alienation), and it legitimises participation and voice. It also confers particular rights and obligations.

But citizenship has also been exclusionary. The nature of citizenship in any community is socially constructed, contextual and fluid. Not all citizens have access to the same rights, and this access is often determined by identity, with some of the central identity categories — such as gender, ethnicity, class, sexuality, ability — being dominant and deemed to be more valued and desirable than others (Kahu, 2022). As Eglin (2020) argues, 'liberalism came to political prominence in societies that were already capitalist, imperialist, racist, patriarchal, heteronormative and ableist. Its attendant rights were understood to be those of the white, heterosexual, male, colonizing, able-bodied, property owner' (p. 13). As many of the chapters in this book attest, the struggle to extend the rights of citizenship to colonised, non-property-owning, female, LGBTQIA+, non-white, and other marginalised groups is an ongoing struggle.

This process has been further challenged by globalisation as the world has become increasingly interconnected through flows of ideas, commodities, finance and people. These exchanges have led to significant increases in living standards in some parts of the world, most notably China and India, and made a very small percentage of people very rich. However, it is clear that the world is struggling with the social, cultural, economic and environmental challenges of globalisation. Economic stagnation, extreme inequality, mass unemployment and underemployment, precariousness, poverty, hunger, wasted output and lives have led to what Foster (2019) describes as a planetary ecological 'death spiral' (p. 1).

This spiral is evident in the Rito chapters. As the chapters on climate change attest, we have reached a new and dangerous stage in planetary evolution with rising temperatures, extreme weather, rising oceans and mass species extinctions leading to the rapid deterioration of our physical, social and economic environment. As Angus (2016) argues, capitalism's inexorable drive for growth, which has been powered by the burning of fossil fuels, has driven our world to the brink of disaster. This drive for growth and the concomitant pressure on the Earth's resources is also the cause of significant hostility, as we can see in the chapters on conflict. Meanwhile, the world faces the ongoing challenge of poverty and worsening inequality, which is both caused by and leads to conflict and amplifies the impacts of climate change. In all of this, it is increasingly clear that both individual and collective rights are still not enjoyed by large parts of the global population (Eglin, 2020).

As discussed in Chapter 3, these challenges have contributed to a significant backlash against globalisation as witnessed in the protests of the 'anti-globalisation movement' of the late 1980s, through to the anti-austerity and anti-capitalist movements of the 2000s, the class-based mobilisations that followed the financial collapse of 2007–2008, the Occupy Movement in 2011 and the Global Climate Strikes of 2019 (Eglin, 2020). Indigenous movements and groups have often been at the forefront of these, such as the Zapatista uprising of 1994. More recently there has been a backlash against the granting of rights to many, and the twenty-first century has seen the rise of right-wing and far-right populist movements. This right-wing response to neoliberalism and globalisation favours an exclusionary vision of citizenship where perceived outsiders are not worthy of citizenship rights and has led to the 'building of walls and other disgraceful means of closing borders' (Eglin, 2020, p. 7) to protect the 'rights' of the privileged.

Complicating global citizenship

In the midst of this, the idea of global citizenship has risen in popularity as a means to highlight moral commitments to and engagement with others. The term 'global citizen' has been used to explain this growing sense of global belonging and interdependence, and the rights and responsibilities that flow from it. When the challenges we face locally are linked to collective global challenges that cross borders and oceans, and when the rights of one group are impacted by the actions of others who may be thousands of miles away, our responses to them must also be both local and global in scope. A global conception of citizenship can help us see those links and can facilitate the connections and cooperation necessary to address global challenges.

But global citizenship has also become a problematic term. Most contemporary and popular conceptions of global citizenship are rooted in Western, liberal traditions, advancing particular (Western) political interests. As Eglin (2020) argues, the concept of citizen is closely associated with the liberal state, while the concept of global citizen has come to be associated with neoliberalism. He argues that contemporary forms of global citizenship are ideological, serving the interests of global capitalism and multinational corporations.

Moreover, as discussed in Chapter 4, these forms of global citizenship are generally framed by the modern/colonial imaginary (Pashby et al., 2020) and neoliberal global citizens continue to be complicit in the perpetuation of global inequality, seeing the world and the global challenges through a lens that is ahistorical, depoliticised and ethnocentric, offering simple solutions that reflect northern paternalism and salvationism (Andreotti, 2012). Arguably, the concept of global citizenship as it has been popularised in the twenty-first century reflects and expresses the relationship between the largely white, 'developed' north and the largely non-white, underdeveloped south (Eglin, 2020, p. 11). This means that efforts to promote rights and responsibilities that apply to all human beings can be seen as a form of neo-colonialism and cultural imperialism masking the impacts of colonial violence and splitting the world in two — those who are privileged, and capable of being active global citizens, and those who are in need of support.

This is why, as discussed in Chapters 4 and 6, global citizenship is often associated with 'white saviourism', where the global citizen is constructed as a benevolent helper, delivering a gift to the 'other' who is in need. As Potter (2010, in Eglin, 2020) argues, the concept of global citizenship is compromised by:

> the restriction of the possibility of its realization to a small minority of the world's mostly rich, mostly male, mostly white, mostly straight, mostly Northern and mostly able-bodied people ... it has an ideological affordance in itself. Capitalism, imperialism, racism, patriarchy, heteronormativity and ableism work to ensure that a designated few realize the dream while the rest of us, in being seduced by it, are thereby mystified. (p. 13)

Despite this, we argue — with Eglin (2020) — that neoliberal capitalism and the Global North do not own the concept of global citizenship. But we need to look beyond these loud, dominant voices for other forms of global connection and citizenship to help us address the wicked global problems we face today.

Decolonising global citizenship

Throughout this book, we have highlighted the agency and actions of a range of groups from within and outside global governance and power structures, including a range of Indigenous responses. In Chapter 19, Forster and Belgrave explored the idea of agency and active citizenship, noting that while individual responsibility is crucial to making change, altering the structures that constrain action is equally important. This is a significant challenge, particularly where — as noted above — what may seem to be a 'good' response morally and ethically is fraught and may even contribute to ongoing injustice.

This is why this book presents a range of voices and perspectives, and weaves Indigenous knowledge with Western knowledge, affirming both ways of knowing as legitimate, but prioritising the voices of Indigenous people and those most affected by global processes and challenges. Our aim was to avoid the pitfalls of much of the discourse of global challenges and citizenship, which focuses on victimhood, with Indigenous and marginalised groups spoken for and portrayed as in need of help. Highlighting and sharing the voices of those directly concerned not only enables us to see the problems as defined by those affected but also to become aware of the myriad solutions and responses missed by mainstream media and scholarship, enabling much more positive, hopeful and mana-enhancing (empowering) conversations about rights and responsibility (McLennan et al., 2021).

Highlighting these voices and responses in this book, and centring our discussion of global citizenship here in Aotearoa, is part of our contribution to unsettling settler colonialism and decolonising global citizenship (McLennan et al., 2021, 2022). Decolonisation is a political and epistemological movement aimed not only at the liberation of colonised peoples, but at transforming ways of thinking, knowing and doing (Ndlovu-Gatsheni, 2015). The core of decolonisation, for Indigenous people, is the material matter of the return of land and sovereignty (Tuck & Yang, 2012), and this emphasis is evident in the chapters by Hepi et al. (Chapter 6), Kaiser & Kenney (Chapter 9), and Forster et al. (Chapter 17). Beyond this, decoloniality involves 'working toward a vision of human life that is not dependent upon or structured by the forced imposition of one ideal of society over those that differ' (Mignolo, 2017, p. 459). As Linda Tuhiwai Smith (2012) has argued, decolonisation is a 'long-term process involving the bureaucratic, cultural, linguistic and psychological divesting of colonial power' (p. 175). This involves the production and diffusion of alternative discourses, knowledges and creative acts aimed at breaking down 'hierarchies of difference that dehumanize subjects and communities and that destroy nature' (Maldonado-Torres, 2016, p. 10). The iho atua and many of the aho, and the emphasis on Indigenous perspectives throughout this book are one way in which we aim to contribute to this process.

We acknowledge that this is a limited effort, part of a long and messy process, and the dropped stitches, tangled threads and unfinished edges presented in this book reflect the gnarly, complex and fluid nature of decolonisation. This is a 'messy, dynamic, and a contradictory process' (Sium et al., 2012, p. ii) that imagines and works towards another world while remaining conscious of the dominance of Western thought and material relations. As such, we are also responding to Stein and others' (2020) call 'to identify opportunities and openings for responsible, context-specific collective experiments that enact different kinds of relationships, and different possibilities for (co)existence, without guarantees' (p. 45). Our approach to global citizenship is one that is deeply embedded in the local context but also strongly connected to the global. Indeed, we argue that globalising the local and localising the global is perhaps the only way in which global citizenship can be indigenised and decolonised.

In this endeavour we draw from Anna Tsing (2005) who asks, 'Might it be possible to use other scholarly skills, including the ability to tell a story that both acknowledges imperial power and leaves room for possibility?' (p. 267). We also draw on Gibson-Graham's new ways of 'doing thinking', an 'ontological re-framing' (2006, pp. xxix–xxx) which is open to new ideas, and which works to uncover what is possible and creative, but which does not deny critique, '. . . a mode of thinking that is generative, uncertain, hopeful, and yet fully grounded in an understanding of the material and discursive violence and promises of the long history of development interventions' (Gibson-Graham, 2005, p. 6).

While the challenges of the planetary 'death spiral' are immense, and climate change and the Covid-19 pandemic appear to have pushed the planet to the brink, we see possibility in the voices from the periphery, and in the responses and actions of myriad individuals, groups and institutions within and across the many 'scales of action'. Our uncertain, but generative and hopeful approach to global citizenship is inspired by the legacy of generations of Māori leaders and activists who hoped for and worked towards a better future for all, even in the midst of the violence of colonisation and the heavy losses and pain this entailed. We also return to the concept of manaaki, the notion of caring for one another that is reflected in the raranga metaphor. This strengths-based, long-term strategy reminds us of the importance of protecting and looking after all members of the global family. It is global citizenship in action, it is welcoming, respectful and purposeful; elevating the mana or authority and presence of others to strengthen, build resilience, good health and wellbeing, and to continue the collective fight for justice and peace.

References

Andreotti, V. de O. (2012). Editor's preface: Heads up. *Critical Literacy: Theories and practices, 6*(1), 1–3.

Angus, I. (2016). *Facing the Anthropocene: Fossil capitalism and the crisis of the earth system.* Monthly Review Press.

Eglin, P. (2020). Introduction. In D. D. Chapman, T. Ruiz-Chapman, & P. Elgin (Eds.), *The Global Citizenship Nexus: Critical studies* (pp. 3–21). Routledge.

Foster, J. B. (2019). Capitalism has failed: What next? *Monthly Review, 70*(9), 1–24.

Gibson-Graham, J. K. (2005). Surplus possibilities: Postdevelopment and community economies. *Singapore Journal of Tropical Geography, 26*(1), 4–26. https://doi.org/10.1111/j.0129-7619.2005.00198.x

Gibson-Graham, J. K. (2006). *A Postcapitalist Politics.* University of Minnesota Press.

Kahu, E. (2022). Identity and citizenship in Aotearoa New Zealand. In E. Kahu, R. Shaw & H. Dollery (Eds.), *Tūrangawaewae: Identity & belonging in Aotearoa New Zealand.* (2nd ed.) Massey University Press.

Maldonado-Torres, N. (2016). *Outline of Ten Theses on Coloniality and Decoloniality.* Fondation Frantz Fanon. https://doi.org/10.5811/westjem.2011.5.6700

McLennan, S. J., Dodson, G., Kahu, E., Neill, C., & Shaw, R. (2022, forthcoming). 'It's complicated': Reflections on teaching citizenship in Aotearoa New Zealand. In B. Lythberg, C. Woods, & A. Bell, *Ally Strategies — what is the work of settlers towards decolonisation?* Routledge.

McLennan, S. J., Forster, M., & Hazou, R. (2021). Weaving together: Decolonising global citizenship education in Aotearoa New Zealand. *Geographical Research*, March, 1–14. https://doi.org/10.1111/1745-5871.12484

Mignolo, W. D. (2017). Delinking: The rhetoric of modernity, the logic of coloniality and the grammar of de-coloniality. *Cultural Studies, 21*(2–3), 449–514. https://doi.org/10.1080/09502380601162647

Ndlovu-Gatsheni, S. J. (2015). Decoloniality as the future of Africa. *History Compass, 13*(10), 485–496. https://doi.org/10.1111/hic3.12264

Pashby, K., da Costa, M., Stein, S., & Andreotti, V. (2020). A meta-review of typologies of global citizenship education. *Comparative Education, 56*(2), 144–164. https://doi.org/10.1080/03050068.2020.1723352

Sium, A., Desai, C., & Ritskes, E. (2012). Towards the 'tangible unknown': Decolonization and the Indigenous future. *Decolonization: Indigeneity, education and society, 1*(1), i–xiii. https://doi.org/10.1007/s10964-013-0081-8

Smith, L. T. (2012). *Decolonizing Methodologies: Research and indigenous people* (2nd ed.). Zed Books.

Stein, S., Andreotti, V. de O., Suša, R., Amsler, S., Hunt, D., Ahenakew, C., Jimmy, E., Čajková, T., Valley, W., Cardoso, C., Dino, S., Pitaguary, B., Pataxó, U., D'Emilia, D., Calhoun, B., & Okano, H. (2020). Gesturing towards decolonial futures: Reflections on our learnings thus far. *Nordic Journal of Comparative and International Education, 4*(1), 43–65. https://doi.org/10.7577/njcie.3518

Tsing, A. L. (2005). *Friction: An ethnography of global connection.* Princeton University Press.

Tuck, E., & Yang, K. W. (2012). Decolonization is not a metaphor. *Decolonization: Indigeneity, education and society, 1*(1), 1–40. https://doi.org/10.1093/acprof:oso/9780199253487.003.0014

About the contributors

EMELINE AFEAKI-MAFILE'O MNZM is a social entrepreneur who founded Affirming Works in 2001, which provides essential services to Pacific people in Auckland. This led her to contribute to public policy in New Zealand and the Pacific. Afeaki-Mafile'o and her husband, Alipate, provide opportunities for farmers in Tonga to produce Tupu'anga products, including organic coffee, vegetable chips and vanilla. Together they started the Community Café, with proceeds funding social service programmes across Auckland. In 2006 Afeaki-Mafile'o was named a Blake Emerging Leader and in 2013 she won the Woman of Influence Community and Social Enterprise Award. She has been a member of the Westpac Sustainability advisory panel since 2019 and is an invited member of the leadership group for the Mana Kai Initiative, instigated by the Aotearoa Circle.

SIAUTU ALEFAIO-TUGIA (Samoan lineage of Matautu-Tai, Sasina, Manunu ma Fagamalo) is an Associate Professor in the School of Psychology at Massey University. Her research focuses on Pacific-Indigenous psychology, Pacific diaspora and quality of life, community-humanitarian disaster resilience and family violence. She combines extensive practice and academic experience to reinform psychology from Pacific-Indigenous knowledge frameworks. Associate Professor Alefaio-Tugia is a Rutherford Discovery Fellow and has been awarded major research grants from, and acted as adviser to, various New Zealand bodies including Ministry of Social Development (MSD), Ministry of Education, Counties Manukau Police Pacific Advisory Board and Department of Corrections.

MALCOLM ANDREWS (Fijian lineage from the villages of Wainaloka, Makolei, vasu Kasavu Savusavu-Vanualevu) is the acting director of partnership at the Pasifika Medical Association and a current postgraduate student at Massey University. He has completed his Master of Arts (Psychology) and is undertaking his doctoral studies in 2022.

JAMES ARROWSMITH is a professor in the School of Management at Massey University. He has published over 50 articles in top-ranked journals and been awarded over $1 million in grant funding in New Zealand and from the United Kingdom's Economic and Social Research Council. Professor Arrowsmith has acted as a consultant for employers, government agencies and trade unions, including for a recent series of projects for the International Labour Organisation, advising Pacific Island countries on labour reform. He is co-director of MPOWER — Massey University's People, Organisation, Work and Employment Research group. He is on the editorial board of five leading HR and employment relations journals, is co-editor-in-chief of *Labour and Industry: A journal of the social and economic relations of work* and associate editor of the *International Journal of Human Resource Management*.

GLENN BANKS is a professor of geography and head of school in the School of People, Environment and Planning at Massey University. He has spent more than 30 years working on issues of mining and resource extraction in the Pacific, with a focus on the effects on communities in the region. His other research interests include international development aid and the global wine industry.

DAVID BELGRAVE is a lecturer in citizenship and politics in the School of People, Environment and Planning at Massey University. He is a graduate of the University of Auckland, Massey University, Australian National University and Victoria University of Wellington. His research interests include New Zealand public policy, East Asian security, the Cold War and environmental politics. He is a former history researcher for Waitangi Tribunal claimants, where he focused on environmental history and land law. He is a co-editor of *Tūtira Mai: Making change in Aotearoa New Zealand* (Massey University Press, 2021).

VANESSA BRAMWELL is a PhD candidate in politics and a tutor at Massey University. Her research examines normative ideas about children affected by armed conflict in United Nations workstreams, and how such ideas might impact service provision in conflict zones. Bramwell teaches across Massey University's citizenship papers as well as in politics and security studies, and she has recently written several chapters for edited collections on the subject of children affected by armed conflict.

STUART CARR is a professor of psychology in the Industrial and Organisational (I/O) Psychology Program at Massey University. Professor Carr co-facilitates the End

Poverty and Inequality Cluster (EPIC), which includes a focus on transitions from precarious labour to decent work and living wages. Intersecting with EPIC is Project GLOW (Global Living Organisational Wage), a multi-country, multi-generational, interdisciplinary study of the links between decent wages (in purchasing power parity) and sustainable livelihoods for the eradication of poverty — the primary UN Sustainable Development Goal (SDG1).

SHINE CHOI teaches political theory and international relations at Massey University. Her research has focused on how an illiberal state such as North Korea creates the international as a space of politics. Her other research areas include non-Western IR theory, intercultural relations, visuality and aesthetics, postcolonial feminist theory and critical/creative methods. She is co-editor of the series *Creative Interventions in Global Politics* (Rowman & Littlefield) and serves as an editor for the *International Feminist Journal of Politics* (2022–2025).

TOM DOIG is a lecturer in creative writing at the University of Queensland, and the author of three creative non-fiction books. *Hazelwood* (Penguin Random House, 2020) was a finalist for the 2020 Walkley Book Award and the 2021 Ned Kelly Awards, and was awarded Highly Commended in the 2020 Victorian Premier's Literary Awards. *The Coal Face* (Penguin Books Australia, 2015) was joint winner of the 2015 Oral History Victoria Education Innovation Award. *Mörön to Mörön: Two men, two bikes, one Mongolian misadventure* (Allen & Unwin, 2013) is a humorous travel memoir. Dr Doig is also the contributing editor of the interdisciplinary collection *Living with the Climate Crisis: Voices from Aotearoa* (Bridget Williams Books, 2020).

MARGARET FORSTER (Ngāti Kahungunu, Rongomaiwāhine) is an expert in Māori knowledge systems and Māori engagement. As an Indigenous educator and researcher her work draws on Māori world views, understandings, and knowledge to respond to contemporary issues and contribute to positive Māori development.

SAMANTHA GARDYNE is a lecturer at Massey University where she also co-ordinates the Master of Sustainable Development Goals. Her research interests include education for sustainable development, sustainable livelihoods and, more recently, sustainable consumerism. She hopes to inspire students to think differently, to question what they have always accepted and, hopefully, to decide to live in such a way that they might make a difference to the world around them.

BETH GREENER is a professor in international relations at Massey University. Her research focuses on international security issues, particularly the role of the state as a security provider. She has published widely on issues including peacekeeping, international policing and non-conventional military roles, and she is currently engaged in a research project looking at gender and the military.

JARROD HAAR is a professor of human resource management at Auckland University of Technology and has Māori tribal affiliations of Ngāti Maniapoto and Ngāti Mahuta. His research focuses on wellbeing (especially job burnout), work–family–life issues (especially work–life balance), Indigenous (Māori) employees, leadership, and innovation. He is ranked a world-class researcher (PBRF), has won industry and best-paper awards, and won multiple research grants (Marsden, FRST, Ngā Pae o te Māramatanga). His current grants include a Health Research Council (wellbeing and the precariat), a National Science Challenge (Science for Technological Innovation), and Ngā Pae o te Māramatanga (Māori and Work). He has over 400 refereed outputs (including 128 journal articles). He is a Fellow of the Royal Society of New Zealand Te Apārangi.

RAND HAZOU is a Palestinian-Kiwi theatre practitioner and scholar. His research explores theatre engaging with rights and social justice. His research interests lie in applied theatre, refugee theatre and decolonial theory and practice. In 2004, he was commissioned by the UNDP to travel to the Occupied Territories in Palestine to run workshops for Palestianian youths. In Aotearoa, he has led teaching and creative projects engaging with prison, aged-care and street communities. In 2017, he was appointed the inaugural course co-ordinator for Tū Rangaranga.

DARRIN HODGETTS is a professor of societal psychology at Massey University, where he researches urban poverty and health inequalities. His recent publications include *The SAGE Handbook of Applied Social Psychology* (SAGE, 2019), *Asia-Pacific Perspectives on Intercultural Psychology* (Routledge, 2019), *Social Psychology and Everyday Life* (2nd ed., Bloomsbury, 2020) and *Urban Poverty and Health Inequalities: A relational approach* (Routledge, 2017).

TRACEY HEPI (Ngai Tūhoe, Ngāti Tūwharetoa) and her whānau live in Ashhurst, Manawatū. She teaches Oceanic Literatures as well as many of the core courses for Massey University's BA programme. Her research interests are Māori speculative fiction (horror, science fiction and fantasy), and how teenage girls create media, which is the focus of the Marsden project Seen and Heard: Understanding the media girls consume, create, and share in Aotearoa.

NICHOLAS HOLM is a senior lecturer in media studies based on Massey University's Te Whanganui-a-Tara Wellington campus. His research explores the political role of popular culture and entertainment media in a capitalist context, with a particular focus on humour and comedy. He is the author of *Advertising and Consumer Society* (Bloomsbury, 2017) and *Humour as Politics* (Palgrave Macmillan, 2017).

INGRID HORROCKS is a professor of creative writing and English based on Massey University's Te Whanganui-a-Tara Wellington campus. She has a PhD from Princeton University and her essays on writing and climate change have appeared in *The Spinoff*, *The Guardian* and *Lithub*. Her latest book, a blend of memoir, essay, travel and nature writing, is called *Where We Swim* (Te Herenga Waka University Press and University of Queensland Press, 2021). Her creative writing teaching includes a new course on contemporary eco-fictions and non-fictions, designed with Laura-Jean McKay

HARVEY JONES is a computer programmer/analyst in the School of Psychology at Massey University. He develops and maintains the websites associated with the school and its research activities. He is also responsible for creating and operating online surveys conducted by researchers using the extensive options provided within Qualtrics, a cloud-based survey tool. His experience and knowledge of data management, team communication options and IT support requirements supports academic research.

LUCY KAISER (Kāi/Ngāi Tahu, Kāti Mamoe, Waitaha) is a social scientist at GNS Science and the Joint Centre of Disaster Research at Massey University. She is also a pūkenga at Te Toi Whakaruruhau o Aotearoa, New Zealand's Māori Disaster Research Centre. Her research interests include Indigenous emergency management, disaster risk reduction and risk communication research. She is currently a PhD candidate and is investigating how Murihiku (southern) tangata whenua are planning for and responding to the impacts of climate change.

CHRISTINE KENNEY (Te Āti Awa, Ngāti Toarangatira, Ngāi Tahu) is a professor of disaster risk reduction, and director of external relations in the School of Psychology at Massey University, as well as director of Te Toi Whakaruruhau o Aotearoa, New Zealand's Māori Disaster Research Centre. Professor Kenney is also a member of New Zealand's ministerial committee on emergency management, chair of the UNDRR Indigenous Disaster Science caucus and a co-author of the 2022 Global Assessment Report (GAR).

DAVID LITTLEWOOD is a lecturer in history in Massey University's School of Humanities, Media and Creative Communication, and has been the Manawatū campus offering co-ordinator for Tū Rangaranga: Global Encounters since 2019. His research focuses on how involvement in the two world wars impacted on New Zealand society. His first book was *Military Service Tribunals and Boards in the Great War: Determining the fate of Britain's and New Zealand's conscripts* (Routledge, 2018), and he is currently working on a follow-up that analyses New Zealanders' experiences of conscription during the Second World War.

AXEL MALECKI is a lecturer with the School of People, Environment and Planning at Massey University. His research interests coalesce around political geography, development studies and population geography with particular emphasis on the relationship between international migration and development, as well as the relationship between mature liberal democracies and the governance of migration. He has also held posts at Victoria University of Wellington, where he taught in the Master of Migration Studies Programme.

SHARON MCLENNAN is a senior lecturer in citizenship and development studies at Massey University. She was a part of the team that designed and developed the Tū Rangaranga: Global Encounters course in 2016–2017 and has been the distance offering co-ordinator from the beginning of the course, and the course co-ordinator since 2019. She has teaching and research interests in critical and decolonial approaches to the study and practice of international development and global citizenship. She also has ongoing research interests in global health and health resilience.

APISALOME MOVONO began his career at the University of the South Pacific in Fiji and is now a senior lecturer at Massey University, where he continues his passion for the Pacific by researching and promoting development that is fair, resilient and sustainable for future generations. He is the co-founder of the Laucala Beach Sustainability Society and is an active conservationist and community development advocate for his people in Fiji and the Pacific region.

CAROL NEILL was a course co-ordinator in Tū Rangaranga: Global Encounters at the Albany campus from 2019 to 2021 and is now a senior lecturer in the School of Education at Auckland University of Technology. Carol has a PhD in history from Massey University and has researched widely across aspects of New Zealand's political, economic and social history. In recent years her research has extended to history and citizenship education, in particular, considering how New Zealanders seek to reconcile colonisation history with their understanding of social and political challenges that present today.

JANE PARKER is a professor of employment relations and human resource management in the School of Management at Massey University. She is co-editor in chief of *Labour and Industry*, an associate editor of the *Journal of Organisational Effectiveness*, and is on the editorial boards of *Human Relations* and *Employee Relations*. Jane is a member of the executive committee of the International Labour and Employment Relations Association (ILERA) and an associate fellow of the Industrial Relations Research Unit at the University of Warwick, England. She publishes widely on employment relations and human resource management matters, including social movement unionism, worker freedom, employee consultation, and diversity and inclusion. Jane is also the co-director of Massey's People, Organisation, Work and Employment Research (MPOWER) Group, and recently led a major funded study on gender equity in Aotearoa's public service.

CATHERINE RIVERA has a PhD in social anthropology from Massey University. She was a tutor on Tū Rangaranga: Global Encounters from 2017 to 2021. Her academic research focuses on civil society and democratic participation, social justice, youth activism, and religious diversity in Aotearoa New Zealand.

DAMIEN ROGERS is a senior lecturer at Massey University. He holds a PhD in political science and international relations from the Australian National University and a PhD in law from the University of Waikato. His research interests concern how and why individuals and groups respond to various types of political violence, including armed conflict, terrorism and mass atrocity.

PETRA SATELE (Samoan heritage from the villages of Faleapuna and Vailuutai) was born and raised in West Auckland. She completed her Master of Science in psychology at Massey University, where she is continuing her research on Pacific Indigenous resilience as a PhD candidate. Satele is the NIUPATCH (Navigate in Unity Pacific Approaches to Community Humanitarianism) project lead and research navigator for Pacific resilience.

SY TAFFEL is a senior lecturer in media studies and co-director of the Political Ecology Research Centre at Massey University. He is the author of *Digital Media Ecologies* (Bloomsbury, 2019). His research focuses on digital technology and the environment, digital media and society, automation, and digital labour.

KRUSHIL WATENE (Ngāti Manu, Te Hikutu, Ngāti Whātua o Orākei, Tonga) is an associate professor in philosophy at Massey University. Her research addresses fundamental questions in moral and political philosophy, particularly those related to wellbeing, development and justice. Her primary areas of expertise include mainstream theories of wellbeing and justice, obligations to future generations, and Indigenous philosophies. Her research contributes to high-level discussions of Indigenous concepts in global justice theorising, grounded in research that demonstrates the central role of local communities. She holds a PhD in philosophy from the University of St Andrews. She is currently a Rutherford Discovery Fellow, undertaking research on intergenerational justice.

AMANDA YOUNG-HAUSER is a lecturer in the School of Psychology at Massey University's Auckland campus. She has a background in community psychology and is involved in multiple research projects concerning sustainable livelihoods, the precariat and wellbeing, and gender (in)equities. Her research interests include social (in)justice, restorative justice, the (un)doing of relationships, narrative theory and research, intimate partner violence, crime and punishment, and the prevention of child sexual abuse.

Index

Page numbers in **bold** refer
to images.

Abu-Shanab, Nadia 232
active citizenship 299, 300–03,
307, 309, 315, 316
Māori 302, 305, 307
trade-offs 301–02
advertising 208
Afeaki-Mafile'o, Emeline 290,
291–92
Affirming Works (Affirming
Women) social enterprise
291–92
agency 300–01, 315–16
agriculture 36, 210, 211, 218, 302
ahikā 90–91
aid programmes 71
air travel 26, 55, 130–31, 301
Alefaio, Siautu 290–91
Amazon rainforest 108, **109**
ancestors 16, 17, 33, 66, 91, 99, 117,
127, 152, 168
Annan, Kofi, *In Larger Freedom*
report 83, 196
anti-globalisation movements 55,
58, 314
ANZUS alliance 37
Apple
code of corporate
conduct 220–21
iPhone 207, 208–09, 213,
216–17
Ardern, Jacinda 40, 186
aroha 67, 181
art interventions 223, 224, 233–35
Asia: Aotearoa's growing Asian
orientation 37
'Asian Values' debate 85, 87
assimilation 33, 74, 184
Athens 68–69
atrocity crimes 184, 185, 190,
191–93, 197, 203–04
see also Responsibility to
Protect (R2P)
international criminal
tribunals and 'hybrid'
institutions 185, 192–93,
194
atua 17, 64, 66, 82, 97, 117, 274
Auckland
hyper-diversity 46

Pasifika population 282,
284, 285, 287
Australia
foreign policy of Aotearoa 37
Māori migrants 40

Bagosora, Colonel 200
Bangladesh 51
Banksy
artworks 234–35
'Floating Balloon Girl' 223
The Walled Off Hotel,
Bethlehem 227–29, **228**,
230–31, 233, 234
'Banksy Effect' 223
Beijing Declaration and
Platform for the Action of the
Fourth World Conference on
Women 259
Ben-Barak, Idan 231
Bethlehem 227–29, **228**, 230–31
biculturalism 49, 278, 304
Bill of Rights Act 1990 91, 93
'blood diamonds' 211
Bloomfield, Ashley 87
Bolivia 218
Borrowdale, Andrew 87
Bosnian Muslims massacre,
Srebrenica, 1995 185, 190, 194,
199, 202, 203
Boycott, Divestment and Sanctions
(BDS) against Israel 231–33
Boyd incident 30
Bradley, James 175, 178
Brandt Line 59
'Bretton Woods' system 37
Brexit 58, 59, 182
Britain *see* United Kingdom
(Britain)
Brundtland Commission 193
BTS Army 49
Building Act 2004 146
Bush, George 198–99

Cambodia 192
capital flows 46, 47, 48, 60
capitalism 85, 87, 206, 207, 239,
241–42, 314, 315
carbon dioxide 118, 119, 124, 145,
150, 298, 301
disproportionate
responsibility for
emissions 251

child labour 210, 241
child soldiers 211
China 38, 54, 86, 191, 203, 213, 216,
218, 241, 313
Chinese migration to Aotearoa 36,
38, **39**
Christchurch mosque attacks,
2019 40, 180
Chun Yee-Hop 38
citizenship
see also active citizenship;
global citizenship
and belonging 64, 68, 224,
313
and climate change 122, 125
complications 313–14
conceptualisation 20, 75
conditional nature
of colonial Māori
citizenship 67
and identity 71, 75
and inequality 246
Māori views 16, 37, 64,
66–68, 75, 91, 97, 312
nation-state context 20,
68–69, 70–71, 73, 74, 75,
100–01, 224, 312
not an inclusive term 69, 313
rights 313, 314
Western tradition 68–69, 70,
73, 74, 75, 100–01
Civil Defence and Emergency
Management Act 2002 146
civil rights 69, 87, 122, 253
civil society 40–41, 48, 101, 104–
05, 220, 221, 245, 256
see also non-governmental
organisations (NGOs)
civil wars 199, 203, 209, 210
climate change
see also Māori: climate
change impacts and
responses
activism 120, 154, 156,
165–67, 170–72, 314
and citizenship 122, 125,
164–65, 170, 301
community and individual
responses 124, 317
creative writing 161, 164–79
digital technology
contribution 217

327

garment industry emissions 52, 53
global connections 20, 49
government action 124, 143–47
imagining possible futures 174–75, 178
impacts 118, 119
Indigenous peoples' impacts and responses 104, 119, 120, 122–23, 142–43, 156
inequality 119, 142
international action 107, 123–24
overview 116, 118, 313–14
private sector action 124
probability of conflict 183
and rights 119, 122–23
sea-level rise, Kiribati 56–57, 57
'super wicked problem' 298
Climate Change Response Act 2002 145–46
Climate Change Response (Zero Carbon) Amendment Act 2019 124, 145, 146
Coca-Cola 48, 49
Cochabamba Water War 218, **219**
Cold War 85, 182, 198, 199
collective
opportunities for co-existence 317
and reduced likelihood of conflict 188
responsibilities 15, 20, 21, 70, 97, 98, 220–21, 274, 300, 301, 302
rights 15, 20, 21, 85, 87–88, 301, 314
collective security 198, 204
see also United Nations (UN)
colonialism
see also decolonisation; neo-colonialism
addressing benefits secured through colonialism 78
impacts 17, 28–29, 50, 75, 120, 142, 199, 234, 239
neoliberalism as a form of colonisation 47, 58
in Pacific poetry 176
in processes of contemporary globalisation 60, 315
and understanding of human rights 83, 85
colonisation of Aotearoa
British belief in 'civilising mission' 32, 184
compulsory study in schools 186

Māori resistance 33, 55, 82
negative impacts 16, 32–34, 36, 41, 50, 51, 66–67, 180, 266–67, 268, 278, 287, 301, 303, 304, 305, 317
suppression of Māori sovereignty 16, 67, 82, 89–90, 91, 93, 180, 309
Taranaki 34, **35**
commodity chains 44, 46
commodity production *see* production
commodity thinking 206, 207–09
communication networks 23, 26, 46, 50, 239
community
engagement 101, 104–05
local initiatives 58, 245–46
membership 20, 313
support networks 41
Community Café, Auckland 292
conflict minerals 214, **215**
Conflict Minerals Regulation 2021 (EU) 220
conflicts
see also names of individual conflicts
Aotearoa's participation in international conflicts 180
causes 183–84
commodity conflict 209–10, 211, 216, 217, 220
culpability 200
frequency 182–83
and global citizenship 188
and globalisation 49, 298
and human rights 184–85, 253
international action to address 107
responses 185, 188, 303
consumption 207, 220, 249, 251, 258, 298, 302
relations of consumption 208, 209
Convention on the Elimination of All Forms of Discrimination Against Women (CEDAW) 259
Convention on the Prevention and Punishment of the Crime of Genocide (1948) 192
Convention on the Rights of the Child (CRC) 209, 210
coral bleaching 135
corporate social responsibility 105
cosmopolitanism 70, 75
cost of living 287
Covid-19 pandemic
Aotearoa's response 40, 44, 267

Delta variant 271, 277, 278–79
Fiji 131
and globalisation 46, 48, 54–55, 317
impact on those in precarious employment 54, 241, 267, 274, 277
individual and collective rights in tension 87–88, 182
iwi-led checkpoints 270, **271**
Māori community impacts and responses 54, 264, 265, 267, 270–71, 275, 276–77, 278–79
mobilisation of the far right 59–60
nationalism and populism 59–60
online networking 44, 50
Pacific islands 130
Pasifika impacts and responses 54, 272–73, **273**
poverty and hunger faced by garment workers 51, 53
reduction in GHG emissions 118
unequal economic burdens 183, 267
vaccination 271, 276–77
COVID in the Islands: A comparative perspective on the Caribbean and the Pacific 272
creative writing, and climate change 161, 164–72
imagining alternative worlds 172–75, 178–79
crimes against humanity 191–92, 194, 196, 197
cultural appropriation 51
cultural globalisation 48–9
culture, as a dimension of development 255

Dallaire Institute 200
Dallaire, Major-General Roméo 200, **201**
Dayenu 232
decolonisation 67, 82, 89, 176, 234, 266, 301, 302, 303–09, 315–17
Democratic Republic of the Congo (DRC) 209, 210, 211, 214, **215**, 217, 241
descendants, relationships to 99
desertification 122, 183, 210
development discourse 250
digital interactions 44, 104
digital technology, climate change contribution 217

328   TŪ RANGARANGA

dignity 45, 71, 83, 87, 198, 249, 252, 253, 254, 287
discrimination 51, 184, 191, 237, 249, 253, 254, 256, 257, 261, 271, 309
    see also gender; racism; and under Indigenous peoples
diversity of society 40, 46, 49, 186, 203, 252, 311
Dodd-Frank Act 2010 (US) 214, 220
Dugard, John 227

Earthrise 72, **72**
ecology 212
    see also political ecology
economic-centred outlook on progress and development 107, 120, 132, 251, 258, 279, 314, 317
economic developments leading to social change 37, 40
    see also neoliberalism
economic globalisation 47–8, 58, 203
Edgecumbe flood, 2017 147, 148
education 51, 84, 85, 93, 101, 123, 266, 302
    inequality 104, 122, 184, 227, 239, 242, 244, 253, 254, 258, 259, 266, 286, 288
emergency management 146–47
employment inequities 259, 266
Enlightenment 29, 70, 198
environment
    see also exploitation of resources; human–nature relationship
    colonisation impacts 142
    electronic waste 216
    environmental movement 71, 72
    globalisation risks 46
    Indigenous responsibilities and responses 67, 68, 142, 150
    mining industry impacts 211, 214
    production processes 213, 216
    protection policies 58
    rights 94
    socio-environmental responsibilities 58, 96, 98, 301
Environment Canterbury 146
ethnic cleansing 194, 196, 197, 202
European exploration 28–29, 109, 303, 304
European Union (previously European Economic Community) 36, 37, 48, 59, 220, 240

exploitation of resources 32, 36, 49, 63, 74, 75, 100, 120, 239
    Amazon rainforest 108, **109**
    political ecology of extraction 209–12, 220

far right 55, 59–60, 314
fashion industry 52, 53
Fiji
    climate change impacts 134, 135, 137
    Covid-19 137
    lunar calendar (Vula Vakaviti) 133–34
    Marine Protected Areas 135
    Naviti Resort 128, **134**
    tourism 125, 128, 131, 133, 134, 135, 137, 138
    traditional knowledge and livelihoods of communities 133–34, 137
    Vatuolalai village 128, 131, 133–35, **134**, 137, 138
First World War 36–37, 70, 85, 183, 184, 224
food security 106, 135, 137, 142, 183, 244, 252
Foon, Meng 308–09
foreign policy 36–37
fossil fuels 118, 119, 124
France, Meagan, 'extinction' 161, 164
Fruean, Briana 168

Gaddafi, Muammar 202
garment industry 51, 52–53
Geddes, Winifred 148
gender
    inequality, equality and empowerment 58, 244, 249, 256, 258–61
    pay gap 260
General Agreement on Tariffs and Trade (GATT) 37, 40, 48
genocide 185, 190, 192, 194, 196
global citizenship
    collective responses to atrocity crimes 192
    complications of global connections 20, 60, 63, 69, 312–15
    conceptualising 70–71, 314–17
    and conflicts 188
    critical perspectives 73–75
    decolonising 16, 315–17
    definitions 71, 224
    as a form of neo-colonialism 73, 74, 315
    government of Aotearoa 204
    and neoliberalism 73–74, 104, 315

    rights and responsibilities 15, 20–21, 70–71, 75, 78, 100–01, 104–05, 107, 110, 224, 300, 309, 311–12, 314
    'soft' global citizenship 73
Global Conflict Tracker, Center for Preventive Action 182
Global North 59, 73, 74, 202, 213, 237, 249, 258, 315
Global South 58, 59, 74, 216, 315
globalisation
    see also anti-globalisation movements; economic globalisation; social and cultural globalisation; and under Indigenous peoples; also under Māori
    Aotearoa's leadership in global developments 40–41, 303
    Aotearoa's web of global connections 41, 298, 300, 312
    changes to connections and allegiances 20–21, 41, 313
    and civil wars 199
    defining and conceptualising 46
    individual New Zealanders as global leaders 41
    leadership by multilateral organisations 37, 41, 48
    negative impacts 49, 50–5, 58, 60, 94, 199, 203, 213, 237, 239, 279, 303, 313
    political globalisation 48
    positive impacts 50, 60
    responsibilities 100–01, 104–05, 107, 110
    right-wing response 314
    risks 44, 46
    role of migration and travel 40, 46, 48, 60
    roots of modern globalisation 26, 44
    slowing 56–60
globalising the local 16, 41, 317
Great Chain of Being 102, **103**
greenhouse gases (GHGs) 53, 118, 119, 123, 124, 128, 130, 150, 217

harakeke 14, 15, 311
He Puapua (Charters et al., 2019) 93, 277
    health 75, 93, 101, 106, 122, 127, 183, 213, 216, 218, 227, 317
    see also Covid-19 pandemic; and under Māori
    inequalities 54, 184, 240, 242, 244, 253, 254, 259, 265–67, 279

INDEX   329

Heke, Hone 33
Hīkoita te Ao (Smith) 162, **163**
Hine-ahu-one 27
Hinenuitepō 117
Hinetītama 117
Hipkins, Chris 186
Hiroshima bombing 191
Holocaust 192
hongi 27
housing 104, 122, 128, 142, 145, 242, 244, 253, 266, 275, 278, 301
human–nature relationships 98–99, 100, 107, 110, 133–34
see also non-humans
human rights 21, 51, 71, 75, 93
Aotearoa's responsibilities and duties 204
approach to inequality and poverty 241, 244, 252–54
and climate change 119, 122
in commodity production 209–10, 214
in conflict with state sovereignty 88
and conflicts 184–85
families of rights 84–85
human needs and nature 83
individual or collective rights 85, 87–88
Responsibility to Protect 193, 196, 203
sustainable development approach 249
tourism industry challenges 129
Treaty of Westphalia, 1648 197–98
Human Rights Act 1993 86
Human Rights Commission, New Zealand 86, 92, 286
humanitarianism 29, 32, 203
assumptions about needs 105

ideas, flow 46, 50
identities 60, 63, 75, 199
see also national identity; and under Indigenous peoples; also under Māori
connected to land, water and non-human entities 99
identity politics 203
iho atua (origin narratives) 15, 16, 17, 18–19
Ihumātao protests 76–77, **77**
imperialism 89, 100, 120, 183, 184, 225, 305, 313, 315
cultural 73, 315
Indigenous Knowledge Systems (IKS) 16–17, 107, 110, 133, 137, 138, 142–43, 316

Indigenous peoples
see also colonialism
activism 76, 108, 314
climate change impacts and responses 104, 119, 120, 122–23, 142–43, 156
commodity extraction impacts 210–11
creative works 174
decision-making practices 58
family and community commitments 104
global citizenship concerns 74, 316
globalisation 16, 46, 50–51, 60, 67, 74, 316
historical global connections 26, 28, 68
identities 63, 70, 74–75
intellectual property 51
marginalisation and discrimination 90, 92, 93, 101, 239, 265, 316
neoliberalism 50–51
philosophies and frameworks 96, 98–99
responsibilities 67, 96, 98–100, 107, 110, 316
rights 21, 41, 49, 67, 74–75, 76–77, 83, 129–30, 220, 316
self-determination 89
and Sustainable Development Goals 255
tourism impacts 129–30, 131
treatment by European explorers 28–29
individuals
neoliberal individualism 47–48, 74
responsibilities 20, 70, 98, 220, 221, 301–02, 316
rights 20, 21, 85, 87–88, 301, 314
Western conception of individualism 85, 87, 101
inequality 46, 51, 52, 54, 237, 239, 248–49, 250
see also discrimination; gender; poverty; wealth and income gaps; and under education; also under health
causes and extent 239–41
and citizenship 246, 315
climate change causes and impacts 119, 142
gender 244, 249, 256, 258–61
and human rights 241, 244, 252–54

international action to address 107
mapping poverty and inequality 242, **243**
Northern lens 73, 237
of opportunity 252, 253
responses 244–46, 249, 251–52, 265, 301
source of conflict 183, 184, 253
influenza pandemic, 1918 268–69, 270
Ingoe, Maia, 'School Strike 4 Climate: A Fight for Future' 170–72
Intergovernmental Panel on Climate Change (IPCC) 118, 123, 127–28
International Convention on Intervention and State Sovereignty (ICISS) 193
International Court of Justice 226, 231–32
International Criminal Court (ICC) 185, 188, 193
International Criminal Tribunal for Rwanda 185, 193
International Criminal Tribunal for the Former Republic of Yugoslavia 185, 193, 194
International Indigenous Peoples' Forum on Climate Change (UNFCCC) 143
International Labour Organization (ILO) 286
International Monetary Fund (IMF) 37, 48, 58, 240
Internet 217
intersectionality 244, 249, 254, 256, 258
influences reinforcing deprivation 257
iPhone 207, 208–09, 213, 216–17
island nations
see also Fiji; Kiribati; Pacific Ocean and islands
climate change impacts 119, 122, 127–28, 183
Israel 225, 230
see also Palestinian–Israeli conflict
Israeli Separation Wall 223, 226, **226**, 227–29, **228**, 230–32, 233
iwi/hapū management plans (IHMPs) 150
Iwi Leaders Forum 275

Jackson, Moana 304–05
Jetñil-Kijiner, Kathy, 'Dear Matafele Peinam' 166–67, 168, 170

330 TŪ RANGARANGA

Ka Puta Ka Ora (Māori
  Television) 264, 270
kaitiakitanga 144, 146, 147, 152,
  156
kaupapa (values) 142
kaupapa Māori services 275
kāwanatanga 276–78
Kāwanatanga Karauna (state
  governance) 277
King, Philip 30
Kingitanga movement 33, 67
Kiribati 56–57, **57**, 136
Kosovo 194, 202
Kyoto Protocol 145

land
    see also Māori land
  Indigenous relationships 99,
    107
Last Warning Campaign
  (LWC) 108
leave no one behind (LNOB) 254,
  256–58, 258, 261
Libya 190, 202
'living standard framework' 40
living standards 101, 105, 245,
  275, 313
living wage 286–87, 289, 294
Living Wage Movement Aotearoa
  New Zealand (LWMANZ) 287
Local Government Act 2002 146
localising the global 16, 41, 317
Logan-Riley, India 120, **121**
Lorde 41, 232–33

Mafile'o, Alipate 290, 292
Māhia Beach, Tuia 250 flotilla of
  ships 305, **306**
mana-enhancing relations 17, 27,
  274, 316
Mana Moana Project 154, **155**
mana tangata 64, 97
mana whenua 66, 76, 90–91,
  146, 302
manaaki 15, 238, 265, 274, 276, 317
Māori global encounters grounded
  in 27
platform for ethical behaviour 16,
  27, 181
manaaki manuhiri (care of
  visitors) 67
manufacturing *see* production
Māori
    see also colonisation of
      Aotearoa
  activism 41, 55, 58, 120, 154,
    156, 304–05, 317
  citizenship views 16, 37, 64,
    66–68, 75, 91, 97, 312
  connections with Pacific
    Island communities 16, 28

consultation and
  engagement 302
Covid-19 impacts and
  responses 54, 264, 265,
  267, 270–71, 275, 276–77,
  278–79
dairy industry impacts 211
early global connections and
  trade 19, 32, 33
encounters with
  Europeans 29–30, 32, 102,
  120, 303–05, 307–08
global impacts on the Māori
  world 45, 51, 58, 82, 267
global interests and
  concerns 67
health and social service
  providers 51, 67
health outcomes 27, 32, 51,
  67, 91, 141, 150, 265–67,
  270–71, 278
identity 19, 63, 266, 270,
  275, 278
kinship and community
  obligations 64, 66
neoliberalism impacts 50–
  51, 54, 58
origin narratives (*see* iho atua
  (origin narratives))
outward migration 40
population 33, 283
responsibilities 64, 75, 97, 98
rights 64, 66, 75, 90–91,
  93–94, 220
self-determination 17, 32, 89–
  90, 220, 270, 275, 276, 277
self-management 51
tangihanga 270
urban migration 37
whakapapa relationships 98,
  147
Maori (28) Battalion 37
Māori: climate change impacts and
  responses
  activism 156
  coastal communities 141,
    144–45, 151
  involvement in national
    climate change
    frameworks 123, 143–47
  iwi-led strategies 150–53,
    156
  mātauranga Māori combined
    with Western science 147,
    150, 151
  partnering with government
    agencies 151
  responses 147–56
  risks 141
Māori development 275–76
Māori: land (whenua)

collective ownership
  replaced by individual 33
confiscations 33, 34, 76,
  239, 309
European acquisition 33, 34,
  36, 50, 239
returning to communal
  ownership 58
spiritual significance and
  connection to ancestors 27,
  33, 63, 66, 239
Māori Women's Welfare
  League 67, 275
Matar, Haggai 227
mātauranga Māori 58, 92, 142, 147,
  150, 151
Māui 97, 117, 299
mauri (life essence of a
  resource) 147, 238, 299, 301
McDonaldisation 49
McKay, Laura Jean, *The Animals in
  that Country* 172–74
migration 46
  anti-immigrant
    sentiments 59
  Aotearoa, outward
    migration 40, 41
  forced 183
  and inequality 254
  for labour purposes 40,
    47, 282
  as a result of climate
    change 122
migration inward, to Aotearoa
  Chinese 38, **39**, 309
  diversity 40
  Pacific 36, 40, 282–83
Milošević, Slobodan 194
mining industry 211–12, 214
Moana (film), and climate
  change 168, **169**
Moleta, Clare, *Unsheltered* 174–75
Montevideo Convention 122
moral equivalency 228
multiculturalism 49
multilateralism 48
  organisations 37, 41, 48
Musket Wars, 1820s–1830s 32

Nagasaki bombing 191
nation-states
    see also states
  barriers to cooperation 100,
    105, 107
  context of citizenship 20,
    68–69, 70–71, 73, 74, 75,
    100–01, 224, 312
  cosmopolitanism 70
  decline 71
  and globalisation 48, 58,
    75, 100

INDEX 331

Māori relations 67, 277, 278
mining industry impacts 211
social structures and
policies 279
National Climate Change Risk
Assessment 145–46
National Emergency Management
Agency 148
national identity 37, 60, 63, 182,
278, 304
National Institute of Water
and Atmospheric Research
(NIWA) 151
National Policy Statements
(NPS) 144
nationalism 55, 59–60, 184, 199,
202
Native Land Court 33
NATO 194, 202–03
neo-colonialism 47, 58, 73, 74, 89,
185, 315
neoliberalism 40, 46, 47–48, 54,
60, 94, 101, 105, 213, 217, 239,
240–41, 279, 314
connection to global
citizenship 73–74, 75, 315
as new colonialism 47, 58
New Zealand Coastal Policy
Statement 2010 144–45
New Zealand Emissions Trading
Scheme (ETS) 145
New Zealand Māori Council 275
New Zealand Wars 33, 67, 180,
186, **187**
Ngāi Tahu 150, 151–53
Ngata, Tina 305
Ngāti Awa Volunteer Army
(NAVA) 147, 148, **149**
Ngāti Hau 148
Ngāti Porou 151
nitrogen circulation 212–13
NIUPATCH (Navigate In
Unity: Pacific Approaches
to Community-
Humanitarianism 290, 291
Noa, and Tapu 238
non-governmental organisations
(NGOs) 58, 206, 216, 220, 221,
245, 275, 290
see also civil society
non-humans
see also human–nature
relationships
creative writing about non-
humans 172–74
global connections 48
responsibilities of
humans 98
rights 21, 93–94, 107, 110
normalisation 231, 233
nuclear-free policy 41

Office of Treaty Settlements 91
Offill, Jenny, *Weather* 165
Ōkurei Point ūrupa erosion,
2019 147

Pacific Ocean and islands
see also Fiji; island nations;
Kiribati; Pasifika in
Aotearoa
adapting to change 138
Aotearoa's growing Pacific
orientation 37
climate change impacts
127–28, 130–31, 136, 138,
166–70, 301
Covid-19 pandemic 130, 138
poetry 176–77
Polynesian voyaging 16, 28,
41, 127, 304, 305
relational principles and
values 132
spirituality and climate
change 132
tourism 128–31, 138
widespread exchange
community 41, 68
Palestine, New Zealand's
position 233
Palestinian Campaign for the
Academic and Cultural Boycott
of Israel (PACABI) 232, 233
Palestinian–Israeli conflict 224–
25, 227, 230, 233
pandemics
see also Covid-19 pandemic;
influenza pandemic, 1918
impact on Indigenous
peoples 268–69
spread via globalisation 54–
55
Papatūānuku 18, 27, 64, **65**, 66, 117,
174, 238, 278
Papua New Guinea 44, 132, 210,
211
Paris Agreement 123, 124, 145
Pasifika in Aotearoa
activism 41, 289–91
Covid-19 impacts and
responses 54, 272–73, **273**
'Dawn Raids' 282–83
employment 40, 282, 283,
284, 286, 287
income 284, 286
inequality 283, 286, 287, 288
Māori connections to
communities 16, 28
migrants 36, 40, 282–83
neoliberalism impacts 54
pay gap 288
population 283–85
poverty and poverty

reduction 283, 286, 287,
289, 292, 294
social service
programmes 291–92
urban neighbourhoods 40
Pataka Art+Museum, *Here: Kupe to
Cook* exhibition 307, **308**
peace 17, 48, 70, 74, 86, 106, 185,
188, 190, 192, 203, 248, 252, 317
peace activism 58, 71, 188
peacekeeping operations 180, 185,
192, 194, 199, 200, 202, 204
personhood of natural entities 107
poetry
on climate change 161, 164,
166–67, 170, 178–79
Pacific poetry 176–77
Pol Pot's crimes against
humanity 192
political ecology 206, 212, 216
of extraction 209–12, 220
political rights 85, 87, 89, 122, 253
poll tax levied on Chinese
migrants 38, 309
population of Aotearoa
European 33
Māori 33, 283
Pasifika 283–85
populism 59–60
potentiality 45
poutiriao 66
pouwhenua 90
poverty 49, 51, 104, 237, 246
see also inequality; living
wage
causes and extent 239–41
difficult trade-offs 244
and human rights 241, 244,
252–54
international action to
address 107, 248
Māori and Pasifika 50–51
mapping poverty and
inequality 242, **243**
responses 71, 245–46,
248–49, 251–52
women and girls 259
power 60, 81, 83, 100, 101, 105,
107, 203, 207, 235, 240, 249, 256,
258, 259–60, 303
precariat 46, 51, 54, 119, 240–41,
277, 279
Covid-19 pandemic
impact 54, 241, 267, 274
Indigenous peoples 267
privatisation 47, 51
production
see also exploitation of
resources
child labour 210, 211, 241
connection to rights and

responsibilities 207, 217, 219–21
human rights 209–10, 213, 216
infrastructure 216–17
internationalisation 47, 50, 213
labour rights 209, 210, 211, 213, 216, 241
life cycles 212–16, 217, 220
relations of production 208, 209
strategies to mitigate social and environmental costs 220–21
toxic processes 213, 216
unsafe practices 49, 51, 52, 63, 241
unsustainability 249
protests 41, 246, 314

quality of life 240, 282, 283, 286, 287, 291, 292, 294

racism 176, 241, 256, 265, 266, 267, 271, 308–09
radical hope 175, 178
Radio New Zealand, New Zealand Wars Collection 186
rāhui 147, 150
rangatiratanga (Māori authority) 66, 90, 91, 92, 117, 265, 270, 274, 275–76, 277, 279
see also tino rangatiratanga (absolute tribal authority)
Ranginui 18, 64, **65**, 66, 117, 238
raranga metaphor 14–15, 16–17, 300, 311, 317
Rata, Arama 305
Raukūmara Pae Maunga Restoration Project 151
Reagan, Ronald 40, 47, 240
Refugee Convention, 1951 (UN) 56
refugees 75, 183, 184, 225, 232
Renewables in Cities 2019 Global Status Report 124
Resource Management Act 1991 144, 145
resources
see also exploitation of resources
as a driver of conflict 183
limitations 251
responsibilities
see also active citizenship; collective; individuals; and under global citizenship
global context 20, 21, 70, 100–01, 104–05, 107, 110, 224, 300, 314
Indigenous peoples 67, 96,

98–100, 107, 110, 316
Māori 64, 75, 97, 98
relational 98–100
shared 75, 78, 304, 309
as solutions 300, 301
to the state 301
and structural injustices 75, 78
tourists 130–31
Responsibility to Protect (R2P) 88, 185, 193, 196–98
framing the use of armed force in international affairs 202–03
high threshold of human suffering before action 203
roots 198–99, 202
rights
see also civil rights; collective; human rights; individuals; political rights; universal rights; and under global citizenship
as action 300
alternative approaches 81, 83
as capabilities 84
and citizenship 17, 20–21, 75–76, 84–85, 88, 89, 90, 91, 300, 309, 313, 314
and climate change 119, 122–23
concept 21, 75, 81–87
discourses 21
Indigenous peoples 21, 41, 49, 67, 74–75, 76–77, 83, 129–30, 220, 316
mainstream view 81
Māori 64, 66, 75, 90–91, 93–94, 220
non-humans 21, 93–94, 107, 110
positive and negative rights 84
responsibilities to respond to rights issues 71, 300, 301
Rist, Gilbert 250
Rogernomics 47
Russia (including Soviet Union) 29, 86, 183, 191, 199, 203
Ruwhiu, Leland 274
Rwandan Genocide, 1994 185, 190, 199, 200, 203

Sachs, Justine 232
Sāmoa 268–69, 282
Santos Perez, Craig 178–79
School Strike 4 Climate movement 170–72
Second World War 37, 41, 67, 70, 83, 85, 182, 184, 185, 199, 248
self-determination

see also under Māori
climate change impacts 122–23, 128
Indigenous peoples 89
and state sovereignty 88–89
services, globalisation 50
Shaw, Richard 34
Silicon Valley 213, 217
slavery 29, 52, 53
'slowbalisation' 55
smart phone production 207, 208–09, 213, 216–17, 241
Smith, Huhana, Hīkoita te Ao 162, **163**
social and cultural globalisation 48–9
social enterprises 105, 291–92
social justice 20, 84, 256, 274, 276, 277, 305, 307, 309
social media 46, 48, 76, 220
social policy 40
social responsibility 105
solesolevaki 134, 137, 138
solidarity 233–34
global solidarity 234
SOUL — Save Our Urban Landscape 76–77, **77**
South Pacific Tourism Organisation (SPTO) 128–29
spirituality 99–100, 239
Srebrenica, Bosnian Muslims massacre, 1995 185, 190, 194, 199, 202, 203
stakeholder engagement 302
state sovereignty
in conflict with human rights 88
and political suppression 89
and self-determination 88–89, 93
states
see also nation-states
definition 122
legal responsibilities to the state 301
poverty and inequality responsibilities 245
responsibility to protect from atrocity crimes 197
Treaty of Westphalia, 1648 191, 197–98
Statute of Westminster, 1949 37
Structural Adjustment Programmes 240
structural change 84, 89, 212, 245, 250, 300, 301–02, 316
structural violence 241
superdiversity 40, 49
superiority and inferiority beliefs as a cause of conflict 163–84

INDEX 333

colonial assumptions 29, 32, 105, 184, 315
sustainability 193, 301
  origins and development 249, 251–52
Sustainable Development Goals (SDGs) 105, 106, 249
  climate action 123, 124
  gender equality and empowerment 259, 260, 261
  and Indigenous peoples 255, 277
  relating to poverty and inequality 245, 253–54, 256, 261–62, 265, 287
  trade-offs 256, 258
Syria 190, 203

Tairāwhiti (Gisborne) 170–72
TalanoaHUBBS 289–91, **293**, 294
Tānemahuta 181, 238
tangata whenua 15–16, 21, 27, 66, 67, 90, 312
  tangata tiriti relationship 307–08
tantalum 209, 210, 213
Tapu and Noa 238
taunahanaha 90
Te Ao Hurihuri 45
te ao Māori (Māori world views) 64, 142, 151, 181, 302
Te Ao Mārama — Te Ao Hurihuri — Te Ao Hou 45
Te Arawa 147
Te Kore — Te Pō — Te Ao Mārama 45
Te Pahi and Te Pahi Medal 30, **31**
te reo Māori 33, 92
  revitalisation activities 58, 275
Te Rōpū Whakakaupapa Urutā 267, 270
Te Rūnanga o Ngāi Tahu 151–53
Te Tāhū o te Whāriki strategy 151–53
Te Tangi a Tauira 2008 150
Te Whānau-ā-Apanui 151
Tearfund 52
Teitiota, Ioane 56–57
telecommunications technology 26
Thatcher, Margaret 40, 47, 240
Thirty Years War 184
tihei mauri ora 181
tikanga (customs) 92, 142, 146, 147, 270
tino rangatiratanga (absolute tribal authority) 32, 51, 67, 82, 89–90
  see also rangatiratanga (Māori authority)

te Tiriti o Waitangi 32, 49, 67, 90, 93, 123, 143–44, 276, 277, 278, 304, 307–08
  as a bill of rights 91
  and UNDRIP 92, 93, 278
Tonga 290, 292
tourism
  see also Fiji
  Bethlehem 230–31
  climate change impacts 125, 128
  economic and social factors 129–30
  ecosystem disturbances 129
  occupation tourism 231
  Pacific 128–31
  solidarity tourism 231
  tourist responsibilities 130–31
trade 36, 37, 41, 54, 71
  'free trade' agreements 47
  Māori 32, 33
  Pacific region 37
  policies driving industrial expansion and consumption 258
  protectionism 254
transcultural identities 49
travel 40, 46, 54, 128, 301
  see also air travel
Treaty of Versailles 183
Truman, Harry 191, 248
Trump, Donald 58, 59, 214, 220
Tuia 250 303–05, **306**, 307–09, **308**
  Māori responses 305, 307
Tukuitonga, Colin 272–73
Tupaia 28
Tupu'anga Coffee, Tonga 290, 292
tūrangawaewae 15, 21, 50, 63, 90, 91, 312

unemployment 54, 104, 266, 284, 287, 313
United Kingdom (Britain)
  see also Brexit
  Aotearoa's move away from British models 37, 41
  Aotearoa's participation in imperial wars 180
  colonial assumptions of superiority 29, **32**, 184
  economic connections of Pākehā settlers 36
  foreign policy of Aotearoa 36–37
  migration and travel from Aotearoa 40
  migration to Aotearoa 36
  neoliberalism 40, 47, 240
United Nations (UN) 37, 48, 71, 76,

100, 105, 156, 182, 221, 225, 240
  2030 Agenda for Sustainable Development 106, 249, 253, 261
  Charter 88, 192, 193, 196, 197, 198, 199
  Commission on the Status of Women 129
  General Assembly 196–97, 198, 233
  Human Rights Commission 86
  Human Rights Committee 56–57
  Human Rights Council 86, 119, 122, 123
  Office of the Special Adviser on the Prevention of Genocide 197
  Security Council 190, 192, 193, 196, 198–99, 202, 203–04
United Nations Assistance Mission for Rwanda 200
United Nations Declaration on the Rights of Indigenous People (UNDRIP) 76, 84, 90, 92, 93, 129, 210–11, 265, 274, 277, 278
United Nations Framework Convention on Climate Change (UNFCCC) 123, 143, 145
  Conference of Parties (COP) 123
  COP25 summit 156
  COP26 summit 120, **121**
United Nations World Summit Outcome Document (2005) 196–97
United States
  Aotearoa's defence relationship 180, 204
  bombing of Hiroshima and Nagasaki 191–92
  development agenda 240
  drought 218
  foreign policy of Aotearoa 37, 41
  GHG emissions produced by military 119
  hegemony 85
  migration and travel from Aotearoa 40
  neoliberalism 40, 47, 240
  presidential election, 2020 182
Universal Declaration of Human Rights (UDHR) 21, 70–71, 84–85, 92, 94, 100, 198, 209–10, 252, 265
universal rights 21, 75, 90, 93, 94

van Neerven, Ellen, *Heat and Light* 174
Vanuatu National Sustainable Development Plan (NSDP) 130

wāhi tapu (sacred places) 141, 145
Waitangi Day 55
Waitangi Tribunal 90, 91, 156
The Walled Off Hotel, Bethlehem 227–9, **228, 229,** 230–31, 233
war crimes 196, 197
  description 191–92
  trials 185, 188
water, traded as commodity 218, **219,** 220
wealth and income gaps 240, 242, **243,** 250
'welfare dependency' 51
wellbeing 101, 277, 279
West
  approaches to laws, policies and politics 110
  braiding Indigenous and Western knowledge 17
  citizenship perspectives 68–69, 70, 73, 74, 75, 100–01
  conception of individualism 85, 87, 101
  economic-centred outlook on progress and development 107, 120, 132, 251, 258, 279, 314, 317
  expansion of ideas, values, lifestyles and technology 51

scientific advancement and industrial production 239
scientific information 142, 147, 150
Western liberalism 73, 74, 83, 182, 228, 302, 313, 314–15
Westernisation 49, 51, 105
Whai Rawa 275
Whakamaua: Māori Health Action Plan 2020–2025 (Ministry of Health) 91
whakapapa 45, 63, 90, 98, 147, 270, 302, 304
  of action 299
whānau ora 276
Whanganui River, Te Awa Tupua 107, 110
'white saviourism' 105, 315
wicked problems 298, 309, 315
women's rights to equality 256, 258–61
Wong, Kirsten 38
World Bank 37, 58, 218, 240
World Health Organization (WHO) 221, 274, 277
World Trade Organization (WTO) 37, 40, 58

Zananiri, Sary 231
Zero Carbon Bill 2019 124, 145
Zionism 224, 225

First published in 2022 by Massey University Press
Massey University Press
Private Bag 102904, North Shore Mail Centre
Auckland 0745, New Zealand
www.masseypress.ac.nz

Text copyright © individual authors, 2022
Images copyright © as credited, 2022

The text excerpts in this book have been sourced from a wide range of parties, as credited. Reasonable efforts have been made to trace the copyright holders and obtain permission to reproduce these texts. In cases where this has not been possible, copyright owners are invited to contact the publisher. The support and permissions provided are gratefully acknowledged.

Design by Kate Barraclough
Cover and typesetting by Sarah Elworthy

The moral right of the authors has been asserted

All rights reserved. Except as provided by the Copyright Act 1994, no part of this book may be reproduced, stored in or introduced into a retrieval system or transmitted in any form or by any means (electronic, mechanical, photocopying, recording or otherwise) without the prior written permission of both the copyright owner(s) and the publisher.

A catalogue record for this book is available from the National Library of New Zealand

Printed and bound in Singapore by Markono Print Media

ISBN: 978-1-9910160-1-0